The Study of Real Skills
Volume I

The analysis of practical skills

The Study of Real Skills
Volume I

The analysis of practical skills

Edited by

W. T. Singleton MA DSc

Professor of Applied Psychology
University of Aston in Birmingham

Published by
MTP Press Limited
St Leonard's House
St Leonardgate
Lancaster, Lancs
England

ISBN 0 85200 199 1

Typeset by The Lancashire Typesetting Co Ltd, Bolton
and printed by R. & R. Clark Ltd, Edinburgh

Contents

Contributors

Lisanne Bainbridge
Department of Psychology, University of Reading, Building 3, Earley Gate, Whiteknights, Reading RG6 2AL, UK

P. Branton
22 Kings Gardens, West End Lane, London NW6 4PU, UK

Wing Commander G. W. F. Charles
Procurement Executive, Ministry of Defence, Flight Systems Department, Farnborough, Hants., GU14 6TD, UK

J. D. Eccles
Welsh National School of Medicine, University of Wales, Dental School, Heath Park, Cardiff CF4 4XY, UK

B. A. Lacy
The Old Stables, Park Lane, Harefield, Middlesex, UK

B. R. Lawson
Department of Architecture, University of Sheffield, The Arts Tower, Sheffield S10 2TN, UK

J. Matthews
National Institute of Agricultural Engineering, Wrest Park, Silsoe, Bedford, MK45 4HS, UK

R. B. Miller
Colonial House, South Road, Poughkeepsie, New York 12601, USA

B. Pettersson
Skogsarbeten Drottninggatan 97, S-11360 Stockholm, Sweden

J. T. Reason
Department of Psychology, University of Manchester, Manchester M13 9PL, UK

W. T. Singleton
Applied Psychology Department, University of Aston in Birmingham, Birmingham B4 7ET, UK

R. B. Stammers
Applied Psychology Department, University of Aston in Birmingham, Birmingham B4 7ET, UK

R. G. Taylor
Applied Psychology Department, University of Aston in Birmingham, Birmingham B4 7ET, UK

R. G. Thorne
Procurement Executive, Ministry of Defence, Flight Systems Department, Farnborough, Hants., GU14 6TD, UK

D. Whitfield
Applied Psychology Department, University of Aston in Birmingham, Birmingham B4 7ET, UK

Preface

The origins of this book are in my first attempts to understand psychology as a post-war student in the Cambridge of the late 1940s. Sir Frederic Bartlett and his colleagues in the Psychology Department were talking and writing about the concept of the skill as the fundamental unit of behaviour. This made entire sense to me but not apparently to very many other people because the movement dwindled rapidly with the retirement of Sir Frederic in 1952. It got lost within performance studies which were essentially behaviouristic and stimulus–response in origin, a quite different style of thinking from the gestalt approach of skill psychology. This is not a simple dichotomy of course and skill psychology does go some way towards the analytic approach in accepting that a science needs to have a basic element, a unit from which the complexities of real behaviour can be constructed, into which it can be analysed and in terms of which it can be described and understood. The trick is to pick the right unit and I think that skills is an appropriate unit for human behaviour. Note the plural, although these units are elements they are not identical any more than the ninety-odd elements of the physical world are identical.

The issue is sometimes clarified by considering the analogy with the attempt to describe a house. The simplest observable elements here are the brick, the piece of stone or the piece of wood. It would clearly be absurd to go to a more microscopic unit than these, it isn't efficient to describe a house in terms of its component particles such as electrons or chemical compounds. Even the brick is too small, this is the wrong element for getting at the essentials of a house, it doesn't fundamentally matter whether a house is made of brick or stone or wood. The effective description of a house is as a collection of rooms and thus the room is the basic element we need for the study of houses. We can push the analogy one stage further, the first step in describing a room is not to measure it but to state what it is for, is it a dining room, a kitchen, a bedroom or a living room or some combination of these? Similarly for human behaviour, the stimulus–response pair may occasionally be useful but for most higher level behaviour it is too microscopic. So also is the chemistry of muscle action or the electrical activity in a nerve. In the basic skill we have an element we can start to understand by describing its purpose and having done this we might go on to measurement. Examining the combinations and interactions of these elements might then encompass the description of real purposive human behaviour.

So much for the fundamental model. The other characteristic of a science is the fundamental method. I left Cambridge at the end of 1953 to take up the problem of applying psychology to the study of the work of ordinary people in the industrial Midlands. I found, as many others have found, that the laboratory experiment was not enough. One had to start by observation and measurement in the real situation and the topic of measurement was not some universal human subject but a particular set of individuals with a history, background, aspirations and attitudes as well as performance levels. Such measurement was inevitably untidy and it could sometimes be reinforced and clarified by manipulating a selected few of the variables in a more controlled laboratory situation. One of these studies which went on intermittently for some years is described in Chapter 5. It seems to me that the experiment can never be more than the successor and servant of the study of the real situation and that the concept of the general man is too remote an abstraction for the understanding of particular human behaviour. It may well be that the same principles have long been accepted in other disciplines namely that scientific progress depends on relating the laboratory to reality and on knowing when to stop generalizing and start categorizing. These things are worth restating because they are so readily obscured by the mass of reported psychology experiments which are merely successors to earlier experiments using the healthy, educated, young man as the universal human operator or worse still, the laboratory animal as the universal behavioural organism.

This book is about ordinary people coping with the physical world, partly in order to do so and partly by doing so they develop specialized attributes which we call skills. It is not a text book in the sense that a particular facet of human knowledge has been structured and referenced in a form from which the average student can memorize material to pass an examination. Nor is it a collection of case studies with the extraction of knowledge and principles left to the skills of the reader. Because the study of skill is in the early stages of development I have invited a range of specialists to describe the work they have done on the analysis of particular kinds of specialized human activity. The jobs cover the range of human occupations from dominantly manual to partially creative. The investigators come from different backgrounds and have different objectives, about half would admit to being psychologists. They have in common an interest in human skill and a consequent style of study which contains this particular way of thinking. I have tried to introduce this way of thinking by explaining what I think skill studies are about, by tracing some of their origins in experimental psychology and finally by attempting to extract some common principles from the series of studies. It is planned that this book should be the first in a series dealing with progressively more complex aspects of skill.

Studying ordinary skilled people has its own difficulties and limitations. One particularly frustrating aspect is that once such studies are completed and reported it is so easy to criticize them and to underestimate the perseverance, expertise and creativity which went into conducting them. Having tried it myself I have the greatest admiration for the achievements of the authors of the separate chapters in this book. I would like to thank the authors specifically for their contributions and more generally for the opportunity and privilege to be associated with them in this collective effort to further the understanding of human behaviour through the study of human skills. I would also like to thank my secretary, Anne van der Salm, not only for much typing and retyping but also for her extensive part in communicating with the authors and publishers and in general by keeping the project tidy. Finally, I would like to acknowledge co-operation in the form of permission to reproduce material by:

HMSO (Table 1) (Figures 10.1, 10.2, 10.3)
The Royal Society (Quotation, p. 33)
Forskning-stiftelsen Skogsarbeten (Figures 2.1, 2.2, 2.3, 2.4)
National Institute of Agricultural Engineering (Figures 3.2, 3.3, 3.4, 3.5, 3.6)
Engineering Industry Training Board (Table 4.1)
T. W. Kepton Ltd. (Figures 5.1, 5.3)
Shoe and Allied Trades Research Association (Figures 5.2, 5.4)
Wales National School of Medicine Dental School (Figures 6.1, 6.2, 6.3, 6.4)
British Railways Board (Figures 8.1, 8.2)
British Airways (Figure 9.1)
Redifon Flight Simulation Ltd. (Figures 9.2, 9.3)
Civil Aviation Authority (Fig. 9.4)
U.S. National Aeronautical and Space Administration (Table 10.2)
Neilson McCarthy Ltd. and Wiggins Teape Ltd. (Figure 11.1)
Taylor and Francis (Figures 11.2, 11.4, 11.5, 11.6)
Institution of Chemical Engineers (Figure 11.3)
The Motor (Quotation p. 321)

Introduction

THE CONCEPT OF SKILL

The term 'skill' is widely used in industry and in psychology. In the working world there are said to be three grades of operative; the skilled, the semi-skilled and the unskilled. The distinctions are in terms of length and kind of training. A skilled man has served an apprenticeship, a semi-skilled operative has had some training, an unskilled job is one which any person can do immediately (Table 1). This categorization will not bear close examination even within one industry. Different trades have different lengths of apprenticeship but the duration seems to depend more on tradition than on the amount of material to be absorbed. The length of training for a semi-skilled operative might be anything from 2 days to 2 years, and the distinction between an apprenticeship and a training period is based on long established custom and practice in the industry or trade concerned. It is usually true that, given the necessary physical capacities, anyone can do an unskilled job but could the appropriate performance level be maintained or achieved at all? We can all pick apples but few of us would like to live on the money we would earn by our speed at picking apples. Logically, since all jobs are subject to some improvement with practice the problem of whether this practice ought to come from experience or from formal training would be better settled by systematic investigation rather than by the arbitrary habit of regarding particular jobs as skilled, semi-skilled or unskilled.

In practice, of course, it is not as simple as this. We are talking about people with pride in their work and their skill, they establish institutions and traditions which are weighted in favour of continuity rather than regular reappraisal. This, however, is another story. This book is about man interacting with the physical world rather than men interacting with each other. A further confusion arises because although apprenticeship schemes appear to be about the acquisition of skill, on closer study it emerges that they are really concerned with attitudes rather than skills. The objective of the long training period is not so much to generate a man who can do things at a given level of speed and quality but rather a man who always will do things at this level and will never do them below this level. In this sense a skilled man is a man of integrity and rigid standards of quality of workmanship. This is, of course, entirely admirable. but it is not skill as the psychologist uses the term.

Table 1.   A Ministry of Labour classification (1967)

Group 5 *Other skilled manual occupations*	Group 6 *Other semi-skilled manual occupations*	Group 7 *Labourers and unskilled occupations*
Carpenters	Bottlers	Agricultural workers
Joiners	Printing machine assistants	Porters
Compositors	Plastic moulders	Dock labourers
Process engravers	Assemblers	Messengers
Steel erectors	Shepherds	Lift attendants
Bricklayers	Foresters	Kitchen hands
Plasterers	Paint sprayers	Caretakers
Glaziers	Warehousemen	Office cleaners
Tilers	Storekeepers	Window cleaners
Crane drivers	Packers	Laundry workers
Rubber moulders	Boiler firemen	
Photographers		

Although the industrial use of skill classifications is complex and to some extent arbitrary the term is most frequently used in the narrow way in ordinary language. Taking spectator sports as one example, observation and discussions of skilled performance is quite close to the way in which skill is talked about in applied psychology. We can all admire the performance of fast skills, whether it be a concert pianist, an acrobat, a tennis player or a racing motorcyclist. It takes only a little training or insight to observe with equivalent pleasure the higher levels of subtler skills, the middle-aged labourer using a shovel, the motor mechanic tightening a bolt or the assembly operator fitting a rear window into a car. All these and a multitude of other activities have in common the basic characteristic of skill–economy. Usually there is no sign of wasted effort, the moving limbs and body are controlled but not stiffened and tightened by overactive muscles; there is no haste, there is usually speed in the sense that the total achievement in a given period is impressive but nothing seems to happen suddenly or unexpectedly to the performer.

All this is unfortunate for the professional entertainer in that the more highly skilled he is the easier the task appears to be and he is often reduced to introducing deliberate mistakes so that the audience are made increasingly aware of his real difficulties. Another cure for the complacent observer is for him to try it himself and he will find, of course, that although he may be able to move and react just as quickly as the skilled operator his achievement falls depressingly short of that which looked so easy. There are so many things which need to be looked for, so much to be held in mind, and so many things to be done either simultaneously or in quick succession. All skilled activity involves these three components of selection of relevant data, using it to make decisions on what to do and then doing it. After the first movement its consequences become part of the information used to decide on the next one and so on. With some experience one can carry out a movement and shape it so that the succeeding one will follow smoothly. This is why skills are said to be serial and not just sequential. What is being done now cannot be considered in isolation from that which has just been done and that which is just going to be done. Skill then can only be understood in terms of organized patterns and directed series and any attempt to consider a particular stimulus–response combination in isolation is a simplification at the expense of losing the essence of the whole business.

There is another industrial classification which will not bear close analysis. Skills are said to be either mental or physical. This has all sorts of ramifications in our social and industrial structure; staff and operatives, white collar and blue collar workers, office and factory, manual and mental labour, all stem from this oversimplified dichotomy. The analysis made already leads inevitably to the conclusion that no skill exists without both control and action, the former involves the central nervous system—that is mental activity, and there would be no evidence that anything is happening or has happened unless there is some output which can only arise from muscular activity. In other words, all skills are mental and all skills are physical. It is true that highly practised skills such as walking do not require continuous or even regular conscious control but the slenderest acquaintance with diseases of the nervous system is enough to persuade anyone of the importance of control in the regulation of such a skill.

At the other extreme the highest level of mental activity can only find expression through muscle action although again the highly practised muscle groups which are involved for example in speaking or writing are apt to be overlooked. Similarly the practice of a skill is impossible without information from the outside world. For the skills of thinking most of this information may have been stored for some time but it only entered storage by activity of the sense organs. For so-called muscular skills some sense organs must be operating all the time to keep the human activity in phase with whatever is happening in the immediate environment. To summarize this second characteristic of skill, there is no input to the human operator except through the senses, there is no control except by the central nervous system, there is no output except by muscles and there can be no manifestation of skill without all three.

What is meant by differences in skill between individuals or over time for a given individual is to do with different ways of acquiring data, different ways of thinking and different patterns and sequences of action. The differences must be due mainly to the different education, training and experience of each individual, in other words to learning. Acquisition of skill is a very broad category of learning. From this point of view there are only two kinds of behaviour patterns; the instinctive and the skilled. A statement such as 'his headlights caught a dark shape and he braked instinctively' might be alright for a novelist but it would never do for a psychologist. We drive cars by skill and not by instinct. An instinct is an innate pattern of behaviour, in some animals and birds it can be beautifully elaborate, but it is not subject to drastic modification by experience. Skilled behaviour is the complement of instinctive behaviour. The further one moves along the phylogenetic scale (Figure 1) the greater the importance of skill and the lesser the importance of

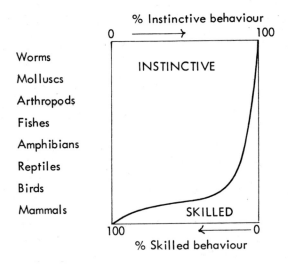

Figure 1   Instinct and skill on the phylogenetic scale

instinct. As with all psychological dichotomies there is a continuum rather than a rigid separation of two types of behaviour. Instinctive behaviour is innate and consistent, skilled behaviour is learned and variable but obviously we can have an innate drive served and modified by skilled behaviour patterns.

This emphasizes the fourth basic characteristics of skill, namely that there is always a purpose. Skilled behaviour makes sense because it progresses the individual towards some goal which is important to him. The drive is not necessarily an instinctive one, indeed most goals are themselves learned. Nevertheless the variety and variability of the behaviour associated with real skilled performance achieves coherence in the underlying purpose.

In summary, skilled behaviour has four characteristics:

1. It is continuous, there is always an extensive overlap and interaction. Even in principle, it cannot be analysed by separation into discrete units along either space or time axes
2. It involves all the stages of information processing indentifiable in the organism, basically inputs, processing and outputs
3. It is learned and therefore highly variable within and between individuals
4. There is a purpose, objective or goal providing meaning to the activity.

INPUT, OUTPUT AND COGNITIVE SKILLS

Although the three functions; inputs, processing and outputs are all essential to skilled performance their relative importance differs markedly in different tasks. This provides us with one crude classification of skills in terms of the dominant function within the process. Typifying the *output dominated skills* are the fast motor skills found in ball games and industrial assembly operations. There are *input dominated skills* such as those required in industrial inspection and monitoring tasks. There are skills where the input is obvious, the output is trivial and the skill depends on the differential weighting and combinations of inputs or assemblies of inputs, in other words on information processing. These are called thinking or *cognitive skills*. Cognition implies knowledge and in this context it is important to note the distinction long recognized by philosophers, between 'knowing how' and 'knowing that'. 'Knowing that' is unfortunately much the commoner state in our society, it is theoretical and academic, it enables one to write and discuss, to pass examinations and to acquire prestige but not necessarily to operate effectively in the real world. In contrast 'knowing how' is direct and operationally based—it involves personal involvement and successful experience, such knowledge cannot necessarily be demonstrated verbally and it is not readily transmitted to others, this is cognitive skill. 'Knowing that' is important, it facilitates communication and provides understanding, it is the business of the critic as opposed to the artist, the spectator as distinct from the player, it is not skill. Many people would claim, with some justification, that there are such things as *social skills* which do not fit into these categories but these are clearly along a different dimension and are outside the scope of this book.

Dominance in this sense is more than an indicator of relative importance. If the skill is said to be output-dominated it means that the output elements are the key features around which input and processing elements are structured, timed and generally fitted. Key features are the formulation of the structure as distinct from its purpose. To complicate matters even further the objective may be sufficiently structured or immediate to form a succession of key features. To anthropomorphize the problem, the individual or inner man must somehow keep track of what he is doing. This is critical in skilled activity because it is so homogenous, everything depends on everything else within the activity, there are no endings, no beginnings, no simple causes and effects. There must, however, be some landmarks, some navigation aids that the inner man can steer by. These are what are called the *key features of the skill*. They are not easily identifiable because they are not consciously selected by the operator and they vary enormously between skills and between stages of learning for a particular skill. Sometimes they are stages in the achievement of the objective as mentioned above. Sometimes they are output elements, for example in a game of tennis when the player's activity is focused on getting the racquet in contact with the ball at a particular point in space and time and when the racquet is moving with a very precise direction and speed. All other preceding inputs and outputs for many seconds are related to this particular key feature. Sometimes they are input elements when all the outputs are phased in with a given pattern of inputs, for example, for the spectator, ball-room dancing on the television is a coherent activity but switch off the sound and it becomes very peculiar. Without music or some other rhythmical time base it is also impossible to perform. The laboratory-based research worker is a good example of the skilled operator using central key features; he has a model of some aspect of human knowledge which he manipulates and develops on the basis of data coming from the laboratory which is itself generated partly by his own output activities. This, then, is the justification for the categorization of skills as input, cognitive or output.

PERCEPTUAL AND MOTOR SKILLS

A different categorization can be devised by starting from physiological and developmental considerations. The body is an extraordinary complex skeletal system of some two hundred bones linked together and activated by a much larger number of muscle groups. This system has a number of characteristics. Firstly in a mechanical sense, considered as a collection of masses, it is unstable and positive control and effort is required to maintain it in dynamic equilibrium. Secondly it has enormous flexibility in mobility because of the peculiar system of locomotion, essentially two legs functioning in a reciprocating mode. Thirdly, it is capable of extraordinary dexterity because of the unique construction of five-digit hands, one opposing the other four attached to arms with complex joints in wrists, elbows and shoulders. This is the physical basis of the virtually infinite range of activities indulged in by the human operator.

This versatility has a price which is the complexity of the requisite control system. All these muscles and joints have to function as a tightly integrated whole. The way in which this is achieved is grossly underrated for three reasons: The system is very reliable, it is almost entirely unconscious and the skills involved were acquired very early in life so that the labour of acquiring them has been forgotten. They seem to reach their peak in the 15 to 20 years old group and it is salutary to compare the motor performance of someone of this age with either a 3 year old child or an 80 year old pensioner. No elaborate performance measures or stressful tasks are needed. The contrast is marked even by casual observation of these subjects walking along a level road. A teenager in extreme fatigue will walk more and more like the child or the pensioner, that is the smoothness will diminish and the movements will become less integrated and less predictable although not necessarily less fast. If one observes a baby a few months old there is plenty of energy and activity but not very much selection. The unskilled state is not to do nothing but rather to do everything.

Skill develops by selectivity and by the integration of activities. For example the very young baby will spend hours moving an arm and watching it move, this is the phase of associating the feeling of moving the arm with the sight of the arm moving. It will then spend more hours banging things, thereby associating data from the sense of movement, the sense of touch, vision and hearing into the one impression. Over the first 2 years of life the baby progresses from the most primitive activities of staring, headlifting, through eye-following and sound location, reaching, banging, creeping, walking, running, to the elaborate integrations required for throwing and fitting things together. Up to the age of 5 activities get steadily more and more elaborate and anticipatory so that ultimately postural adaptation, precise manipulation and selective finger actions are achieved. The child then has the rudiments of skilled action and further developments are based on improved space perception and on the building up of larger and larger limits of activity which can be reeled off without conscious attention. In computer terminology one would say that the sub-routines become more and more elaborate. As the child grows older it develops more specific skills such as those involved in games, music making and car driving, but from the motor point of view these are just greater elaborations and longer chains of the basic skills acquired in the first 5 years.

The essence of this kind of skill is that if things go according to plan no conscious attention is required. In effect a decision is made so that action is initiated, thereafter the control of the action is done by checking against some kind of internal model, plan or programme and successful checks simply allow the activity to continue. An unsuccessful check or a mismatch results in the appeal to more elaborate control systems which may well be conscious. For example, suppose one is walking along the road and a foot goes into an unseen hole, or when going upstairs or downstairs one steps on to a step which isn't there, in these circumstances chatting or daydreaming, or whatever, comes to a halt and the whole control system switches over to the clarification of what has gone wrong starting by searching for new data using the visual system. Similarly, it is possible for a skilled knitter to knit and watch the television, but when something unexpected happens, as when a stitch is dropped, then the flow of intricate finger manipulation stops and the eyes and the attention are abruptly switched from the television to the knitting. It is clearly efficient for the organism to be able to delegate routine activities in this way, there is an inevitable loss of flexibility but enormous gain in that the distant senses (eyes and ears) are freed for other activities and the routine motor activity is checked by feed-back of data from the actions themselves mainly through the kinaesthetic system. This is the mechanism of motor skills. A motor skill is a routine which is available to translate a simple decision into an integrated collection of actions incorporating not only the necessary manipulation and mobility but also the adaptive postural scheme to maintain body stability.

At the information input end of the organism there is the complementary problem of integrating together a lot of streams of data so as to provide a meaningful model which can generate a decision. There has to be very drastic filtering and combining going on simultaneously. From the point of view of an individual performing a particular task, the world is full of irrelevant information. All these data impinge on the sense organs. In the case of man the significant senses are those of sight and hearing with minor confirmatory additions from touch, taste and smell. The first problem is to select what is relevant and organize it into a structure or model which has some meaning. In man these basic models seem to be organized along the lines of the visual system. This is presumably what is meant by visual imagery. Again, using the anthropomorphic metaphor, the inner man seems to build an internal model of the world, usually the visual world, with reinforcing data through the other senses. It is rather like doing jig-saw puzzles, the inner man can only fit one piece at one instant but he may be engaged in constructing a number of pictures. All the pieces for many pictures are jumbled together. Most pieces are not important to any of his pictures and what is more, many different pictures can be constructed from the same pieces. A further complication is that the pictures are never finished and never static, every new piece modifies the picture and this process can go on indefinitely. As with the motor performance, most of the process is entirely unconscious.

Suppose I am standing on a street corner waiting for my wife. This being England, it is probably cold and wet. I attend to these climatic sensations only until they have driven me into the position on the corner where I get the best compromise of maximum shelter and maximum visibility. Thereafter, unless the weather changes dramatically, I ignore all sensation due to it. I build another visual picture which combines the geography of that part of the city with either a general knowledge of my wife's habits at that time of the day or the memory of her telephone message saying where she was coming from. There is noise all around me from the traffic, the shops, the pedestrians and so on. I ignore this also because it has no relevance unless I hear someone speaking directly to me or I hear, for example, a squeal of brakes which might mean I am in the path of a skidding car. I look at all the people coming towards me from the most likely direction of my wife's approach. I can't state very precisely what I am looking for but the visual filter is still extra-ordinarily efficient. It rejects all data about most individuals perhaps on the basis that they are male, or, if female, that they are much smaller or bigger, younger or older, than my wife. It is not a complete rejection, because if one of my colleagues walks past I will recognize him and say hello. If one of our neighbour's wives goes past I will raise my hat. I might not, of course, and she will go home and complain to her husband that she saw me but I 'looked right through her'. Eventually my wife appears—how do I recognize her? It may be the clothes and the hair I first identify—but she could have bought a new outfit and changed the colour and style of her hair and I would still recognize her. My guess would be that apart from facial characteristics which physically are really very small differences from other faces, I rely mainly on the way she walks and that there is some change in her posture and expression when she sees me. This complex visual activity proceeds without any conscious effect or control on my part; my only awareness is the pleasant sense of recognition and completion.

There is no rest for the perceptual systems of my wife and myself. As soon as they have achieved what is for these systems the trivial task of bringing together two individuals in a city of more than a million people they generate other models incorporating potential places to eat, their standards recently, the relative accessibility, the time available and so on all leading to a joint decision about our next action. To consolidate our respective models of this problem we talk to each other. Not very much perhaps but enough to ensure that we have the same criteria and we are thinking within the same range of choices. This can hardly be a visual model topographically matching the real three-dimensional world. It is probably a mixed model partly pictorial, partly symbolic. If she mentions a particular restaurant I will add this to my model possibly in terms of the name itself as written or spoken possibly by a visual image of the entrance, the head waiter, the meal we last had there or some peculiar combination of all these. The visual search skill is one which the organism acquires in the first few years, indeed, mostly in the first few weeks of life. The use of symbolism is a much later development coinciding perhaps with the learning of language. The use of symbolic representation enormously increases cognitive abilities. The ability to construct symbolic models and to manipulate symbols, both iconic and linguistic, is the unique characteristic of human behaviour.

To recapitulate, human information processing can be conceived as starting with diffuse streams of data which are filtered, combined and focused on a decision, following which there is divergence again into the multiplicity of actions consequent upon the decision. The translation of the incoming data into the decision requires perceptual skill, the translation of the decision into complex bodily activity requires motor skill. In this classification these are the two main kinds of skill. Motor skills can be called sub-routines or programmes which result in a series of co-ordinated actions.

A new motor skill is acquired by a more elaborate or simply a large combination of more elementary skills. Perceptual skills are not so uniformly hierarchical. There is a hierarchy based on the elementary search techniques, selectivity, the separation of organized and relevant from disorganized and irrelevant (figure from ground in other terminology) and on the more and more complex pictorial representations. This hierarchy is not a continuous one in that there is a qualitative distinction between pictorial models and models involving symbolism. The perceptual skills are senior to the motor skills in many senses, they occur first in the sequence of information processing, they are more complex, they can override and they are the locus of consciousness. Motor skills can be entirely automatic and unconscious. Perceptual skills only partially so. Note that in this scheme there is no clear division between the input organization and the data manipulation or cognition. The information processes leading to a decision are not easily separable into stages within a sequence.

THE HIERARCHICAL NATURE OF SKILL

The suggestion that there are skills within skills has at least two quite different interpretations, both of which make sense.

The more mundane one is the implication of skills as building bricks which are put together to generate more complex skills. Any skill which goes on for more than a matter of seconds is bound to be made up of many subsidiary skills and the way these are linked together in time or space is just as important as the elementary skills themselves. Taking a car round a corner may involve steering, gear changing, and braking as well as more abstract skills such as maintenance of body balance and an intuitive appreciation of the dynamic behaviour of that vehicle under those conditions. None of the components can be fully understood unless or until they are integrated together in the complete sequence of actions. All the components are necessary parts of the whole, some of them may be equally necessary parts of other skills and many of them are skills in their own right.

A different interpretation of the hierarchical nature of skills arises from the suggestion that although for a given skill we can talk about input, processing and output, we can, at a lower level, identify other input, processing and output sequences within each of these three. For example, in sitting at my desk writing this the skill involved is essentially cognitive. The inputs have arrived over many years from observation, reading, lectures, discussion and generally communicating with others interested in skill. The mode of output is of no consequence, it makes no difference whether I use a pen, a typewriter or a tape-recorder. Yet although the important process is entirely information processing I can describe it as if it were a total skill. It seems to me that I am like a man in a crowded aviary trying to catch the birds. All kinds of ideas are flying round in my mind, all I can do is isolate one or two of them, grab them and get them recorded before they fly out of reach again. Note that I am talking about thinking itself as if it were a serial process of input, processing, and output. Similarly I can talk about an input process such as that involving visual scanning as an activity involving raw data (the input) which is selectively acquired (that is, it involves control and processing) and which is fed in an organized way (an output) to the more complex information process associated with the larger skill. Equally I can describe what for the larger skill is just an ouput as a serial process. For example a simple hand movement practised to the point where no visual monitoring or conscious control is required still requires specificity of speed and direction which must involve control with all the attendant input, processing and output of data.

THE MEASUREMENT OF SKILL

Comparative achievement might seem the obvious measure of skill, but this is only true in a statistical sense. In the simplest case of a game between two players the 'better' one does not win all the time, he need only win more than half to keep his reputation as the one with the higher level of skill. Before this measure becomes reliable a large sample of behaviour is required and this tends to take up a lot of time and expense if scoring of the particular skill is elaborate. In an industrial case for example, it is extremely difficult to find a measurable criterion of achievement which can be unambiguously related to level of skill. The amount of work done to a particular standard in a given time is usually more closely related to the amount of work available and to external incentives rather than to the skill of the operator.

This balancing of work load suggests another consideration not yet mentioned, the skill of a team as opposed to that of an individual. The production engineer is taught to assign batteries of machines and operatives for mass production so that the operation times balance. In practice this is an arithmetical impossibility. The lowest common multiple of even a small number of operation cycle times is such that an impossibly large number of machines and operative would be required if all bottle necks and idle times are to be avoided. They are avoided in practice because operatives adjust their working rate to suit the amount of work available. One of the real difficulties of automation is that machines without operatives do not demonstrate this adaptive faculty. The effect of incentives such as piecework payment introduces the confusion of skill and effort. The lesser skilled of two operatives may do more work and earn more by greater effort. This sort of variable needs to be isolated within our study of skill. We can safely conclude that level of achievement is a misleading measure of level of skill unless extraneous variables are detected and controlled and at best we can only express results in terms of probabilities.

Consistency is another possible criterion. Superficially this is attractive, our intuitive view of the skilled man is that he keeps going steadily, inexorably and precisely, like a machine in fact. This is related to the absence of haste but it is not the same thing. There is some evidence to suggest that the reverse is true within appropriate limits. Consider for example a pilot approaching a runway using an instrument landing system. It might be thought that we could measure skill by the closeness to which the pilot sticks to the optimum line of approach. It has been shown that highly experienced pilots when compared with inexperienced ones show greater deviations from this optimum because they make corrections less often. The skilled pilot knows how far he can depart from the ideal without endangering his aircraft, the less skilled one does not have this awareness and confidence and thus makes more corrections than are strictly necessary. The phenomenon is widespread and accounts for the common irritation which the learner finds in watching a skilled operator, 'how does he get such a good result from performance in such a casual and variable fashion?' He gets it by knowing what matters and what doesn't but his objective from moment to moment is certainly not complete consistency. The exception to this principle is the automatic kind of activity which is unfortunately still imposed on many industrial workers. Repetitive press or drill operations and simple assemblies come into this category. The worker can repeat the cycle with remarkable consistency for long periods and tolerate the job because it can be done without conscious attention. This is a prostitution of the human operator and to suggest that they actually enjoy it is a criticism of our educational system rather than an adequate defence of our industrial practice.

There is one sense in which consistency reflects skill. The skilled man is more resistant to disturbing forces such as stress of many kinds and to the limitations of his tools. It is common practice to attempt to counteract the possible effects of stress by over training, that is by increasing the level of skill beyond that which is normally required. This strategy is used, for example, by the military in the hope of maintaining performance in conditions of personal danger or of extremes of heat and cold, noise or vibration. It is used also in the training of complex machine operators such as pilots and process controllers. The skill of these operators is not apparent and presumably is not measurable except on the rare occasions when the load rises very much above the normal level.

It has already been emphasized that skill is to do with direction and timing. The skilled operator has always relied on two techniques which have recently been regarded as discoveries in management control theory—management by objectives and management by exception. Perhaps we should add a third one —management by sequential triggering. The skilled operator has learned to identify the events which can simultaneously signal the end of one phase of activity and the start of another and this is one facet of the essential smoothness of skill. Unfortunately 'smoothness' is not easily measureable except as low third and fourth order derivatives of movement. The strategy of reacting to signals only when necessary as a trigger for corrective action (management by exception) again contributes to smoothness and also to consistency. This can sometimes be measured as relative rarity of corrective action. The undeviating pursuit of an objective is not detectable in performance except by resistance to distraction as mentioned above in the context of stress. The overall smoothness is thus not achieved by speed of reaction but by anticipation of events, partly from extrapolation from preceding events and partly from the established model of the total situation. This can sometimes be detected by subtle measurement of the spread of the skill in the sense of how far in the past and future events are influencing current action (Figure 2). At least it becomes clearer why the time domain is such an important feature of all skilled performance. There can be a further complication in the perception of relevance—the highly skilled man may restrict his past influences and future predictions because their potential affect is too slight to warrant the trouble of taking them into account.

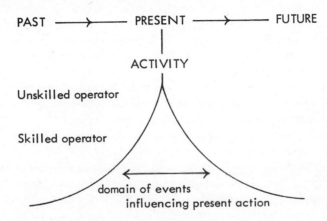

Figure 2   The spread of effect in time as skill increases

THE INTEGRAL NATURE OF SKILL

Attempts to separate input, output and cognitive or perceptual and motor skills are useful in clarifying the origins of skilled behaviour but it is obvious that only outputs are measurable with reasonable definity, objectives can be obtained by observation and discussion, inputs by inference and sometimes by design if they are entirely artificial. For example, it is not possible to determine the inputs of a car driver, but it is possible to determine the inputs, including the timing, for a process controller who has a display based on his demands for information from a computer store. The critical decision point is only ascertainable by asking the operator to state when he has made one and, in any case, the whole concept of the decision dividing perceptual from motor activities might be nothing more than a convenient rationalization.

Perceptual skills might appear to be fundamentally different from motor skills in at least two respects: one is a model and the other is a routine, one often involves symbolism and the other doesn't. With closer study these distinctions become less clear. Models and routines are both connected with the business of control by exception. They have in common that no change is made until there is a contra-indication of success from a signal. Symbolism, at least as far as imagery is concerned, is not the prerogative of perceptual skills, motor skills could not proceed without the presence of the continuously developing body image. All this suggests that if there is a way of analysing and separating skills we have not yet located it.

METHODOLOGY OF SKILL STUDIES

It emerges that the study of skill is elusive with a frustrating quality of 'now you see it, now you don't'. This is perhaps because, as already noted, perception involves isolation of figure from ground and in a skill there is no figure separable from the ground or if there is it changes all the time like clouds in a sky or a melody in music. If there is a relevant historical scientific category it is clearly field theory rather than particle theory, gestalt rather than stimulus–response.

The trouble is that science is already ossified by the traditions and success of the physical sciences, we like to analyse things, to identify and separate the fundamental elements. But this procedure is a sure way of losing the essence of skill. We like to have numbers to describe our findings and to record our conclusions but numbers imply categories and we are not yet very clear about categories in skill. There will not be many numbers in this book. We like to use mathematics but most classical mathematics is either clumsy, irrelevant or even misleading when applied to skill. It is interesting to speculate about why mathematics should be so powerful an aid to physical sciences and so puny in its support for behavioural sciences. It seems to be mainly due to the difficulty of coping with the concept of purpose in mathematical terms. This is quite fundamental to behaviour and yet is irrelevant to the physical world which apparently can be described by meaningless and chance exchange of energy. The essence of behaviour is that it has a direction and a goal and although this is incorporated in the concept of skill it is not something we can approach with mathematical tools at present.

There are also some myths about science which impede progress. One is that the scientist proceeds by generating a hypothesis and then proving whether or not it is true in his laboratory. The results of each experiment generate further hypotheses which are in turn subject to experimental test. The practical situation is much less tidy. The creative psychologist, and probably all other scientists also, does not proceed in such a logical manner. He has ideas which are collected into models. He checks these by observation and discussion with colleagues. The main uses of laboratory data are to warn him when he is going in the wrong direction and to encourage him to think more realistically about specific issues. The question 'What is the evidence in support of . . . ?' is useful for elementary examination questions but it has little place in the development of a science. A concept is supported because it feels right and only rejected when the evidence is against it. The feel for what is right comes not from the laboratory but from observation and action, particularly problem-solving outside the laboratory. For the psychologist this means the clinic, the factory, the battlefield, and so on. Anywhere, in fact, where there are people who apparently can be helped by psychological insight.

Another myth is that each professional scientist is a member of a large rational, professional group which carries on inexorably developing the body of knowledge, with each individual making his tiny permanent contribution. Psychology at least is not like this. It is highly fashion conscious. At any one time some theories are in vogue, some are falling into disrepute and some are just emerging. Ideas about skill have developed gradually and very slowly throughout this century. Since about 1960 there has been little progress because of the current fashion for the laboratory measurement of human performance. Such work is not about the higher levels of skill because the typical subjects used are not skilled operators. Much of it is misconceived because of the obsession with numerical data at the expense of description and classification.

However, these human performance psychologists have been very busy in their laboratories and it would be unreasonably doctrinaire to ignore their efforts and their achievements. The first chapter is about these activities and thereafter the book is devoted to descriptions of studies of skilled operators coping with the physical world. Most of the studies were not done for fun or even for the furtherance of science, they were deliberately organized to help those being studied and through them the rest of us who depend on their efforts. The final chapter returns to the fascinating biproduct just introduced —the developing concept of skill itself.

1

Laboratory Studies of Skill

W. T. SINGLETON

ORIGINS OF SKILL STUDIES

It is one of the principles of skill psychology that man is very much a categorizer and this applies to students of skill as much as to any other skilled activity. To understand and describe the research on skill and on human performance it is necessary to have some structure. The conventional structure is to follow the path of information through the organism and distinguish between inputs, central processing and outputs. It is not possible to do this very neatly and for some topics these distinctions are clearly invalid. To reduce artificial separations this chapter is subdivided into output, input and throughput, thus avoiding the problem of defining the interfaces at which peripheral functions become central functions. There are various phenomena where time is the key variable and so it is necessary to have a fourth category of temporal aspects of skill. Although much of what is described has emerged from laboratory studies it is important to keep these in perspective and some discussion is provided of the limitations of the laboratory based experimental method. In particular the hiatus in progress which has become increasingly obvious over the past decade needs to be recognized and analysed.

OUTPUT, ASPECTS

Co-ordination at the level of muscle groups can hardly be called skill in that it is built into the structure of the nervous system. This can be demonstrated by electrical stimulation of the motor cortex, stimulation at different points will generate different movements sometimes involving the same muscle groups. That is, assignment of space in the motor cortex refers to patterns of movement rather than to particular muscles (Morgan *et al.*, 1950). However, when movements are co-ordinated in succession as well as in space then there must be some underlying purpose and consequently there must also be some skill.

Human performance studies have usually not been concerned with movement as a component of progression towards a goal but rather as an isolated controlled entity without any wide context. Physiological studies (Paillard, 1960) indicate the variety of possible muscular activity underlying superficially identical movements. Thus there is an inherent problem of control and this has been studied on the basis of both servo-theory and information theory.

The servo-theory approach (McRuer, 1968; Kraiss, 1972) is one of simulation; electrical or mathematical models are devised which behave in the same way in space and time as do joints or total limbs. The models can also include eye movements which are tracking the hand movements (Vossius, 1972). In these terms manual movements involve second order linear systems but there are non-linearities the definition of which can aid in the identification of the actual biological systems which must be in operation.

The information theory approach (Fitts, 1954) postulates that the time required for a movement is determined by the uncertainty or required accuracy as measured, for example, by the ratio of 'target' width to the length of the movement. Experimental data fits the formulation reasonably well which suggests that the limiting factor on movement times is in the central control and monitoring rather than in the mechanics of the limb. Little is known about the postural aspects of maintaining a position of equilibrium. This depends on tonic muscles as opposed to the phasic contractions which generate movements and it may be that there are two distinct motor systems; tonic and phasic. Head (1920) suggested that control of posture depends on the maintenance of a body image or schema which is continuously modified by feedback data from successive movements and when necessary also by visual and auditory data. Implicit within this concept is the notion of continuity in space and time, each sense datum has meaning not in isolation but in relation to preceding data.

Motor skills, that is complex patterns and sequences of effector activity, have been studied extensively both in adults and in children. In adults research has centred on the control of such movements by examining the effects of removing or distorting one or more sensory channels, e.g. Provins (1958) examined the effect of anaesthetizing the relevant part of a finger on exerting pressure and tapping. Smith *et al.* (1969) displaced, disoriented and delayed visual feedback using television circuitry. Provins found that accuracy rather than speed was disturbed and Smith found that although performance is reduced perhaps the most striking effect of disturbed visual feedback is the reduction of learning. It has been established for both laboratory and industrial tasks (Seymour, 1966) that during learning the element times most subject to reduction are those where there is 'perceptual load', it seems that it is the control function which is subject to change with learning rather than the movement itself.

Singleton (1953) showed the reverse effect with fatigue, namely that the control decision times increase and the increases (that is, the deterioration) are greater for more complex decisions. Raju (Singleton, 1968) showed that with learning the control and checking activities for an accurate movement spread to the preceding and succeeding elements of the task respectively, with increased skill an activity becomes more truly serial rather than merely sequential. Children provide the opportunity for the study of the development of motor skills (Connolly, 1970; Anglin, 1974). It emerges from these studies that there are interesting spatial aspects of reference of movements to the mid-line of the body and to the mouth, timing aspects in what Bruner calls the orchestration into serial order and spatio-temporal aspects in the integration of simpler constituent skills into more complex skills.

INPUT ASPECTS

The study of babies and children also provides useful evidence about the progressive development of perceptual activities. The basic motor skills are established in the first 5 years or so and thereafter increasing complexity even of output activity depends on support from perceptual skills. The basic motor skills seem to culminate at about the age of 5 or 6 with the development of postural adaptation and precise finger manipulations (Munn, 1965). Thereafter the obvious improvements can be traced to increased lateral cerebral dominance which forms the basis of symbolic skills and to the improved space perception needed for control and more particularly for anticipation.

The most striking phenomena in the context of perception are the constancies: size, shape, brightness, colour and position relative to the observer. For *size* it is self-evident that an object moving towards or away from the observer must have a changing size of retinal image yet there is no impression of size variation. Similarly a rotating circular plate does not appear to change in *shape* from a circle to an ellipse to a line and back again as the projected image does. Changing light reaching the eye does not necessarily result in an apparent change in *brightness*. A piece of coal in sunlight will emit more light than a piece of paper in moonlight but they still look black and white respectively. *Colour* constancy is not so completely effective for variations in the amount and colour of incident light but there are subtle compensatory mechanisms which account for the difficulties in getting good 'natural' colour photographs. The most striking phenomenon of all is in the *stability of the visual world*. The eyes move continually in relation to the head, the head in relation to the body and the body in relation to the physical world yet we apparently receive directly stable images of a stable world. How this is done physically by the sensing and integrating of data from all the relative motions still remains something of a mystery. From the psychological point of view all the constancy phenomena suggest that we should consider the human operator not so much as a direct responder to separate sensations but rather as a builder of models of the real world which facilitate the translation of sensory information into adaptive decisions. Further evidence for the essential indirectness of the perceptual response is provided by visual illusions (Gregory, 1966, 1970). Distortions, inconsistencies and other peculiarities of seeing things can be analysed and traced to mistaken inferences about the data coming in through the eyes.

The models of reality which we use to interpret what is happening and what to do about it are the basis of perceptual skills. The most sensitive and succinct description of the development of perceptual skills is due to Gibson (1966). He prefers to discuss perceptual systems rather than sensory or perceptual channels. He considers that the basic system is the one which is to do with orientation; the main sources of data in man are the vestibular apparatus which detects force or acceleration (mainly gravity) and, together with supporting data from the sense of touch within the skin, provides the basis of body posture and equilibrium. This in turn provides a mobile, flexible but stable platform for the auditory and visual systems. The platform depends also on the haptic system which is basically concerned with touching but depends not only on receptors for pressure and temperature in the skin but also on proprioceptors in muscles, joints and ligaments, and deals with movement or kinaesthesis as well as touch. Finally there is a taste / smell perceptual system but this is of relatively minor importance for man. In summary there are five systems: orienting, haptic, auditory, visual and taste / smell.

The development of perceptual skill also has been described in detail by Gibson. He suggests that the *first stage* consists of discriminating the range of possible inputs. An organism can begin to make sense of an input from an awareness of how this input fits within the total range. Here also is the beginning of classification. The *second stage* consists in the establishment of covariation of inputs. Some inputs occur together with other inputs, some inputs often succeed other inputs. This is how the inputs through different senses become associated. The *third stage* is the isolation of external invariants, in given input situations constancies are detected and are reinforced, structure is identified and isolated. It would be misleading to suggest that there is some inner intelligent little man looking for these things and noting them down as they are detected. Rather it is the nature of the input system itself which accentuates these structures. We can almost say that the individual does not see in spite of body movements, head movement, eye movements and eye tremor. On the contrary, these changes are a necessary condition for seeing in the perceptual sense because they are part of the process by which invariance is identified.

Consider for example an insect exploring an object using antennae. The antennae do not stay still, they move continuously, touching and probing looking for continuity and constancy. Consider a dog smelling at something —it doesn't make one big steady sniff, it snuffles around with rapid successive sniffs which are presumably a necessary process to identifying the structure of the dog's particular odour percept of the object. Similarly a man's eyes do not gaze steadily at an object, if they did they would not detect it, seeing involves shimmering around the object so that evidence is available about invariance. In fact it is more than just evidence, the invariance itself emerges from the process.

The *fourth stage* is learning what Gibson calls affordances of objects, that is their meaning in the sense of their consequences for the observer, whether for example they are manipulable, dangerous, edible or what. Note that these also are categories so that this is another kind of categorization. The *fifth stage* is in detecting invariances in events. As Gibson puts it, 'the child learns how things work as well as how they differ'. He first develops simple casual concepts such as colliding and pouring but goes on to more abstract ones such as inertia and energy in mechanical, chemical and electrical forms. Finally, the *sixth stage* is one of increasing economy by selective attention. The concentration on the essentials and the ignoring of the irrelevant and the redundant. These stages are not a series in the sense that the order is invariant and each stage takes over neatly from the previous one. The series does, however, reflect a hierarchy, it describes how a child learns to perceive. It describes also how an adult approaches the perceptual problem of understanding a novel situation, and by reversal what happens in fatigue.

The business of economy and efficiency in perceptual processes is a useful starting point also for a consideration of the various kinds of models or structures which the observer develops. The simplest kind are pictorial in the sense that the models correspond in some way to the real world itself with the three dimensions of space and one of time. Note, however, that the observer is not restricted to an infinitely narrow here–now dividing the past from the future as envisaged by the physicist. The future is here already in that the observer is anticipating events and has expectations for which relative probabilities change as the events unfold and the past is very much with him in that he understands the present evidence because of its relationship to the immediate past evidence. The inter-relationship rather than the events themselves is the source of meaning. These dynamic pictorial models are effective but they tie the observer very closely into the environment. To retreat from it and to be more economical the models become less and less close to reality and take on more of the character of images containing the essentials which can be called icons. The observer can go further into the world of symbolism particularly using language. This is the distinction which Bruner makes between iconic and symbolic representation.

To summarize the hierarchy of model building, the most primitive models as used by the baby are enactive in that the observer is the centre of the universe. Pictorial models then develop in which the fixed reference is the physical world with the observer mobile within it. In the cause of economy these models get more and more iconic in that non-essentials are omitted so that the model departs from reality but the real escape from the restrictions of the immediate environment occurs when the icons become entirely symbolic and are connected to reality only by conventions. New conventions develop also about the relationship between symbols; in linguistic terms there is syntactics and pragmatics as well as semantics. To use Fogel's (1963) terminology these conventions provide us with symbolic constructive models to add to our symbolic descriptive models. We can manipulate the symbols themselves. These are the perceptual skills we need to develop and control the technological world.

THROUGHPUT ASPECTS

Memory

The separation of input and output aspects of skill is convenient and clear enough for the peripheral functions where information enters and leaves the human operator but at the more central level the distinction fades and there are functions which cannot be readily distinguished in this way.

The most obvious one is memory, without memory, in the sense of the record of past experience, individuals could not function at all, although sometimes the term is used in a much narrower sense. For example, when the front parts of the temporal lobes are removed or destroyed the memory is said to have disappeared (Nathan, 1969). Cases are quoted such as the young man who treated his mother as a stranger and addressed her as 'madam'. Yet this implies that he could still see and recognize a woman, he remembered the social conventions of how one talks to a woman and he had not forgotten how to speak English. There is a danger in taking too much notice of the few striking cases commonly quoted by the clinical neurologists, presumably when dealing with thousands of patients they come across all kinds of variations and confusions of the classical syndromes.

However, there is one very common and consistent finding from neurology; damage such as a general blow on the head in an accident is likely to lead to loss of memory for what happened immediately before the accident, possibly only for a few seconds, possibly for a day or more but longer-term memory is not affected. The suggestion emerges that there are two kinds of memory, short-term and long-term. This makes operational sense if one thinks of long-term memory as the repository from which one gains the benefits of past experience while short-term memory provides the means for continuity within current activity. Laboratory studies of short-term memory began with 'memory span' measurement in the early part of this century

(Woodworth, 1938). The subject is presented with relatively meaningless material such as strings of digits, or letters or nonsense syllables which he is asked to reproduce almost immediately. There is obviously a limit to how long a stream he can reproduce accurately and this is the memory-span. It turns out to be about eight items but varies with the individual, the material, the situation, the precise calculation convention for taking account of inter-mittent successes and so on.

One of the interesting findings which emerged was the importance of grouping. For example, a group of six digits is more readily memorized if it is deliberately treated as a succession of two trios or three pairs rather than a homogenous string of six. These studies were revived and extended following the introduction of information theory into psychology, which provoked the 'bits versus chunks' controversy (Miller, 1956) on the question of whether the capacity of short-term memory is more reliably measurable in terms of items or in terms of amount of information. The concept of chunks incor-porates the subjective group of items as opposed to the objective individual items. Crossman (1961) pointed out that there are two aspect of memorizing, the contained items and their order, and that the human subject seems to treat the two memory tasks as different. Other interesting findings were that items which sound the same are more readily confused than those which look the same even for visually presented material, (Conrad, 1963) suggesting that the short-term store is phonemically rather than visually based. Baddeley (1966) showed that for long-term memory confusion was on the basis of meaning rather than acoustic similarity thus reinforcing the concept of two separate mechanisms. Brown (1958) demonstrated the relevance of other activity interpolated between presentation and recall thus introducing the importance of rehearsal as a contributing factor. The stage was set for an enormous range of experiments with minor variations of conditions and measures. One can present material to one ear and masking material to the other ear (Broadbent, 1957), to one eye and masking material to the other eye (Schiller, 1965), either all at once or in groups (Michon, 1964), one can require recall in different orders (Kay and Poulton, 1951) and so on. In short one can generate a whole branch of literature, if not knowledge, around the short-term memory problem. Baddeley *et al.* (1971) are reduced to the extraordinary strategy of distinguishing between primary memory and secondary memory on the one hand and short-term memory and long-term memory on the other hand. The former pair are hypothetical storage systems and the latter pair are defined by experimental conditions. Whether or not the short-term memory exists in nature, it has been created by the sheer mass of laboratory work by the experimental psychologists.

A storage system more relevant to human skill has been explored using terms such as dynamic memory or running memory. Instead of asking the subject to accept and reproduce a single string of material he holds a steady string and is expected to add an item on every time he takes an item off.

For example, Kay (1963) presented a series of lights in random order and required the subject to respond not to the light which was on but to the previous one, or two back or three back and so on, the subjects found it very difficult to take one item out of store without losing the others. One-back is not difficult and as Whitfield has pointed out can be advantageous because the stimulus can be regarded as anticipatory in that it is one ahead of the response (Singleton, 1968).

There has been surprisingly little work on long-term memory, partly because such experiments inevitably either take a long time or are uncontrolled in the input sense and partly because the classical experimental work in this field by Bartlett (1932) set such a high standard that others have been reluctant to try to emulate him. Bartlett demonstrated that long-term memory is schematic rather than literal. Reproduction is based on reconstruction rather than recall and the development of memory systems can follow either the receptor modes or the effector modes. Bartlett used Head's (*op. cit.*) concept of a schema to describe the process he envisaged. Schema are continuously modified constructs which the organism can 'turn round on' and reproduce something by inferring from the present state that such and such must have happened. It would obviously not make any sense to try to measure the capacity of the long-term memory and there seems to be increasing doubt amongst experimental psychologists about the feasibility of separating the performance of short-term and long-term memories (Craik, 1971).

There are many other facets of memory experiments pursuing ideas different from either short-term and long-term or primary and secondary. Sperling (1960) has shown that subjects can perform effectively when given a brief presentation *followed* by instructions of which part of the presentation is to be recalled. On this basis it is reasonable to postulate a visual pre-perceptual store. There is probably an analogous store for auditory inputs (Broadbent, 1957). Fitts and Posner (1967) call these sensory stores. They seem to function rather like extended after-images and Sperling (1963) has shown by blocking the visual after-image using a backward masking technique (that is filling the visual field with a black/white squares image) that the stored material can be scanned at a rate of about 10 ms per item, the capacity of the system is about 10 items. The preliminary store of visual data is called the iconic store, the corresponding store for auditory data is called the echoic store (Neisser, 1967).

Motor memory has been studied by examining the accuracy of a repeat production of a given force or a given displacement. Again it seems that interpolated activity in the form of an irrelevant intervening movement can cause greater forgetting although forgetting does occur even during unfilled retention intervals (Pepper *et al.*, 1970).

Limited capacity

There are several different senses in which the human operator can be said to have a limited capacity. Limited storage capacity in the short-term has been discussed above and there is also the concept of limited channel capacity. Although this is obviously a communication theory concept it seems from the laboratory data that there are two different limits, the maximum rate at which information which can be processed and the maximum rate at which items can be processed (Attneave, 1959; Garner, 1962). In servo-theory, as distinct from information theory terminology it is also possible to describe the limited band-width of the human operator and in more detail to express the various time delays to which the human operator is characteristically subject within a general transfer function relating inputs and outputs. Although these studies and theories are extremely elegant and sophisticated (Sheridan *et al.*, 1974) they are not immediately relevant to studies of skill because there has been little attention to the learning variable. They can be used to predict and describe highly skilled behaviour, e.g. in executing an aircraft manoeuvre, but only if the information presentation and the operator's options are highly constrained by the nature of the situation. Kelley (1968) lists three main criticisms of mathematical models of the human operator. They omit the key human functions of data reduction (that is selecting and coding on the basis of relevance), they do not incorporate the concept of representation or modelling of the task by the operator and they assume that the operator response is a function only of his input at about that time.

Single-channelness

There are extensive studies and speculations in the psychological literature about whether or not the human operator can do more than one thing at a time. They have been comprehensively described by Welford (1968). There are two phenomena which suggest that the operator may function only as a single channel: Craik (1948) noticed that in continuous tracking an operator appears to make intermittent corrections at around half-second intervals rather than to track continuously, Telford (1931) found that when two stimuli are presented within half a second the reaction to the second one tends to be delayed and he suggested that there is a 'psychological refractory phase' of about half a second during which, having just made a response, the operator cannot make another one. It has been shown by other experiments that this delay is not eliminated by practice (Hick, 1948), that it is central rather than sensory because it occurs when one signal is visual and the other is auditory (Davis, 1957) and that it is central rather than muscular in that it still occurs when the two responses in succession are made by different hands (Davis, 1956).

It is possible for 'grouping' to occur, if two stimuli occur almost simultaneously they can both be dealt with and this raises the question of what is meant by doing one 'thing' at a time. One aeronautical engineer has asked the pertinent question 'how can the human operator be a single channel mechanism when he can fly an aeroplane which has six degrees of freedom?' The one 'thing' is certainly not a degree of freedom or any other one of an orthogonal set of parameters, it is not objective at all it is more to do with manipulating one mental model at a time. Being highly subjective there are bound to be extensive individual differences. One 'thing' for a skilled man may be half a dozen 'things' for an unskilled man. Welford suggests that the label refractoriness is unfortunate in that it implies that the mechanism is out of action for the short time interval after the first stimulus, and he considers that it is engaged on something else, namely checking the first response. This would explain why the refractory period is about twice the ordinary reaction time.

There have been many other theories, e.g. that there really is a refractory phase to allow recovery from action, that percepts are quantized in sampling periods of just over one quarter of a second and that one quantum is terminated by a stimulus, that the effect is due simply to temporal uncertainty and that the operator just doesn't expect the second event to occur so quickly after the first and so on. This is just the kind of problem which provides the experimental psychologists with a reason for embarking on the generation of yet more extensive and rather tedious literature. This literature is reviewed by Broadbent (1971). Having recognized that this phenomenon exists under the artificial conditions of successive presentation of discrete stimuli and perhaps in response to a single axis continuous stimulus its further exploration in the laboratory doesn't seem to have an consequences for the study of real skills.

Experimental psychology has suggested one technique for the measurement of load on the human operator. If his single channel is not fully utilized then variations in external conditions such as task complexity, or internal conditions such as effort will not be detectable by performance changes. If on the other hand the channel can be kept fully loaded than there should be changes in performance with changing conditions. Thus if the operator is engaged in a primary task such as driving a car which does not normally fully utilize his capacity one can give him a secondary task such as mental arithmetic, measure changes in secondary task performance and use these as indicators of something changing in the primary task. Reviews of this literature have been provided by Welford (1968) and Rolfe (1971). The early promise of this technique has not been sustained, there are fundamental difficulties in the similarities, differences and interactions of the two tasks which make reasonable inferences from such data almost impossible.

Speed of performance

It might seem that the basic measure of speed for a human operator is the reaction time where a stimulus appears at some unpredictable instant for which the required response is a sudden ungraded movement. Interest in the measurement of this situation was revived with the introduction of information theory into psychology and was strengthened by evidence suggesting that the human operator's rate of gain of information is constant. That is, the greater the range of possible stimuli (with consequently more information per stimulus) the slower the reaction time. Hick (1952) showed that this was so for different numbers of possible but equiprobable stimuli and also that when subjects deliberately went faster and increased their error frequencies thereby reducing their required information intake the human operator information transmission rate remained about the same. Hyman (1953) showed that the relationship held when probabilities were changed by varying the relative frequencies within a set of lights and also by introducing patterns into sequences of lights. Several models have been proposed as to why this should be so. These are described in detail in Welford (1968). One of Hick's original proposals was a *serial classification model* in which the operator is assumed to carry out successive binary classifications, e.g. given eight possible stimuli he first divides them into two fours, then the four into pairs and then selects one of the pair. If each choice takes the same time this accounts nicely for the logarithmic increase in reaction time with number of stimuli, but the model has to be made much more complicated to account for unequal frequencies of possible signals.

Another proposal is a *simultaneous scanning model* in which the operator is assumed to compare all incoming signals with all possible identifications but in this case the comparison times are subject to random variations and the greater the number of comparisons going on in parallel the longer, on average, the process will take to complete. These alternative models are mentioned not so much because of their operational relevance to skill studies but rather because they nicely illustrate how the human performance psychologist starts with an apparently simple phenomenon, generates various possible explanations and then tries to think of more detailed controlled situations and performance measurements which will increase the weight of evidence for or against various theories. It usually turns out, as in this instance, that further evidence reveals increasingly the complexity of what appeared at first sight to be a simple phenomenon. For example, it has been shown that the increase in reaction-time with number of choices does not always occur if sufficient learning is allowed, nor if the relationship between stimulus and response is highly compatible. (Leonard (1959) used vibration applied to the finger tip as a stimulus and pressure from that same finger as the appropriate response.) Nor is it clear in which situations discrimination of the stimulus or selection of the response is the dominant variable or whether it is the interaction which matters.

Crossman (1955) examined the relationship between reaction time and discriminability and showed that reaction time varied with the proportional difference between the two stimuli, e.g. separating cards with two spots from those with four spots took about the same time as separating those with four spots from those with eight spots but it takes a longer time to separate three spot cards from four spot cards and shorter time to separate two spot cards from eight spot cards. Similar results have been obtained by others for length of lines, degrees of greyness and so on. The phenomena have been discussed mainly in terms of decision theory imported from statistical economics. The general idea is that a class of stimuli requiring a unique response will be normally distributed and this distribution may overlap with that for another class of stimuli requiring a different response or no response. The operator's problems is to select his cut-off point within the overlap of these two distributions so as to optimize the relative numbers of incorrect and correct responses. This optimizing function will depend on the relative importance of reacting to a non-stimulus (false positives) and not reacting to a stimulus (omission errors). There is now a vast literature on this subject (Broadbent, 1971) but, apart from suggesting that kinds of errors need to be classified and separated, the contribution to knowledge seems to be that when an operator finds a discrimination difficult he takes longer and he is less confident about his decision. These can hardly be described as devastating psychological insights.

TEMPORAL ASPECTS

Speed of serial activity

Measures of discrete aspects of human performance such as reaction time, movement time and refractory periods would suggest that the speed of complex human activity will necessarily be rather low. That this is in fact not so is an interesting research topic in itself. How does the human operator achieve such speed given such poor capacities? Several techniques have been identified by laboratory analysis. Fleishman *et al.* (1963) gave tests of visual/ spatial orientation and kinaesthetic sensitivity to forty subjects and then measured their performance in a two-handed co-ordination test. The relative performance of the subjects changed through the learning phase. At first there was a high correlation of speed with visual/spatial score and this gradually decreased but the correlation of speed with kinaesthetic score increased with learning. That is, the high performing individuals to start with were those with the highest visual/spatial scores but, with greater practice, they were gradually overtaken by those with a high kinaesthetic score. This is one demonstration of the introspectively and observationally established principle that with greater learning the operator relies less on vision and more on kinaesthesis. The standard claim for a high level of learning: 'I can do it with my eyes shut' is in line with this principle. Reliance on kinaesthetic rather than visual information provides greater speed potential for several reasons. Kinaesthetic reaction time is marginally faster than visual, but more importantly kinaesthesis avoids delays due to the inertia of the physical world (e.g. knowing by experience that a given displacement-pressure on an accelerator pedal will eventually cause a given change of speed, is clearly a much faster feedback of information than waiting for the speed to actually appear as a visually detected change in speedometer reading). It also eliminates the need for eye movement and attention shift times—there are apparently no such equivalent times for the kinaesthetic system.

Another technique already mentioned in relation to short-term memory is the increasing overlap of the constituent items of the series. The sequence of *plan–execute–check* for each element of the activity provides extensive scope for increased speed if the *check* can be eliminated or at least reduced in importance, and if the *plan* for the next element can overlap with the *execute* for the previous one. This, however, is verging on anticipation, which warrants a separate section.

Learning

The familiar learning curve in which time of performance for any task when plotted against extent of practice shows a decelerating rate of improvement, disguises many interrelated phenomena. To start with it is an average which has eliminated large and interesting variations. The differences between dominantly visual performers and dominantly kinaesthetic performers for a motor task has been described above. The learning curve for an individual is never smooth, it always shows erratic ups and downs in achievement which presumably reflect complex interactions between personal variables such as effort, arousal and method with physical variables such as random changes in materials, components tasks and the environment. There are learning curves within learning curves which can sometimes be detected by plateaux. The learner exhausts the possibilities of one strategy which takes him to a steady level of performance but he then evolves a new strategy and goes off down another learning curve, e.g. the trainee typist must first learn to associate actions of particular fingers in particular keyboard locations with the stimulus of a particular letter and performance will follow a learning curve and reach a plateau. Thereafter she begins to perceive common sequences of letters and consolidates corresponding patterns and sequences of finger movements and this enables her to go through another learning phase. In practice the plateaux may not be obvious because one learning phase overlaps with the next.

For most real tasks the situation is not so easily analysable and the only generalizations which are possible are operational statements about what happens to cycle times. Crossman (1959) for example suggests that skill is acquired by selective reinforcement of successful methods. The average speed is improved by increasing the probability of a fast procedure. This is revealed in the frequency distribution of cycle times not so much by a shift of the whole distribution but by a skewing towards the shorter times, the mode shifts more and more below the mean (Dudley, 1963). This effect occurs even for very short cycle times and it is not clear how the learner can detect and react to such small time differences. Crossman suggests that he may do it by using the decay of short-term memory as the 'clock' or alternatively that he does not do it by time at all but by relative effort. That is, he pursues the principle of minimum effort which usually coincides with minimum time. In this sense skill is a more and more exact adaptation to the task. All this, of course, applies most readily to situations such as industrial assembly tasks where the cycle time is a relatively unambiguous measure of performance. There are many other kinds of task, e.g. those involving control, where skill is connected more with timing than with time. The golfer, for example, may have a preliminary problem in how to hit the ball fast enough to project it to the appropriate range but his main learning phase is in developing precision rather than speed, timing rather than time. Instructors can help considerably in ensuring that learners have the most appropriate objective at each stage in the learning process.

Considering the fundamental importance of the role of instruction in all training and education there has been remarkably little relevant research. King (1959) points out that the instructor can be an undesirable barrier as an intermediary in information transmission between knowledge of performance and the performer, and when possible the requisite instruction should be built in automatically as part of the feedback, but this does not negate the importance of formal instruction in setting appropriate attitudes, methods and objectives. Gagné (1962) emphasizes the role of instruction in what he calls filtering and shunting. *Filtering* is distinguishing signals from noise in the context of the particular task and *shunting* is transforming inputs into appropriate outputs at the lowest possible level in the hierarchy of the nervous system; these are separate aspects of what is known in other terminology as developing the appropriate *set*.

All this is easiest to envisage in terms of motor skills but these are at the lower end of the learning hierarchy. Gagné (1974) proposes five major categories of learned human capabilities: motor skill, verbal information, intellectual skill, cognitive strategy and attitudes. *Motor skills* involve timing and smoothness of muscular movement, *verbal information* is the business of naming, labelling and memorizing facts. *Intellectual skills* begin with the classical educational requirements of reading, writing and arithmetic but develop into an extensive and more or less specialized hierarchy of essentially cognitive manipulations. Gagné, however, defines *cognitive strategies* as skills concerned with the self organization of learning, that is controlling ones own behaviour in attending, learning, remembering and thinking. Acquiring these skills is 'learning how to learn'. *Attitudes* are learning dispositions which characterize individual differences but they also change with learning. Whether attitudes are a separate dimension from skills is not yet clear.

It remains possible, however, to make some general statements about the effect of learning on skills separating output, input and throughput aspects. For outputs the characteristics of unskilled behaviour are confused order, variable timing and inappropriate accuracy (usually too little but sometimes too much), but for the skilled performer the order, timing and accuracy are much more exact. For inputs the unskilled performer has not identified and separated the relevant from the irrelevant, whereas the skilled performer attends only to what is relevant and ignores all other data. Where possible he relies much less than the unskilled performer on vision and more on touch and kinaesthesis. For throughputs the skilled performer progressively reduces his conscious attention, or, to put it another way, he reduces the level at which information processing is done as much as possible (shunting). It will be noted that there is an overall strategy of minimal effort and usually minimal activity, although in some circumstances he may trade off a little extra activity in favour of not having to do so much information processing or control. For example, in a fault-finding procedure the skilled operator will usually vary his routine in terms of relative likelihoods of faults but he may occasionally work through a full routine which he knows is not essential to avoid the difficulty of selecting the specifically relevant.

Anticipation

As Bartlett (1958) puts it, 'In every kind of skilled action from the simplest to the most complex, there is some kind of apprehension of the direction in which the evidence is moving or of the varied directions in which it might move.' He distinguishes three kinds of anticipation: receptor–effector, perceptual and symbolic. The simplest, called *receptor–effector anticipation* is made possible by the potentiality of overlap in time between receptor and effector processes. One nice illustration is in a three-choice task devised by Leonard (1953). He had three lights arranged in a triangular path. With the lever at one vertex of the triangle, one of the other two lights would come on as the stimulus requiring a movement of the lever in the corresponding direction. The lights came on in a random sequence triggered by each lever movement and so the subject had a discrete, successive, but not serial, two-choice task. He had to move the lever in response to a stimulus and then react to the next stimulus which appeared on the completion of the movement. In an alternative task there was an additional stimulus light which indicated the required direction of the successive movement. Thus the subject could during a move, plan his next move. With this advance information which made anticipation possible the whole performance became faster and smoother. The reaction times which necessitated staying at the corners were eliminated because the subject could react to the next stimulus during the previous movement. This is receptor–effector anticipation but, regardless of the task and the degree of learning it cannot operate very effectively more than one move ahead because the receptor time is less than the effector time and a one-event lead is all that can be utilized without potentially disrupting the accuracy of sequencing.

It is possible to look effectively further ahead by utilizing *perceptual anticipation*. This term was coined by Poulton (1952) to describe the utilization of structure to identify trends and extrapolate to the future. One of the simplest forms of this is tracking a sinusoidal wave-form where the regularity of the stimulus makes possible extrapolation into the future. In general the operator detects some indication of structure such as periodicity, symmetry or grouping and assumes that the future will be a continuation of the past. He may also detect and utilize structure in information about the future if this is available (the preview case) (Poulton, 1964). In this way the subject can, to use other terminology, set up a model of the future, including his own behaviour, and switch to a control strategy of detecting errors in that which he has already programmed. He reels off this motor activity in phase with the stimulus situation but also uses an override correction facility when something unexpected occurs. *Symbolic anticipation* was first illustrated in experiments by Mackworth *et al.* (1959) which were intended to simulate tasks such as air traffic control. The operator is coping with a number of streams of information and to do this, in addition to taking action in relation to the most immediate needs he scans the future and 'tags' various events in the order in which he is most likely to have to deal with them. In other words he restructures the presented information into a symbolic queue, the order of events in the queue can change as the need for action approaches.

This kind of anticipation is much utilized in car driving. The driver scans the approaching stimulus field and rejects many items but tags others as potentially needing action or at least further watching in a flexible sequence. As the events unfold some are discarded as unimportant and others are placed in a sequence which becomes more and more determinate as the need for action arises. Road signs and other warning signals are designed to enhance this capability. These three forms as described by Bartlett are along one dimension of anticipation. There are others which are less readily susceptible to experimental investigation and demonstration but which are nevertheless important in real skills. For example, what might be called *cognitive anticipation* is possible because of the extensive previous knowledge and experience of the physical setting in which a skill is practised. This 'feel' for the future behaviour of the system might be intuitive or scientific, or some mixture of the two, but it is characteristic of the highly skilled man that he relies extensively on these expectations and probabilities attached to the range of future events. The skills of controllers of complex machines and processes centre on this ability.

There is a variation of this concerned with people rather than things which might be called *behavioural anticipation*. If, for example, a car driver is approaching a group of persons on the pavement, he will give them a wider berth if they are 10 years old than he will if they are 40 years old because he knows that children are much more likely to run off the pavement than are adults. Similarly a decision whether or not to pass another car on a winding road will be influenced by factors such as the relative power of the car and the age of its driver.

The many forms of anticipation have in common that they are techniques for acquiring and updating more effective models of the situation the operator is coping with on the particular dimension of prediction.

Fatigue and stress

The distinction between fatigue effects and stress effects have never been agreed with any precision. Broadly speaking fatigue is chronic, stress is acute (but it must also be acknowledged that at present fatigue is rather dated as a concept and stress is the more fashionable). Both terms suffer from a superficial analogy and assumed relationship between physical, physiological and psychological parameters. Fatigue is fundamentally a subjective feeling. If one continues with any task one begins to feel tired and to wish to stop doing it. This seems to be an adaptive inclination because if one stops doing it the feeling diminishes and eventually disappears so that one is ready to start doing it again. There is also a more generalized feeling, not related to particular tasks which is diminished by not doing anything constructive for a while, one goes to sleep or in the longer term takes a holiday.

To get the whole business on a more scientific basis the obvious approach is to devise a simple highly repetitive task for which there is an unambiguous performance measure. To this end the ergograph was designed in which a finger or a hand pulls regularly against an external resistance, e.g. lifts a weight, and a trace is recorded of this periodic movement. There are many physical effects corresponding to the subjective feelings which can be detected from the traces. The amplitude of movement gradually decreases and eventually becomes zero, the decrement is more rapid for a high load, there is a recovery time for a given task and this increases with the total time or load imposed by the task. More complex phenomena can also be noted: there is an optimum time or total work output beyond which the required recovery time is disproportionately larger, the decrement can be reduced by trying harder and, if one finger is being used the effect spreads to adjacent fingers in that other fingers show a more rapid decrement when exercised immediately afterwards. These principles have been shown to extend to heavy physical work in industry (Bonjer, 1971). The greater the proportion of maximal effort used the less the endurance time, about one third of the maximum is acceptable for an eight hour day. There are complicated interactions between physiological and psychological parameters, even with the ergograph it can be shown that the decrement in performance is influenced by the subjective as well as the objective load. If the subject thinks he has a lighter load he will go on longer and he will show recovery when told that his load has been reduced even though in fact this has not happened.

Skill fatigue was first explored in detail in the classic Cambridge Cockpit experiments (Davis, 1948). Pilots carried out a synthetic flying task for several hours, their performance was recorded and their more general reactions were noted. The performance measures indicated very complex changes in errors, some aspects of performance showed no deterioration over 2 hours, other aspects of the same performance were up to 50% worse after this period. Within one aspect of performance error frequency fell towards the end but the average duration of an error increased. There was little relationship between how well the pilots performed and how well they claimed they were performing. There were large individual differences in general behaviour, some pilots became overactive, excited and irritable, others became withdrawn, bored and inert. Bartlett (1943) used these data to develop a new approach to the concept of fatigue and his paper, in fact, laid the foundations for the new studies of skill which he developed in other papers (Bartlett, 1948, 1951(a), 1951(b), 1953). As he put it:

> Suppose instead of rather blindly taking over methods which were just and correct when applied to the case of simple muscular fatigue, that people had honestly asked themselves what looks to be the character of the skills involved when we say we get tired in the pursuit of complex activities in daily life, in industry, or in the practice of specialized skill in the fighting services. They would have got a picture wholly different from that of repeated movements set up in response to recurrent and unvarying stimuli. They would have found co-ordinated actions the constituents of which can, and frequently do, change places. They would have found a type of behaviour in which it has become of enormous importance to time the constituents correctly, so that each can flow readily into its neighbour. They would have found interruptions and rests no more uniform than actions. They would have seen stimuli to such co-ordinate action which are not a repetitive succession but a field, a pattern, an organized group of signals capable of changing their internal arrangement without loss of their identity as an organized group.

In Bartlett's view the main indicator of fatigue is a progressive lowering of standards of performance, what a man is able to do as measured by an isolated test does not change but what he actually does within continuous performance is subject to deterioration. In addition, his timing diminishes in precision, there is more variability although not necessarily a lower average speed, all the right things will still be done but there is an increasing likelihood that the order will be wrong. Corresponding to these disorganizations of the response the stimulus field ceases to be an integrated whole and dissociates into parts which are dealt with separately, there is a concentration on the more important sources of data and an increasing probability that other sources will be ignored. Paradoxically there is a greater awareness of irrelevant stimuli associated, for example, with the sensation of bodily comfort or of distractions in the surroundings. This general picture is intuitively appealing but it is not easy to consolidate into more exact formulations which can either be checked in the laboratory or used to develop predictions of real behaviour. Welford (1958) has applied the general principles to the study of ageing which has much in common with fatigue. Murrell (1962) has developed the concept of the *actile period* which is defined as an optimum period of performance in repetitive work the end of which is signalled by increased variability of performance.

Partly because of the unsatisfactory lack of precision in fatigue studies, stress studies have been more and more popular over the past two decades. Stress appears to be a more concrete concept because, by contrast with fatigue, which began as a subjective feeling and was taken up by the psychologists and physiologists and eventually by the physical scientists, stress began as a physical sciences concept and has moved through physiology to psychology. The idea is straightforward. When a piece of physical material such as a metal wire is subject to an imposed load, called the stress, it suffers some deformation such as an extension which is called the corresponding strain. The ratio of stress to strain is constant over a certain range (Hooke's Law). Within this normal range when the stress is reduced there is a corresponding reduction in strain, but if the stress is taken beyond a point called the elastic limit then the strain remains even when the stress is removed, a permanent distortion has been caused. Finally there is a level of stress at which abrupt fracture occurs called the breaking point.

There are no *a priori* reasons whatever why there should be an analogous situation in human behaviour, but the idea has proved attractive to many people. Not surprisingly, stresses, strains and breaking points in relation to people are commonly bandied about by the layman but one could expect psychologists to be rather more careful to define their terms. Unfortunately they have not been and there is no common agreement about the definition of stress. It is accepted that there are several kinds of stressor: environmental ones such as heat and noise which are physiological, danger and frustration which are psychological, and task originating stressors such as hard physical work and information overload—again physiological and psychological respectively. There are also perhaps more general internal ones due to disturbance of circadian rhythms such as sleep loss and time zone change. The distinction between stresses and strain is also useful (Singleton *et al.*, 1971) if one retains the engineering convention and defines stress in terms of externally imposed loads, and strains as bodily or behavioural reactions to the imposed load.

Unfortunately this distinction is ignored by the physiologists. For example, the original heat stress indices, such as effective temperature, are measures of stressors but the newer ones such as the heat stress index are based on sweat rates and are measures of strain in the above terminology (Singleton, 1972). Similarly so-called Selye stress (Levi, 1974) is defined in terms of reaction to stress, presumably because the only measures of 'psycho-social stress' available are the indirect ones such as internal physiological indications of endocrinal activity. The literature on stress is now very extensive for both effects on performance (Poulton, 1970; Welford, 1974) and effects on health (Appley and Trumbull, 1967; Gunderson and Rahe, 1974). Although these books are excellent summaries of the state of the art it must be admitted that the topic is still very unsatisfactory both conceptually and in terms of usefulness.

Vigilance and arousal

The technological developments of instrumentation and radar during World War II resulted in the design of a new type of task where the operator was not required to do anything except to respond in some simple manner to a stimulus which was both rare and difficult to detect. Such tasks are now found also in industry, some of the watch-keeping type in the high technology process industries and some in mass production manufacturing where routine inspection is required. The first experiments were carried out by Mackworth (1950). He devised an experimental situation in which subjects were required to watch a pointer stepping around against a plain white background taking one hundred steps to complete a revolution and making one step every second, occasionally (less than once per minute on average and irregularly) the pointer would make a double step, the subject's task was to press a key when this happened. Mackworth used this situation to investigate changes in performance in time, the effects of instructions, interruptions, drugs and temperature. He did similar experiments with an auditory task designed by K. J. W. Craik in which the subject listened to a ping every 3 s but occasionally got an 'echo' ping half way between two of the regular ones. The results were remarkable in demonstrating a low success rate and a very rapid fall-off of proportion of signals detected. On average subjects missed about 15% in the first half hour and between 25% and 30% over the remaining $1\frac{1}{2}$ hours.

As with other phenomena which superficially at least are readily simulated in the laboratory a considerable literature has grown up but surprisingly little has been added to the original Mackworth findings (Mackworth, 1969, 1970; Broadbent, 1971). In general when an operator is performing a monotonous task in which a fleeting non-obvious signal must be detected, his attention is likely to wander off after 10 or 15 min. His performance can be improved by incentives, drugs, increasing the signal, optimizing the environmental parameters of noise, heat and lighting and provision of some variety. Any change of conditions likely to increase or maintain alertness will improve performance. The study of vigilance reintroduced into psychology the importance of alertness, arousal or activation. There has been a concurrent physiological interest in this concept but unfortunately it turns out that measures of the three possible kinds of arousal: bodily state, performance and feeling do not always correlate highly. Lacey (1967) for example shows that what he calls somatic and behavioural arousal commonly correlate but can be dissociated particularly by the effects of drugs. It follows that the safe comprehensive strategy when attempting to obtain indicators of human behaviour is to measure simultaneously psychological, biochemical, physiological and anatomical parameters (Singleton, 1971a).

The difficulty of measuring arousal is not, of course, a sufficient justification for underestimating its importance as one of the main dimensions of the human state at a given time. Arousal control is one of the underlying modulating factors in skill, it helps the individual to maintain his principle of maximum economy or minimum effort. The arousal level is adjusted more or less automatically to meet the needs of the perceived situation but there is a further complication in what Murrell (1971) calls auto-arousal, here the individual deliberately alters his own arousal state when there is a mismatch between required and actual achievement. It may not be possible to sustain the distinction between automatic and voluntary control of arousal and the relationship between arousal and effort has not been explored but within this confused picture there is something of consequence for the understanding of behaviour in general and skill in particular.

LIMITATIONS OF HUMAN PERFORMANCE STUDIES

It is clear that the intensive study of human performance in the laboratory has not been without its dividends in terms of increasing understanding of how people behave in the laboratory. There are difficulties in extending these ideas to everyday behaviour, some stemming from the inherent artificiality of the laboratory situation and others stemming from the discrepancies between the factors which it has been fashionable to manipulate and those which seem important in ordinary work. There are two main measures of performance; speed and errors. A worker does something rapidly because his pay depends on the amount he produces or because he must in order to keep in phase with some external system such as activities of other people or the powered movements of hardware. He functions at some optimum level determined by the specific conditions of the system and although it may be a near maximum level in some complex sense determined by interactions between a large range of factors, some external, some internal, it is not the kind of maximum which is explored, for example, by measuring speed of reaction time or short-term memory span. For him a mistake is something which has real consequences: he damages himself or others or it costs him money or status.

Contrast this with the standard laboratory instruction 'go as fast as you can without making any mistakes'. Speed and errors are essentially meaningless for the experimental subject in the sense that however he performs there can be no consequences of great significance to him. In terms of the relevance to laboratory tasks there have often been oversimplifications: sometimes in the cause of logical simplicity (which is not necessarily the same as psychological simplicity), and sometimes for ease of measurement. For example, the so-called simple reaction time situation where a subject presses a key in response to the hopefully unpredictable appearance of a light is not at all simple in that the subject may evolve the most complex strategies to improve his estimates of what will happen when. The skill aspect has been either disguised or eliminated rather than simplified by the attempted removal of the possibility of anticipating the stimulus and grading the response. For more operational criticisms of the relevance of laboratory experimentation see Chapanis (1967, 1971), Chiles (1971) and Singleton (1971b). However, while the findings of the experimental psychologists need to be approached with caution generated by the above criticism they are still of considerable interest in themselves and retain some implications for real skill studies.

In discussing experimental psychology it is important to distinguish between the Gestalt type and the Stimulus–Response type. Gestalt psychology started with three German psychologists, Wertheimer, Koffka and Kohler, in the early years of this century. They had some rather involved theoretical ideas but they were all elegant experimenters. They relied on introspective evidence supported by experimentation and they were not afraid of studying high level human behaviour. Wertheimer (1945) wrote an interesting book on productive thinking, Koffka (1935) was particularly interested in perception and memory and Kohler was concerned with learning particularly by insight. While criticizing behaviourism Kohler (1947) wrote: 'the right psychological formula is therefore: pattern of stimulation–organization–response to the products of organization', there is an obvious rapport here with the concept of skill. The experiments by Bartlett (1932) are characteristic of the gestalt method in that there is extensive reliance on thinking out the problem and using experiments as an aid to research thinking rather than as important ends in themselves.

The pursuit of relevance in the experimental situation leads to lack of precision of control and often complete absence of consideration for statistical significance. In rejecting these criteria the experimenter must naturally rely to a greater extent on the elegance and general fitness for purpose of experiments but such intellectual effort and discipline has its own rewards. The theories of learning developed by Lewin and Wheeler (Hilgard, 1948) follow the gestalt tradition and again fit with skill theories. Tolman's Sign–Gestalt theory is an interesting integration in that Tolman is regarded as a behaviourist but this is essentially a field theory.

Stimulus–Response or S–R psychology started from the belief that there was a fundamental element of behaviour, the stimulus–response pair, for which the properties should be explored in minute detail so that eventually all behaviour could be explained by more and more complex combinations of these pairs. The precedent here, of course, is chemistry, a successful science based on the study of a limited number of elements and the description of all physical substances as combinations of these elements. In psychology, the main originator of this approach was Pavlov (1927) who wrote 'It is obvious that the different kinds of habits based on training, education and discipline of any sort are nothing but a long chain of conditioned reflexes.' This approach suited the climate of the times particularly in America. It seemed to provide a basis for the study of behaviour which avoided both the endless disputes between philosophers about body/mind problems and the tiresomely unquantitative characteristics of introspective psychology which relied on variables such as feelings and emotions. As Watson (1914) put it in his manifesto on behaviourism:

> It is possible to write a psychology, to define it . . . as the 'science of behaviour' and never go back on the definition, never to use the terms consciousness, mental states, mind, content, will, imagery and the like . . .
> It can be done in terms of stimulus and response, in terms of habit formation, habit integration and the like.

The result was a vast literature on conditioning as the basis of learning (Hilgard and Marquis, 1940), and culminated in the principles of behaviour enunciated by Hull (1943), who starts from the established functions of neural impulses, such as reinforcement and inhibition, and uses them to erect an elaborate set of postulates about molar behaviour. For example, postulate 16 states that 'when reaction potentials to two or more incompatible responses occur in an organism at the same time, only the reaction whose effective reaction potential is greatest will be evoked'. As Hilgard (1948) comments 'The postulate does not solve the problem (of patterns), it takes the problem from the field of perception and buries it in the nervous system.'

It will be appreciated that the author has considerable admiration for the skill psychologists who carry out experimental work following the methods pioneered by the gestalt psychologists, but he is much less sanguine about the preponderance of work in the human performance field which is in the behaviourist and stimulus–response tradition. We need experimental psychology because it can provide some solid anchor points which aid in the understanding and prediction of human behaviour in adapting to the physical world and more particularly the technological world.

There are, however, several serious dangers. The similarity of the methods to those used in the physical sciences provide a superficial rigour and validity which is not entirely justifiable. People are not samples of materials or plots of wheat from which simple measures can be acquired, manipulated and extrapolated from. The mystique of complex apparatus and complex statistical methods confuses rather than clarifies the issues. On the other hand the relative simplicity of the methods, in the sense that they can readily be taught and learned, together with the apparent success in making progress encourages too many people to make careers in this kind of activity. Experimental psychology is easy to carry out competently by the criteria that journals will accept reports and colleagues cannot fault the technique. It is, however, very difficult to carry out with validity and creativity to the point where an advance of knowledge can be claimed. Broadbent (1971) defends the behaviourist approach to psychology on the grounds that such concepts facilitate communication and make it easier to 'interrogate nature to obtain fresh information'. He is dubious about the value of common sense because there are many equally plausible common sense approaches and one needs the discipline of the experimental evidence to 'exclude whole classes of other possible theories'.

Unfortunately too much reliance on experimental evidence not only excludes theories which are contradicted by the evidence but also theories which are not readily susceptible to exploration by experimental methods. This is, in essence, why the study of skill is a neglected subject. Take for example the concept of attention. Moray (1969) has written a scholarly book on this topic and he himself quotes a lucid definition of attention by William James 'the taking possession by the mind, in clear and vivid form, of one out of what seems simultaneously possible objects or trains of thought'.

This concept needs exploration because it described an important aspect of skill. Consider a sales representative driving down a motorway. His attention would appear superficially to be devoted to receiving data mainly through the eyes about the progress of his vehicle along the road in relation to other traffic. This is the situation on which the experimental psychologist likes to concentrate. Unfortunately it is only the tip of the iceberg in terms of the cognitive activity of the salesman. The way in which he is driving is dominated by his personality and by his objective. He has an appointment at some factory; he will determine his driving style by asking himself questions such as does he have plenty of time or is he likely to be late, how important to his company is it that he should avoid being late thus improving his chances of making a sale? Having devised a strategy in this wide context he need not concentrate his attention wholly on driving. He may switch on the radio, thereby providing an unrelated sensory input or he might simply sit back and reappraise the progress of his career, what are his chances of promotion over the next few years and how it will be affected by a sale today. Promotion might mean moving to a different part of the country and this will initiate a train of thought about the progress of his children's education and the kinds of careers they seem suited for. The number of trucks he passes might stimulate him to think about the country's economy or the effects on the environment of pollution due to internal combustion engines. Such ideas might in turn lead on to the progress and likely survival time for western civilization.

Moray can tell us nothing of consequence about this kind of behaviour because, being an experimental psychologist, he describes only the experiments which have been done in laboratories. He has to exclude everything about skill because as he points out 'all work reported in this book should be regarded as work on unpractised subjects' and more fundamentally he has lost the essence of attention because in order to stick to the laboratory evidence he has to quite artificially restrict the phenomenon to 'selective processes in vision and hearing'. A few such books are desirable but the real complaint is that too large a proportion of the resources devoted to psychology are being dissipated in this narrow way. For one current illustration of the ultimate of this approach to psychology see Rabbit and Dornic (1975). The argument that it is the only respectable way we know is hopefully countered by the remainder of this book. Whether or not this hope is realized there have to be other ways of finding out about human behaviour to supplement laboratory based experimental psychology if psychology is to have any kind of adequacy in dealing with ordinary behaviour.

References

Anglin, J. M. (1974). J. S. Bruner, *Beyond the Information Given* (London: George, Allen and Unwin)

Appley, M. H. and Trumbull, R. (1967). *Psychological Stress* (New York: Appleton Century Crofts)

Attneave, F. (1959). *Applications of Information Theory to Psychology* (New York: Holt–Dryden)

Baddeley, A. (1966). The influence of acoustic and semantic similarity in long term memory for word sequences. *Qt. J. Exp. Psychol.*, **18**, 302.

Baddeley, A. and Patterson, K. (1971). Relation between long-term and short-term memory. *Br. Med. Bull.*, **27, 3,** 237

Bartlett, F. C. (1932). *Remembering* (Cambridge: University Press)

Bartlett, F. C. (1943). Fatigue following highly skilled work. *Proc. R. Soc. B.*, **131,** 247

Bartlett, F. C. (1948). The measurement of human skill. *Occup. Psychol.*, **22,** 31–38, 83

Bartlett, F. C. (1951a). Anticipation in human performance. *In* Akman *et al.* (eds.) *Essays in Psychology Dedicated to David Katz* (Uppsala: Amlquist and Wiksell)

Bartlett, F. C. (1951b) The bearing of experimental psychology upon human skilled performance. *Br. J. Indust. Med.*, **8,** 209

Bartlett, F. C. (1953). Psychological criteria of fatigue. *In* W. F. Floyd and A. T. Welford (eds.), *Fatigue* (London: H. K. Lewis)

Bartlett, F. C. (1958). *Thinking* (London: George Allen & Unwin)

Bonjer, F. H. (1971). Temporal factors and physiological load. *In* W. T. Singleton, J. G. Fox and D. Whitefield (eds.), *Measurement of Man at Work* (London: Taylor & Francis)

Broadbent, D. E. (1957). Immediate memory and simultaneous stimuli. *Qt. J. Exp. Psychol.*, **9,** 1

Broadbent, D. E. (1971). *Decision and Stress* (London: Academic Press)

Brown, J. (1958). Some tests of the decay theory of immediate memory. *Qt. J. Exp. Psychol.*, **10,** 12

Bruner, J. S. (1974). *In* J. M. Anglin (ed.), *Beyond the Information Given* (London: George Allen & Unwin)

Chapanis, A. (1967). The relevance of laboratory studies to practical situations. *Ergonomics*, **10,** 557

Chapanis, A. (1971). The search for relevance in applied research. *In* W. T. Singleton, J. G. Fox and D. Whitfield (eds.), *Measurement of Man at Work* (London: Taylor & Francis)

Chiles, W. D. (1971). Complex performance: the development of research criteria applicable to the real world. *In* W. T. Singleton, J. G. Fox and D. Whitfield (eds.), *Measurement of Man at Work* (London: Taylor & Francis)

Connolly, K. (1970). *Mechanisms of motor skill development* (London: Academic Press)

Conrad, R. (1963). Acoustic confusions and memory span for words. *Nature* (London), **197**, 1029

Craik, K. J. W. (1948). Man as an element in a control system. *Br. J. Psychol.*, **38**, 142

Craik, F. I. M. (1971). Primary memory. *Br. Med. Bull.*, **27**, 3, 232

Crossman, E. R. F. W. (1955). The measurement of dicriminability. *Q. J. Exp. Psychol.*, **7**, 176

Crossman, E. R. F. W. (1959). A theory of the acquisition of speed skill. *Ergonomics*, **2**, 2, 153

Crossman, E. R. F. W. (1961). Information and serial order in human immediate memory. *In* C. Cherry (ed.), *Information theory* (London: Butterworth)

Davis, D. R. (1948). Pilot Error. *Air Ministry Publication, AP3139A* (London: HMSO)

Davis, R. (1956). The limits of the psychological refractory period. *Qt. J. Exp. Psychol.*, **8**, 23

Davis, R. (1957). The human operator as a single channel information system. *Q. J. Exp. Psychol.*, **9**, 119

Dudley, N. A. (1963). Work-time distributions. *Int. J. Prod. Res.*, **2**, 2, 137

Fitts, P. M. (1954). The information capacity of the human motor system in controlling the amplitude of movement. *J. Exp. Psychol.*, **47**, 381

Fitts, P. M. and Posner, M. I. (1967). *Human Performance* (Belmont: Brooke–Cole)

Fleishman, E. A. and Rich, S. (1963). The role of kinaesthetic and spatial–visual abilities in perceptual motor learning. *J. Exp. Psychol.*, **66**, 6

Fogel, L. J. (1963). *Biotechnology* (New Jersey: Prentice Hall)

Gagné, R. M. (1962). Human functions in systems. *In* R. M. Gagné (ed.), *Psychological Principles in System Development* (New York: Holt, Rinehart and Winston)

Gagné, R. M. (1974). Taxonomic problems of educational systems. *In* W. T. Singleton and P. Spurgeon (eds.), *Measurement of Human Resources* (London: Taylor & Francis)

Garner, W. F. (1962). *Uncertainty and Structure as Psychological Concepts* (New York: Wiley)

Gibson, J. J. (1966). *The Senses Considered as Perceptual Systems* (London: Allen and Unwin)

Gregory, R. L. (1966). *Eye and Brain* (London: Weidenfield and Nicolson)

Gregory, R. L. (1970). *The Intelligent Eye* (London: Weidenfield and Nicolson)

Gunderson, E. K. E. and Rahe, R. M. (1974). *Life Stress and Illness* (Springfield, Ill: Thomas)

Head, H. (1920). *Studies in Neurology* (Oxford: University Press)

Hick, W. E. (1948). The discontinuous functioning of the human operator in pursuit tasks. *Q. J. Exp. Psychol.*, **1**, 36

Hilgard, E. R. (1948). *Theories of Learning* (New York: Appleton, Century, Crofts)

Hilgard, E. R. and Marquis, D. G. (1940). *Conditioning and Learning* (New York: Appleton Century Crofts)

Hull, C. L. (1943). *Principles of Behaviour* (New York: Appleton Century Crofts)

Hyman, R. (1953). Stimulus information as a determinant of reaction time. *J. Exp. Psychol.*, **45**, 188

Kay, H. (1953). Experimental Studies of Adult Learning. PhD thesis quoted in A. T. Welford (1958). Ageing and Human Skills (Oxford: University Press)

Kay, H. and Poulton, E. C. (1951). Anticipation in memorising. *B. J. Psychol.*, **42**, 34

Kelley, C. R. (1968). *Manual and Automatic Control* (New York: Wiley)

King, S. D. M. (1959). The operator as a self-regulating system. *Ergonomics*, **2**, 7, 171

Koffka, K. (1935). *Principles of Gestalt Psychology* (London: Routledge and Kegan Paul)

Kohler, W. (1947). *Gestalt Psychology* (New York: Liveright)

Kraiss, K. F. (1972). A model for analysing the co-ordination of manual movements. *In* R. K. Bernotat and K. P. Gartner (eds.), *Displays and Controls* (Amsterdam: Swets and Zeitlinger)

Lacey, J. I. (1967). Somatic response patterning and stress: some revisions of activation theory. *In* H. M. Appley and R. Trumbull (eds.), *Psychological Stress* (New York: Appleton Century Crofts)

Lashley, K. S. (1950). In search of the engram. *Symp. Soc. Exp. Biol.*, **4**, 454

Leonard, J. A. (1953). Advance information in sensori-motor skills. *Q. J. Exp. Psychol.*, **5**, 141

Leonard, J. A. (1959). Tactual choice reactions. *Q. J. Exp. Psychol.*, **2**, 76

Levi, L. (1974). Psychological stress and disease: a conceptual model. *In* E. K. E. Gunderson and R. H. Rahe (eds.), *Life Stress and Illness* (Springfield, Ill: Thomas)

Mackworth, J. F. (1969). *Vigilance and Habituation* (Harmondsworth: Penguin)

Mackworth, J. F. (1970). *Vigilance and Attention* (Harmondsworth: Penguin)

Mackworth, N. H. (1950). Researches on the measurement of human performance. *MRC Special Report No. 268* (London: HMSO)

Mackworth, N. H. and Mackworth, J. F. (1959). Remembering advance cues during searching. *B. J. Psychol.*, **50**, 207

McRuer, D. T. (1968). A neuro muscular actuation system model. *IEEE Transactions*, **MMS 9**, 3

Michon, J. A. (1964). Temporal structure of letter groups and span of perception. *Q.J. Exp. Psychol.*, **16**, 232

Miller, G. A. (1956). The magical number seven plus or minus two. Some limits on the capacity for processing information. *Psychol. Rev.*, **63**, 81

Moray, N. (1969). *Attention: Selective Processes in Vision and Hearing* (London: Hutchinson)

Morgan, C. T. and Stellar, E. (1950). *Physiological Psychology* (New York: McGraw Hill)

Munn, N. L. (1965). *The evolution and growth of human behaviour* (London: Harrap)

Murrell, K. F. H. (1962). Operator variability and its industrial consequences. *Int. J. Prod. Res.*, **1**, 39

Murrell, K. F. H. (1971). Temporal factors in light work. *In* W. T. Singleton, J. G. Fox and D. Whitfield (eds.), *Measurement of Man at Work* (London: Taylor & Francis)

Nathan, P. (1969). *The Nervous System* (Harmondsworth: Penguin)

Neisser, U. (1967). *Cognitive Psychology* (New York: Appleton Century Crofts)

Paillard, J. (1960). The patterning of skilled movements. *In* J. Field, H. W. Magoun and V. E. Hall (eds.), *Handbook of Physiology. Vol. III* (Washington: American Physiological Society)

Pavlov, I. P. (1927). *Conditioned Reflexes.* (Oxford: University Press). Quoted in E. R. Hilgard and D. G. Marquis (1940). *Conditioning and Learning* (New York: Appleton Century Crofts)

Pepper, R. L. and Herman, L. M. (1970). Decay and interference effects in the short-term retention of a discrete motor act. *J. Exp. Psychol. Mon.*, *Suppl.* **83**, **2**, 1

Poulton, E. C. (1952). Perceptual anticipation in tracking using two-pointer and one-pointer displays. *B. J. Psychol.*, **43**, 222. Also The Basis of Perceptual anticipation in Tracking. *B. J. Psychol.*, **43**, 295

Poulton, E. C. (1964). Postview and preview in tracking with complex and simple inputs. *Ergonomics*, **7**, 257

Poulton, E. C. (1970). *Environment and Human Efficiency* (Springfield Ill: Charles C. Thomas)

Provins, K. A. (1958). The effect of peripheral nerve block on the appreciation and execution of finger movements. *J. Physiol.*, **143**, 55

Rabbitt, P. M. A. and Dormic, S. (1975). *Attention and Performance V* (London: Academic Press)

Rolfe, J. M. (1971). The secondary task as a measure of mental load. *In* W. T. Singleton, J. G. Fox and D. Whitfield (eds.), *Measurement of Man at Work* (London: Taylor & Francis)

Schiller, P. H. (1965). *J. Exp. Psychol.*, **69**, 2, 193

Seymour, W. D. (1966). *Industrial Skills* (London: Pitman)

Sheridan, T. B. and Ferrell, W. R. (1974). *Man–Machine Systems* (Cambridge: MIT Press)

Singleton, W. T. (1953). Deterioration of performance on a short-term perceptual motor task. *In* W. F. Floyd and A. T. Welford (eds.), *Fatigue* (London: H. K. Lewis)

Singleton, W. T. (1968). Some recent experiments on learning and their training implications. *Ergonomics*, **11, 1,** 53

Singleton, W. T. (1971a). The measurement of man at work with particular reference to arousal. *In* W. T. Singleton, J. G. Fox and D. Whitfield (eds.), *Measurement of Man at Work* (London: Taylor & Francis)

Singleton, W. T. (1971b). Psychological aspects of man–machine systems. *In* P. B. Warr (ed.), *Psychology at Work* (Harmondsworth: Penguin)

Singleton, W. T. (1972). *Introduction to Ergonomics* (Geneva: WHO)

Singleton, W. T., Fox, J. G. and Whitfield, D. (eds.), (1971). *Measurement of Man at Work* (London: Taylor & Francis)

Smith, K. U. and Sussman, H. (1969). Cybernetic theory and analysis of motor learning and memory. *In* E. A. Bilodeau (ed.), *Principles of Skill Acquisition* (New York: Academic Press)

Sperling, G. (1961). The information available in brief visual presentations. *Psychol. Mon.*, **74**

Sperling, G. (1963). A model for visual memory tasks. *Human Factors*, **5,** 19

Telford, C. W. (1931). The refractory phase of voluntary and associative responses. *J. Exp. Psychol.*, **14,** 1

Vossius, G. (1972). The functional organisation of object directed human intended movement and the forming of a mathematical model. *In* R. K. Bernotat and K. P. Gartner (eds.), *Displays and Controls* (Amsterdam: Swets and Zeitlinger)

Watson, J. B. (1914). *Behaviour.* (New York: Holt). Quoted in R. S. Woodworth (1949). *Contemporary Schools of Psychology* (London: Methuen)

Welford, A. T. (1958). *Ageing and Human Skill* (Oxford: University Press)

Welford, A. T. (1968). *Fundamentals of skill* (London: Methuen)

Welford, A. T. (1974). *Man under Stress* (London: Taylor & Francis)

Wertheimer, M. (1945). *Productive thinking* (New York: Holt, Rinehart and Winston)

Woodworth, R. S. (1938). *Experimental Psychology* (New York: Holt, Rinehart and Winston)

2

The Forest Worker

B. PETTERSSON

HISTORICAL DEVELOPMENT IN SWEDEN

During the latter half of the nineteenth century a large number of sawmills were established, particularly in northern Sweden. Later on pulpmills were built to supplement the sawmills and to enable utilization of wood chippings. Today, most enterprises have both sawmills and pulpmills. The forest industry is of great importance to the Swedish economy, accounting for around 25% of the total value of exports. Sweden is a small country, but, nonetheless, it has a relatively high share of the world's export market of forest products.

Of the Swedish forest land, 50% is owned by private forest owners, most of whom are farmers with small woodlots and small lots of farmland. At the time when wood started to be used for industrial purposes, around 80–90% of the Swedish population made a living from farming, mining, etc. Most of the farmers would work part of the winter in the forest and the rest of the year on their farms. Consequently, the forest enterprises which were expanding at that time also recruited their labour force from among the small farmers.

There were two main categories of forest workers: the teamsters and the cutters. At that time, forest work was not regarded as a trade in the same way as other crafts. There was no real prestige in forest work and it was poorly paid. However, the teamster or horse handler had a slightly higher status than the cutter and was often in the position of employer to him. He was really a sort of contractor, who accepted assignments to carry out felling in a certain logging area on behalf of a forestry company and who was therefore also responsible for recruiting the number of cutters necessary. The equipment was simple: The teamster had a horse and log sled or double sleigh and the cutter had an axe, saw and barking spud.

Development during the last few decades has rapidly changed the picture of Swedish forestry described above. The emphasis given to exports has put the industry in a difficult position. It finds itself squeezed between the export price of forest products on one side and the high Swedish wage rates on the other. This has probably been the single most important cause of the current, rapid mechanization in forestry in Sweden.

Figure 2.1   Forest worker at the end of the nineteenth century (By courtesy of Forsknings-stiftelsen Skogsarbeten)

The rate at which wages have increased during the last two decades has meant that the mechanization of forestry has become increasingly more attractive. During the 1950s barking was mechanized. The middle of the 1950s also saw the introduction of the chain saw. Around 1960, the special extraction machines for logging were introduced, and extraction was mechanized rapidly during the 1960s. Specialized machines, most of which are forwarders, account for more than 80% of the wood extracted today (Anon., 1974).

During the 1960s, various solutions for the mechanization of limbing and bucking were tested and some of these are now in practical operation. The 1970s will see the extensive mechanization of limbing and bucking (cutting into standard lengths). In addition, felling will also probably be mechanized quite extensively. Owing to mechanization and rationalization, the amount of wood cut per man-day in 1975 was about ten times that of 20 years ago. The forest worker is generally a well trained and professional worker employed throughout the year. But, on the other hand, the number of forest workers has decreased in proportion to the capacity increase per man.

PRESENT DAY TASKS AND SKILLS—THE CUTTER

Despite mechanization, the most common category of forest worker today is the cutter, but the equipment and methods he uses have little in common with those of his predecessors at the end of the nineteenth century. His most important equipment consists of two or three lightweight power saws—if one should break down, the cutter need not waste time on extensive repair work. For the greater part of the year he spends his time felling trees by power saw but during the summer he usually alternates this with a certain amount of silvicultural work such as planting and young stand cleaning.

The work of a cutter today is done outdoors, in all seasons. This implies that during the winter, a cutter is subjected to temperatures of $-20\ °C$ or more. He often has to plod through snow deeper than 60 cm. The work consists of walking across forest land carrying a power saw, weighing between 7–8 kg, together with a fair amount of additional equipment such as service equipment for the saw, and a felling lever, etc.

The work also includes the cutting of strip roads through the stand, the selection of trees in accordance with specific directions, the felling of trees into the strip road, limbing, marking the trees for bucking in accordance with special directions, bucking, rolling logs away from the strip road and the dragging and stacking of pulpwood in piles of at least $0.5\ m^3$ (stacked wood) at the strip road. Further, the work includes the daily maintenance of the power saw such as topping up with lubricating oil and fuel, filing the chain and other service work. The cutter is also responsible for ensuring that tree marking and marking for bucking is carried out in accordance with the directions and that safety regulations are followed.

On his way to the tree the cutter must decide a suitable felling direction. The decision is based on factors such as the direction in which the tree leans, crown overhang, distance to strip road, obstructing trees, etc. The cutter has great possibilities to direct the fall of the tree by, for example, cutting the trees in a suitable order, by locating the felling notch correctly and by using felling levers and other aids. A well done directional felling facilitates considerably subsequent operations such as the manual extraction of wood to strip road. A poorly done directional felling increases the risk of lodging, i.e. the tree becomes hung up in one or more standing trees. Lodging may cause accidents and is in general very time consuming. A great deal of the difference between a 'good' and an 'average' cutter stems from the planning of the work—especially the planning of the directional felling.

During felling the cutter must also look for ground obstacles as the butt end of the tree may kick back and cause accidents. This may be the case when the tree falls across a large rock or previously felled stem. If possible the tree should be felled in such a way that it comes to rest at a comfortable working height. The subsequent limbing with power saw is facilitated if the cutter does not have to bend down and if he can rest the weight of the saw on the stem during limbing. During limbing the saw is moved along the stem according to a certain pattern cutting one limb at a time (Figure 2.2).

Figure 2.2 Forest worker, cutter in the 1970s (By courtesy of Forskningsstiftelsen Skogsarbeten)

A common cause of accidents in limbing was kick-back from the saw injuring the left hand or arm of the cutter. Kick-back generally is caused by the point of the guide bar hitting a limb or a butt forcing the saw upwards at great speed. A kick-back may result in an accident within 0·1–0·2 s. This means that the cutter has no possibility to react consciously or by reflexes. However, by introducing technical devices to stop the chain at kick-back which work more or less automatically, it has been possible to reduce this type of accidents by about 80% within a few years.

After limbing the cutter does the necessary crosscutting. Before doing so he has to find out from which direction to cut and he must ask himself whether it is posible to cut the stem from above or whether it is necessary to cut from below. He therefore has to assess whether the stem rests in tension so that the saw might get stuck, or if he can cut through the stem without such problems. This is often very difficult and it calls for the cutters full attention to sounds or vibrations from the saw or the stem. The inexperienced cutter often runs into difficulties here. When deciding where to buck the tree the cutter must also make an economic assessment of the relative value of different assortments. In doing this he has to consider a number of factors such as taper, knots, defects such as rot, etc. This work element—the so called 'marking for bucking'—is of great importance to the total value yield of a tree.

For many years now, cutting has been one of the types of work in Sweden accounting for the highest number of industrial accidents. The main reason is that a piece of potentially very dangerous equipment is used, the power saw, and under conditions which are relatively difficult to control. The accidents occurring are also of a relatively serious nature and fatalities and permanent disabilities are not uncommon. Consequently, the cutter is furnished with extensive personal protective equipment such as helmet, earmuffs, eye protectors, safety gloves, leg guards and often safety shoes with steel toecaps.

The work is physically demanding. The cutter has hitherto been paid piecework rates but this changed to a more time based system during 1975. He must drag pulpwood logs weighing between 20 and 70 kg each. This means that he must be physically fit and during the greater part of the day he will have a pulse of around 100–120/min. Consequently, his energy consumption is between 4000 and 5000 calories per day, i.e. almost double that of a person with a normal office job. However, it is possible for a cutter to make his work a lot easier through good planning, for example, selection of trees, selection of felling direction and working technique. It is also possible for the work of a cutter to influence greatly the value of the wood extracted from a given stand.

Capacities and skills required

A cutter must have a high capacity for physical work. Even if the work is facilitated by means of good planning and proper techniques, it is not possible to achieve a normal work standard if his oxygen absorption capacity is not at least as high as the average for the Swedish adult population. He must also be physically active. The cutter must be able to plan his work and must also have a good working technique. Great weight is especially given to a steady and safe manner of working. In addition, the cutter must be familiar with the demands for various wood assortments and should also be able to look after a power saw, for example, to file the chain, to carry out smaller repairs, etc.

PRESENT DAY TASKS AND SKILLS—THE LOGGING MACHINE OPERATOR

The logging machine operator operates either an extraction machine, e.g. a forwarder, or another logging machine, e.g. a feller, limber, bucker or limber-bucker (Figure 2.3). The work of a logging machine operator includes route planning based on sketches and reconnaissance in the terrain, operating in runs across the logging area, felling the trees and the processing of felled trees accessible from each set-up. The various operations are automated to a certain degree. The work also includes daily inspection and maintenance, a certain amount of fault-finding, smaller repairs and the preparation for and participation in more extensive, on-site repairs.

Figure 2.3 Forest worker, feller operator, in the 1970s (By courtesy of Forskningsstiftelsen Skogsarbeten)

When the operator has to move his machine through the terrain he must be familiar with the mobility characteristics of the machine, i.e. how it reacts under varying ground, surface and slope conditions respectively. On the basis of this knowledge and after having studied the terrain ahead he can select a suitable route. The operator profits from some years of previous experience as he can then more readily avoid getting stuck or causing damage to his machine as well as the stand where he operates. During the operation the operator must know his machine and be on the alert to unfamiliar sounds from engine and transmission so that he can avoid breakdowns in time.

When the operator has selected a suitable set up the second part of his job starts, namely loading, unloading or processing. From the selected position he is now to carry out the necessary operation in the shortest time possible. It could, for example, be a question of feeding in previously felled trees by means of a loader boom into a processing unit for limbing and bucking (Figure 2.4). The operator works with control levers which place high demands on his psycho-motor talent as well as his ability to react. The high feeding speed of the machine sometimes places too high a demand on the operator. A common feeding speed on a so called 'processor' is 2 m/s.

Figure 2.4 Logging machine, limber-bucker, in the 1970s (By courtesy of Forsknings-stiftelsen Skogsarbeten)

Thus, in a very short period of time the operator has to assess the quality of the tree—taper, defects etc.—relate this to the relevant marking-for-bucking instructions, decide where to buck the tree and finally, by means of his controls, initiate the bucking operation. It is impossible to carry out this job continuously without any errors and during the last few years part of the job has been automated.

Many problems such as the one described still remain in mechanized logging work, however. Between 65 and 70% of the work is carried out from the cab and the remaining 25–35% outdoors in conjunction with reconnaissance and service and repair work. The operator is subjected to shaking and vibration in the cab and during summer the temperature can be uncomfortably high. Machine maintenance and repair work is also fairly dirty work. It is the responsibility of the machine operator to ensure that no unauthorized person encroaches on the operating area of the machine. He is also responsible for seeing that bucking is carried out in accordance with the bucking directive. Further, he must inspect and maintain the machine so that it does not become damaged as a result of neglected maintenance. His machine may be worth up to £100 000.

Capacities and skills required

The physical demands on a machine operator are considerably less than those on a cutter. However, a certain amount of heavy lifting work may be involved, e.g. during repair work. These demands limit the possibilities of employing women as machine operators today. The intellectual requirements are primarily associated with the necessity of absorbing the knowledge necessary to understand the design of the machine (Andersson *et al.*, 1968). Perception and psychomotor demands are fairly high. A machine operator must be able to identify relevant signals, to assess the form and quality of the trees, judge speeds, etc. In addition, he must have quick reactions and be able to control his movements, e.g. when operating the boom controls. Good co-ordination is also necessary during boom operation and off-road driving (Hall *et al.*, 1972). The personal qualities include presence of mind, owing to the critical situation which can arise in the event of machine breakdown. A sense of responsibility towards the safety of fellow workers and towards costly machines, initiative and a capacity for teamwork are other important personal qualities.

EDUCATION AND TRAINING

Basic Training

The basic training which forestry workers undergo comprises a part of the general educational system in Sweden. After 9 years at comprehensive school, the forest worker undergoes a 2-year basic training course. The aim of the training is to provide the basic knowledge and skills necessary for working in forestry as regards silviculture, logging and extraction. After basic training, the pupil can either apply for a job or continue with more advanced training.

The principal subjects dealt with are logging, theory of machines, forest production, wood measurement and wood technology, but other subjects are also included such as ergonomics and nature conservancy together with subjects of a more general nature, e.g. Swedish, English and Mathematics.

Re-training

The majority of Swedish forest workers have not had the opportunity to undergo the 2-year basic training course. Most of the cutters are more or less self-taught and have only gone on further training courses of a few days or weeks. On the introduction of mechanization, these men will have to be transferred to the job of machine operator. They will then be sent on a shorter basic training course—so-called re-training—lasting between 6 and 10 weeks. The aim of this training is to make the changeover to machine operator easier and is focused mainly on technical subjects such as the theory of machines and engines. After completion of re-training, the pupil can then be trained for the machine he is to operate.

Further training

Further training comprises an important part of the rapid technical development that Swedish forestry is currently undergoing. This training generally comprises short courses in boom operation, the repair and maintenance of a given machine, etc. On the introduction of a new type of machine, e.g. a limber-bucker, the training may be arranged as shown in Figure 2.5. In further training a great deal of weight is given to the integration of the training for various personnel categories such as supervisors and forest workers.

During theoretical training, a certain amount of emphasis is given to proficiency training, conducted in the form of formal training following the

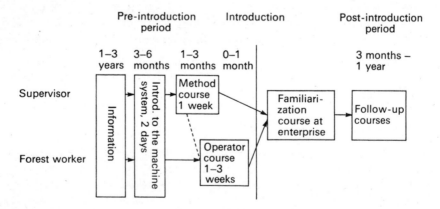

Figure 2.5 The training of forest workers and supervisors on the introduction of highly mechanized logging systems

'part by part' method, and by means of simulators. However, the aim of basic training or re-training is not to provide the pupils with full proficiency, a great deal is left to the training on the machine itself or at the enterprise.

THE FUTURE

As mentioned earlier, forestry is currently undergoing rapid mechanization in Sweden, it is estimated that by 1985 about 80% of all logging will be carried out by mechanized methods. The machines currently employed in logging are primarily machines for felling and for limbing-bucking. The prerequisite for the rapid and successful introduction of mechanization is that all forest workers, service men, supervisors, etc. undergo extensive training. Another prerequisite is that the development work is carried out with due considera-tion being given to the human capacity and limitations, both physical and psychological.

Mechanization implies without doubt a reduced accident risk. But the machines should not be allowed to become so technically complex nor to be so demanding on the operator that, for example, older persons or persons with a reduced working capacity cannot be employed as machine operators. A great deal of attention is currently being focused on these matters in work on the development of logging technology. With an interval of 5 years between them, two ergonomic evaluations have been carried out on all types of logging and extraction machines in operation. Ergonomic checklists with guidelines and recommendations for a number of different fields are utilized by the machine manufacturers and the machine users during design and purchasing of machines (Aminoff et al., 1975). As a result of the experience gained from these ergonomic examinations, the continued technical develop-ment work has been focused on solving the most essential ergonomic problems, currently judged to be maintenance work (accident risks, awkward working position and heavy lifting), lighting conditions, the operating climate in the cab and vibration.

The extensive change which forest worker activities is currently undergoing can also be expected to have an effect on the psychological work content. For example, a study by Gardell established that the work of a cutter, despite the fact that it is physically exerting compared to most other jobs in industry, is regarded as being relatively independent and free from work confinement and monotony (Gardell, 1968). What psychological effect then has mechanization had on forest work? The changeover to mechanized logging has not only resulted in different work assignments but also in dif-ferent working conditions (Hall, 1973). One of the most important changes is that many workers have left physically active jobs for one in which they spend most of their time sitting down. This has resulted in many machine operators becoming overweight, they have not adapted their eating habits to their new working conditions.

Further, the work process has taken on a faster tempo with the result that the forest worker now has less scope to influence his own performance at work. Technical competence has become more important than forestry experience in pace with the improvement of the machines' off-road mobility properties and in the same way demands for work quality have been replaced by quantity demands. In this context it can be mentioned that many forest workers find it personally disturbing to have to sacrifice quality demands in order to meet demands for productivity.

The scope for self-determination of each individual forest worker has been narrowed with increased mechanization. Working hours have become less flexible and an individual's working tempo now depends on the performance of his machine, on productivity calculations drawn up by supervisors and on the planning and working tempo of others. Despite the fact that teamwork should be an integral part of mechanized logging, it does not seem to have been developed very far. Generally speaking, each individual carries on separately with his own task, and because of the interdependence of the operating procedure, the workers often end up either consciously or subconsciously hurrying each other to prevent themselves from being the one who causes waiting time. Conversely, more marked teamwork is to be found in machine servicing, in fault-finding and in machine repair work.

Accordingly, the results of studies carried out indicate that the need in mechanized logging is for development towards better teamwork and increased participation in mutual planning activities by all group members. Many machine operators, for example, are of the opinion that they can make valuable contributions to the planning of work ahead of machine operation. An essential task of Swedish forestry should be the concern for utilizing these resources found within its organization to the advantage of forest worker job satisfaction and to the advantage of the economic results of the activities.

References

Aminoff, S., Hansson, J-E. and Pettersson, B. (1975). Ergonomic checklist for transport and materials handling machinery. Logging Research Foundation, Stockholm

Andersson, L., Bergström, L., Krantz, A., Lennerheim, G. and Pettersson, B. (1968). Selection of tractor operators by psychological test. Logging Research Foundation, Report No. 7, 1968, Stockholm

Anon. (1974). *Logging in Sweden.* Logging Research Foundation, Stockholm

Gardell, B. (1968). Skogsarbetares arbetsanpassning. PA-rådet. Meddelande No. 59, Stockholm

Hall, B., Persson, A. and Pettersson, B. (1972). Training of processor operators. Logging Research Foundation, Report No. 11, 1972, Stockholm

Hall, B. (1973). Skogsarbetet ur psykologisk synvinkel. Logging Research Foundation, Economi No. 11, 1973, Stockholm

3

The Farm Worker

J. MATTHEWS

INTRODUCTION

Farm statistics

The nature and organization of agriculture varies tremendously from country to country. Agricultural holdings may vary in size from a fraction of a hectare (1 hectare is about $2\frac{1}{2}$ acres) to many tens of thousands of hectares, and the labour requirement varies from several men per hectare in a horticultural or greenhouse enterprise, or perhaps where pigs or poultry are kept intensively, to one man per hundreds of hectares in arable or perhaps some types of fatstock farming. In England and Wales for example, where farming types are extremely mixed there are about 220 000 holdings of which approximately 120 000 are of between 3 and 50 hectares. 20 000 are under 3 hectares and approximately 80 000 over 50 hectares, with 2000 over 500 hectares in extent. Elsewhere in the world the average area of holdings varies from a little over one hectare in Malta or Barbados for example, to 400 hectares in the Argentine. A considerable proportion of holdings in the UK do not supply an adequate livelihood for the owner, who needs to have some other source of income. Similar part-time activity is common in many European countries and even on quite large holdings in N. America. The farms in England and Wales constitute approximately 15 million hectares of land of which approximately 7 million are arable, 5 million grassland and the remainder very rough grazing. The land supports approximately 10 million cattle, 7 million pigs, 18 million sheep and 110 million head of poultry and as such allows the country to produce a little over half of its food requirement (Ministry of Agriculture, Fisheries and Food, 1974).

Employment statistics

For comparison with the farm statistics above the employment data for England and Wales is shown in Table 3.1. These are taken from Ministry of Agriculture, Fisheries and Food 1973 statistics. The figures for farmers, partners and directors should be treated with reserve, but overall the data show that total numbers of people engaged is just over half a million with employees totalling 300 000. Of these, approximately 160 000 are part-time only. Those categories increasing significantly in numbers are the farm managers and the female regular employees. The data excludes farmers' wives and children although on many holdings, particularly the smaller ones, they play a very significant part particularly during the busier seasons. There is regrettably no reliable information on the ages of workers or on changes in the age pattern. The period when many of the older farm workers did not drive tractors has virtually passed so that one may expect a fairly wide and even age distribution in most branches of farm work.

Table 3.1   **Farmers and farm workers employed in England and Wales, December 1973**

	Thousands
Farmers, partners and directors, whole-time	165
part-time	42
Salaried managers	6
Regular whole time workers, male	164
female	21
Regular part-time workers, male	28
female	34
Seasonal or casual, male	31
female	29
Total	520

Both farm and labour statistics are particularly difficult to quantify accurately worldwide since, in less developed areas in particular, separate holdings are less easy to define and a large majority of the population is engaged in agricultural pursuits for some part of its time. The percentage of the economically active population engaged in agriculture varies from 1% in Kuwait to 96% in Niger. Table 3.2 summarizes the agricultural populations as proportions of the total in various territories (F.A.O. 1971). The agricultural population includes the employee and his family.

WHAT IS A FARM WORKER?

The worker's activities

Traditionally the farm worker has been expected to accept an extremely wide range of duties and possess the skills to undertake them. These activities included items such as milking, or feeding pigs, which were done daily, and others associated with a particular crop which were undertaken for a period of perhaps a few days or a few weeks together each year. In recent years there has been more specialization among farm staff with many workers classed as stockmen or tractor drivers but overall the majority would still be considered as general farm workers and be expected to deal with machinery operation, manual work and probably with stock. Farm workers' abilities are commendable not only because of the wide range of activities but because skills have normally been gained not from any formal training but largely from experience and in the majority of cases without the attainment of a very high level of formal education. Furthermore the seasonal activities are usually associated with rush periods so that skills learned from earlier seasons must be rapidly remembered and applied.

Table 3.2 Agricultural employment in various territories

Territory	Total population	Agricultural population	Percentage
Europe	444	100	23
USSR	231	73	32
North America	214	13	6
Central America	80	41	51
South America	166	73	44
Asia (excluding China)	1133	730	64
China	764	481	63
Africa	314	231	74
Oceana	17	3	19
	3363	1745	52

By way of example the general farm worker may milk the cows twice a day, this requiring skill in husbandry to identify sickness and to determine feed quantities. He may, in between, drive the tractor or other machines on one or more of a variety of tasks and he may also be expected to carry out manual work in shifting bales or sacks or digging up potatoes for instance. The same man may need to assist a cow in having a calf thereby acting as a nursing auxiliary, he may shear sheep using skills not dissimilar to the hairdresser and he may be capable of welding, or operating simple machine tools to assist in maintenance of the farm's machinery and buildings. The engineering skills have generally replaced some of the most admired of the earlier skills of the farm worker, namely the ability to build a neat stack of hay, the skills of thatching and of laying a hedge which not only looks attractive but also grows in such a way that animals are kept securely in the field.

Nowadays it is common to find on the larger farms staff whose skills generally fall into one of the three areas of stockmanship, machine operation or manual work and it is under these categories that the work is described in more detail later in the chapter. On larger farms also there is some management hierarchy although this is generally less formalized and, because of the smaller size of the labour forces, less structured than in other industries. There may be, for example, a head stockman or even a head dairyman on a farm which has both milk and fatstock cattle. A farm foreman may be employed and have responsibilities for day to day allocation of labour, for supervision of work and some instruction. On all farms the decisions on use of the land, purchasing policy for animals or equipment, staff recruiting and produce marketing will normally be taken by the owner or manager. It is more than likely that he will also decide on dates for planting and harvesting crops, and on the feeding of the animals. Figure 3.1 shows the possible

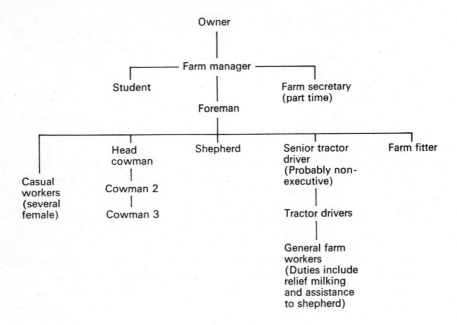

Figure 3.1   Possible management hierarchy on larger farm

hierarchy for a large mixed farm but it should be borne in mind for every farm of this size there are thousands of farms with only the employer and at most one worker. In the past rank was gained purely on the basis of age and experience but over the last 20 or so years with more farm workers having some type of agricultural college training, managers, foremen and even head stockmen or machinery operators may have gained their position through college learned knowledge.

Working conditions on the farm

Working hours are often long with an early start common particularly for dairy workers and with periods of late night working largely on a seasonal basis in summer. A 6 and even 7 day working week is practised, although throughout the year it is more common for farm workers to work 5½ days per week. Annual holidays are normally 2 weeks but in some cases 3 weeks are given. The basic wages are poor but with the long hours worked and some fringe benefits these are not a good guide to the man's total earnings. The man is often supplied with a cottage at a relatively low rental and may be given milk, vegetables and perhaps more personal assistance than would be expected from other industries.

Piece workers and contract workers are employed. For example much of the picking of brussels sprouts, which when snow and frost cover the plants is a particularly arduous task, is carried out by piece workers earning high incomes. Contract workers are most common in milking, although in the majority of cases these men are employed by a worker supply organization. They are then available to the farmer either on a short-term basis for permanent staff holidays or emergencies or on a more permanent basis where the agency will be responsible for their recruiting and provision and will normally accept from the farmer a fee related to the performance of the cows.

Farm work includes both indoor and outdoor activities. Much external work must be done in inclement weather but as the large majority of it is mechanized and increasingly machines are fitted with cabs or other shelter, relatively little work is done in direct rainfall. The exception would be work in connection with sheep and rounding-up cattle, for example, together with vegetable picking during the winter. In colder climates outdoor clothing is normally worn even within the cabs or shelter of machinery since it is normally necessary to leave the cab relatively frequently to deal with, for example, blockages or breakages. In summer it is seldom in the UK that the climate outdoors is uncomfortably hot for work but this can sometimes be the condition inside cabs due to radiant heat through the glass. The environments within buildings can vary considerably since some farm buildings are brick built and heated whilst others may be little more than an open shelter with considerable draughts and temperatures below freezing. Where indoor work is continued for long and regular periods, for example, inside a milking parlour or a fruit inspection and grading store, some heating is usually provided but this is often not to normal factory standards.

Mud and dust are common environmental components, the mud in fields, gateways and yards frequently making it difficult to move. Dust is met both in the operation of field machinery, particularly in spring cultivation and combine harvesters dealing with cereals, and inside buildings where hay, cereals or feedstuffs are being moved. Masks are sometimes provided, but less often worn, and it is very common for the worker to be completely covered in a layer of dust by the end of the day. There are unsatisfactory noise levels on tractors and other field machines (N.I.A.E., 1971) and also in some buildings housing crop processing or feed preparation plant, or even those containing animals (Talamo *et al.*, 1973). Evidence of noise-induced hearing loss among tractor drivers was obtained in the 1960s but since then there has been action in many countries to restrict noise levels by law on new tractors—generally to 90 dBA. These regulations are not being applied to combine harvesters and other self-propelled machines but here exposure times are shorter and noise frequently a little less. The plant in farm buildings could also be a hazard to hearing but in a minority of cases, since this equipment is normally employed only for a short period each day or on a seasonal basis of a few weeks per year.

Apart from the health hazard to hearing, there is also evidence from some countries of a high incidence of spinal deformities and stomach complaints among tractor drivers, caused in all probability largely by the vibration and jolting of the vehicle which works over relatively rough terrain (Matthews, 1973). Most tractors are fitted with suspension seats to ease the discomfort but it appears unlikely that a comfortable seat will be developed without some more complete suspension of the vehicle or the driver's cab. This component of the environment is probably important also in determining speed of work, hence it is a problem receiving much attention from researchers. Other identified health hazards are lung diseases from the dust and particularly from the spores resulting from materials such as hay, straw or cereals which heat during storage (Lacey, 1972) and diseases such as brucellosis which can be contracted from the farm animals. A great deal of lifting and handling of awkward loads including, for example, field implements and fence components is expected and strains and accidents caused in lifting are common (Ministry of Agriculture, Fisheries and Food, 1973). The analyses of fatal and non fatal farm accidents shows machinery to be the most important source of accidents whilst accidents with animals and falls from buildings, stacks and machines are also common.

INFLUENCES AFFECTING CHANGES IN SKILL REQUIREMENTS

The work

Mechanization has increased fairly rapidly in agriculture, particularly in field work during and immediately after the 1939–46 war, and in animal husbandry much more recently. This has been brought about partly by the development of machines to carry out more and more of the farm processes and partly by increase in costs and reduced availability of hand labour. A good example of the increased mechanization is in milking. During the 1930s the majority of cows were hand milked. Simple milking machines where buckets were stood by the cows in conventional stalls were introduced in the

1940s. Since then milking parlours have gone through three further stages, firstly pipeline systems where the cows pass through stalls at ground level, secondly the 'herringbone' type of milking parlour with a pit for the operator so that the cow's udder is at a convenient height for him to attach the machine and do the other tasks such as washing, and, finally, the rotary parlours where cows are carried around during milking on a type of roundabout, again to provide for a minimum of manual effort and maximum number of cows per hour.

Reduction in employees on the farm in the United Kingdom is shown in Figure 3.2. The reasons for reduction in this labour force are connected with mechanization, but as there has been no redundancy it is likely that the workers available have dropped in the same way as the trends in the figure.

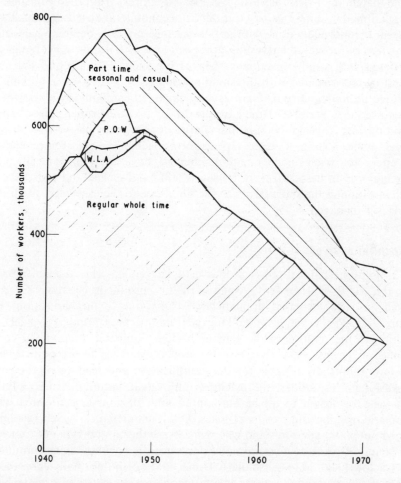

Figure 3.2 Trends in engagement of employed workers in the U.K. (By courtesy of the National Institute of Agricultural Engineering)

The reasons for this are probably largely the poor wages on the farm, the long hours, including weekend work, which are becoming increasingly less socially acceptable, and the poor environment in which the work is carried out with inclement weather, mud, manure and so on. Farming methods have also changed considerably. The maintenance of hedges, for example, which on many farms once occupied one member of the staff throughout the winter period is now virtually, in the United Kingdom at least, a mechanized procedure. Hedges which once were not only both trimmed with hand tools, but also relaid regularly, are no longer laid and the trimming is carried out by cutting devices attached to a tractor. Hay and straw are both baled almost without exception so that there is no longer the need for skill of pitching and loading wagons with hay or of building ricks with loose hay or straw.

The thatching of ricks has also disappeared entirely from the farm since it was so time consuming as to be totally uneconomic and, where stacks are covered, it is normally done with polythene sheeting. The combine harvester has replaced traditional harvesting processes and with it have gone the skills associated with stooking, moving sheaves by pitchfork, rick building and several tasks associated with threshing machines. Very little hand milking is practised although dairy men are usually capable of milking by hand where this is necessary because of the cows health or for some other reason. Also within the last 20 years the hand harvesting of root crops has vitually disappeared, hand hoeing is being replaced by machinery, whilst mechanized harvesters for blackcurrants and raspberries have been introduced. The large majority of dessert fruit is, however, still hand picked and prospects of mechanization in the short term are not good due to the ease with which the product is damaged.

Mechanization trends

The ratio of mechanical power available to workers has changed continually over the last 3 or 4 decades. Along with this, production per worker employed has also increased dramatically largely due to mechanization (see Figure 3.2). The example of milking parlour mechanization is typical. In addition to the changes in the general parlour equipment, individual components of the task have progressively been mechanized to the point where it is now technically feasible for the identification and feeding of the cow, the washing of the udder, the machine removal at optimum time and the milk yield recording to all be automated and, of course, associated with automatic opening and closing of gates. Ditch maintenance, which was once carried out with hand tools and where necessary the hand digging of trenches and laying of pipes, is now normally done using a backhoe digger mounted to a tractor. Field drainage similarly is mechanized and normally carried out by a contractor, probably using laying techniques which require pipes only to be handled from the trailer to the machine above ground level. Twenty years ago sugar beet seeds were planted in excess of the number of plants required and it was usual for the individual seed clusters sown to give more than one plant. The excess was then removed using hand hoes. Weeding was also normally accomplished by the same hand tool processes. Monogerm seed and precision seeders now allow crops to be planted such that the final stand is directly achieved although this is not always the optimum technique in practice because of the possibility of unfavourable soil conditions causing seed not to germinate. Nevertheless automatic singlers capable of detecting plant positions and using chemical or mechanical methods to remove unwanted plants are available and hand work is largely disappearing.

Development of control requirements

Early agricultural machines were not particularly sophisticated or complicated in functioning and, apart from the normal driving skills of steering, gear changing and braking, controls were limited to those necessary to lift the machine out of work at the end of a bout or to adjust, for example, depth or width of working. Present field machines and plant however can require considerable skill either in simultaneous operation of several components of the machine or in a conventional process control type of role likely, for example, in grain drying or feed preparation plant. On a combine harvester the driver, as well as steering along the line of the crop, must continually monitor and where necessary adjust:
1. The height of the cutting bar and table
2. The height of the header (the rotating sails which knock the crop back onto the table)
3. The forward speed of the machine to maintain optimum throughput and threshing efficiency
4. The horizontal position of the header
5. The level of grain in the tank and the discharge auger.

In addition he must, by audible and other cues, assure himself that the threshing mechanism is functioning correctly and must generally be in touch with tractor drivers bringing trailers to empty the machine. In a grain drying plant, typical of crop processers, the drying process time may be as long as 2 hours under some circumstances. With such a process time and normally the ability only to monitor intermittently the moisture content of the dried grain, considerable skill and knowledge of control processes is necessary to avoid the operator's actions resulting in either wild hunting of the machine and the consequent moisture content or long delays in changing the throughput rate such that grain is over or under dried. Automatic controllers are now available but, due to the considerable variability of the biological materials, the management of such a drying plant on a daily or longer term basis also requires considerable skill. This is because its optimum use in the harvest season is essential, particularly when weather conditions are bad, if all the crop is to be adequately dried before deterioration sets in. Under these circumstances the person managing the equipment must decide how many hours per day it should be operated and whether it should continue during the night. He must also decide whether the grain should be passed through twice in order to partially dry it quickly after it is received from the field in extremely wet conditions and how varying crops, which must not be mixed, shall be received and processed in such a way that there is not a critical shortage of intake hoppers or holding bins. Finally, in addition to the drier itself, there is usually an arrangement of conveyors, cleaning equipment and possibly weighing equipment all of which must be monitored to ensure its correct functioning.

PRESENT DAY TASKS AND SKILLS—STOCKMEN

Milking and other dairy work

A good dairyman is probably one of the most skilled workers in agriculture requiring a variety of skills, some traditional and some more recently developed. A typical dairyman's job includes milking the cows twice daily, supervising their health and welfare in the role generally known as animal husbandry, supervising the calving, subsequently looking after calves and young stock and frequently carrying out other farm work such as hay or

Figure 3.3 Animal health and welfare monitoring within a building holding 500 animals (By courtesy of the National Institute of Agricultural Engineering)

silage making. The degree of specialization will generally depend on the size of farm, and on the largest enterprises the dairyman may not be involved in any tractor work. On the smaller farm he is however, very likely to be involved in harvesting forage crops and may also be expected to do tractor work on other tasks such as fertilizer or spray application or even arable farm work.

The job of milking is complicated and requires considerable training or experience. Milking equipment, and hence the way the task is set, can vary considerably. Excluding hand milking, which is scarcely practiced in most technologically developed countries, the degree of sophistication may vary from a simple cowshed or mobile bale parlour into which the cows walk in small batches with the milk perhaps being collected by the equipment into a bucket at the side of each cow to be subsequently emptied and if necessary recorded, to a rotary parlour equal in capital cost perhaps to the cost of 100 cows. In the rotary parlour the cows will walk aboard a large rotating platform designed so that their udder is at a convenient height for the man to attach the machinery and milking will proceed while this platform rotates so that cows return to the vicinity of the operator in a time by which the milk has been removed. The task of the operator will depend not only on the sophistication of the equipment but also on the number of cows with which he has to deal and the degree to which parts of the task have become automated. The man may work alone or the milking parlour may be manned by a pair of operatives. A typical milking duty includes the following tasks most: of them being performed with the cow standing higher than the man for easy reach to the udder (Figure 3.4).

Identification. The individual cows must be identified as they enter the parlour in order that they may be given the correct quantity of food and the milk yield is subsequently recorded. Normally food is related to the amount of yield over the last few days and in a herd it is likely that 4, 5 or even more different quantities may be given to individual groups of cows. Depending mainly on the herd size, identification of the cows may be by their physical features, such cows normally being known by individual names. It may be by a number branded onto the cow or by some type of tail tag or other attached identification which may also include a colour code for the amount of food given. The largest herds in the United Kingdom contain 300 or more cows and clearly in these cases individual recognition with remembered names is impossible.

Feeding. Having identified the cows by name or number, the quantity of feed must be dispensed either by operation of push buttons or manual trips or even in some cases by shovelling the food into a manger. In the case or large herds it may be necessary after having identified the cow to consult a chart recording the amount of food.

Washing and drying. The cow's udder has to be washed with a wet cloth and dried effectively, often with paper towels. This is not only done to ensure hygiene by removing mud and possible sources of germs but also to stimulate the cow to let down milk when the machine is applied. Therefore a good washing technique is essential, as it is also essential that it is done just before applying the machine.

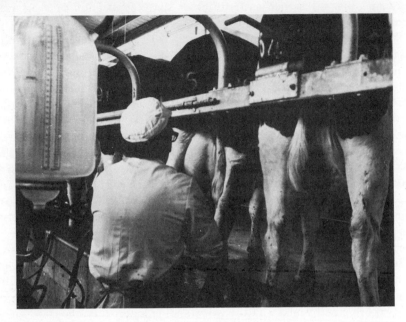

Figure 3.4 Attaching the milking machine in a modern herringbone parlour (By courtesy of the National Institute of Agricultural Engineering)

Attaching the milking machine. The cluster of the milking machine with four teat cups and connecting pipes must be attached to the cow, the man needing to take some care to avoid risks of the cow kicking. In many cases the teats must be located and the cups attached by feel only.

Monitoring of cows' health and breeding. During the time the cow is in the parlour, and particularly throughout the period of physical contact with the animal, the man must look for any signs of ill health. These might include leaving food, general listlessness or fidgetiness, looking out of condition with, perhaps a loss of weight or coat, lowered head and obviously diseased or sensitive parts particularly the teats, or injuries. This is a vital task since in a contagious disease like mastitis it may not only be the individual cow which will suffer if these signs are missed, but a large proportion of the beasts in the whole herd. Also the man must look for signs of oestrus since it is vitally important that the cow is inseminated at the correct time if milk yields are to be optimized. The man will also have the opportunity to observe the cow when with the herd and particularly in relation to oestrus, signs then may include cows mounting one another. Clearly an experienced cowman or a highly trained one can identify health and oestrus at an earlier stage than a naïve man.

Remove machine. The judgement of the time when the machine should be removed from the cow is also important. Both under and over-milking are commonly thought to result in a reduced yield during the remainder of the lactation period. The reduction in milk flow can normally be observed but as each of the four quarters of the udder may take a different time to empty, the judgement as to when the machine should be removed is frequently a difficult one and requires training and experience. Devices which automatically remove the machine at the correct time are now being introduced but manual machine removal is likely to persist on the majority of farms for some time.

Milk yield recording. On occasions, most frequently once or twice a week, the yield of individual cows is recorded to help with the subsequent determination of feed quantities and the analysis of the performance and economics of the herd. The subsequent analysis of this data may be one of the tasks of the milker or he may be concerned purely with writing down quantities.

Teat dipping. Before the cow is released it is common to dip the teats in a disinfecting chemical to aid mastitis control.

Cow exit and entry. At the end of the process gates must be operated to release the batch of cows in the parlour and to replace them by a new group. The man will frequently need to hustle the new cows into their correct standing positions and again firmness and confidence in dealing with animals is vitally important. At the end of each milking period a number of other associated tasks such as cleaning out the milking machine and the parlour must be carried out.

The majority of milkers learn their skills on the job, working with more experienced men, although some training is available at agricultural colleges. Essentially it is a job requiring a great deal of patience and care, a confidence and interest in animals and a willingness to work long hours, since morning milking starts at 6 or 7 a.m. and afternoon milking may not finish until 5 or 6 p.m. It is accepted that the confidence of the cowman can considerably affect the performance of the herd and Seabrook has carried out some work in which he has shown that herd yield is related to personality factors (Seabrook, 1972). Specifically, an introvert personality appears more suitable for successful milking and herd husbandry. It has often been alleged that the milker's task leads to considerable stress, mainly mental stress due to the requirements of the task, but an analysis of the sources and symptoms of stress by Tomlinson, suggests that it is not excessive (Tomlinson, 1971).

THE SHEPHERD

The shepherd's work is less mechanized than that of the dairy worker. He also spends a greater proportion of his time working out of doors. The animal husbandry skills are similar to those of the man working with cows since he must be alert to signs of illness or injury among his flock. He must supervise the insemination by the rams and be prepared to assist throughout the period of lambing. Provision of adequate and correct food is another vital factor and it will be of most importance in the period just before lambing when sheep must be brought to a state of high fitness and ruggedness. The shepherd is likely to be needed at the time of lambing to deal with orphan lambs, having them accepted by another mother, perhaps even by skinning dead lambs and covering the orphan with the skin of a potential foster mother's dead offspring.

His other skill is that of shearing. This can of course be developed to a particularly high degree, even to the point where workers compete in national or international competitions. The skill is normally greatest in the larger sheep rearing territories of Australia and New Zealand but nevertheless the British farmworker may be required to shear upwards of 100 sheep each year and with a skill enabling him to average one sheep per 6–8 minutes. Particular skills are involved in manipulating the cutters to take off all the wool but not to cut the animal in order to remove the fleece as nearly in one piece as possible, and of course to carry out the task rapidly.

PIGS AND POULTRY

The majority of these creatures are nowadays kept in accommodation which leads to very intensive stocking. Most pigs are kept in pens, each housing perhaps 10 to 30 pigs, within larger buildings. The pigs in each pen are likely to be of a similar age but differ in age from those in other pens such that a steady flow of animals into the building from weaning and out of the building for killing is maintained. Most poultry are housed in cages within larger buildings, each cage holding perhaps four or five birds. The worker must therefore spend much time within a building holding a very large number of creatures. This is usually artificially lit, particularly in the case of poultry, where the length of day is artificially controlled by the lighting. The environment normally incorporates a reasonable climate, the heat from the animals being used to provide an adequately high temperature and excessive heat being removed by fans. The buildings may, however, be dusty with feather debris sometimes a hazard to health.

Particular skills required are mainly of two types. There is need for a manipulative skill in handling the animals or birds, especially if this is to be done rapidly and effectively for placement or removal from the pen or cage, for treatment such as injections or inspection and, where breeding is carried out, for assistance of the mother or offspring at this critical time. The other main skill is the ability to diagnose illness. It may also cover, however, injury or the bullying of one animal by its penmates. Again in breeding, oestrus detection may be important. Further, careful visual observation is necessary at all times to ensure adequate feeding and water supply for the animals or birds and to see that they are all consuming their food or drink correctly. Again the man doing this work may have other duties around the farm, particularly duties in connection with the preparation and processing of foodstuffs and work in connection with the removal of effluent.

PRESENT DAY TASKS AND SKILLS—MACHINE OPERATORS

Tractors

The ubiquity of the tractor means that the driver needs to have a wide range of skills in addition to the normal basic ones of driving and maintenance. The tractor is used as a transport vehicle, for hauling implements in the field and, with a number of different attached implements, for such jobs as loading, digging ditches or trenches or cutting hedges, or as a power unit. The basic driving task, although not demanding the ability to control the vehicle at high speeds or in traffic, needs instead the ability to drive in a straight line across the field, to judge the width of a cut accurately by driving a fixed distance from the previous route and skill in negotiating gateways and buildings with trailers or other machines behind the tractor. These machines must also frequently be reversed as for example when backing a tipping trailer into a storage building or to an intake hopper.

The tractor driver's maintenance tasks include the usual lubrication, tyre inflation and cleaning. He may in addition be expected to carry out simple repairs and rectifications such as replacing broken parts or cleaning out fuel injectors.

Each of the implements or pieces of attached equipment used with the tractor will require the operator's skill for adjustment and correct operation. The power used in ploughing, for example, can be significantly affected by the accurate setting of the plough share and mould board whilst mowers require carefully sharpened knives and the correct adjustment of height of cutter bar. Another aspect requiring skill where a seed, fertilizer or herbicide must be applied is the correct adjustment of the machine to arrive at the desired application rate over the area of the field. Because of the differences in properties of different materials, for example, different varieties of wheat or formulations of granular fertilizer, different speeds of application and variations in machine performance such as that caused by wear, the application rate cannot normally be set against an absolute scale. It is necessary for the operator to make an approximate adjustment, to measure the application rate over a smaller area and then to adjust appropriately to gain the correct application for the complete field. The tractor driver therefore requires driving skills, skill in setting and operation of all the machines used with the tractor and sufficient estimating and calculating skill to dispense the materials correctly.

Figure 3.5 Co-ordinated tractor work; forage chopping and loading in the foreground, tractor with trailer behind (By courtesy of the National Institute of Agricultural Engineering)

Self-propelled machines

The driver's task is generally similar to that of the tractor driver. A self-propelled machine is a specialized machine incorporating its own power unit and controls, most often used for harvesting tasks. It is dealt with separately, however, since the actual operating task may be more taxing than that of the tractor and is worthy of separate consideration. The most common example of such a machine is the combine harvester for cereals and the task of the driver of this machine is described below.

Steering—The machine must be steered up and down or round the field so that the cutting table, which may be typically between 10 and 14 feet wide, takes a full swath of crop without being driven such that any misses the table and is left standing in the field. On reaching a corner fairly violent steering is needed to turn the machine round and set it for the next side. This may involve reversing in order to make the turn in a small space in which case on most machines the operation of the clutch and a change of gear is necessary, although a recent addition is a simple pedal which allows direction to be changed without clutch operation.

Speed control—The speed of the combine harvester must be maximized so that the crop is harvested as rapidly as possible but speed must not exceed that at which the grain is efficiently removed from the ears and straw. In most cases the operator must judge this from experience of the performance of his combine harvester and the knowledge of where losses are likely to be excessive. In doing this he will usually use the audible cues available from the functioning of the threshing mechanism and the engine indicating the loading of material in the mechanism and the power consumption. The machine may, however, be fitted with a grain loss monitor which indicates on a single dial increasing or decreasing losses and in this case the operator's control of speed will be somewhat simplified, although he will have to observe the meter continually and make adjustments quite frequently. On most machines speed adjustment is a continuous process achieved by a lever which may also combine other functions detailed below. In some cases, however, speed is proportionate to displacement of the lever; in others speed continues to change for as long as the lever is displaced.

Table height control—The height of the cutting table knife must be continuously monitored and adjusted where undulations in the ground or possibly sections of crop which have been laid flat by rain or wind make this necessary. This control is often combined on the same lever with forward speed but with a different action. Difficulties of adjusting the table height are that a different optimum height may be necessary in different areas of the crop due, for example, to wind or rain flattening some regions, whilst the best height may also vary across the table so a best mean must be judged.

Reel height—The reel is mounted above the cutting knife and its purpose is to deflect the crop onto the table from where it is conveyed into the machine. The height of the reel must also be adjusted as the height of the heads of the cereal crop is likely to vary, particularly where this has been affected by wind or rain.

Reel position—A less frequent adjustment, nevertheless one made during work, is to the fore-and-aft adjustment of the reel position. Again this is made in response to crop conditions particularly the direction in which the stalks are leaning.

Tank emptying—The combine harvester tank typically holds the product of 20 to 40 minutes work. It is emptied by auger normally into a trailer which for maximum efficiency is driven alongside the machine when the combine harvester is still operating. The combine harvester operator must therefore observe the level of grain in his tank, ensure that the trailer arrives and he can empty before this overflows, notice the arrival of the trailer underneath the auger emptying device and operate the start and stop of this to clear his tank.

General monitoring—In addition the man must by visual and audio monitoring check the correct functioning of his machine. This normally means ensuring that there are no breakages or belts coming detached and that grain and straw are being discharged in a reasonable manner. In addition he must check that the knife is functioning correctly so that a good clean stubble is left without, for example, strips of crop left where the cutter has become blocked with soil.

Some information on the frequency with which the principal controls are operated and the rate of information monitoring has been obtained (Zander, 1970) and is given in Table 3.3. Simultaneous control of so many functions makes this a difficult and frequently inefficiently performed task. An important factor is that the work is seasonal, the man therefore carries out this job for 100 hours or less spread out over a period of 3 or 4 weeks in the autumn. The vagaries of the weather can introduce their own stresses to the job and together with the frequently worked long hours in a day the operator's skills and alertness are likely to be at risk.

Table 3.3   Some details of the combine harvester driver's task

		Turnings	*Percentages*
Steering wheel movements		0–1/6	37
		1/6–2/6	34·7
		2/6–3/6	19·3
		> 3/6	9·0
		Control	*Percentages*
Other control frequencies		Table height	74·8
		Reel height	12·8
		Forward speed	12·4
		Source	*Bits/s*
Information speeds		Terrain	2
		Crop	9
		Working width	2
		Threshing quality	4
		Noise	2

Farmstead plant operators

This plant includes crop processing and conveying equipment, animal feed preparation mixing or dispensing equipment and more specialized farm machinery, for fruit or vegetable grading or packing for example. Essentially the operator's task with crop or feed processing equipment is one of knowing how to start and stop the machinery correctly, of monitoring its correct functioning when in use, particularly in regard to blockages, breakages or detached belts or chains, etc. and the more simple aspects of maintenance.

One particular example where further skill is required is in the supervision and operation of crop drying plant. This may be for grass or grain, but the latter, which is more common, will be described in some detail as an example.

A continuous flow grain drier is used to reduce the moisture content of harvested grain to a safe storage level. It is normally installed in a farm barn along with a system of conveyors and perhaps grain cleaning equipment so that grain received in trucks or trailers from the field into a storage pit can be passed through the cleaner and drier and directly into storage either in bins or large heaps on the floor. The drier normally blows constant temperature hot air through the grain, the temperature being set to the highest value which will damage neither the germination nor brewing or baking properties of the grain. The moisture content of the grain as received from the field varies and therefore the main task of the operator is to vary the rate of grain throughput in the drier such that the drying time is sufficient for the moisture content to be reduced to the safe storage level. Under-drying results in a risk of deterioration in storage through moulding and over-drying a loss of revenue in that the weight of the grain available for sale is less and there is normally no payment bonus for the lower moisture value. In addition of course unnecessary fuel is used in the drying process.

The moisture content of grain received from the field may for example be 21% and the safe storage level 15%. Throughout the day, however, due to the drying effect of the sun or wind or due to different degrees of ripeness between one part of the field and another the incoming moisture content may perhaps vary from 24 to 18% (Matthews, 1964). The drying therefore needs to remove between 9 and 3% of moisture which may in turn be equivalent to time in the drier varying from 20 minutes to 1 hour 30 minutes. This change in moisture content may be gradual but may also include some significant steps as the harvesting process moves to a different plot. The man must despite all this attempt to keep the output moisture within say $\pm \frac{1}{2}\%$ of the objective. The particular difficulties are as follows:

1. It is normally possible only to sample the outgoing moisture content at intervals since continuous recording moisture meters of adequate precision are usually regarded as too expensive for farm use.
2. The man has only his experience to provide for him the information on the relationship between the percentage of moisture removed and the time the grain is in the drier, or, alternatively, the degree of adjustment of the control, perhaps on a variable size orifice, which he must adjust to vary throughput rate. This is because different samples of grain dry at different rates and it is not possible for the makers of the equipment to calibrate for different amounts of drying.
3. The relatively long process time means that it is very easy for over-correction or under-correction to be made and for the effect to be so delayed that serious errors in the setting change only become apparent much later.
4. During a wet harvest season in particular processing will often continue for 18–24 hours a day and there is therefore considerable strain on the supervising staff.

In addition to the throughput controls the man supervising the plant must continually assure himself that conveyors and other equipment are working correctly. It is relatively easy to suffer blockages from foreign bodies brought in from the field. He must check the cleaning equipment occasionally removing sacks of reject materials. He must watch for the time when the storage bin becomes full and the product must be moved to another bin. He must finally check the flame and burner of the drier and assure himself that the hot air temperature is being maintained. In addition he may also be responsible for the broader strategy of the drying, deciding for example whether a crop which is particularly wet should be passed through the drier for partial moisture removal to be temporarily stored until there is more time available on the dryer to complete the drying process. Alternatively he must decide to continue the complete drying at the risk of having too much material from the field for the capacity of the intake hopper. He may also in a period where harvesting has been held up by the weather but is then permitted to go ahead rapidly find himself with many batches of material with the need for additional transference from one site to another and the need to plan the complete drying most efficiently.

This task has been given in some detail since it does indicate that there is some need for the man in this type of work to be a strategist, with some knowledge of process control and even servo mechanisms if he is to avoid hunting in the drying process. He needs to be capable of working the long hours, making instrument measurements and often at the same time having sufficient manual strength to handle sacks of grain. With all these tasks to do it is nevertheless common within the farm hierarchy for this man to be considered less responsible than the man who is operating a combine harvester.

Handtools

One of the most skilled handtool tasks on the farm used to be cutting grass or cereals using a scythe. Virtually no use is made in modern agriculture of this tool and handtool skills probably have ceased to become particularly important in that the tools used are generally those which would be found either in any normal workshop or even the domestic garage or garden toolshed. The farm worker still occasionally uses the fork and the rake, although generally for tidying up rather than carrying out a demanding task. Workshop tools are used for machinery maintenance and frequently welding is carried out on the farm. In addition power drills, grinders and spraying equipment are common. Many farms possess a chain saw which can be used for cutting up fallen branches or trees and perhaps for some work in connection with hedge maintenance or building.

PRESENT DAY TASKS AND SKILLS—HORTICULTURAL WORKERS

Manual tasks

Probably more than in any other section of farming, manual work persists as part of the duties of the horticultural worker. In part this is because the enterprises are often small but the bigger influence is probably the difficulty of mechanizing the picking of such crops as cucumbers, tomatoes or flowers bearing in mind the fragility of the crop and the fact that harvesting must be selective since the crop does not all ripen at the same time. In addition, where crops are grown in greenhouses, access is difficult and machinery again limited. Horticultural workers' tasks normally include cultivation, planting, weeding, spraying, picking and some produce grading and packing. Some of these tasks are partially mechanized. A large amount of the labour force is seasonal, such staff often being housewives engaged for the picking season and perhaps for such other fairly lengthy tasks as tree pruning or produce grading.

All the tasks concerned with harvesting the crop require skill in judging the ripeness or quality of the product, manual dexterity in plucking it in the correct way so that plant and product are not damaged, and training in the economy of motions so that the task may be carried out throughout the working day without undue fatigue or fall-off in effectiveness. Such skills are probably learned mainly by instruction from fellow workers or foremen on the job. Where produce has to be graded for the market as in the case of apples or tomatoes, official specifications for the different grades have generally been drawn up by government or international bodies. These describe in some detail the acceptable shape, size and degree of blemishes on the fruit. Pictures are often available but again a great deal is left to the interpretation of the worker. Observations have shown that large numbers of misgradings are common (Stevens, 1970) although it may be that this is not as serious as it might appear for the retailing bodies since the same population (i.e. housewives) is usually the purchaser and such mistakes of misinterpretation made in the grading stage may well be in line with their subsequent judgement of the product although not strictly in line with the grade specification. In grading and packing manipulative skills of a fairly high order are again necessary if high throughputs are to be achieved. At the moment the product is normally moved between the grade channels manually although mechanical movement of the fruit in response to push button selection is being developed.

Machine manning and operation

Much horticultural work is carried out using soil cultivation with motorized walking cultivators for which the operator needs considerable skill and an adequate level of strength to guide the machine and maintain a correct depth of work. The magnitude and direction of forces which need to be applied to the handles of the machine will obviously vary with the soil state and, inside a glasshouse in particular, a great deal of manoeuvring may be necessary to effectively cultivate all the soil and avoid pathways and building components. This basic machine may also be used with attachments for weeding, spraying and other tasks.

On many horticultural enterprises a four-wheel tractor will be used for cultivation. The tractor will also be used for planting although manual operations will generally be required on the planter to separate and arrange planting materials. For example brassica plants are normally transplanted from the initial seed bed into a final arrangement in the field. In order to facilitate this planting of the individual transplants the operators of the machine—one for each row—select and separate plants from a bundle and place them singly into gripping mechanisms which then rotate to place and cover them in the soil. This task requires considerable manual dexterity to achieve a high work rate but no other particular skill. Potatoes may also be manually arranged into cups on a potato planter although completely mechanical machines are also available. On a potato harvester it is usual for teams of workers to sort the tubers from the soil, stones and other trash while the material is travelling slowly over a conveyor belt (Figure 3.6).

Figure 3.6 Working on a potato harvester (By courtesy of the National Institute of Agricultural Engineering)

Machine design varies but a common design is one with two parallel conveyors, one carrying mainly trash and the other mainly potatoes. The two or more operators, usually standing on either side, will then remove further trash from the potatoes or move potatoes from the trash conveyor onto the one for the crop. There are no very skilled judgements to be made and manual dexterity with endurance and willingness to work with muddy hands and often in a poor climate are the main characteristics required.

EDUCATION AND TRAINING

Education

Education for agriculture includes both technical and business studies, the latter becoming increasingly important. Physics, chemistry, biological sciences and engineering are clearly all important. For those with a management role the business content of courses needs to include organization and management of staff, financial budgeting and accounting and at least some development of the ability to value animals, crops, machinery and land. Formal education is available from Ordinary National Diploma level to First Degree and Higher Degree level, with specializations in agriculture, dairying, horticulture, poultry, agricultural engineering and other topics. The National Diploma courses are available generally at the County Agricultural or Technical Colleges whereas agricultural degree studies are included in the curricula of several universities and other colleges.

Training

The Agricultural, Horticultural and Forestry Industry Training Board was set up to provide skills training in agriculture. It operates both formal entry training schemes for those taking up work in agriculture and horticulture and various specialized training courses. In 1971 the Board launched a 3 year scheme known as the New Entrant (Apprentice) Training Scheme in Agriculture and Horticulture designed to suit the needs of both the employee and the particular farm on which he or she is employed. This scheme allows the possibility of transfer to another employer or holding in order that the training may widen his experience. The training is given chiefly on the holding under the guidance of the employer or his more skilled workers. The scheme is not limited entirely to new entrants but may also be employed for those who have already spent time in the industry providing their standard or competence is relevant to the training given. In addition to the training on the farm it is a condition that the trainee be released for a minimum of 144 hours of further education during each of the three years, this being usually day or block release at a suitable College of Education. There he is taught the basic knowledge relating to the practical work. During the 3 year period practical proficiency tests to show that a high degree of skill has been acquired at essential tasks are set.

Short courses

Short courses for groups are held at colleges or other appropriate places, ranging from manufacturer's premises to individual farms. The length of these courses may be from less than one day to several days. They are usually designed to deal with specialized topics and a particular feature of them is that they should attract not only those with little experience but also practising farmers and farm workers from the surrounding area. In addition weekend or day courses or conferences are a popular feature at many agricultural colleges where they can attract up to several hundred participants from surrounding areas.

THE FUTURE

The labour force

The present labour force will in all probability continue in most countries to decline further to be replaced by mechanization although the reduction, which in the UK over the last 10 years has been approximately 20%, is unlikely to be quite as large in the next decade. In the longer term it seems likely that farms will be mainly of two types. The smaller holdings, although large by present day standards, will be operated mainly by the owner and family with peak work demands being catered for by the employment of contractors. The larger enterprise will be organized more on factory lines and will probably have large numbers of staff with management and foremen hierarchies. There is no compelling reason why either of these enterprise types should be more probably dealing with animals or with arable farming. However, sheep are likely to be concentrated mainly in the smaller family farms. Less use will probably be made of casual workers, as there is further mechanization of fruit and vegetable harvesting. Within the animal husbandry sphere the use of contract herdsmen, either for dairy or for other animal types, to allow permanent staff to take leave will increase.

Mechanization which has permitted the dramatic decrease in labour over the last two or three decades will have some further scope for reducing manual effort and, by increasing the size of equipment, for reducing the number of tractor and other machinery operators required. A prime example of the impact of mechanization is in dairying and where the rate of one man milking cows which once was perhaps 6 per hour and now can approach or even, in some cases, exceed 100 cows per hour, is likely to increase a little further, perhaps to 150/200 cows per man hour, with the use of automated equipment perhaps for all tasks except the placing of the machine on the cow's udder.

The average horse power of tractors which has increased perhaps by 40% in the last 20 years will go on increasing. Machines are now being sold with engines of greater than 300 horse power in many territories. There is a distinct possibility that within the next two decades the number of tractors in use and hence the numbers operating could be reduced by one third or more. The use of this greater power is made possible by the development of wider implements and higher work rates. In addition implements are being combined, for example in cultivation and drilling, such that the tractor needs to cross the field less times to complete the task of having the crop sown. Driverless tractor operation is already technically feasible for some tasks, notably those where the plants are fixed as in an orchard (Finn-Kelcey *et al.*, 1967) and there is no inherent technical reason why equipment should not be devised to replace the operator on the large majority of tractor work. The economic justification of such equipment is, however, far from proven and it does seem likely that for most tractor work, where the fields are used for different crops in succeeding years and implements are of many different types, each of a different width, the human operator will be required for many years yet. Alternatives employed mainly experimentally but to a limited extent in practice are to provide either mechanically or electronically for one operator to control two machines, either when riding on one of them or from a central control tower.

Implements which use a human operator as part of the functioning are likely to become completely automatic. This applies largely to harvesters where for potatoes, X-ray equipment is being used to detect potatoes or stones and control the separation (Palmer, 1973). On transplanters, plants may be grown in small soil composition capsules which are then capable of being mechanically handled on the machine for planting.

The largest influence of further mechanization or automation on manual work is likely, however, to be in connection with livestock. Automatic feeding systems are now quite common for pigs and poultry kept under intensive conditions. Filling of the troughs with food may be initiated by simply pressing a button or may be coupled to a timer to occur completely automatically. In some installations, mainly experimental, the complete food mixing, weighing and distributing process for several groups of animals, each requiring different quantities or types of food, have been sequentially automated (N.I.A.E., 1973). Manure removal may also be completely mechanized and, although egg collection still remains mainly manual, there is no technical reason why this too should not be automatic. Perhaps the one area where manual skills and activity appear to be required for a long period is in the monitoring of the health and general well-being of the animals. This is particularly so in breeding situations but the time may be envisaged when, rather than the worker spending a great deal of time in the generally unfavourable atmosphere of the house, which is often at high temperature and may well contain much dust and perhaps also toxic spores, remote viewing of the animals could be arranged using closed circuit television.

The horticultural sphere perhaps provides the most difficult technical problems to complete mechanization. The selection of ripe produce from a bush or tree where the degree of ripeness varies as with a tomato plant, would be made technically fairly difficult by the random arrangement of the fruit and the interference with leaves and stems of plant. The location and grasping of the fruit, which is likely to be extremely fragile, is also difficult so that perhaps a more likely way in which the work may be altered is in the use of belts or gantries such that the plants may be moved within the greenhouse to a convenient position for manual picking. The use of mobile platforms and other picking aids in the field to aid access to fruit on trees is also likely to increase.

Trends in skills

The skills required of individual workers will surely continue to change. In general agricultural work in the more distant future manual skill requirements would seem to be limited to sheep shearing, machinery maintenance where parts have to be moved or lifted and some aspects of animal handling where the beasts or birds must be carried or cajoled. It is unlikely that bale or sack handling will continue to be a manual task except on the smaller farms whilst power-assisted controls on machinery will again reduce physical efforts. Manipulative skills will probably remain important in several separate areas. The man dealing with stock will continue to need his skill in handling and treating animals, in attaching the milking machinery and dealing with birth and welfare of the young. On the horticultural enterprises picking, pruning and quality grading of produce are likely often to be manual for some time to come if dessert or salad quality must be maintained and improved. Associated with the manipulative skill in this area is a considerable requirement for judgement and visual acuity.

The operation of both field machinery such as combine harvesters or barn machinery such as crop drying or feed preparation or processing plant is likely to involve a combination of manual control and process control skills. On both types of machinery automatic controlling elements will probably reduce the need for the man to exercise very high levels of skill in the process control field where all too easily at present, control 'hunting' can be initiated or under-correction made. As machinery becomes more sophisticated and is combined to greater extents to carry out more processes in one pass of the material, the monitoring skills of the man will probably be stretched further. Both visual and audible cues are likely to be used in monitoring but there will probably be an improvement in the quality of displays.

The area of skills in which the requirement will increase most is likely to be in diagnostic skills where increasingly the search will be made for optimum crops and optimum animal growth. A greater range of chemical and other treatments will be available in both areas but increasing skill will be required to judge the need and the best time for the application of these treatments. Response to the treatment and its continuation, repetition or cessation must also be diagnosed. Management skills will also be needed increasingly to organize optimum use of machinery and man-power or to forecast and plan ahead for the main operations such as cultivation, planting or harvesting. Further economic judgements, for example, increased crop yield balanced against increased nitrogen fertilizer cost or continuation of keeping a batch of poultry despite their feed cost when egg production begins to decrease, will need to be made more precisely.

Working conditions

With haymaking and harvesting work in particular so much governed by the weather and restricted to short seasons, it is difficult to see how a 'nine-to-five' job can be created for agricultural workers. For this reason and because of the trend towards ever increasing sophistication of the machinery and therefore high capital value, it is likely that shift working will become more common so that machinery can be used to its full extent during the hours of daylight and possibly also during darkness and more crop may be harvested at the optimum time. The agricultural worker's wage, in many countries one of the lowest of any occupation at present, will probably increase more in proportion than other wages as the labour force becomes less satisfied with the reasons given for low wages. These are that farming is a relaxed and interesting job, that housing is available and that there are some fringe benefits such as free produce from the farm.

The working environment will undoubtedly be improved. The current trend of increasingly sophisticated cabs on tractors and machines with heating and air filtration and, in the hotter climates, air cooling will continue. Better buildings are being erected with higher roofs, more light and better ventilation. The presence of dust leads to much criticism and its seems possible that *Codes of Practice* will be established specifying necessary ventilation and the availability of masks to reduce this discomfort and hazard. The noise limits established for the operator's position on tractors in several countries may be followed in the longer term by limits or at least Code of Practice recommendations for working positions in buildings whilst ride vibration and jolting on field machines may well be very significantly reduced by the use of suspensions, again under the presence of regulations or Codes of Practice.

Education and training

The period will surely be reached where all new full-time employees will receive some career training. Those employed in supervisory roles are likely to be trained at specialized farm colleges but other staff will probably be given day release to attend a local technical college which will offer courses in animal husbandry, mechanization, agronomy, horticulture or combinations of these individual areas. Such basic training will presumably be supplemented by specialist and refresher courses attended by workers of all ages on such specific subjects as combine harvester operation, pig breeding or the growing of potatoes for example.

More sophisticated machinery will require more detailed and intense training of the operators if the best use is to be made of it. In part this will probably be carried out by manufacturers of such equipment who will run courses at their training centres, or perhaps locally, prior to the appropriate season for the use of the new machine. Such courses may use films and even simulators to help the operators achieve good performance. With seasonal activities the need for recourse to such measures as simulation is more likely as prior to the season the crop will not exist. Such training may be supplemented by improved instruction manuals and instructions on the machine.

Research development and application

Animal husbandry research and development is probably resulting in a decrease in the worker skills required and this trend is likely to continue. For example, improved knowledge of the diet and environmental requirements of animals or birds before or during the birth of the young has resulted in less difficulties during the birth and less fatalities. Correctly designed buildings with adequate heating, which will continue to improve, also reduce the risks and the manual intervention needed. Disease in animals is more easily treated with modern injections and less nursing of a sick animal is therefore involved. It is likely that instruments and improved tests will reduce the skill needed in detecting illness or oestrus and increasingly breeding is improving the uniformity of the animals such that with predetermined rations the dates for optimum slaughter can be set with little judgement.

In the arable sphere an increasingly large array of products is available as herbicides, pesticides or fungicides to deal with all contingencies. Fortunately alongside this the chemical companies are increasingly supplying information and advice to farmers and their staff on the selection and use of these products. Nevertheless with competing companies and the increasing economic importance of gaining optimum yield the diagnosis of weeds, diseases or pests is becoming more important and farm staff will surely be better trained in the use of chemical treatments. The same applies to fertilizers where, with increasing costs of the basic elements, it is important that fertilizer is correctly applied in type and in quantity. Botanical research is leading to continually increasing yields from all types of plant. Such advances can often bring difficulties in other areas. For example the straw may be weaker and the crop suffer more seriously in heavy rain or wind with consequent need for much more skill if it is to be correctly harvested. One area in which this research has so far failed to yield sufficient information is in the definition of an adequate seed bed for crop growth. There are so many variables, including for example particle size of the soil, pore sizes, water infiltration, moisture content, nutrient distribution, presence of pests and, above all, the influence of weather between planting and harvest, that such a definition appears almost impossible. In this situation the judgement of an adequate seed bed is very much subjective, based on experience. It would appear likely that for a very long time such judgements as cultivation treatment, planting date and treatment of the crop subsequent to planting will need to be made.

Where crops are grown in controlled environments such as in greenhouses, research is permitting the individual aspects of the environment to be, not only more closely controlled, but to be inter-related for maximum growth and yield. It is likely that this will all be done automatically but skill will be required in supervision of these more sophisticated controls, in fault detection and in some maintenance.

Engineering research, although enabling a number of manual workers to be reduced significantly brings with it the need for greater skill in machine operation, in fault diagnosis and maintenance and in the use of less familiar devices such as electronic and hydraulic circuits, simple computing elements and data processing and recording equipment.

References

Br. Stand. 3904 (1965). Recommendations for the location and direction of motion of operator's controls for self-propelled agricultural machines

Br. Stand. 1495 (1970). Agricultural tractor details for light and medium tractors

Food and Agriculture Organisation of the United Nations (1971). *Production Yearbook, Vol. 24*, Rome

Finn-Kelcey, P. and Owen, W. M. (1967). Leader Cable Tractor Guidance. *Proc. Agric. Eng. Symp., London*

Lacey, J. (1972). Actinomycetes and Fungus spores in farm air. *J. Agric. Lab. Sci.*, 1, 2

Lovegrove, H. T. and Evans, D. J. (1970). Ergonomics in the development of operational skills. *J. Proc. Inst. Agric. Eng.*, 25, 1, 37

Mainzer, W. (1966). Accident prevention in the cowshed. *Br. J. Ind. Med.*, 23, 24

Matthews, J. (1964). Performance of an automatic moisture control unit fitted to a farm grain dryer. *J. Agric. Eng. Res.*, 9(2)

Matthews, J. (1973). The measurement of tractor ride comfort. *Soc. Auto. Eng., Paper 730795*

Matthews, J. and Knight, A. A. (1971). Ergonomics in agricultural equipment design. *Nat. Inst. Agric. Engng., Silsoe, UK*

Meadows, A. W., Lovibond, S. H. and John, R. D. (1959). The establishment of psycho-physical standards in the sorting of fruit. *Occup. Psychol.*, 33, 217

Ministry of Agriculture, Fisheries and Food (1973). Annual analyses of fatal accidents and diseases in agriculture. *MAFF, London*

Ministry of Agriculture, Fisheries and Food (1974). December 1973 Agricultural returns for England and Wales. London, February 18th

National Institute of Agricultural Engineering (1971). Proceedings of the Subject Day on tractor and cab noise. *Report No. 1*. Silsoe, UK

National Institute of Agricultural Engineering (1973). Proceedings of the Subject Day Livestock Feeding and Weighing. *Report No. 11*. Silsoe, UK

Palmer, J. (1973). Development of a field separator of potatoes from stones and clods by means of X-radiation. *J. Agric. Eng. Res.*, 18(4)

Seabrook, M. F. (1972). A study of the influence of cowman's personality and job satisfaction on yield of dairy cows. *J. Agric. Lab. Sci.*, 1(2)

Sparrow, T. D. (1972). The use of agricultural manpower. *J. Agric. Lab. Sci.*, 1(2), 3

Splinter, W. E. and Suggs, C. W. (1963). Simulation and field studies of human errors in multiple loading transplanting. *Paper to Annual Meeting of Am. Soc. Agric. Eng.*

Stevens, G. N. (1970). The human operator and quality inspection of horticultural produce. *J. Inst. Agric. Eng.*, 25(1)

Talamo, J. D. C. and Stayner, R. M. (1973). Some aspects of environmental noise in farm buildings and plant. *Nat. Inst. of Agric. Eng.*, *Departmental Note DN/TE/199/1435*

Tomlinson, R. W. (1970). The assessment of workload in agricultural tasks. *J. Proc. Inst. Agric. Eng.*, **25**(1), 18

Tomlinson, R. W. (1971). A survey of psychological and mental stress on cowmen in Herringbone Dairy Systems. *Nat. Inst. Agric. Eng.*, *Departmental Note DN/TE/158/ 1440*. Silsoe, UK

Tomlinson, R. W. and Cottrell, F. B. (1970). Investigation by Laboratory simulation of some factors influencing the picking of fruit from mobile platforms. *J. Agric. Eng. Res.*, **15**(1), 39

Zander, J. (1970). Studies of combine harvester operation. *J. Inst. Agric. Eng.*, **25**(1), London

4

The Metal Working Machine Tool Operator

R. G. TAYLOR

MACHINE TOOLS—TERMINOLOGY AND PRINCIPLES

This chapter concentrates on metal working machines. Machine tools exist to facilitate the production of components: Compared with the engineer's hand tools they offer greater power, speed and accuracy. They are nearly always driven by individual electric motors (for power and speed) and are based on massive, rigid frames (for accuracy). In metal cutting the aim is to provide close control over the relative motion of a tool or cutter and a workpiece. In metal forming, accuracy is obtained by the use of carefully aligned and shaped pairs of tools, known as dies, between which metal is shaped under pressure. Components are designed to suit metal cutting when very high accuracy is required, or only a small number of identical components is to be produced. For long runs of less accurate work the faster and less wasteful forming processes are preferred.

Principles of metal cutting

Figure 4.1a shows the basic principle of turning. The meaning of the terms cutting motion, feed motion and depth of cut will be clear from the figure, which shows the arrangement for 'sliding' feed (feed parallel to the axis of the rotating workpiece). 'Surfacing' feed, at right angles to this, would produce a flat end on the workpiece: Intermediate feed directions would produce conical tapers of various angles.

Internal surfaces or bores can be turned with suitable tools, when the workpiece is supported only at the left-hand end, or a non-rotating drill can be

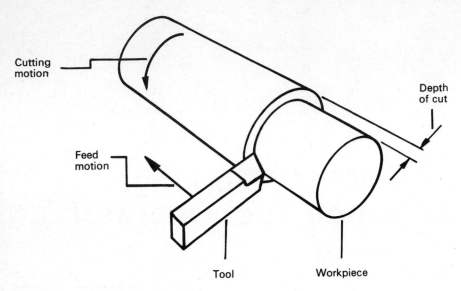

Cutting
motion

Depth
of cut

Feed
motion

Tool

Workpiece

Figure 4.1a   The principle of turning

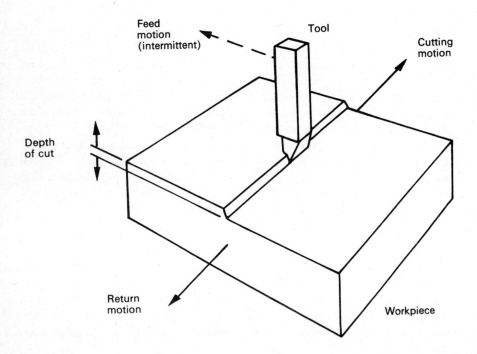

Feed
motion
(intermittent)

Tool

Cutting
motion

Depth
of cut

Return
motion

Workpiece

Figure 4.1b   The principle of planing

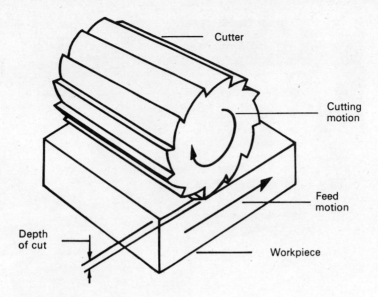

Figure 4.1c   The principle of milling

fed in from the right to make a hole along the workpiece axis. External and internal screw threads can be cut with a suitably profiled tool, provided that the feed motion is accurately proportioned to the cutting motion.

The lathe in all its different forms is the machine used for turning. The main difference between the types of lathe, apart from size, is the allocation of skilled tasks between the direct operator and the toolsetter. The screwcutting centre lathe shown in Figure 4.2a leaves all the skilled tasks with the operator, viz:

> Choice of workholding method
> Choice of tool
> Choice of spindle speed (worked out from cutting speed and diameter of work)
> Choice of feed rate (cuts per mm or revolutions per cut) and direction
> Choice of number of preliminary roughing cuts and depth of final finishing cut.
> Control of length of cut and final diameter.

Semi-automatic lathes are known as capstan and turret lathes. Figure 4.2b shows a bar-feed capstan lathe, in which the loading of components is eliminated. Each new component is machined on the end of a long bar of material fed in through the headstock spindle. When finished, the component is 'parted-off' by means of a knife tool carried on the cross slide. Up to five

Figure 4.2a   A centre lathe

Figure 4.2b   A capstan lathe

previous operations are carried out by tools mounted on a six position turret in the tailstock position. For each of these tools the length and depth of each cut are preset. Cutting is carried out by feeding the turret towards the work. At the end of the return stroke the turret is automatically indexed to bring the next tool into position. The sixth position on the turret contains an adjustable stop against which a new length of bar is fed ready for the next cycle of machining. The operator's tasks are reduced to:

Choice of spindle speed
Choice of feed rate (or application of hand feed)
Operation of cross slide to part-off component
Operation of bar-feed control.

The skilled pre-setting of the tools and stops to control the length and depth of each cut is the task of the toolsetter. The operator's job is referred to as 'semi-skilled'. Automatic lathes take this process to its logical conclusion, eliminating the operator from the system. Boring machines work on the inverse principle: the work is clamped to a stationary bed and the tool rotates to cut accurate internal diameters. Planing machines are used for producing flat surfaces on large workpieces, such as the cylinder blocks of ships' engines (the principle of planing is shown in Figure 4.1b). These workpieces are made in small quantities so that no automatic functions are provided. The critical skills involved in planing concern the clamping and measuring of the large and relatively flexible workpieces. Shapers are much smaller machines, in which the tool oscillates to provide cutting and return motions, and the workpiece moves to provide the feed motion.

The basic action of milling is shown in Figure 4.1c. Since the whole length of each successive tooth cuts metal, flat surfaces can be produced much more quickly than by single-point methods such as planing and shaping, and finer surface finishes can be obtained. When the required surface is other than flat, special form-milling cutters are used. Grooves and bevelled edges (chamfers) can be milled in this way. Instead of being clamped to the table, the workpiece may be supported on a turntable, or between centres as in a lathe. Form cutters can then be used to mill gear teeth, serrations, spiral grooves, etc. on circular workpieces. The action shown is that of a horizontal milling machine, illustrated in Figure 4.3. In the vertical milling machine the cutter is held at the top only and rotates about a vertical axis. The universal machine is similar, except that the angle of the cutter axis is adjustable. Both versatile and production types are available. The production miller is pre-set (like the semi-automatic lathes) so that the operator's task reduces to the loading and unloading of workpieces. The so-called plano-miller is a planing machine with the single-point tools replaced by milling heads.

In drilling machines a rotating twist-drill is fed vertically downward to cut a cylindrical hole into or through the workpiece. In the most skilled types of drilling the operator marks out the positions of the required holes on the

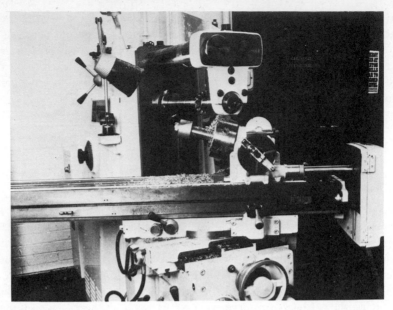

Figure 4.3 A horizontal milling machine

surface of the work, chooses a set of drills of increasing diameter to provide the initial pilot hole and then by steps up to the final diameter, and positions the drill over the mark accurately. He chooses a suitable feed and speed for each drill: hand or mechanical feed may be used. In production work any of these skilled tasks may be eliminated. A multi-spindle drill can be preset to drill several holes at once in accurate spatial relation, the work being held in the right place by a fixture. A jig may be provided: this not only holds the work in place but also contains hardened collars ('drill bushes'), which guide the drills onto the work and obviate the need for pilot holes. Feeds and speeds may be preset. As before, the skills of the toolmaker and toolsetter are employed to increase the speed and accuracy of the operation and this has the effect of reducing the skills demanded from the direct operator.

Most of the machines mentioned so far have their equivalents in the range of grinding machines. The tool or cutter is replaced by a rapidly rotating abrasive wheel. The surface grinder resembles a horizontal milling machine and the cylindrical grinder is similar to a lathe, for example. Very hard materials may be ground: one common use of the process is the machining of tools and cutters for use in other machine tools.

All the processes referred to above may be carried out dry or wet, i.e. with the cutting action bathed in a stream of soluble oil mixed with water, known generally as a cutting fluid or coolant.

The operator may be relieved of many tasks by the application of numerical control, which is effectively computer control, to any or all of the functions of a machine tool. This is used where a very intricate and accurately dimensioned workpiece is to be produced in small numbers, as is often the case in the aircraft industry.

Principles of metal forming

Many metals are ductile, as opposed to brittle: they can be made to bend, stretch, or flow into a new shape. Drawing is the art of stretching a flat sheet of metal between a punch and a hollow die so that it assumes a hollow shape determined by the shape of the clearance between punch and die when the punch is fully inserted into the die. Automobile body panels are usually made in this way. The machine used is the power press, which may be hydraulically or mechanically actuated. Making the toolsets (punch and die) for this process is regarded as highly skilled work, but operating the press is classified as unskilled: the tasks are simply the loading of blanks into the press and the unloading of components. This work is often done automatically if the quantity of work warrants the cost.

Forging is a skilled task in which a hot metal billet is hammered into shape in the way that a blacksmith would do it, i.e. by turning the billet under the hammer at intervals until the required shape (judged by eye) is achieved. In industry the hammer is mechanically operated. Stamping is less skilled than forging. A hot metal blank is placed on a shaped die and another die attached to a heavy weight is dropped on top of it, squeezing the blank into the shape of the space between the dies in a single blow. Many machine parts requiring high strength are made in this way initially and are subsequently 'finished' on surfaces requiring high accuracy by means of an appropriate metal-cutting process. Impact extrusion takes advantage of the fact that cold metal will flow more readily if it is deformed very rapidly: by closing a punch and die at great speed a solid pellet of aluminium can be converted into a thin-walled cylindrical vessel. Using the impact principle the head of a bolt can be formed on the end of a bar of steel equal in diameter to the shank of the bolt. To produce a bolt by turning, one would have to start with a bar equal in diameter to the head of the bolt, cutting away about half the original metal to produce the shank. Instead of cutting a thread on the bolt, this can be produced by a forming process: the shank is rolled between grooved dies. These processes, cold heading and thread rolling, are completely automatic.

Conclusion

The over-riding aim in the design and development of all production processes is to minimize the cost per component. This is done by saving material: hence the increasing use of forming as opposed to cutting processes, and by saving wages: hence the tendency to depend less on skilled direct operators and to make processes automatic where possible. The real skills required of the operator of a particular machine depend on tne length to which these trends toward greater productive efficiency have been taken. There are two main reasons why skills are still required: the volume of production may not justify the expense of automatic machinery, and there are still tasks where no mechanized alternative to human skill has yet been developed—tasks such as assembly and inspection, where perception is critical, for example. The main considerations in the design and marketing of machine tools are technical performance and price. Thus the machine is designed as a machine/work-piece system primarily, rather than a man/machine system. The set of real skills deployed by a machine-tool operator is something of a chance assemblage: he is brought in to perform the tasks which cannot be done more cheaply by the machine.

METAL WORKING TASKS

The engineering factory is a complex organization of people engaged in diverse tasks. Chains of information processing tasks intersect with hierarchies of responsibility to achieve the end result of a flow of saleable products. Figures 4.4 and 4.5 show how this organization evolved. In Figure 4.4 is

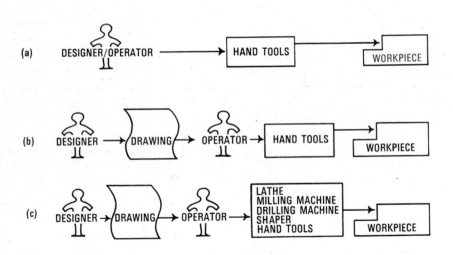

Figure 4.4   Separation of design from production

shown the gradual separation of the designer from the product caused by the introduction of technical drawing and the subsequent development of machine tools. Figure 4.5 shows the current situation in a large mass-production factory. The information required to specify the exact form of the product

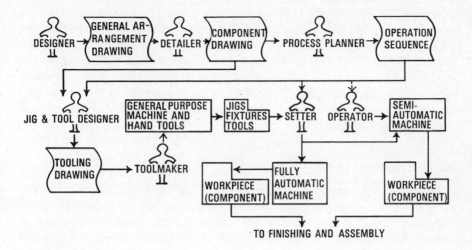

Figure 4.5 The flow of product defining information in a factory, showing the use of versatile, semi-automatic and automatic machine tools

passes through two stages of drawing, and then the specification of the operation sequence and the provision of jigs and fixtures before reaching the operator. Because so much of the decision making for the product and its method of manufacture has been done before the operator becomes involved, his job requires little cognitive skill. It has been reduced to a set of sensori-motor tasks. These may require skill in psychological terminology but in industrial parlance the job is called 'semi-skilled'. Training is often informal and takes weeks rather than years.

The tasks which industry considers 'skilled' are those involving planning and choice and the ability to read an engineering drawing. These have either 'staff' or 'craft' status. The first four jobs in Figure 4.5 are staff jobs: the jobholders work in offices, their tools pencil and paper, and their training takes place partly 'off-line' in technical college or university. The toolmaker and setter, as well as the millwright, maintenance fitter and electrician (not shown), hold craft jobs. They work in the factory proper and their training consists of a lengthy apprenticeship. Socially, there is a quasi-military hierarchical structure: the technical and managerial staff are the 'officers', the craftsmen, together with the foremen and chargehands are the 'NCOs' and the direct operators are the 'men'.

In small organizations the technical and 'line management' functions may be combined, for example, in the chargehand/setter. Alternatively the levels of the hierarchy may be merged, as in the job of the setter/operator. In another variation, the firm specializes in 'one-offs'—special products made to order and all different—and in this case the direct operator is actually a craftsman, using versatile machine tools to translate engineering drawings into components. For numerically controlled machine tools, the process planner of Figure 4.5 is replaced by a programmer, who either specifies the required control tape directly or programs a computer to do so. The operator is relieved of all measuring tasks and may also be relieved of feed and speed selection and tool changing, depending on the sophistication of the system. Complex profiles may be machined, beyond the skill of any operator using a normal machine tool.

Kinds of operator

The semi-skilled operator. As an example of the skills needed to operate a semi-automatic machine tool we may take the bar-feed capstan lathe. Singleton (1964) presents a link chart showing the control actions, their initiating stimuli and the feedback stimuli which indicate successful completion of each action. For the turret-mounted tools the operator has to select a spindle speed and a mechanical feed rate, either from experience or according to instructions. He must traverse the turret by hand, using the capstan wheel, until the tool is almost, but not quite, touching the workpiece. Then he must engage the mechanical feed drive, which is stopped automatically when the pre-set length of cut is reached. For tools mounted on the cross slide the operator has the extra task of selecting the next pre-set stop (on the turret this is automatic). He must then engage the cross-slide feed, wait until the feed stops and then withdraw the cross slide manually, by winding a crank. Each withdrawal of the turret automatically brings the next tool into position and changes the turret stop, which controls the length of cut. The cross slide is always used to part-off the completed workpiece from the bar, but may be brought in earlier to perform some other cutting operation. The last position on the turret contains the bar-feed stop. When this is in position, and after parting-off, the operator must release the chuck which clamps the bar to the headstock spindle, operate the control to advance the new end of the bar to the stop and re-clamp the chuck. The whole sequence is repeated. During all cuts it is necessary to adjust the rate and direction of flow of coolant as required.

The operator has to use judgement in positioning the tool close to the work before engaging mechanical feed: the further away it is, the more time the machine will spend 'cutting air', but the closer it is, the greater the risk of unintentional collison. He may have to use judgement in selecting spindle speeds and feedrates, or these may be specified for him. On simple machines without mechanical feed he must apply the feed by hand, judging the force applied to the capstan to get the right compromise between surface finish and time taken. He will always have to judge the coolant flow, compromising between tool-life and making too much mess. The non-judgemental part of his skill consists in operating the controls in the correct order through every cycle and getting into a rhythm which avoids the machine having to wait for his next action any longer than necessary.

The versatile machine tool operator. The skills involved in the craft of versatile machine tool operation are at two levels: planning skills and executive skills. At the planning stage the operator must choose the order in which he will make the cuts. If he starts with a rough billet of metal the first cut may produce a flat surface to act as a firm base while subsequent cuts are taken. Then he must choose the work-holding methods and the tools to be used. Finally he must choose feed rates and cutting speeds. At the level of execution the operator has to make many judgements. For example, Orna (1971), gives a comprehensive list of the executive skills found in studies of milling. There are forty-five of these, falling into three main groups: work-holding, cutting and measuring. They involve judgements of movement, distance, pressure, impact, vibration and surface finish. Vision, touch, kinaesthesis and audition are the sense modalities through which the judgements are made. The overall objective is to do the job as quickly as possible within the required limits of dimensional accuracy and surface finish.

The numerical control operator. It might seem that the operator of a numerically controlled machine would need to be skilled in work-holding methods and nothing else, since other judgements are embodied in the machine program. In practice, however, the operators of such machines are usually chosen from the ranks of experienced versatile machine tool operators. The high cost of the machine and the consequent high value of the finished workpiece are such that it is very important both to keep the machine working and to avoid scrapping any workpieces. In the present state of the art this often means that the operator has to over-ride the program, either by changing the programmed feeds and speeds in the interests of accuracy and surface finish, or by amending an incorrect dimension. He has controls which enable him to make these modifications, and one of his tasks is to 'de-bug' new programs. He also needs to diagnose faults in the machine. When trying out a new program he will first run through it with the cutting motions displaced from the workpiece, to check whether any disastrous collisions between tools and workpiece have been programmed in error. When the machine is cutting, he will monitor its performance in order to take corrective action where necessary and, if possible, save the workpiece from irreparable damage. His job is made more difficult by the fact that all the controls are electrical in their action and are on a control cabinet rather than on the machine itself: it is thus more difficult to avoid making control errors. Although the intention behind numerical control was to de-skill the operator's job, this has not yet happened: it is currently one of the most highly skilled of all machine-tool operating jobs.

The metal forming operator. Forging is highly skilled, but other tasks in metal forming are much less so. In drawing and other work with presses the key-note is dexterity in placing the blank under the tool and removing the finished workpiece. There is a legal requirement that the dies of presses shall be securely fenced to protect the operator. The operator is thus isolated from the process itself and his skill reduces to loading and unloading quickly and rhythmically.

Conclusions

The over-riding trend in engineering has been towards de-skilling jobs. The strategy is to rely on a stable élite corps of decision-makers and a quickly-trained floating population of operators. This allows each operator to be maximally productive and hopefully minimizes the cost of the product. We are perhaps at the end of an era of cheap materials and energy and expensive labour. In future, materials and energy may cost more and the emphasis may shift from saving labour to saving material and energy. This would lead to greater use of operators' skill potential. Another trend which points to higher levels of skill in the future is the quest for intrinsically motivating jobs (Herzberg, 1968), in which a man can achieve greater self-actualization through his work. Skill levels are thus in a state of balance between the established, de-skilling, division of labour and the new pressures and priorities just mentioned.

THE MAN-MACHINE INTERFACE

The transactions between a machine and its operator consist of transfers of material, energy and information, in both directions. Transfers of material and energy from machine to man are largely concerned in accidents: transfers from man to machine (e.g. loading the workpiece, operating manual controls) involve considerations of posture and work-physiology (Easterby, 1964; Alcock, 1961; Singleton, 1964). Clearly, fatigue, difficult posture and accidents militate against the expression of skill, but the most direct effect on skill is that of information transfer. Skilled performance depends on speed, accuracy of movement, smooth integration of perceptual and motor events and freedom from error. The problem of interface design is that of choosing (or designing) and arranging the machine's control and display elements in such a way as to enhance all these aspects of skill.

Design of displays and controls

Identification of elements. Both speed and error rates are important in the sub-task of deciding which display element to read or which control element to operate. The worst case consists of a matrix of identical elements: here the task resembles the classical multiple-choice reaction task, in which the time to identify one element depends on the logarithm of the number of (equiprobable) stimuli. Especially on large special-purpose machine tools either pushbuttons or dials are often arranged in an equi-spaced row or matrix. This is likely to give the slowest identification and the greatest probablity of error. Identification can be made faster if advantage is taken of any inherent structure there may be in the task to provide a corresponding structure in spatial arrangement of interface elements. If exact temporal sequences are found in the task (e.g. for start-up or shut-down) this suggests the provision of a corresponding spatial order in the arrangement of the controls and displays involved. Even in less-structured tasks there may be some temporal correlation in the use of elements: any clustering of correlations suggests a corresponding division of elements into sub-groups containing those which are often used together. A division into sub-groups according to association with particular machine functions (speed selection, feed selection, rapid traverse, etc.) will have the effect of reducing the search space for the next element needed.

In that the techniques of grouping make identification faster they probably make it easier, in the sense of reducing error probabilities. However, further security can be achieved by providing the operator with confirmation that he has actually selected the particular control or display that he intended to select. For controls, the naïve operator will be able to use labels (either text or standard symbols—BS 3641: 1971/2) to check the identity of controls. The provision of labels implies that the operator looks at each control as he is about to operate it, thus precluding the independence of perception and action which we have said is a key part of skilled performance. To give non-visual feedback of the identity of controls we can resort to very wide spacing (about 200 mm minimum) or to shape-coding, so that the feel of the control is associated with its function.

Operation of controls. Controls found on machine tools may be of direct mechanical type or indirect hydraulic or electrical. They may be discrete (two or more positions governing a corresponding number of states of the machine) or continuous (infinitely variable position between limits governing the value of some machine parameter). Discrete controls need understandable labelling of their individual positions for the benefit of learners, but the operator who is working up to normal speed will wish to forsake the labels and operate the control with kinaesthetic feedback. This implies: a good 'detent' action between positions, as few positions as possible on each control, rotary controls if there are more than two positions and a good angular separation between positions. Continuous controls will normally be associated with a display of the controlled parameter. This may be a scale and pointer directly attached to the control, an instrument displaying the controlled parameter, or movement of the actual tool or workpiece. In all cases there is a tradeoff between speed and accuracy. Corlett (1961) has examined the conditions for maximizing accuracy when a rotary mechanical control is directly coupled to a concentric scale-and-pointer display. In other cases the ratio of control movement to display movement can be chosen so as to give the minimum sum of 'slewing time' and 'adjustment time', within the limits imposed by accuracy required and manual force available.

Reading displays. Visual displays may be real (tool and workpiece) or artificial. The artificial display chosen to present certain information depends on the nature of the information and the use to which it is to be put. On machine tools positional information in increasingly being given in digital form. This information may be used for comparison with a digitally presented dimension on a drawing. Where possible the choice of origin and direction of increase should be such that the displayed value is equal to the written value when the dimension being machined is correct. This will eliminate the time taken and the possibility of error in intermediate calculation by the operator. Where accurate values are not required (e.g. spindle speed, motor power consumption) it is a mistake to use digital presentation. An analogue (scale and pointer) display not only gives the value of the parameter: it also shows the position within the range and the speed and direction of change directly and in a form which can be used by the operator without his having to translate it into numbers. Research on the relative direction of motion of a control and its associated display has been reviewed by Loveless (1962): the importance of using a correctly experienced population in this work is shown by Singleton (1971) quoting work by the present author. A comparison of analogue and digital displays for a particular application (Micrometer) is given by Murrell and Kingston (1963).

Conclusions

There is a considerable amount of published information on the psychophysics of displays and the forces which can be applied to controls, but these aspects do not touch the central problem of producing an interface which will enhance skilled performance without impeding the learning of that performance. The aim is to achieve a smooth, rapid, accurate and error-free performance from the combination of man and machine. For this, research and development on complete interfaces involving the acquisition of skills over a realistic time scale would be necessary. One of the experiments reported by Singleton (1968) is of this character, but it does not seem to have been followed up.

SKILLS ANALYSIS AND TRAINING

The nature of skill

Whether in industry or in the psychological laboratory, skilled performance connotes behaviour which has been refined by practice until high speed, low error rate and high resistance to disturbance have been achieved. Industrial training schemes use the criterion of 'Experienced Worker Standard' to define the levels of speed and quality which are the goals of training. Alternative training methods are judged by the time taken by trainees to reach this standard. The use of this criterion involves the assumption that the experienced worker, who probably had no formal training, has reached the highest level of skill possible by means of extensive practice alone. It is at least possible that optimum training could lead to higher levels than this: the raising of standards would then be an alternative to the shortening of training times as the goal of training. While industrial development of training methods is concerned with the *level* of skill, judged by results, psychologists are interested in the *nature* of skill: what it is that differentiates skilled performance from the attempts of a beginner. Singleton (1968) reports three experiments on the nature of skill in laboratory tasks, while Seymour (1966) reports a series of investigations using a simulated capstan lathe. The results in each case tend to confirm the views of Bartlett (1947) on the nature of skill:

1. Perception and action are both modified by practice
2. Practice is only effective when knowledge of results is given
3. The relation between perception and action changes with practice from a simple chain of stimulus–response pairs to a much freer linkage between a smooth flow of perceptual acts and a smooth flow of motor acts
4. This freedom is exploited to allow attention to dwell on a perceptually difficult or critical element without any disruption of concurrent motor activity
5. This freedom is made possible by the substitution of auditory, tactile, or kinaesthetic cues for visual ones in the elements of the task coming before and after one one requiring extra visual attention
6. Behaviour becomes goal-directed: results are achieved uniformly despite increased variation in behaviour on elements of the task. The variation is due to less stringent self-monitoring by the operator and to reaction to external disturbances which, in an unpractised operator, would have precluded achievement of the required result.

The analysis of industrial tasks

Developments from work study. Industrial analysis of tasks has been carried out ever since F. W. Taylor (1911) proposed the idea of the 'one best way' of carrying out a task. The traditional work-study approach which developed from this concentrates almost entirely on minimizing the time and energy used in carrying out a motor sequence. Various attempts have been made to expand the analysis of tasks to include perceptual activity. Singleton's (1964) 'link design chart' brings in the perceptual cues which trigger each individual motor act and those which signify the successful completion of each act.

The purpose of this chart was to aid the design of the man–machine information interface. This type of chart would have to be expanded if it were to show the changing sensori-motor pattern of a developing skill. In practice it tends to be drawn up *a priori* and is probably based on the methods of work applicable to a beginner. The link chart is based on the logical sequence of events entailed in the task as the designer sees it. Seymour's (1966) 'Sensori-motor process chart', on the other hand, is time based, having columns for left and right hand movements together with a 'vision' column in which appear the successive foci of visual attention corresponding in time with the hand motions. This allows the strict correlation between visual perception and motor acts to be relaxed, as shown in Seymour's example of a packing task, where skilled operators looked ahead of the task element currently being performed by the hands, in order to get 'set' for the next element. Columns for other senses are provided, as well as a 'mental work' column for recording acts of decision making or judgement. The type of chart to be used depends on the nature of the task: for machine-paced work in which the operator is performing delicate handling operations the sensori-motor process chart is essential, but for work on semi-automatic machines where the task is mainly that of starting and stopping and selecting machine motions the link chart may be adequate.

Skills analysis. The purpose of skills analysis in industry is the design of optimum training programmes. For repetitive work of many kinds this has been done by the recording of the performance of 'experienced workers' on a chart of the sensori-motor type. The name 'skills analysis' is unfortunate: skill resides not in the individual elements of perception, decision and action but in the way they are put together by the skilled operator. Much 'skills analysis' is no more than a sophisticated analysis of task elements, in the tradition of work measurement.

In the machine-tool context, the Perkins Engine Company has carried out considerable research on methods of training based on skills analysis, sponsored by the Engineering Industry Training Board (Orna, 1971). The specific method of analysis found to be successful at Perkins involved the use of ex-operators as analysts. Tasks were recorded on videotape and immediately studied in detail by the analyst and the operator working together. From the analysis key points of difficult perception, judgement and dexterity were extracted for subsequent use in the design of training programmes, and the (inflexible) order of task activity was found. After consistent success with this method applied to 'semi-skilled' operators, it was tried with craft apprentices, including future versatile machine-tool operators, Success was not achieved, and a new approach was sought. The problem was that there was too great a discrepancy between end-of-training performance and experienced worker performance on craft jobs such as electrical maintenance and versatile machine-tool operation. This difference was assumed to be in '. . . perceptual organization which results in continuous adjustments to the process, the

prediction of errors and successes, and the ability to look ahead . . .', attention to feedback, continuous decision-making within a set of rules which the
operator 'has developed and made his own on the basis of experience' and the
making and following of personal plans of action. In short, current analysis
and training methods neglected the intellectual components of skills, and
consequently failed where this component was critical, i.e. in craft occupations.

In the terms used by Miller *et al.* (1960), these high level skills require
study of the 'image' (the mental model which the operator has of the task)
based on perception and feedback of results of actions, as well as of the 'plan'
(actually a complex heirarchy of plans) which controls his actions. The versatile operator must have an image which is accurate enough to allow prediction of the results of his actions, and he must be able to develop his own plans
for coping with novel situations. The alternative to a workable image and
plan is a set of stimulus–response connections which, once learned, are
completely inflexible. This would be adequate for a semi-skilled task but not
for craft work. Miller *et al.* (*op. cit.*) stress that individual differences in
planning style are very great: this squares with the insistence on *personal*
plans in the Perkins work.

Training

For semi-skilled work, at least, the principles of training are fairly well
established (see for instance Seymour, 1966). The general principle is to work
up from elementary operations to the complete task. One method often
advocated is the 'progressive part' system. Elements are learned first, followed
by groups of elements adjacent in the serial order of the task, and so on
until the task is being practised as a whole. It has been found by experience
that this is better than learning the complete task from the start, or jumping
straight from well-learned elements to the complete task. Seymour suggests
(from experiments on the simulated capstan lathe) that a method involving
first the learning of especially difficult elements followed by the complete
task is best (Seymour, 1966). It is not difficult to set up a training scheme of
one of these types incorporating the necessary evaluations of the trainee's
performance by means of tests at each stage, thus providing control information for the trainer and knowledge of results for the trainee.

As the Perkins studies show, this traditional approach is useless for the
training of craftsmen. Versatile machine-tool operators have acquired their
skills in the past by means of an apprenticeship. Working for, and eventually
with, an experienced craftsman is a viable training method but it takes a very
long time (5–7 years). Gipsy fortune tellers learn their art by watching their
mothers practice it: eventually they can do it too, but they are incapable of
explaining how it is done. It seems obvious that an analysis of the skills
involved could expedite their training and that of machine-tool craftsmen.

There is no reason to suppose that a good craftsman is also a good teacher, or that he can even analyse and explain his own skills unaided.

The Perkins researchers used electrical maintenance as a test vehicle for training in cognitive skills: a thorough analysis was carried out with particular emphasis on planning and decision-making. A new training programme incorporating instruction and testing in these skills was evolved, tested, and found effective. For our purposes the study of milling which followed is more to the point. However, for practical reasons a full analysis of the planning skills was not carried out. Nevertheless, a training programme for milling was devised using principles proved in earlier exercises in which specific attention was paid to planning skills. As well as the changes in programme content, a shift in learning methods was introduced, the accent changing from instructor-centred to trainee-centred learning. This perhaps seemed more appropriate to the learning of planning and decision skills, for with planning goes responsibility. Another reason for the change to guided-discovery exercises, discussion seminars and the like was that trainees with the capacity to become craftsmen were heartily bored by the one-way communication of lectures and demonstrations. Whatever the reason for the adoption of these new learning methods, they are in line with the dictum of Miller *et al.* (1960) that individual differences in planning styles are great.

With the changes in content and style suggested above, a milling programme was tested in a factory against a traditional programme (given to a control group) and proved to be superior. After experiencing the programme, trainee milling machine operators could tackle an 'unseen' workpiece, arriving at an acceptable workholding plan and cutting sequence and then carrying these out to approved standards of speed and product quality. Table 4.1, which is taken from the Perkins/EITB report (Orna, 1971) summarizes the difference between the 'old' and 'new' (or semi-skilled and skilled) approaches to analysis and training. It would be interesting to know whether it is the new content or the new methods which contribute most to the new programme's success. The discovery method of learning must take place in a restricted context: possibly a greater knowledge of how we acquire planning hierarchies would lead to a general training in planning which would transfer to situations far removed from machine-tool operation. The same speculations apply to training for predicting and decision making.

DANGER AND ACCIDENTS

The operational approach

Any workpiece where machinery is used abounds in dangers which may lead to harm (injury or disease) to workers. The translation of danger into harm may be precipitated by the presence and/or interaction of several factors: the contribution of the variable nature of skilled performance is considered

Table 4.1 Old and new craft-training methods compared (From Orna, 1971)

	Initial approach	Revised approach
Analysis	1 Physical skills 2 Fault diagnosis 3 Knowledge	Total task structure and related skilled behaviour
Training objectives	To learn the operational elements of the task and the use of the tools. Mainly manufacture of workpieces	To learn the total behaviour necessary to meet task objectives
Training content	To practise physical skills and to learn knowledge and procedures	To comprehend the task structure, to develop rules and strategies, and to practise their applications
Degree of flexibility	Closely specified 'one best method' and set knowledge topics	Different approaches, improvisations, manipulation of rules to overcome limitations in the environment
Training methods	Job instructor, instruction schedules, audio-visual programmes, demonstrations, practice	Job instructor, group discussions, experimentation, self evaluation of learning results
Instructor and trainee roles	Mainly learning by listening and copying. Instructor controls teaching process	Co-operative endeavour. Learning through discovery guided by instructor. Trainee plays large part in control of his own learning and of training programme
Measurement of effectiveness	Periodic. Phase and final tests (practical and theory)	Continuous. Learning objectives in behavioural terms must be met at every learning stage
Utilization of feedback	Mainly for grading purposes	Immediate adjustment of on-going training processes is possible. Subsequent improvement in programme content and training methods
Integration of total training process	Limited. Lack of linkage with task objective and post-training experience	Complete. Task objective, analysis of structure and behaviour, learning objectives, post-training experience, are all interlinked by design and by feedback
Further hypotheses		
Transfer of skills. Versatility	1 Within the process, e.g. milling—good 2 Within the trade, e.g. machining—limited 3 To other tasks, e.g. jig design—almost none	1 Within the process—complete 2 Within the trade—good 3 To other tasks—some
Effect on post-training experience period	Nil	Reduces post-training period, and thus overall training time

by Swain (1973) and by Singleton (1975); Atherley (1975) discusses the effects
of management's strategies and underlying attitudes; Booth (1975) outlines
the role of machine design; and an extra factor which is usually present is
chance, in the sense that the degree of harm in particular cases cannot be
predicted from the nature of the danger. In their classic study of 'critical
incidents' in flying Fitts and Jones (1947) show that it is easy to confuse these
precipitating factors: what were thought to be pilot errors often turned out
to be weaknesses in machine design.

The extended study undertaken by the National Institute of Industrial
Psychology (Powell *et al.*, 1971) in a machine shop and other workshops
shows that the dangers in a task are highly specific, not only to the type of
task but even to the details of it, for example: component tolerances, variation in machine settings, etc. In the capstan lathe section of the machine shop
the most common injury was a foreign body in the eye, although the most
common class of injuries was from the machine and tools (33%). In the press
section the most common injury by far was a cut from a component, this
occurring within the most common class (72%): injuries from material and
components. The type of person most likely to be injured, in both cases, was
either the beginner in the shop or the operator who changed tasks often.
Types of danger which are characteristic of machine tool operation are listed
in Table 4.2, together with examples of the way they are embodied in the
machine and of the type of harm that may result from them. In practice there
are more general dangers to be found in the workplace: poor 'housekeeping',
leading to tripping over and striking against objects (a very common, but not
usually serious, type of accident), transport dangers such as slipping of crane
slings and collision with vehicles, dangerous postures leading eventually to
lower-back injury, and dangers inherent in the man–machine information
interface leading to errors in operation with consequent precipitation of other
dangers.

The amount of operator involvement necessary to convert danger into
harm varies with the nature of the danger. There are three distinct approaches
to the reduction of harm: secure fencing of dangerous parts, provision of
protective clothing, and control of the operator's behaviour through training,
incentives and discipline. None of these methods is completely effective: the
appropriate combination of them depends on the opportunities presented by
any particular combination of machine and job. The safety of operators can
only be guaranteed by an effective 'safe place of work' strategy. This puts
little onus on the operator and requires that danger be removed or sealed off
completely. While many production machine tools can be operated in this
way, it would be difficult to apply the strategy to versatile machines without
cutting off essential information channels between the workpiece and the
skilled operator. The same applies to production machines when operated by
the toolsetter: he must have a close view of the action in order to make the
necessary fine adjustments. On large machines he may have to rely on an

Table 4.2 Machine tool dangers

Danger	Examples	Harm
Sharp edges	Tools, semi-finished work, swarf	Skin laceration
Traps (close approach of parts)	Press-tools, certain machine slides	Crushing of fingers or limbs
In-running nips (closely spaced rotating parts)	Pairs of rollers or gearwheels; pulley and belt (including conveyor belts)	Clothing, hair on fingers drawn in: crushing and other injuries
Rotating parts	Chucks, workpieces, grinding wheels	Laceration of abrasion
	Shafts, drills, workpieces	Entanglement of clothing or hair: various injuries
Escape of material (normal)	Waste material:	
	Swarf (wet)	Skin laceration
	Swarf (dry)	Burns, eye damage
	Grinding particles	Eye damage
Escape of material (accidental)	Tools or workpieces broken or pulled from clamping devices by excess cutting force or collision while traversing: broken or loose parts of machines (including bursting of grinding wheels)	Laceration, bruising, fractures, etc.
Escape of toxic substances	Cutting fluids (certain types)	Bacterial infection, dermatitis, carcinoma
	Swarf from machining:	
	Asbestos	Lung disease
	Beryllium	Lung disease
	Lead	Cumulative poisoning
Escape of energy (noise)	Drop-forging, stamping, presswork, compressed air exhaust, rotating stock bar on automatic lathe, etc.	Hearing loss after prolonged exposure
Escape of energy (electrical)	Faulty maintenance or installation	Electrocution

assistant to operate the controls while he is close to the cutting or forming action. A misunderstood instruction in such a situation can cause serious harm to the toolsetter. Here a 'safe system of working' is appropriate. For instance, while the guards are off the machine all its motions except the ultra-slow 'inching' or 'crawling' speeds would be automatically disabled.

Where there is no physical way in which the danger and the man can be kept apart we must rely on attempts to control the inherent variability of human behaviour: 'safe person' strategies mean building into the operator's skill the necessary behaviour to achieve safety, both in the operation of the machine and in the conscientious use of protective clothing and devices. Clearly this is a problem of training, for it is during initial training that the operator's priorities are set and it is to the first-learned method of performing a task that the operator will revert when under stress.

The psychological approach

There are a number of psychological concepts and terms relevant to safety, in particular stress, arousal and fatigue. In the industrial situation we can distinguish three types of factor which can stress the operator:

Factors intrinsic in the task: The load of the task itself: perception, coding, judgement, memory, decision-making and the rate, difficulty and variety of these.

Factors in the immediate environment: noise, vibration, heat, cold, perceived danger, incentives, etc.

Factors extrinsic to the job: e.g. carry-over from the non-work part of the operator's life: lack of sleep, domestic difficulties, etc.

The combined stress pattern on an operator at a given moment is thus multi-dimensional and at differing degrees of immediacy. It is not surprising to find that the effects of combined stresses on skilled performance are not simply additive. Broadbent (1971) shows that stress effects can be additive or independent or even subtractive, and that these interactions are different for different tasks. The explanation usually accepted for this confusing state of affairs is that there is an intervening variable between imposed stress and performance, namely arousal. Measures of arousal have been attempted in terms of EEG, muscle tension, heart rate and hormone balance as well as (by inference) performance. The results show that arousal itself appears to be multidimensional. Broadbent (*op. cit.*) points out that performance-derived arousal is not the same as neurophysiological arousal (the generalized cortical readiness derived from the passage of stimulus information through the ascending reticular formation). He deplores the use of the same word for both. He further suggests that peripheral physiological measures record a combination of arousal and effort. However, it is clear that the relation between performance and arousal is of 'inverted-U' type; too high or too low a level of arousal will degrade performance. The optimum level of arousal for a combination of person and task depends on the difficulty of the task and seems to be also a function of the subject's personality as measured by EPI scores (Eysenck, 1967). This has been shown by Bursill and Shigehisa (1972) for very simple tasks and for the tasks of responding to an IQ test and of paired associate learning by Eysenck (*op. cit.*). In general, introverts need less arousal to reach optimum performance than extroverts, and neurotic subjects need less than stable ones. Difficult tasks are more arousing than simple ones when the difficulty consists in the variety of activity within the task. Hockey

(1970a, b) has shown that high (above optimum) arousal leads to a narrowing of attention, in the sense that aspects of the task not considered central to its performance tend to be ignored.

Bearing in mind that all these findings refer to experimental laboratory tasks, we may cautiously note the implications for machine-tool operation as follows:

Low intrinsic job-stress. We should expect a simple, repetitive job to produce low arousal. Especially in extroverts, this could lead to a wandering of attention from the task in hand and to sub-optimal performance. If, as sometimes happens, a highly complex job contains an occasional period of routine work, e.g. when a toolmaker has to make a batch of identical parts, this effect is likely to be dangerous: a man temperamentally suited to high-variety work and largely responsible for his own safety will be vulnerable in the routine situation.

High intrinsic job stress. This is the normal situation for versatile operators, who have many things to plan and do. If the stress is too high for the individual we should expect a narrowing of attention, especially in introverts. This could lead to failure to notice dangers external to the task in hand (e.g. getting involved in somebody else's accident), or failure to attend to the safety features of the task, if these are not regarded as key features.

Environmental stress. Workers in factories where machine tools are installed will be protected from extremes of environmental stress for the sake of their health. The protection provided for operators continuously exposed to hazardous levels of noise, heat, etc. may not be used by occasional visitors to the workshop: the effects of extreme environmental stress may be important in the case of maintenance personnel or patrol inspectors or possibly tool-setters who may perform demanding tasks in a high-stress environment and be over-aroused. The effect of moderate environmental stress cannot be predicted from experimental findings, although factors other than safety would suggest that levels should be kept low.

Extrinsic stress. Hockey's findings suggest that a high level of extrinsic stress would cause the job itself to be relegated to the periphery of attention. This would be a tenuous inference were it not for the fact that there is anecdotal evidence from industry that severe extrinsic stress associated with such factors as bereavement or the breakdown of marriage has caused hitherto reliable workers to make apparently crass errors of omission, sometimes leading to accidents.

In summary, we can say that machine-tool operators on low-skill repetitive tasks need to be protected from danger, including danger resulting from their own actions, since their level of arousal is likely to be well below the optimum for efficient performance. High-skill operators on high-variety tasks need to be protected from stress; they should not be over-motivated or expected to attempt impossible targets in terms of speed or accuracy, lest their arousal should rise well beyond the optimum. Workers who are in a position to make accident-triggering errors may become error prone due to factors in their non-work life: if ways can be found, perhaps via medical or counselling services, for management to become aware of these problems before an accident instead of afterwards, an improvement in safety would result.

Branton (1970) studied in detail the variability of movement times and accuracies for the elements of a capstan-lathe operator's task. The subjects had had 10 years practice at the task. He found that variabilities (and hence probability of error) rose to a peak at times ranging from 55 to 105 min after a work break, and then declined. The highest daily peak coincided with the daily peak for accidents at 11.00 to 11.30 h. He suggests that since this peak occurred at a time of day when performance at laboratory tasks is optimal, it could not be caused by fatigue due to mental overload, but must be due to some effect of monotony. Murrell (1962) also detected this sudden increase in variability of element times in repetitive tasks, referring to the end of an 'actile period'. Branton suggests that the reason for it may be a changeover from closed loop to ballistic control of hand movements after a certain period of re-acquaintance with the task. Singleton (1953) points out that such a change would increase the information processing load of the task, a result which might well be congenial to an operator seeking to mitigate monotony. An alternative hypothesis would be that the relation between intrinsic task stress and performance, via a change in arousal, contains an inertia term.

The skills approach

It has been said that all accidents are caused by human error. This is often taken to mean that blame and retribution should be directed at some person whenever an accident occurs. Thus a counter argument arises from safety professionals that the notorious variability of human behaviour is nobody's fault but is a fact of life and a constraint on the design of the technological environment. It is difficult to escape from the blaming habit when discussing human error: the very words carry a connotation of 'wrongness' which can too easily be taken in the moral instead of the technical sense. However, it is clear that the commission of an unusual act or the omission of a usual act on the part of a skilled worker is a perfectly possible causal factor in some accidents. If a 'safe person' strategy is relied on it may be the main cause, but in other cases it must coexist with inadequate job design, machine design or protection in order to precipitate an accident.

Singleton (1975) makes the point that an error is the result of a disorder of skill. On the perceptual side the wrong 'mental model' may be selected (this could happen where an unfamiliar machine with a novel layout of controls was in use), or incoming data may be wrongly interpreted although the right model is in use (the operator may think that the smell of burning is coming from the cutting action of his machine when actually his pipe has set his pocket on fire). The use of the appropriate mental model as a test-bed for finding out the future consequences of actions is part of perceptual skill. Low performance in this area, for whatever reason, be it incapacity or overload, will render the operator less able to avoid the accident when it arrives. In particular, good anticipation allows information overload to be foreseen and avoided.

Another disorder of skill is the incorrect appreciation of probabilities. This is especially the case with the probabilities of rare events such as accidents. The man who has not yet had his first accident may use his own experience to estimate the probability of accident as zero when it is actually greater than zero. Similarly he may fail to act on a warning signal which has never before occurred because it is not in his mental model of the task. On the motor side it is the very speed and smoothness of performance which may constitute a danger: the man is simply going too fast to react to the single unexpected stimulus that heralds danger. As in perception he can select the wrong model, in motor skills the operator may run off the wrong subroutine: perhaps two subroutines start in a similar way and then diverge. These are some of the ways in which skills can go wrong and lead to errors which in turn may be causal factors in accidents. Both fatigue and ageing, as Singleton points out, can lead to a general degradation of skill: information is either missed or is noticed too late and over-reaction occurs: the trajectory and timing of motor action becomes more variable. Again, the possibility of error is increased.

CONCLUSIONS AND PROSPECTS

We have seen that machine tool operation spans two major classes of industrial work: skilled and semi-skilled. In psychological terms both types of work involve skills of the psychomotor type, but 'skilled' work has additional cognitive components. This difference makes it necessary to alter the approach to skills analysis, to training, and to safety management. At the present time there are far more semi-skilled than skilled workers in industry. The ratio of skilled to semi-skilled workers is determined by the economic criterion of minimizing the total cost per unit of product. It would be a happy coincidence if the resulting distribution of tasks matched the distribution of capacities in the population: in one sense this is bound to happen, since unused capacity is liable to atrophy, but this mental sinking to the level of the job is clearly undesirable.

The task facing industry, if it takes its social role seriously, is to reconcile the efficiency of mass production with the human need for autonomy and responsibility in jobs. This will entail the abolition of semi-skilled work except for a small section of the population of seriously limited capacity, since it is clear that many semi-skilled workers do not take any pride in the job they do. If this comes about we shall be left with automatic machine tools and versatile machine tools only. The manned production machine will hardly exist. The drive towards automation seems to have petered out as the limits of its economic benefits were reached, so the change envisaged must wait for either more ingenuity to be shown in low-cost automation or for social factors to appear in balance sheets or both. In the meantime, we seem to know how to train people for semi-skilled work and we are progressing in our ability to prevent accidents in this class of work. The challenge for the future is to develop means of training for autonomy and responsibility in jobs which may well change fairly often, to understand more about the analysis of cognitive skills and to develop ways of ensuring the safety of workers who are given the authority to organize and vary their own jobs.

References

Alcock, P. H. (1961). Report of work done on a $3\frac{1}{2}$ inch centre lathe with an inclined bed (London: Rural Industries Bureau)

Atherley, G. R. C. (1975). Strategies in health and safety at work. *The Production Engineer*

Bartlett, F. C. (1947). The measurement of human skill. Reprinted in *Occ. Psychol.*, **22**, 83

Booth, R. T. (1975). Design for machinery safety. *Occ. Health*

Branton, P. (1970). A field study of repetitive manual work in relation to accidents at the workplace. *Int. J. Prod. Res.*, **8**, 93

British Standards Institution (1971/2) *BS 3641. Symbols for machine tools Parts 1 and 2* (London: B.S.I.)

Broadbent, D. E. (1971). *Decision and Stress* (London: Academic Press)

Bursill, A. E. and Shigehisa, T. (1972). Heteromodal stimulation, personality and the inverted-U function. *Bull. Br. Psychol. Soc.*, **25**, 70(Abstract)

Corlett, E. N. (1961). The accuracy of setting machine tool handwheels. *Ergonomics*, **4**, 1, 53

Easterby, R. S. (1964). Anthropometric data for machine tool designers. *Proc. 2nd I.E.A. Congress, Dortmund*

Eysenck, H. J. (1967). Intelligence assessment, a theoretical and experimental approach. *Br. J. Ed. Psychol.*, **37**, 81

Fitts, P. M. and Jones, R. E. (1947). Analysis of factors contributing to 460 'pilot-error' experiences in operating aircraft controls. Reprinted in W. Sinaiko (ed.), (1961), *Selected Papers on Human Factors in the Design and Use of Control Systems* (New York: Dover)

Herzberg, F. (1968). *Work and the Nature of Man* (London: Staples Press)

Hockey, G. R. J. (1970a). Changes in attention allocation in a multi-component task under loss of sleep. *Br. J. Psychol.*, **61**, 473

Hockey, G. R. J. (1970b). Signal probability and spatial location as possible bases for increased selectivity in noise. *Q. J. Exp. Psychol.*, **22**, 37

Loveless, N. E. (1962). Direction of motion stereotypes: a review. *Ergonomics*, **5**, 357

Miller, G. A., Galanter, E. and Pribram, K. H. (1960). *Plans and the structure of behaviour* (London: Holt, Rinehart and Winston)

Murrell, K. F. H. (1962). Operator variability and its industrial consequences. *Int. J. Prod. Res.*, **1**, 3, 39

Murrell, K. F. H. and Kingston, P. M. (1963). Experimental comparison of scalar and digital micrometers. *Ergonomics*, **9**, 1, 39

Orna, E. (1971). The analysis and training of certain engineering craft occupations: *Engineering Industry Training Board, Research Report No. 2* (London: E.I.T.B.)

Powell, P. I., Hale, M., Martin, J. and Simon, M. (1971). 2000 Accidents: National Institute of Industrial Psychology, Report No. 21 (London: N.I.I.P.)

Seymour, W. D. (1966). *Industrial Skills* (London: Pitman)

Singleton, W. T. (1953). Deterioration of performance on a short-term perceptual-motor task, in *Symposium on Fatigue*, W. F. Floyd and A. T. Welford (eds.), (London: J. T. Lewis)

Singleton, W. T. (1964). A preliminary study of a capstan lathe. *Int. J. Prod. Res.*, **3**, 3, 213

Singleton, W. T. (1968). Some recent experiments on learning and their training implications. *Ergonomics*, **11**, 1, 53

Singleton, W. T. (1971). General theory of presentation of information. *In* R. K. Bernotat and K. D. Gartner (eds.), *Displays and Controls* (Amsterdam: Swets and Zeitlinger)

Singleton, W. T. (1975). Skill and accidents: in "Occupational Accident Research" (Stockholm: Swedish Work Environment Fund)

Swain, A. D. (1973). *Design Techniques for Improving Human Performance in Production* (London: Industrial and Commercial Techniques Ltd.)

Taylor, F. W. (1911). *Principles of scientific management* (New York: Harper and Row)

5

The Sewing Machinist

W. T. SINGLETON

INTRODUCTION

It is impossible to make statements with any precision about the number of people who earn their living in Britain by operating sewing machines. Government, employers and trade unions keep manpower data in terms of product rather than process. Machines in use may be up to 50 years old so that manufacturers records are not helpful. Thus we know how many people are engaged in making shoes, clothing and so on but surprisingly little about the numbers of specialist machine operators within such occupations. The best estimate seems to be over 15,000 sewing machinists in the shoe industry and more than twice this number making clothes, furniture, handbags, gloves, curtains, etc. more than 50,000 in total. Almost all of them are female, and the numbers have decreased slightly over the past 20 years as productivity has increased. By tradition dating from 'sweat shop' times, they work very hard. A time-study engineer with experience of many occupations will tend to 'rate' sewing machinists very highly. The energy expenditure is not high since the job is essentially sedentary and perhaps the main occupational hazard is a tendency to plumpness. It is possible to have accidents by catching the fingers in the balance wheel and pulley, hair in the thread take-up lever and fingers under the needle, but such incidents are rare and they are painful rather than seriously dangerous so that there is automatic avoidance reinforcement. It is reasonably well paid, usually by piece-work. Operators are invariably in large groups within which there is extensive communication and interaction, some because of interdependence of jobs, some because of common social interests. These interests tend to change with age. The very young unmarried are different from the young marrieds who are different again from the older married, widowed and spinsters. Girls take up the job on leaving school because the work is done in that particular area. It is common in the prosperous medium-sized towns in the Midlands such as Leicester, Northampton and Nottingham, in London and Lancashire and Yorkshire.

Figure 5.1 A clothing factory (By courtesty of T. W. Kempton Ltd.)

A supervisor will often make distinctions between a good worker, a good machinist and a highly skilled machinist. The characteristics of a *good worker* are reliability, hard work and co-operation. Reliability is predominant, one who is never absent, late or wants to go early, is a great asset. So also is one who can be trusted to get on with the work steadily and energetically without supervision. The harassed supervisor is also grateful to those who co-operate readily, do not argue about temporarily changing places or jobs, or the quality of materials and the state of the machine. Note that skill as such hardly comes into this picture. It begins to appear in the good machinist, she is primarily the one whose quality of work is never suspect and secondarily the one who can get through a lot of work. The skilled machinst is the one who combines quality and versatility, who is capable of carrying out a wide variety of jobs to a consistently high standard. Speed is not usually mentioned in this context although it tends to be taken for granted, that is productivity and quality are regarded as co-variants.

THE WORK SPACE

The machinist sits on an industrial chair with her feet on a treadle. This chair is adjustable in height and has an adjustable back-rest which is intended as a lumbar support, connected to the seat by a pillar. Both seat and back-rest are hard for reasons of durability and hygiene but this is often negated by the addition of personal cushions on the seat and cardigans drooped over the back-rest. The treadle which also acts as a foot rest is perhaps 10 cm off the floor which means that the seat should be correspondingly higher, this facilitates standing up and sitting down. There is one other foot control, either a pedal which lifts the presser foot used on cloth sewing-machines or a knee pad which operates the corresponding presser wheel used in leather/plastic sewing machines. The bench is about at elbow height, in area normally 100 cm by 50 cm, with the machine bed set to the right so that the needle-bar is almost in the middle. The most common machine is the flat-bed although there are many others, for example the post-machines and cylinder-arm machines used on shoes.

The focal point of the whole process is the needle moving up and down through the material. There is often an additional small light illuminating this area. The posture is not ideal. The structure of the work space is based on getting the hands near the needle but since much of the work is fine and precise the head and shoulders are usually hunched foward during stitching to improve vision, the back rest is not in use during this phase. The machinists' lap is often an integral part of the work-space, scissors are an essential tool. The work is supplied in trollies or in boxes delivered by conveyor or by human feeder. The machinist usually follows the instructions given on a card which may be in a variety of special codes but she relies also on experience and on conversation with the supervisor.

When the machinist presses the treadle a clutch plate moves off a fixed brake and on to a permanently rotating flywheel so that the machine accelerates rapidly to full speed. This is likely to be about 2000 stitches per min on a shoe machine and up to 7000 stitches per min on a clothing machine. When the treadle is released the clutch moves back off the flywheel on to the brake so that the machine decelerates at a rate depending on the wear of the brake pads, the oiliness of the flywheel and the strength of the return spring. For a badly maintained machine the operator may assist deceleration by pressing the palm of the hand on the balance wheel but this should not be necessary. On the other hand, acceleration and braking must not be too abrupt, a certain smoothness is regarded as optimal. The feet are not usually together in the middle of the treadle, one is in front of the other providing the acceleration while the rear one presses downwards to assist braking. During stitching the hands perform a complex action involving guiding, pushing forward, holding back, gripping sometimes between fingers and thumb but more usually between splayed fingers and the smooth machine base and bench top. There may be two hands guiding or one may guide while the other arranges work either before or after stitching. Exact integration of hand and foot movements is required.

WORKING CONDITIONS

Lighting and ventilation are usually reasonable but could do with some improvement particularly for those in the middle of large rooms. Heating is rarely complained about but there are often disputes about 'draughts' due to traffic through doors and inadequately insulated windows. Noise level is satisfactory in that it is high enough to provide a general feeling of purposeful activity and some privacy but not high enough to interfere with conversation with immediate neighbours. Vibration levels are high enough to provide some feed-back information but no so high that visual fuzziness or other tiresome symptoms are notable.

The job can be monotonous but not so devastatingly so as may appear to the casual visitor. The work is always changing, with different tasks, different styles and different materials. There are tea-breaks and 'music while you work' comes on and goes off at known times thus signalling the particular phase of the day. Several times a day something goes wrong either with the materials or the machine which warrants a discussion and perhaps a stimu-lating dispute with the foreman or mechanic. Managers, designers and other visitors appear and disappear and are often the subject of ribald sotto-voce

Figure 5.2 A shoe factory (By courtesy of Shoe and Allied Trade Research Association)

comment. Conversation is continuous but not regular. The day has a definite rhythm, there are phases when everything seems to be disorganized and little work is being done, other phases (usually mid morning and mid afternoon) when everybody seems to be working very hard with no talking, no moving about, just the regular hum of all the machines accelerating and decelerating, the whole shop falls into an integrated routine like a single biological organism. When this happens the foreman relaxes and also stops moving about, the thing is running itself for perhaps an hour. There are other rhythms over weeks and months which are most obvious from the foremans point of view, at any one time there is a pattern of relative difficulty of control, some groups of operators are helpful, others are being awkward, but this pattern is itself changing all the time. Sometimes the whole shop seems happy sometimes it gets edgy and difficult to control. Occasionally this deteriorates to the point where there is a stoppage, a walk-out or a strike, but such drama is therapeutic in restoring equilibrium. Everyone who works there has some awareness of these cycles of mood and morale and they reduce the monotony for the individuals.

TASK ANALYSIS

The orthodox procedure in task analysis is to define and separate all the different tasks involved in a particular job but for the sewing machinist there is no problem at this level. Her task is simply to stitch things together and attempting to separate different kinds of seams and so on is a fruitless exercise because it varies so much from operator to operator and from day to day depending on the work available. However, by activity sampling and by continuous automatic recording over several days for many operators it was established that the proportion of time spent shoe-machining was around 16% (Singleton, 1956). This seems low and suggests that in terms of efficiency, reduction of machining time per component is much less important than increasing the proportion of time spent machining. For example if an additional 5% of an operators time could be transferred to machining then productivity would increase by more than 25% whereas a reduction of stitching time per component of 5% would improve productivity by only about 1%. If one tries to calculate total efficiency by comparing the actual production of length of seam during a day with that which would be produced if the machine were running at full speed all day the result is absurd. These are superficial calculations in that the close integration of machining and non-machining time is overlooked. More detailed analysis of the pattern of activity reveals that about two-thirds of the time is devoted to machining and stopping during and between runs while one-third is devoted to time between components and in preparation of batches. These results would be different for a clothing machinist where on the whole the rows of stitching are much longer and much straighter.

To investigate the variation of machine speed, an experiment was carried out (Singleton, 1960) in which one skilled machinist was asked to sew around curves of different radii drawn on a synthetic leather. It was shown that sewing speed was a monotonic function of curvature of stitching, this result was confirmed by measures of speed taken from production work. Mechanical measures of the relationship between machine speed and treadle movement revealed large inconsistencies. For one machine the force required to keep the machine just stitching varied from 1 kg to 3 kg at the treadle edge, a change of position of 1 mm could have no effect or could cause the machine speed to change more than half of the total speed range. The treadle edge displacement required to vary speed from zero to near maximum and vice-versa was less than 2 mm.

Detailed observation of operations in factories revealed other inconsistencies in the positioning of scissors, the use of the lap or bench for storage of components, the position and frequency of change of grip and so on.

In general it seems that there is a mechanically complex machine with a crude control mechanism involved in a great variety of work and a corresponding variety of operator working styles. The work is done by the operator with machine assistance confined to a device for generating stitches in succession, a power supply not easily applied and subsidiary additional aids such as scissors, hammers, seam-cutters and so on.

SKILLS ANALYSIS

It is clear from the task description that there must be considerable skill in controlling the machine speed. From the data above, it would be predicted that the task of generating speeds other than maximum is impossible if we did not know that thousands of operators in practice actually do it. The speed control skill was studied in further detail in the factory situation (Singleton, 1960). Continuous records of speed were obtained from machinists carrying out specialized tasks which involved very precise positioning of rows of stitches around curves of varying radii. From these records supplemented by direct observation of the machinists and by films of their treadle movements it emerged that there are at least two techniques for overcoming the inconsistency and abruptness of the control mechanism. The operator does not attempt to obtain a steady speed other than maximum. She can, however, achieve an average speed over a few seconds at any level by moving the treadle to and fro at about the right position presumably controlling the foot movements and frequency of movements by visual and auditory feedback from the machine. The clutch is being touched on and off so that on average, and using the machine inertia, the optimum speed is obtained. A different technique also utilizing machine inertia is to move the treadle and the corresponding machine speed up and down through a more extensive range, phasing this with the curves and changing curvature of the stitching. When this is being practised the machine is never at a constant speed but the acceleration and deceleration phases are fitted beautifully to the changing directions of stitching. Such sewing is a great pleasure to observe and, from discussion with machinists, it seems also to be a pleasure to perform.

Another aspect of the skill is in stopping at exactly the right point. This was examined in the laboratory (Singleton, 1957) using a synthetic sewing task where a machine and its control mechanism were used not to produce stitches but to produce lights running along a panel facing the operator. Stopping points were provided by illuminating a succession of target lights in a second row immediately above the row where 'stitches' appeared. It was demonstrated that the skill existed in that skilled machinists had significantly higher scores than non-machinists, that is machinists were faster and made fewer errors. Machinists were then compared with non-machinists in ability to make precise and consistent short responses in pressing the finger on a switch, pressing the feet on a switch and using hand movement to control a sewing machine. In none of these three situations was any difference detected between the two groups. It seems that the skill is not located in a central mechanism which can function independently of peripheral mechanisms. On the contrary this particular motor skill is very sensitive to changes of either receptor or effector modes.

Attempts to gain insight into the required skills and abilities using psychometric techniques on a considerable scale were made but proved abortive. A large battery of tests were given to some hundreds of machinists and

Figure 5.3   A clothing machinist (By courtesy of T. W. Kempton Ltd.)

attempts were made to correlate test scores with performance in the factory using foreman's ratings and piece-work earnings as criteria. The attempt was abandoned because of the imprecision of definition of what was being measured by the tests—some paper and pencil, some performance—and by the contamination of the criteria by the variables mentioned earlier such as confusion of skill with degree of co-operation and confusion of performance by effort and availability of work. Attempts have also been made to analyse hand movements. Although the importance of this aspect is well recognized and it has a central role in training (Blain, 1958) it is not an aspect where any quantification of description has yet been achieved. What happens to the hands is just too complex to examine and record except by direct observation and filming. Perceptual activity is even more inaccessible to analysis, it is not only visual, auditory and kinaesthetic but there is an unusual touch element in the feel of materials, the exactness of positioning and the grading of sliding grasps. Extensive studies have also been made using method study and time study techniques. One general finding from these is that highly skilled operators do not make faster movements or use higher machine speeds but they are more careful and more systematic than less skilled operators in the way they position components and material to be sewn and after completion of sewing.

In spite of the fragmentary and sometimes statistically unsatisfactory nature of the evidence a skill description for the sewing machinist is possible. In preparing her work she is likely to be systematic and self-consistent but her procedure and work-layout will not necessarily be the same as that of another skilled machinist. The preparation of the machine; spool winding, needle positioning, needle threading, timing adjustment and so on will be fast and deft and will make these tasks look very easy. Posturally again she will not be completely consistent with other machinists but she will not look awkward or uncomfortable. When stitching starts the runs will be relatively long with sudden starts and stops and regular changes of speed. Sometimes the machine is stopped with the needle at the top of the stroke so that the material can be shifted, sometimes with the needle at the bottom of the stroke so that the material can be turned using the needle as a fixed pivot. There will be a minimum of fumbling in picking up material or components and moving them towards the needle bar. The hands will change grip continuously but with no obvious pattern. The upper arms may be parallel with the centre-line of the body, may be at right angles to it or may be at any intermediate angle. Visual attention will not be very rigid and often will appear casual. Removing the work with attendant use of scissor will be notably swift with long dextrous swings.

WORK DESIGN

Technology has made remarkably little impact on this job during this century. Since the invention of the sewing machine the two main changes have been the substitution of mechanical power for muscle power in driving the machine around 1910 and the substitution of separate work benches and electric motors for each machine in place of the drive shafts and pulleys along line benches which were commonly used up to the 1950s. There have of course been less dramatic but quite considerable changes such as smoother machines maintained to a higher standard, better methods of supplying work to machinists, better lighting and the gradual switch from natural to synthetic materials but these have not altered the skills very much. Sewing itself has diminished slightly in importance with the introduction of welding and sticking together of components but it holds its own very well. There has been no change in allocation of function between operator and machine, no automation in this sense. The skilled operator maintains her role because of the versatility of what she can do with her machine (Singleton, 1958). Sewing machines are mainly used in the making of personal things such as clothes, shoes, curtains and upholstery and the public quite properly resists undue standardization and supports regular changes in fashions.

From the above analyses a few predictions about effects of machine modifications are possible. Application of the general engineering principle of improving productivity by increasing machine speed is not a good prospect, the limitations on performance are not due to the slowness of the machine while stitching. This has proved to be the case, maximum machine speeds have not changed for 30 years.

There seem to be two aspects of the skill which might be facilitated by better machine design, the control of speed and the control of the exact stopping position of the needle. Needle-position controls are feasible mechanically using a secondary clutch mechanism and the effectiveness of such controls has been evaluated (Singleton, *et al.*, 1957). There are complications in obtaining valid times for particular tasks with and without these additional controls. The unknown factor is the variation of effort, which can in turn be due to variables such as changing performance because measurements are being taken, the need to maintain expected earnings (earning too much is almost as undesirable as earning too little) and even the desire to be kind and helpful to the investigator. However, by detailed analysis of time and timing it is possible to use a subject as her own control in that elements which can be expected to change because of the machine change can be compared with those on which the machine changes can have no direct effect. In this way it was demonstrated that improvements were possible but not to the extent that would justify adoption of such machines except for specialized operations. It was necessary to design the controls of such a machine very carefully for ease of operation and without this specialized attention to ergonomics such machines are not likely to be successful since the controls are used very frequently, stops and starts can occur at more than 20 per min.

Design of improved speed controls proved surprisingly difficult as an engineering exercise. The required performance of continuous rapid speed variation under load is not soluble except at considerabe additional expense. Thus, although such devices can improve performance (Singleton, 1960) again the improvement is not sufficient to justify large scale additional capital investment. The skilled operator remains the best investment so that the problem is essentially one of training rather than work design.

Figure 5.4   A shoe machinist (By courtesy of Shoe and Allied Trade Research Association)

SELECTION AND TRAINING

It has already been indicated that the orthodox systematic procedure for the design and validation of a battery of selection tests is not appropriate for this job. Inskeep (1971) has confirmed this, following a statistical study of more than 1000 garment workers he was unable to find any significant correlation between dexterity tests and observed productivity. He concluded that the five tests considered were of no value as selection instruments. The acquisition of skill is more to do with what Blain (1959) calls 'Practice and Knack' rather than with large individual differences in capacities, even neglecting the important operational issue of whether any such differences are detectable in test scores. This is not to suggest that no formal selection procedures are possible or are practical. It is common procedure at the entry to machinist training schools to conduct a few tests such as intelligence (non-verbal), visual acuity, manual dexterity and hand–foot co-ordination. Intelligence is something it is useful to have a general indication of, the low scorers may need special assistance in training, e.g. in how to take readings from time-clocks, and the high scorers may get bored by the repetitive nature of much of the training. Vision is obviously important and a standard screening test will detect those who should be advised to visit the optician. Manual dexterity is readily tested by measuring speed on one of the initial training exercises such as needle threading or needle fitting. Eye–hand co-ordination can be measured by any device which requires accurate phasing of hand movements and foot-pedal actuations within a simple fast task. This last have proved important in practice as one of the unitary reasons why girls abandon systematic training courses.

There has been extensive research and development of training courses for machinists. Their origin was the war-time shortage of skilled labour which led to the extensive use of the then novel principle that the way to facilitate the acquisition of skill was to proceed within a formal full-time scheme based on the study of what skilled operators actually did (Seymour, 1968). There are many such schemes known by titles such as 'Training within Industry (T.W.I.)', 'Analytical Training', 'Skills Analysis training' (Seymour, 1959; Barber, 1968; Singer and Ramsden, 1969).

The training of shoe machinists has been developed on a large scale by the Shoe and Allied Trades Research Association (Singleton, 1959; Westley and Jones, 1972). The design of the training scheme was carried out in parallel with the task and skills analysis described above. Surveys were conducted of many factories using both exposure and formal training. The exposure method of placing a trainee next to an experienced operative had many disadvantages. A skilled machinst is unlikely to have all the qualities of a good teacher which include ability to communicate verbally and by demonstration, to maintain motivation and to organize the advancement of learning in some progressive way. Formal schemes also have their difficulties which stem from the clash between the relatively long-term objective of acquiring skill and the short-term objective of meeting production schedules. Priorities of training are invariably lower than priorities of production so that without strong support from senior management the systematic training is too easily disrupted. If the training school is too near the production unit it will be used as a source of additional production capacity, if on the other hand it is too remote it will be difficult to maintain support from production staff and to smooth the difficult transition from training to production. There are no simple or tidy remedies for these universal problems, in addition to the day to day human relations skills the underlying foundation must be a well-designed scheme which justifies itself by results.

For purposes of training, basic skills were divided into four categories: positioning, guiding, machine control and machine servicing. Exercises based on specially constructed training devices were designed for practice within each of these categories. Positioning exercises involve the layout of the bench

for different basic tasks and the rapid sequential positioning of the appropriate pairs of components under a presser wheel which has a control identical to that found in the production machine. Guiding exercises involve a
machine with a specially designed variable speed device set by the instructor
and white lines marked on black material which has to be guided beneath the
wheel, there is no needle in the machine during these exercises. For speed
control exercises an ordinary machine and bench is used with a tachometer
attached to the machine so that the operator has immediate feedback about
the consequences of her foot movements on the treadle, there is no needle
and no material to be sewn. Machine servicing includes setting up tasks
such as inserting needles in needle-bars and threading needles. For each
exercise there is a target speed and for many there is also a target quality
standard. Trainees record their own or their partners progress on each
exercise which is practised for perhaps half-an-hour at a time. Note the
principle of concentrating the trainees attention on a particular task which
during this preliminary training is isolated from all other tasks of the
machinist, there is no distraction and there is unambiguous feedback about
progress. For example, the trainee threads needles until she really can thread
a needle without thought and almost without attention. She doesn't get
bored during this learning because she has a continuous check on how well
she is doing. In fact, such undaunting conditions with immediate knowledge
of results generate a high level of motivation. It is possible within 4 weeks
not only to acquire these basic skills to experienced worker standard but also
to combine them progressively using more advanced exercises as indicated
in Figure 5.5 (Singleton, 1974). The total in-school training course lasts about
6 weeks although the training goes on less formally for some months during
which the progress of the trainee is monitored jointly by the foreman and the

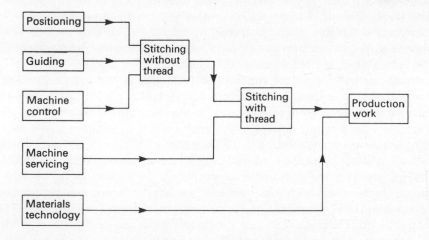

Figure 5.5 Progressive part method for machine sewing

training supervisor. This final phase, including the transition from training school to shopfloor is a very important one, if it is done badly all the benefits of the intensive preliminary training will be lost.

A training school with one supervisor can take about six trainees at a time. Thus in order to make an impact at a national level there was a secondary problem of designing selection and training procedures for instructors. This involved the provision of extensive job aids such as a comprehensive training manual, fault location procedures and manuals partly to aid in training instruction but mainly to ensure that the training which they in turn would be responsible for would not drift too far from the established machinist course. The training courses for instructors have been running regularly for nearly 20 years and are now conducted in other countries as well as in the UK. To date about 500 instructors have been trained to use this scheme. It will be noted that this whole training project requires an inextricable mixture of sensitivity to skill, sensitivity to people and unremitting operational and administrative application going on for decades.

At about the same time that these innovations were being developed in the shoe industry there were similar if less integrated activities in the clothing industry. King (1964) devised a six-stage training course involving: basic skills, handling cloth, operating the machine, basic job elements, learning operations and working at high tempo. Again it proved necessary to go through the second stage of selection and training instructors. At the instructor selection stage job skill was weighted at only about 15% compared with 85% for abilities generally to do with being a good teacher and administrator. Blain (1956, 1958) emphasized that sewing involves complex responses monitored by even more complex sensory cues; visual, auditory and kinaesthetic. It follows that listening and watching have only limited value, personal involvement in a chain of cues and responses is the only way to acquire the skill. The trainer cannot pass on a skill, rather the trainee must re-acquire it. Nevertheless the role of the instructor is crucial not only to provide progressive learning condition but also to facilitate the personal involvement of the trainee which is itself so essential to learning.

Machinist training is not confined to that done at the induction stage. There is extensive interest in training for versatility and in retraining to increase speed. One recent technique to do this latter utilizes *pacing machines*. These vary from simple devices which emit a visual or auditory signal after regular intervals corresponding to the cycle time to more complex ones which emit signals in a sequence corresponding to the sequence of times in which different elements of a task should be completed. The idea is that the operator should pace herself with the machine building up speed and 'stamina'. Investigation and attempted validation of these devices (Oldham, 1972; Ratcliffe, 1972) indicate that they can indeed increase speed of work while they are in use but it is not clear whether or how far this continues when their use is terminated. Problems of operator acceptability are not as serious as might be expected but this depends entirely on the way in which they are introduced. It seems likely that pacers will find a minor place within training school programmes and as one technique within the growing interest in so-called 'self learning methods'. The problem of continuous training so that each member of a particular work-force who wishes to do so can steadily increase her skill and range of skills must remain the responsibility of the foreman, although he may delegate this to a supervisor who specializes in training.

DISCUSSION

Every method which can be used to study the tasks and skills of a production operator has been tried at one time or another on sewing-machinists. The basic methods are observation and interview including all the variations of questionnaires, method-study type charts, films and so on. A reasonable understanding of the job has been obtained but not at the level of precision and numerical description which is often aimed for. We cannot even describe what is happening and why to the machinists hands and we have only the most general ideas about the vast complex of information intake which forms the basis of her perceptual activity. Psychometric methods using test batteries, correlational analyses and so on have not been fruitful. Something has been learned by experimental techniques of controlled isolation and manipulation of variables but such evidence has done little more than provide additional glimpses of the complexity of the situation and the skill. This describes the rather poor scientific status of these studies but operationally it can be argued that we know as much as we need to know to obtain near-optimal workspace designs and training methods. For this particular job the dividend from improved training has, during the last few decades, been much greater than the dividend from better machine design. It looks as though the job will carry on more or less in its present form for a long time. It is not susceptible to fundamental change through technology and the skills involved are not such that it can be carried out economically on a 'do it yourself' basis by the general public. It is difficult to see what should be done next.

Scientifically some concepts from skill psychology have proved enormously beneficial, particularly the principles of feedback and knowledge of results, in the design of training schemes. On the other hand some popular controversies in the psychology text-books have proved to be irrelevant and misconceived, for example, transfer of training, mass versus spaced learning and whole versus part learning. There has been an important contribution from principles of ergonomics to do with optimal dimensions of work spaces including bench heights and sizes, seat heights, good posture, lighting, heating and ventilation. There are some unsolved perhaps insoluble fundamental problems of relating the position of eyes and hands for fine manipulative work.

Operationally we need better production systems rather than better individual man–machine systems. That is, optimal supplies and mixes of work and managers, foremen and supervisors who carefully husband and develop their basic resource—the skills of the work-force. The job is not monotonous and soul-destroying except to the superficial observer. On the contrary, it can be interesting and self-fulfilling, as well as lucrative. The hours are probably still too long and there is great scope for the development of part-time workers. One would guess that regular half-days rather than regular days is the way it should be done to obtain maximum satisfaction and maximum productivity.

References

Barber, J. W. (1968) (ed.), *Industrial Training Handbook* (London: Iliffe)
Belbin, E. and Sergean, R. (1963). *Training in the Clothing Industry* (London: 20th Century Press)
Blain, I. J. (1956). Operator training: suggestions for programme planning. *Occ. Psych.*, **30**, 189
Blain, I. J. (1958). Training sewing machinists. Clothing Institute Technical Report No. 1. *Clothing Institute Journal*, **VII, 2,** Supplement 1–120
Blain, I. J. (1959). Practice and knack, some comments on learning and training in industry. *Ergonomics*, **2, 2,** 167
Inskeep, G. C. (1971). The use of psychomotor tests to select sewing machine operators—some negative findings. *Pers. Psychol.*, **24**, 707
King, D. (1964). *Training within the organisation* (London: Tavistock)
Oldham, G. (1972). Automatic pacing devices. *Clothing Inst. J.*, **XX**, No. 6
Ratcliffe, G. (1972) (ed.). A study of pacing during training of young female machine operators. *AP Report 40, Applied Psychology Department, University of Aston in Birmingham*
Seymour, W. D. (1959). Training operatives in industry. *Ergonomics*, **2, 2,** 143
Seymour, W. D. (1966). *Industrial Skills* (London: Pitman)
Seymour, W. D. (1968). *Skills Analysis Training* (London: Pitman)
Singer, E. J. and Ramsden, J. (1969). *The practical approach to skills analysis* (London: McGraw Hill)
Singleton, W. T. (1956). The interpretation of some performance data obtained in shoe factories. *The Manager, February*, 136
Singleton, W. T. (1957). An experimental investigation of sewing-machine skill. *Br. J. Psychol.*, **48, 2,** 127
Singleton, W. T. (1958). Production problems in the shoe industry. *Ergonomics*, **1, 4,** 307
Singleton, W. T. (1959). The training of shoe machinists. *Ergonomics*, **2, 2,** 148
Singleton, W. T. (1960). An experimental investigation of speed controls for sewing machines. *Ergonomics*, **3, 4,** 365
Singleton, W. T. (1974). *Man–Machine Systems* (Harmondsworth: Penguin)
Singleton, W. T. and Sinister, R. (1957). The design and layout of machinery for industrial operatives. *Occ. Psychol.*, **31**, 234
Westley, K. H. and Jones, F. G. (1972). Training sewing machinists. *Satra Publication, IP22, Kettering*

6

The Dentist

J. D. ECCLES

HISTORICAL BACKGROUND

Dentists have long recognized the need for the development of special skills. Some ancient civilizations, as far back as the fourth century BC, practised replacement of missing teeth on a very limited scale and by the tenth century AD decayed teeth were being prepared, and filled with resinous materials. During the Middle Ages, the barber-surgeons practised extraction of teeth. By the eighteenth century dentistry had made considerable progress and included the treatment of gum diseases and the correction of irregularities in the position of teeth; dentures were carved from blocks of ivory, and later the skills of the goldsmith were used in the construction of gold dentures. Since the beginning of the nineteenth century, advances have been impressive; techniques were developed for building up restorations in teeth by meticulous condensing of gold foil, for the construction of porcelain fillings and crowns, and for making single and multiple cast gold restorations; all of these demanded a high degree of skill.

Early instruments, such as those used for extracting teeth, were clumsy, but improvements in the quality of steel and in manufacturing processes allowed more refined patterns to be developed and more skilful techniques to be used. Advances in technology permitted a gradual evolution of tooth-cutting techniques from the early hand and pedal-operated drills to the electric motor and the air turbine high-speed drill. Each of these exhibited rather different handling characteristics and required some modification of skills. The mouth mirror was invented to enable the dentist to operate on upper teeth without using a cramped working position (Figure 6.1) and this involved another new skill, that of mirror vision. Other types of dental equipment, such as chairs, units and operating lights, made considerable advances in design. The early dentist manufactured many of his own materials, but now dental materials are the basis of a large manufacturing industry and new materials and techniques are continually being introduced.

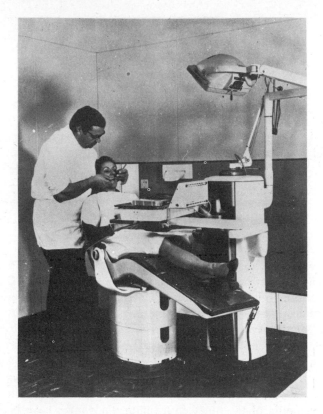

Figure 6.1   Dentist operating in the traditional standing position in which some degree of poor posture and leg fatigue is unavoidable (By courtesy of W.N.S.M. Dental School)

The pattern of dental practice has undergone considerable evolution. Dentistry was originally practised by individuals working single-handed in their own homes and many dentists today operate a similar type of practice. Others, however, have tended to group together into practices where several dentists work as partners or associates in a specially designed or modified building. The pattern of work has changed with an emphasis on the conservation of teeth rather than their extraction. The need for providing efficient dental care has led to the application of ergonomic principles to working methods and surgery design, and to a consideration of the level of skills needed for the particular operations carried out in practice (Figure 6.2).

It was appreciated that some operations could be performed by personnel trained for shorter periods and on a more restricted scale than dentists, and this led to the development of auxiliaries trained in a limited area of skills. These auxiliaries included school dental nurses, who were able to practise a limited range of operations on children; dental hygienists, who were responsible for cleaning teeth and instructing patients in hygiene; and dental therapists, who carried out some forms of treatment working in very close co-operation with the dentist and dental assistants (Figure 6.3). The employment of auxiliaries demanded managerial skills on the part of the dentist who took on the role of leader of the dental health team. The early dentist carried out his own laboratory work, but now skilled technicians perform this work, either in the practice itself or in a commercial laboratory. Some dental technology is still included in a dentist's training so that he can adequately supervise the work of the technician.

As dentistry developed, more emphasis came to be placed on the skills of diagnosis and treatment planning and the crucial area of inter-personal

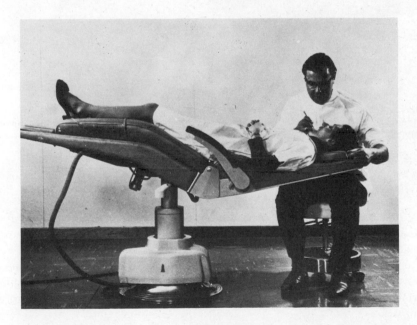

Figure 6.2 Dentist in the modern seated position operating on a reclining patient. His posture is good and unnecessary fatigue is eliminated. The chair is adjusted automatically by push-button controls; other equipment has been removed for clarity (By courtesy of W.N.S.M. Dental School)

relationships with patients. There was a more widespread realization of the importance of preventing dental disease, which required the dentist to motivate his patients. Dentistry was seen to be concerned with the dental health of the community, not just with the treatment of individuals.

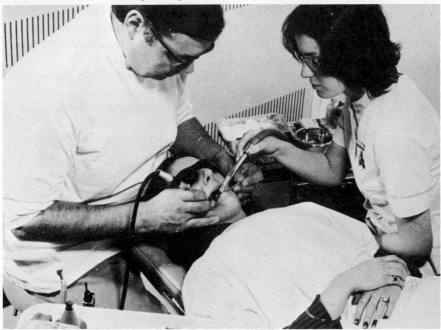

Figure 6.3 Four-handed dentistry with the dentist and dental assistant working in close collaboration. The dentist is using a high-speed drill while the assistant collects the coolant water-spray with a suction tube (By courtesy of W.N.S.M. Dental School)

EDUCATION

The first college of dentistry was founded in Baltimore, USA in 1840 and subsequently a number of private dental schools were opened. Now, most courses in dentistry are given by dental schools associated with a university or comparable institution of higher education. In nearly every country licensure is required in order to practise but in some countries it is still permissible for medical graduates, without formal dental training, to practise dentistry.

The length of the course varies considerably. In the United Kingdom it ranges from 4 to 5 years. In the United States the course is normally 4 years after graduation from college, but the government is now encouraging schools to train dentists in 3 years. In a few countries, such as Italy, it is necessary to study for 6 years and obtain a medical qualification, followed by 2 years of dental training, so that the complete course lasts 8 years.

The content of the course is basically similar in most countries, commencing with preclinical studies in anatomy, physiology and biochemistry, followed by training in medical subjects such as medicine, surgery, pathology and microbiology. The principal dental subjects are conservative dentistry, which deals with restorations in teeth, crowns, bridges and root fillings; prosthetic dentistry, which includes partial and full dentures; oral surgery; orthodontics, the correction of abnormalities in the position and occlusion of teeth; and periodontology, the treatment of diseases of the gums and tissues supporting the teeth. Preventive dentistry, community dentistry, children's dentistry, dental ethics and jurisprudence also form part of the syllabus together with a number of minor subjects.

Training is required in order that the dentist may work efficiently with dental auxiliaries, and the under-graduate syllabus has been extended in this direction. In the United States every dental school now includes in its curriculum a Dental Assistant Utilization (DAU) programme, and similar courses are in operation in other countries on a smaller scale. The development of such a programme is described by Barr (1970) and Bohannan and Cooper (1971), and the evaluation by Rosenzweig et al. (1971). Dental students are also taught to employ and direct dental hygienists. In addition they receive formal training in efficient working methods, in order to make the best use of their skills and operate in comfort without unnecessary fatigue.

Courses in dentistry have two objectives; first, to provide an academic training, and second, to prepare a student to practise dentistry on qualification. Most qualifications satisfy both the academic and practice requirements, but in the United States and Canada each state requires a graduate to pass the State Board Examination before he is entitled to practise in that state. In a few countries, such as Denmark, the graduate must work for a further year under supervision before being entitled to practise independently, and it seems likely that more countries will move towards a post-graduate period of supervised work before full registration.

Recent developments have included the introduction of a flexible curriculum where, by means of extensive self-teaching methods, a student can complete each course as quickly as he is able and so may finish his training in a shorter time than the norm (Bohannan et al., 1972). In the majority of countries, more use could be made of education and training technology. The United States, where some dental teachers have received a formal training in education, has given a lead in this.

SELECTION

The purpose of selection procedures is to identify candidates who will complete the dental education programme successfully, do well in and profit from a dental education, perform creditably in the practice of dentistry, and possess the traits of character and ethical values desired in a professional person (Eselman, 1969). Since dentistry is continually undergoing changes in attitudes, techniques and materials used, those candidates who will also show adaptability to change during a lifetime of practice should be selected.

In an occupation where skills, and particularly psycho-motor skills, are of such importance, much research has been devoted to the selection of entrants who have the potential to acquire a reasonable level of skill, and the rejection of those who do not have this potential. Ideally, such selection should be carried out prior to commencing a course of training, but inevitably some entrants have to be rejected during the course. This may happen only after one or two years have been completed, since the first year of training usually gives teachers little opportunity to observe psycho-motor skills in their students. The cost to all parties in time, money and training facilities is obvious and emphasizes the need for effective pre-entry selection. The reasons for some candidates choosing dentistry as a career are obscure and it may be that expert career guidance at an earlier stage in their education could lead to better use of educational facilities and individual talent. It is also desirable that some effort should be made to measure motivation, a most important factor in performance.

Attention has been concentrated on developing tests and correlating the results of these with performance in examinations, or grades obtained during day-to-day working. Such tests should be designed to measure potential rather than present level of ability. One difficulty is that no information is available on how those who have been rejected might have performed, and this will reduce the level of any positive correlations which are found.

The United States has been by far the most active country in developing aptitude tests. In 1944, the Council on Dental Education of the American Dental Association, appointed a committee to develop a battery of tests to measure the mechanical and academic potential of dental school applicants, and a group of sub-tests, collectively called the Dental Aptitude Test (DAT), was introduced in 1950 on a national basis. This was later adopted in Canada. The manual dexterity part of this test comprised the carving of a cylinder of chalk into a prescribed shape and dimensions, with one end rounded, the other tapering to a small square end, and with a rectangular notch cut on one side. Since 1948, the University of California has applied the California Performance Test to applicants to dentistry. (Brigante and Lamb, 1968). This comprises three tests; modelling in clay, modelling in wax, and carving in plaster. To this has been added the MacQuarrie test of mechanical ability, which several other schools have also adopted. The MacQuarrie consists of seven sub-tests designed to measure spatial visualization, manual dexterity, and perceptual speed and accuracy. Brigante and Lamb (1968) developed a Perception and Control Test comprising a number of sub-tests designed to measure tactile palpation, purposeful hand direction, depth perception, visual acuity, tactile discrimination, hard/soft sensitivity, surface contour matching, finger pressure and finger tension co-ordination, hand steadiness with support, and texture sensitivity. They developed machines designed to measure these factors.

The Dental Aptitude Testing (DAT) programme has developed with time and in 1965 was modified to permit computerized scoring (Ginley, 1966). As the numbers of applicants to dental schools increased, the logistics of arranging for a panel of judges to grade a large number of chalk carvings each year became extremely difficult. For this reason, and because the chalk carving test was considered not so much a prognostic measure as a measure of past experience, and since it was not possible to improve it further, the Council on Dental Education explored the possibility of replacing it by means of a pencil and paper test and such a test, the Perceptual Motor Ability Test (PMAT), was introduced in 1972. It was found to be at least as good as and probably rather better than the chalk carving test (Graham, 1972). The present test includes a school and college ability test, a survey of natural sciences test, a reading comprehension test, together with the PMA test in two and three dimensions.

In the United Kingdom, selection is based on academic performance at school, as measured by the General Certificate of Education results at Advanced and Ordinary Level, on school reports, and usually on an interview. Aptitude testing is little used. Whitehead (1974) compared 'A' level grades of 237 dental students with the results of their final examinations and found a significant correlation. In particular, those who were admitted after two attempts at 'A' levels did not do as well as those who passed at their first attempt, and they obtained a low standard in their final examination irrespective of the 'A' level grades achieved at the second attempt. He also noticed a high failure rate among candidates who entered the dental course as a second choice to medicine. Headmasters' reports, while useful as an indication of personality, tend to be unreliable as predictors of academic performance.

In spite of evidence which suggests that the interview, carried out by untrained interviewers, has little predictive value, it is still used extensively in the United Kingdom. Hobson (1974) makes the point that the interview may be of value in assisting the candidate to choose the dental school at which he would most like to study but, having assessed the cost of an interview, she, in common with many others, questions whether the continued use of this technique is justified. However, the accepted limitations of the interview technique must be viewed in the context of the relative failure of alternative methods of selection, as will be seen later. It would seem unwise to abandon the interview until some well validated technique can be substituted for it, but at the same time the objectives of the interview need to be more clearly defined and interviewers need to be trained. It is only by trying out testing methods under controlled conditions that we can hope to move towards better selection; at the very least we should have more information about the health and visual abilities of applicants.

Research on testing methods

Since the primary object of dental education is to produce a good dentist, it would, ideally, be desirable to compare the results of predictive tests with performance as a dentist after graduation. Brumback and Howell (1971) devised a check list and rating scale for measuring performance in general practice, but for practical reasons tests have usually been compared with performance during the undergraduate course. Such performance may be measured in examinations or by the mean of day-to-day grades (known in the United States as grade-point-average or GPA). Even in professional or class examinations, and more so in day-to-day assessment, there is a high degree of examiner variability. This arises partly from a lack of agreement on criteria and partly from variability in the assessment of performance. Since the Dental Aptitude Test (DAT) is a national examination, its predictions must be compared with grades from numerous dental schools so the lack of reliability is increased (Heller *et al.*, 1965). Training of examiners tends to improve reliability slightly (Houpt and Kress, 1973) but this is difficult when there are many examiners, including part-time teachers, involved. Furthermore it has not been customary to consider the time taken for performance, which is an essential feature of any skill. Neither is it usually possible to assess the actual performance, only the end result. So that results of the predictive value of pre-entry tests must be viewed with these considerable limitations in mind.

The Dental Aptitude Test has been studied by a number of research workers and compared with performance in professional examinations and with GPAs. Manhold and Manhold (1965) found that the manual aptitude portion of the DAT was inconsistent in its ability to predict clinical and preclinical performance. This inconsistency was reflected in the work of Blommers (1956), who found that the DAT manual average correlated with the first year GPA 0·38 for one class and 0·15 for another. Kreit and McDonald (1968) found that the manual portion of the DAT correlated significantly with dental school grades over an 8 year period but was not so consistent from year to year as other variables and reached statistical significance in only four out of eight classes. Hutton (1969) concluded that the manual portion of the DAT was of little, if any, predictive value and that its retention seemed justifiable only in terms of possible public relations value. He mentioned that it was rather common to find potential students being coached to pass this test. Eselman (1969) found that, in a study of 96 students, comparison between the manual score on the DAT and academic success showed little correlation to exist. Dworkin (1970) found a correlation of 0·42 between the manual part of the DAT and technique grades during the first year for one class, but concluded that, overall, the DAT was not a good predictor of dental school performance, possibly because it was required to make predictions on criteria which were too complex and heterogenous, and therefore perhaps unreliable. He also pointed out that the populations to which the DAT was applied were in many respects too heterogenous for reliable statistical comparisons. Phipps *et al.* (1968) found a very low (0·12) correlation between the DAT manual test and clinical performance. Bellanti *et al.* (1972) concluded that, although the DAT manual test correlated moderately well with performance in the preclinical laboratory, the results were still well below a desirable level of prediction.

These findings can be summarized by concluding that the DAT manual test gives some statistically significant but low correlations with performance during training, but its reliability is poor and a number of those who studied it felt that its continued use was not justified.

Vanek (1969) discussed the lack of reliability of many grading methods and the criteria on which these were based. He attempted to develop objective grading methods, such as measurement of cavity depth by a special gauge, and of the surface extent of a cavity by means of a transparent grid on a television image of the cavity. He emphasized the value of such objective methods as a self-testing medium.

Podshadley *et al.* (1969) carried out factor analysis of dental pre-entry tests and isolated nine factors, only two of which were significant. One of these was a manual skill factor with substantial loadings in the three sub-tests of the California Performance Test. They too pointed out how unsatisfactory was the use of the GPA as a criterion of academic success, since many of the grades which formed part of it were not objectively derived and might be influenced by prejudice of the teacher. Zullo (1971a) submitted seven of the 13 sub-test scores of the Dental Admission Programme to a principal component analysis. The existence of three independent factors was revealed; they were called verbal science, abstract reasoning and carving dexterity. In a follow-up study (Zullo, 1971b) he attempted to analyse which specific abilities were measured by the chalk carving and space relations tests of the DAT and by the PMAT, then in experimental form. With the scores on these tests he included scores on the Minnesota rate of manipulation test, Minnesota spatial relations test, O'Connor finger and tweezer dexterity tests, and the Purdue pegboard test. He concluded that six factors were being measured; finger dexterity, small instrument dexterity, manual dexterity, two-dimensional spatial relations and three-dimensional spatial relations. It was his opinion that the chalk carving test had validity in measuring a small instruments dexterity factor. He found the PMAT loaded positively on perceptual or spatial relations factors but not on any of the dexterity factors. Graham (1974) identified several independent factors in the PMAT and defined them as block design, space relations, length of lines, sequence of ideas, three-dimensional drawing, and passing an object through an aperture.

In the United Kingdom, Moore and Peel (1951), and Hopper (1959) found a high correlation between a chalk carving test and performance in operative dentistry. Deubert *et al.* (1975a) applied three paper and pencil tests to students commencing the preclinical technique course. These were a test of mechanical aptitude, a space relations test, and a high level intelligence test. In a pilot study the marks awarded during all the tests on the course correlated significantly with the mechanical aptitude test, and at a lower level with the space relations test, but not with the intelligence test. Grades awarded at advanced and ordinary level GCE examinations did not correlate significantly with any of the tests or scores. Deubert *et al.* (1975b) also devised a Trainability test consisting of cutting a shape in a plastic tooth using high speed and low speed drills. Preclinical students were first given a demonstration and then required to carry out the test under observation. Scores were awarded for a number of factors, and both performance and the finished work were assessed. There was a high level of correlation between almost all the factors and marks in practical class tests in this pilot study but confirmation is required before any conclusion can be reached.

TRAINING

In teaching clinical dentistry, as with any other skill, it is first necessary to specify objectives. Next the methods to be used in training must be decided and the system of feedback from teacher to student defined. The necessity for feedback, and particularly for immediate feedback, as an essential part of teaching psycho-motor skills, has been emphasized by many writers including Rovin and Packer (1971) and Mackenzie (1973). Finally, methods of evaluating learning and the standards achieved should be specified. So far as possible, these should be objective but, where this is not possible, as is often the case in dentistry, a strong attempt should be made to improve the reliability and validity of assessments (Wolcott, 1973).

Objectives

Charvat *et al.* (1968), Nedelsky (1969) and others have attempted to set out general objectives for the training of dentists. Charvat *et al.* listed the following performance requirements. In the *cognitive* domain were (1) knowledge of technical vocabulary, facts, concepts, principles and methods, (2) understanding of these, (3) ability to analyse and interpret data, (4) ability to solve relevant problems, (5) ability to take a history from a patient, (6) ability to retrieve information and to keep records, (7) ability to utilize community resources, and (8) judgement in evaluating a situation, whether clinical or research, for example, in making a diagnosis. In the *psycho-motor* domain they listed (1) skill in performing physical examinations, (2) skill in using laboratory and clinical instruments, and (3) skill in performing technical procedures. In the *affective* domain they included (1) concern for the patient, (2) awareness of professional capabilities and limitations, (3) willingness to establish effective relationships with colleagues and other members of the health team, (4) willingness to develop and apply an inquiring mind, and (5) organization of skills and knowledge to contribute to community and individual patient welfare.

Methods

The traditional methods of training in clinical dentistry have been the lecture, the demonstration, and chairside teaching. Preclinical training in cavity preparation and restorations has for many years been done on a patient simulator or 'phantom head' (Figure 6.4). This consists of a metal or plastic

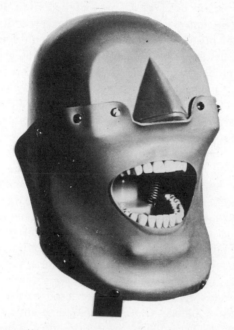

Figure 6.4 Patient simulator of 'phantom head' used by students to practice clinical procedures. The head and teeth are made of plastic material and the cheeks of sheet rubber (By courtesy of W.N.S.M. Dental School)

model head in which are mounted natural or plastic teeth in correct arrangement and articulation. Sometimes rubber cheeks are used to make the model more life-like. This training may be carried out in a separate laboratory, or in the clinic so that the student can get used to the equipment and environment and thus reduce the need for transfer learning. The techniques should be as close as possible to those used in the mouth; for example, the student should use only those operating methods which would be feasible in the mouth and acceptable to a patient. The phantom head course may be continuous, or in the form of short courses alternating with periods of work on patients in the clinic. The latter is a better method of maintaining the student's interest and ensuring that his practice on the phantom head will be more clinically orientated and followed immediately by practice on a patient. Sometimes organizational problems with patients make this difficult and it may happen that many months separate learning on a phantom head from carrying out the same procedure on a patient. Scaling artificial calculus, and radiographic techniques are also taught on the phantom head. One variation of phantom head practice has been the use of preserved pigs' heads for learning oral surgery techniques.

The clinical demonstration on a patient is valuable to show organization, working methods, and procedures near the front of the mouth but only one or two students can see any detail at the back of the mouth. It is best followed immediately by the student carrying out the same procedure on a patient. Again organizational problems may make this difficult since it implies the provision of single items of treatment, rather than integrated dental care which is the aim of modern dentistry. However, there is no doubt more could be done to arrange for teaching and practice to be closely related in time. Chairside teaching involves the student carrying out on a patient some treatment procedures which he has previously learned on a phantom head. The student must cope, not only with the technical skills, but also with the difficulty of performing them on a conscious person who may be apprehensive. Close supervision is essential and teaching must be done with tact to avoid undermining the patient's confidence in the student. In addition to psycho-motor skills the student must learn inter-personal relationships with his patients, organization of his work, treatment planning and decision making, so that on graduation he will be capable of independent practice.

To these traditional methods have been added, more recently, seminar learning, learning by audio–visual means, programmed learning and learning by discovery.

Audio–visual methods of teaching include closed circuit television (Hobkirk, 1974), tape–slide sequences (Barber, 1964), cine films or cine film loops (Pearson and Jepson, 1969) and slide projection and the overhead projector in association with lectures and seminars. Television with videotape recording allows the teacher to demonstrate an operation and saves the teaching time involved in repeated live demonstrations. Television is particularly useful for magnifying those operations in the mouth where it is difficult for more than one or two observers to see clearly. Close circuit television with videotape recording of a student treating a patient can also be used for self-evaluation, particularly of operating positions and general approach to the patient (Robinson et al., 1972). Tape–slide sequences form a useful means of teaching with a saving of staff time and, like other self-teaching methods, allow the student to progress at his own speed, to recapitulate where necessary, and to learn at a time convenient to himself. Computer simulation of a dental practice has been used by Dilworth and Pelton (1972) as a method of teaching practice organization.

Evaluation of training methods

Comparisons of one training method against another have been carried out, but may produce results which are not universally applicable because of variability within each method. For example, comparison of a good lecture against a poor tape–slide sequence will not be valid. Duckworth (1966) compared two small groups of dental students receiving instruction in pathology. One group received instruction in the form of a lecture while the other group received, in addition to a lecture, a practical session and a discussion session. No significant difference was found between the learning of the two groups. Barnes and Holloway (1970) compared three groups learning by means of lectures, small group discussion, and independent reading, and found no difference in the amount of material learned.

Vanek *et al.* (1967) used a self-instructional method in teaching a pre-clinical technical skill, namely cavity preparation, and Light (1967) used programmed self-instruction in teaching root fillings, but neither found any significant difference compared to traditional methods. Mullaney *et al.* (1972) compared two groups of students receiving teaching in root fillings. The first group were taught by traditional methods and the second by traditional methods *and* tape–slide instruction. The second group performed significantly better than the first in the diagnosis of root filling problems but there was no significant difference in the learning of treatment. Kopczyk *et al.* (1973) compared the learning of dental students taught by means of lecture or tape–slide sequence or laboratory seminar and found the best retention with the self-instruction method, which also occupied the shortest time. Most of these authors point out the differences in teaching time between the methods tested. Self-instruction programmes and tape–slide sequences, for example, take up less staff time than do lectures and traditional teaching methods and these findings may be valuable in developing curricula designed to make optimum use of staff. In spite of this, self-teaching methods are best used as aids to teaching, not replacements for teachers.

Many dental schools have built up banks of tape–slide sequences (Lunin and Moreland, 1972) slide loops and self-instruction material. This has had the additional advantage of enabling curricula to be more flexible so that students receiving self-instruction can take tests when they are ready and on successful completion proceed to the next course. This is in contrast to the traditional dental curriculum where students move in cohorts from examination to examination.

Kress and Jacobs (1973) pointed out that relatively little research has been carried out to evaluate alternative methods of practising psycho-motor skills. In a small study on dental graduate students practising cavity preparation, they found no differences between results when several different practice sequences were employed.

Blancheri and Merrill (1963) compared two methods of teaching crown preparation. The same television programme was used in each case, but for the experimental group step-by-step learning was used, where students, having seen one step demonstrated, practised this before watching a demonstration of the next step. The control group saw the whole programme without interruption before commencing the task. No difference in the quality of the results of the two groups was observed, but the step-by-step group had a highly significant shorter mean time to completion than the whole group. The authors interpret this as evidence in favour of step-by-step teaching, but point out that it is only convenient where television monitors are sited in the practice laboratory.

Killip (1965) compared two groups of students learning a motor task, namely cutting a plastic tooth using a handpiece. The first group received instruction before attempting the procedure whilst the second group received identical instruction after they had been allowed to practise the task, i.e. learning by discovery. He concluded that the conventional method produced superior results. However, when both groups were tested on a similar task (transfer learning) the second group achieved the same standard in a significantly shorter time. Killip concluded that learning by discovery produced superior results in transfer learning and increased initiative.

Jones (1974) found that a mirror training exercise did not improve the performance of students carrying out cavity preparation on an upper tooth. This may be explained by the fact that the training was a two-dimensional exercise whereas the cavity was in three dimensions.

Salvendy et al. (1973a) developed an electro–mechanical simulator fitted to a phantom head in the position of a lower molar tooth. This equipment consisted of a sheet with laminations of particular thicknesses so that it gave visual and auditory feedback to the operator and the teacher concerning the correct depth and lateral extent of the cavity. The result was a significant increase in quality and a decrease in time compared to conventional teaching methods.

AN APPROACH TO SKILLS ANALYSIS

In view of the considerable importance of psycho-motor skills in dentistry, surprisingly little research has been devoted to this field, and even this has not been well validated. The majority of the work has involved analysis of simple tasks using cine-photography.

Skills involved in the practice of dentistry are so varied and complex that complete analysis is probably not feasible at this stage. Nevertheless, I have attempted to identify some of the factors involved. An ability to visualize and understand spatial relationships is one of the most important factors. It is used in the study of anatomy and its application in oral surgery, local anaesthetic technique, radiographic technique and interpretation of radiographs, denture design and occlusion, cavity preparation and restorations including crowns and bridges. Colour and shade matching is important in the selection of the correct artificial teeth or crowns. Tactile perception, usually through the medium of instruments, is necessary in the treatment of root canals where it is impossible to see the region being operated on, in cavity preparation to identify sound from diseased tooth substance, in checking the retention and fit of restorations and in checking the occlusion of natural or artificial teeth. Delicate co-ordination and control of hand instruments and hand steadiness is required in cavity preparation, lining of cavities, placing of fillings, scaling of teeth, oral surgery and the treatment of root canals. The ability to recognize parallel surfaces, or to estimate either visually or by tactile means the angle between these surfaces, is needed in the preparation of teeth for crowns, bridges and inlays. Visual acuity is required for detailed procedures; stereoscopic vision is necessary for depth perception, for example, in cavity preparation; and mirror vision is used extensively. Finger tension and co-ordination is essential for many procedures and particularly for the extraction of teeth.

At one time the design of dental units favoured the right-handed operator, but modern dental equipment is more flexible and is equally suitable for the left-handed operator. Many dentists now believe it is an advantage to learn to be ambidextrous, particularly for the extraction of teeth under general anaesthesia when the anaesthetist occupies the space behind the patient's head.

In addition to psycho-motor skills a wide range of other skills is used in dentistry including managerial skills, inter-personal relationships, communication skills, and decision making, but a detailed analysis of these will not be attempted here.

Salvendy et al. (1973b) carried out a skills analysis of the preparation of a simple occlusal cavity in a lower molar tooth mounted in a phantom head. The subjects were seven full-time instructors, and seven freshman dental students who had been given standard teaching by means of lecture/slide instructions. Procedures were photographed using a cine camera at 24 frames per s. Subsequently a frame-by-frame analysis of the film was carried out and a number of variables measured. During the procedures, EMG, GSR and heart rate were monitored. It was concluded that the physiological variables which were measured did not improve the understanding of psycho-motor operations in cavity preparation, which is in line with findings related to other skills. The cine film technique was felt to be a valuable method for skills analysis. It was observed that performance by experienced dentists differed from that of students in that the former made more back and forth strokes using the high speed handpiece, made more changes in drill angle during preparation, lifted the handpiece off the tooth more times during the preparation, and had no slips of the drill compared to numerous slips by students.

Eccles (1972) attempted to analyse the relative importance of vision, hearing and kinaesthesis in feedback during the use of the air turbine handpiece. This handpiece produces a low torque and the pressure of applying it to a tooth must be delicately judged otherwise it will slow down or stall. His results suggested that some operators relied more on hearing, some on vision and some on kinaesthesis, hearing being perhaps the most important. The research demonstrated the adaptability which allows an experienced operator rapidly to accommodate to reduction in any one source of feedback.

FACTORS ADVERSELY AFFECTING SKILLED PERFORMANCE

Age

There is little evidence that the skills of dentists fall off with age, but it is known that older dentists work shorter hours, and more slowly, than younger dentists (Klein et al., 1947). Welford (1962) has pointed out that increasing experience tends to mitigate the effects of slowing with age, for example, through the building up of routines of action and the ability to recognize sequences in events. Such coding lightens the load of decision and it seems likely that dentists use their experience in this way. There is a strong impression that, as experience increases, dentists tend to rely less on vision and more on tactile perception; this is particularly valuable when working in an area where illumination and access are sometimes difficult. It seems possible that this mechanism may help to compensate for some loss of visual acuity which may occur with age.

Fatigue

There seems to be no evidence that fatigue produces a decrement in skilled performance in dentists, but it is reasonable to assume the dentists are not basically different from other workers using psycho-motor skills. Bartlett (1943) has stated that fatigue is marked by a progressive lowering of standards of performance, principally due to loss of central control and one of the effects of this is a loss of timing. There is evidence that dentists do suffer from fatigue (Eccles and Powell, 1967) and if the level of this fatigue is sufficiently great, a fall-off in performance is inevitable. Increasing fatigue also produces irritability (Bartlett, 1943) and it seems reasonable to assume that this may is some cases be sufficient to affect the dentist–patient interaction, particularly in the case of difficult patients, but again there is no evidence of this. Boredom is probably not common among dentists (Eccles and Powell, 1967), since patients differ so much in personality and most dentists have a reasonable variety of work, so boredom is unlikely to have much real effect on skilled performance.

Stress

Distraction may be a factor in inducing stress in dentists. It is generally believed that dentists suffer from stress, but it is difficult to produce evidence.

Noise is probably not an important source of stress to the dentist, but interruptions and the knowledged that a number of patients are waiting to be seen may cause a build up of stress. In addition, the movement of an apprehensive patient during treatment, particularly during a precision operation, may affect concentration and reduce the level of performance. In such a case the dentist may decide on a trade-off and reduce the quality of his work in order to complete it more rapidly with the minimum of disturbance to the patient.

Lack of practice

As with other skilled workers, dentists are conscious of some deterioration in their skills after an absence of some weeks or months, but in the case of the experienced dentist, it takes only a short time for these to return to normal. The problem is more serious with the undergraduate in whom an absence of only a few weeks may produce a severe decrement in skilled performance. This is particularly important in the organization of training courses and tests related to them. Students must be given the opportunity to regain their skills after a vacation before any testing is undertaken.

MANPOWER AND THE USE OF AUXILIARY DENTAL PERSONNEL

Manpower is important in the study of skills in dentistry, since it implies the need to provide sufficient numbers of personnel with appropriate levels of skill. From time-to-time an attempt is made to forecast the future needs and demands for dentists and the different grades of dental auxiliaries.

Dental Manpower is usually expressed in terms of dentist to population ratios. Thus Sweden has a ratio of 1 : 1126, the United States a ratio of 1 : 2045, and the United Kingdom a ratio of 1 : 3673 (F.D.I., 1970). By contrast some countries in Africa have a ratio of one dentist to several hundred thousand of the population. However, the dentist : population ratio is an over-simplified index of manpower. A more refined index would consider the geographical distribution of dentists in relation to the population, the productivity of dentists, and the numbers of auxiliary personnel and their contribution to productivity. Productivity should be seen not only in terms of treatment given but in terms of disease prevented. The quality of treatment is also an important factor. The pattern of organization of dental services is peculiar to each country and it is doubtful if there is one universally best method of providing dental care.

In considering dental manpower needs, a distinction must be made between the *need* for dental care and the *demand* for dental care. In an ideal community where health education has been completely effective, the demand would equal the need, but in practice it often falls far short since a proportion of the population needing care does not desire it, or may not be aware of it. Sheiham

(1974) described several models for predicting manpower requirements. The *supply and demand* model constructs indices of demand and uses these to predict the required dentist : population ratio at a given date. The *functional analysis* model is based on the assumptions of supply and demand and on cost–benefit methods, and involves matching qualifications of dental health personnel to the job requirements. The *target setting* model defines certain objectives, and measures the deficiencies of the present system in relation to these objectives. In practice, the supply and demand model is most commonly used. Klein and Helfrick (1974) projected existing data for manpower needs in USA up to the year 2000 but admit that the validity of projections beyond 3 to 5 years is questionable. The difficulty of predicting manpower needs can be deduced from some of the factors influencing them (Workshop on Dental Manpower, 1968). For example, needs will be reduced if the prevalence of disease is reduced by artificial fluoridation of water or by a major research advance. On the other hand, needs will be increased as the expectation of life increases and dentitions need to be maintained for a longer period.

Even if adequate manpower were available in a country, it would still be necessary to ensure that it was distributed according to demand and need. Cook and Walker (1967) found wide variation in the geographical distribution of dentists in the United Kingdom. In some areas, such as the South, there was one dentist per 2000 of the population, while in parts of the Midlands, Wales and East Anglia there was just over one dentist to every 10 000 persons. They also found clear evidence of an association with the social class structure of the population; the higher the proportion of persons in socio-economic group I, the higher the proportion of dentists, and incidentally the higher the demand for dental care. Some indication of the demand for dental services is given by standardized dental annual consultation rates. Richards (1973) quotes figures of 50 per 1000 persons for the United States and England, and 20 per 1000 for Yugoslavia. Demand will be increased by dental health education and by decreasing cost or providing free dental care, but clearly it is undesirable to increase demand beyond the point where it can be met.

Auxiliary dental personnel

In recent years, with the recognition that dentists by themselves are unable to cope with the dental needs of the community, considerable thought has been given to the cost-effectiveness of methods of providing dental care. This has led to the development of various grades of auxiliary personnel, trained for a shorter time and skilled in a restricted area of dentistry. Some, such as the dental hygienist and the U.K. dental auxiliary, carry out treatment under the direction of a dentist and are classed as operating auxiliaries. Others, such as the dental assistant, are non-operating.

The *dental hygienist* is a person, usually female, who has had formal training in cleaning and polishing teeth, applying local preventive measures in the mouth and giving individual or group instruction in oral hygiene. A hygienist must be registered and may work in private practice, hospital or the public health service, under the control and direction of the dentist. She receives a formal training in a dental school along with dental students or in a special school of dental hygiene. The course usually lasts 6–12 months but may be up to 2 years. Often hygienists have previously trained as dental assistants. Dental hygienists are now used in a large number of countries. Their use is particularly extensive in the United States, where there are some 24 000 (F.D.I., 1970). In the United Kingdom a working party of the British Dental Association has recently recommended a target manpower level of 2500 dental hygienists by 1985. A national ratio of one hygienist to every four dentists has been suggested as desirable.

The U.K. *dental auxiliary* is a person, usually female, trained to treat pre-school and school children in the United Kingdom under the direction and control of a dentist. These auxiliaries are trained over a 2 year period in a special school and are permitted to examine patients and chart dental conditions, clean and polish teeth, place simple fillings in teeth, carry out simple extractions under local anaesthesia and instruct patients in prevention of dental disease. This type of auxiliary was originally developed in New Zealand in 1922, as the *New Zealand dental nurse*, to cope with the severe dental caries problem. They have proved most successful (Friedman, 1972) and some 20 countries have adopted the idea.

The *expanded duty dental assistant* or *dental therapist* is a person, usually female, and often already trained as a dental assistant or hygienist, who receives training which enables her to work on patients in close collaboration with a dentist. She is trained in a dental school or in a special school and is permitted to carry out a wide range of simple procedures in the mouth such as placing simple restorations in teeth. Non-reversible procedures such as cavity preparation are outside her competence and are performed by a dentist. This type of auxiliary was pioneered in the United States in 1964 (Lotzkar *et al.*, 1971). The scheme has been adopted in some 40 of the United States and one experimental project is operating in the United Kingdom (Allred *et al.*, 1973). There is evidence that the work performed by operating auxiliaries is of a good standard and that the cost per item of treatment is decreased (Abramowitz and Berg, 1973; Romcke and Lewis, 1973).

The *dental laboratory technician* is trained to prepare dentures and dental appliances, under the prescription of a dentist. Advanced countries have a ratio of one technician to two or three dentists. In a few countries the dental technician, or *denturist*, is legally entitled to make full dentures directly for the public.

The *dental assistant* is a non-operating auxiliary, usually female, who helps the dentist in his work particularly at the chairside. Her functions include the reception and preparation of patients, sterilization, care and preparation of instruments and the preparation and mixing of restorative and other materials. Dental assistants are used in most countries throughout the world, and present manpower levels in the United States and the United Kingdom are one dental assistant to one dentist. It seems likely that, with improved working methods, a higher ratio of dental assistants to dentists will be needed in the future. The dental assistant may have a formal training lasting 1 or 2 years, either in a dental school or a special school. On the other hand she may receive her training in private practice with optional attendance at evening classes. Only some countries have an obligatory statutory examination for dental assistants. Evidence of the benefits of the skilled use of dental assistant has been produced by Klein *et al.* (1947), and Watermann *et al.* (1952) who showed that skilled use of one chairside assistant reduced the dentist's work load by up to 50%, and two assistants reduced his load by almost 75%.

Provided that dentists and auxiliary personnel are trained to work in close collaboration dental care can be provided on a more cost-effective basis than by the older traditional methods. Arnold (1970) showed that the number of patients he was able to treat in his practice more than doubled as he added auxiliary workers to his staff. In many cases a dental team comprised of dentist, operating auxiliaries and non-operating auxiliaries may be the best method of providing dental care but in other circumstances operating auxiliaries with more remote supervision have proved successful, as in New Zealand. Some dentists have resisted the use of operating auxiliaries which they see as 'dilution' of the profession and feeling is particularly strong against technicians working directly for the public. Further studies on cost-effectiveness are required, particularly long-term studies on wastage rates.

CONDITIONS OF PROFESSIONAL PRACTICE

In order that trained dentists and ancillaries may use their skills for the benefit of the community for as long a period and at as high a level as possible, some consideration of conditions of dental practice is important. In particular, attitudes, job satisfaction, mortality and morbidity rates, and wastage from any source, are relevant.

Evidence from occupational psychology suggests that, although job satsisfaction has no major influences on the quality of work, it affects turnover and the wastage rates, and the same may be true of dentists. There has been very little research on job satisfaction among dentists, but what there is suggests that dentists are more dissatisfied than some other professional groups (Powell and Eccles, 1970). This dissatisfaction appears to be related to the severe pace at which they work and to constraints on their freedom of action associated with a third party payment system.

There is justification for considering dentistry as a high-stress occupation. Suicide rates among dentists are higher than average. In England and Wales the Standardized Mortality Ratio (or S.M.R., which relates to 100 as the population mean) for suicides among dentists was 155 in 1931, 270 in 1951, and 140 in 1961 (Registrar General's Reports, males aged 20–64). Similar high suicide rates among dentists have been reported in the United States in Oregon (Blachly, 1963) and in New England (Glass, 1966). Death from coronary thrombosis among dentists was higher than average in England and Wales in 1951 (SMR = 137), but appears to have fallen well below average in 1961 (SMR = 75). The death rate from all causes among dentists in England and Wales was about average in 1951 (SMR = 97) and in 1961 was well below average (SMR = 64).

Dentists are believed to be more susceptible to musculo–skeletal disability due to the postures they adopt and there is some evidence to support this (Powell and Eccles, 1970). This most commonly affects the back and neck, but it seems possible that the recent change in operating methods, whereby the dentist is seated and works on a reclining patient, may reduce the problem of posture-related morbidity. Other hazards are mercury poisoning (mercury is a constituent of dental amalgam fillings), and infection transmitted from patients, particularly viral hepatitis which is now recognized in the United Kingdom as an industrial disease of dentists for compensation purposes.

CONCLUSIONS

Dentistry, with its combination of cognitive, affective and psycho-motor elements, presents a field of great interest to the student of real skills. Attempts have been made to analyse these skills with a view to devising predictive tests but much more detailed analysis is still required.

There is no doubt that effective pre-entry selection procedures would be of value in rejecting those applicants who, in spite of training, will not make satisfactory dentists, but this is a difficult problem. We have some idea of the qualities required: an ethical approach, motivation, intelligence, adaptability, organizing ability, ability to form good inter-personal relationships, and psycho-motor skills. It is to this last area that most attention has been devoted, but there is still very little firm information which can be used by those responsible for selection. Chalk carving tests have not proved satisfactory—they are too remote from the real skills. Much more research is required to validate predictive tests: we must formulate acceptable criteria and make more objective and reliable assessments of undergraduate performance.

Teachers of dentistry have been reasonably progressive in trying out new methods of training, but there should be more application of experimentally proven methods. As a profession dentists have shown enterprise in evolving ergonomically based methods of work, and in developing and training auxiliaries to make better use of different levels of skills and training, but there is a need to evaluate the cost-effectiveness of these. Conditions of practice should be improved to provide a greater degree of satisfaction in work.

References

Abramowitz, J. and Berg, L. E. (1973). A four-year study of the utilisation of dental assistants with expanded functions. *J. Amer. Dent. Ass.*, **87**, 623

Allred, H., Hobdell, M. H. and Elderton, R. J. (1973). The establishment of an experimental dental care project. *Br. Dent. J.*, **135**, 205

Arnold, G. T. E. R. (1970). Extended duties of dental auxiliaries increase efficiency. *Quintessence Int.*, **1**, 65–72, 77

Barber, T. K. (1964). Synchronised tape and slides as a method of teaching dental technics. *J. Dent. Educ.*, **28**, 43

Barnes, D. S. and Holloway, P. J. (1970). Small and large group teaching in clinical dentistry. *Br. Dent. J.*, **129**, 201

Barr, C. E. (1970). Principles and objectives of DAU instruction to dental students. *J. Dent. Educ.*, **34**, 215

Bartlett, F. C. (1943). Fatigue following highly skilled work. *Proc. R. Soc.*, B, **131**, 248

Bellanti, N. D., Mayberry, W. E. and Tira, D. E. (1972). Relation between selected predictor variables and grades in fixed prosthodontics laboratory. *J. Dent. Educ.*, **36**, 12, 16

Blachly, P. H., Osterud, H. T. and Josslin, R. (1963). Suicide in professional groups. *New Eng. J. Med.*, **286**, 1278

Blancheri, R. L. and Merrill, I. R. (1963). Television in health sciences education: II. The step presentation of dental technic instruction. *J. Dent. Educ.*, **27**, 167

Blommers, P. J. (1956). Prediction of success in the first and second years of the study of dentistry on the basis of certain selected variables. *J. Dent. Educ.*, **20**, 5

Bohannan, H. M. and Cooper, T. M. (1971). The metamorphosis of a dental auxiliary utilisation program. *J. Dent. Educ.*, **35**, 125

Bohannan, H. M., Rovin, S., Packer, M. W. and Costich, E. R. (1972). The flexible dental curriculum. *J. Amer. Dent. Ass.*, **84**, 112

Brigante, R. F. and Lamb, R. E. (1968). Perception and control test: the dental technical aptitude test of the future? *J. Dent. Educ.*, **32**, 340

Brumback, G. B. and Howell, M. A. (1971). Rating clinical performance. *J. Dent. Educ.*, **35**, 179

Charvat, J., McQuire, C. and Parsons, V. (1968). List of performance requirements for dental surgeons. Adapted from: *A review of the Nature and Uses of Examinations in Medical Education* (World Health Organisation. Geneva)

Cook, P. J. and Walker, R. O. (1967). The geographical distribution of dental care in the United Kingdom. *Br. Dent. J.*, **122**, 441–447, 494

Deubert, L. W., Smith, M. C., Jenkins, C. B. and Berry, D. C. (1975a). The selection of dental students. A pilot study using psychometric tests. *Brit. Dent. J.*, **139**, 167

Deubert, L. W., Smith, M. C., Jenkins, C. B. and Berry, D. C. (1975b). The selection of dental students. A pilot study using practical tests. *Brit. Dent. J.*, **139**, 357

Dilworth, J. B. and Pelton, W. J. (1972). Computer simulation of a dental practice using therapists. *J. Dent. Educ.*, **36**, 6, 35

Duckworth, R. (1966). An evaluation of two methods of teaching the principles of pathology to dental students. *Br. Dent. J.*, **121**, 218

Dworkin, S. F. (1970). Dental Aptitude Test as performance predictor over four years of dental school: analyses and interpretations. *J. Dent. Educ.*, **34**, 28

Eccles, J. D. (1972). Feedback in a dental skill. *Dent. practitioner*, **22**, 223

Eccles, J. D. and Powell, M. (1967). The health of dentists. *Br. Dent. J.*, **123**, 379

Eselman, J. C. (1969). Observations on admission procedures. *J. Dent. Educ.*, **33**, 202

Federation Dentaire Internationale (1970). Basic fact sheets

Friedman, J. (1972). The New Zealand School Dental Service: lesson in radical conservation. *J. Amer. Dent. Ass.*, **85**, 609

Glass, R. L. (1966). Mortality of New England dentists 1921–1960. U.S. Dept. of Health, Education and Welfare. Washington

Ginley, T. J. (1966). Present status and future plans of the Dental Aptitude Testing Programme. *J. Dent. Educ.*, **30**, 163

Graham, J. W. (1972). Substitution of the Perceptual-Motor Ability test for chalk carving in Dental Admission Testing Program. *J. Dent. Educ.*, **36**, 11, 9

Graham, J. W. (1974). Factor analysis of the Perceptual-Motor Ability Test. *J. Dent. Educ.*, **38**, 16

Heller, D. B., Carson, R. L. and Douglas, B. L. (1965). Selection of students for dental school. *J. Dent. Educ.*, **29**, 202

Hobkirk, J. A. (1974). Closed-circuit television in British dental schools. *Br. Dent. J.*, **137**, 177

Hobson, P. (1974). The effect of a personal interview on student admission. *Br. Dent. J.*, **137**, 181

Hopper, F. E. (1959). Selection of dental students. *Br. Dent. J.*, **107**, 101

Houpt, M. I. and Kress, G. (1973). Accuracy of measurement in clinical performance in dentistry. *J. Dent. Educ.*, **37**, 7, 34

Hutton, J. G. (1969). Aptitude and personality correlates of dental school performance. *J. Dent. Educ.*, **33**, 474

Jones, J. C. G. (1974). The acquisition of dental skills. An investigation into teaching mirror vision. *Br. Dent. J.*, **137**, 185

Killip, D. E. (1965). Role of discovery in learning manual skills. *J. Dent. Educ.*, **29**, 63

Klein, H., Dollar, M. L. and Bagdonas, J. E. (1947). Dentist-time required to perform dental operations. *J. Amer. Dent. Ass.*, **35**, 153

Klein, R. S. and Helfrich, F, G. (1974). The need for dentists in the United States. *J. Amer. Coll. Dent.*, **41**, 103

Kopczyk, R. A., Lennox, J. A., Kenney, E. B., Kaplan, A. and Trinler, D. (1973). Evaluation of a self-instruction mini-course. *J. Dent. Educ.*, **37**, 4, 40

Kreit, L. H. and McDonald, R. E. (1968). Preprofessional grades and the Dental Aptitude Test as predictors of student performance in dental school. *J. Dent. Educ.*, **32**, 452

Kress, G. C. and Jacobs, S. S. (1973). Effects of practice-sequence strategy on cavity preparation skills. *J. Dent. Educ.*, **37**, 12, 20

Light, E. I. (1967). Programmed self-instruction in endodontics. *J. Dent. Educ.*, **31**, 455

Lotzkar, S., Johnson, D. W. and Thompson, M. B. (1971). Experimental program in expanded functions for dental assistants: phase I base line and phase 2 training. *J. Amer. Dent. Ass.*, **82**, 101

Lunin, M. and Moreland, E. F. (1972). Independent learning center in a dental school. *J. Dent. Educ.*, **36**, 5, 20

Manhold, J. H. and Manhold, B. S. (1965). Final report of an eight-year study of the efficacy of the Dental Aptitude Test in predicting four-year performance in a new dental school. *J. Dent. Educ.*, **29**, 41

Mackenzie, R. S. (1973). Defining clinical competence in terms of quality, quantity, and need for performance criteria. *J. Dent. Educ.*, **37**, 9, 37

Moore, B. G. R. and Peel, E. A. (1951). Predicting aptitude for dentistry. *Occ. Psychol.*, **25**, 192

Mullaney, T. P., Duell, R. C., Smith, T. A. and Blair, H. A. (1972). Programmed simulation of clinical endodontic problems. *J. Dent. Educ.*, **36**, 11, 37

Nedelsky, L. (1969). *Teaching and testing in dental education*. 2nd ed. University of Illinois

Pearson, S. L. and Jepson, L. (1969). Short film loops in the teaching of conservative dentistry. *J. Dent. Educ.*, **33**, 509

Phipps, G. T., Fishman, R. and Scott, R. H. (1968). Prediction of success in a dental school. *J. Dent. Educ.*, **32**, 161

Podshadley, D. W., Chen, M. K. and Shrock, J. G. (1969). A factor analytic approach to the prediction of student performance. *J. Dent. Educ.*, **33**, 105

Powell, M. and Eccles, J. D. (1970). The health and work of two professional groups: dentists and pharmacists. *Dent. Pract.*, **20**, 373

Registrar General's Decennial Supplement. England and Wales Occupational Mortality Tables 1931, 1951, 1961

Richards, N. D. (1973). Utilisation of dental services in *Social sciences and dentistry*. Richards, N. D. and Cohen, L. (eds.). Fédération Dentaire Internationale

Robinson, G. E., McDevitt, E. J., Wuehrmann, A. H. and Sinnett, G. M. (1972). Evaluating dental student performance with time-lapse photography. *J. Dent. Educ.*, **36,** 8, 17

Romcke, R. G. and Lewis, D. W. (1973). Use of expanded function dental hygienists in the Prince Edward Island dental manpower study. *J. Canad. Dent. Ass.*, **39,** 247

Rosenzweig, S., Egelhoff, C. and Webb, N. (1971). An evaluation of the dental auxiliary utilization program. *J. Dent. Educ.*, **35,** 3, 169

Rovin, S. and Packer, M. W. (1971). Evaluation of teaching and teachers at the University of Kentucky College of Dentistry. 1. Development of evaluation criteria. *J. Dent. Educ.*, **35,** 496

Salvendy, G., Goodrich, T. H., Hinton, W. M., Cunningham, P. R. and Ferguson, G. W. (1973a). Electromechanical simulator for acquisition of psychomotor skills in cavity preparation. *J. Dent. Educ.*, **37,** 12, 32

Salvendy, G., Root, C., Cunningham, P. R., Ferguson, G. W., Hinton, W. M., Baum, S. and Khan, L. (1973b). Skills analysis of cavity preparations: Class I in mandibular right first molar. *J. Dent. Educ.*, **37,** 10, 11

Sheiham, A. (1974). Planning for Manpower requirements in dental public health. In *An introduction to community dentistry*. Slack, G. L. and Burt, B. A. (eds.) (Bristol: Wright)

Vanek, H. G., Chen, M. K. and Podshadley, D. W. (1967). Evaluation of a self-instructional method used in preclinical operative dentistry. *J. Dent. Educ.*, **31,** 34

Vanek, H. G. (1969). Objective evaluation of dental school technic products. *J. Dent. Educ.*, **33,** 140

Waterman, G. E. (1952). Effective use of dental assistants. *Publ. Health Rep.*, **67,** 390. Washington D.C.

Welford, A. T. (1962). Changes in speed of performance with age and their industrial significance. *Ergonomics*, **5,** 139

Whitehead, F. I. H. (1974). The relationship of advanced level qualifications to subsequent academic performance of dental students. *Br. Dent. J.*, **137,** 173

Wolcott, R. B. (1973). Operative dentistry's responsibility to the profession: achieving, determining and maintaining competence. *J. Dent. Educ.*, **37,** 10, 38

Workshop on Dental Manpower, Proceedings of (1968). The need, demand and availability of dental health services. *J. Amer. Coll. Dent.*, **35,** 188

Zullo, T. G. (1971a). A factor analysis of perceptual and motor abilities of dental students. *J. Dent. Educ.*, **35,** 356

Zullo, T. G. (1971b). Principal components analysis of the Dental Aptitude Test battery. *J. Dent. Educ.*, **35,** 144

7
The Passenger

J. T. REASON

INTRODUCTION

A chapter entitled 'The Passenger' in a book dealing with various aspects of
human skill surely deserves some explanation. At first sight, the notion of
'passenger skills' appears to juxtapose two seemingly dissonant elements:
the evident passivity of the person being transported in some conveyance
with the highly organized activity which is the essence of skilled behaviour.
One way to resolve this apparent contradiction in terms is to begin by
defining what is meant by a 'skilful passenger' in the present context. *A skilful
passenger is one who through an understanding of the adverse effects associated
with vehicle motion and also of his own built-in protective mechanisms is able to
take active and effective measures to preserve his state of well-being.*

That passengers have the capacity to exercise a wide measure of control
over their own well-being became evident to the present writer while investigating the problem of motion sickness—perhaps the most unpleasant and
certainly the most widespread of all the ill-effects induced by passive motion.
As a consequence of their usually unwitting actions, it was apparent that
passengers could significantly enhance or reduce their basic susceptibility to
motion sickness. From a practical point of view, these observations indicated
that passengers have at their immediate disposal a powerful behavioural tool
for combating motion sickness. But it was equally clear that this tool could
only be wielded effectively if the passenger had a clear understanding both of
the essential nature of the nauseogenic stimulus and of his own capacity to
accelerate or impede the development of adaptation—the acquisition of
which constitutes the only sure defence against motion sickness.

Accordingly, the chapter is divided into two main parts. The first and larger part deals exclusively with the problem of motion sickness. Since the first step in developing coping skills is to *understand* the nature of motion sickness, we shall begin with a brief discussion of its causes and the mechanisms of protective adaptation, and then go on to consider by what means the passenger can modify his own level of susceptibility. The second part deals more speculatively with two other transport problems, vehicle-induced anxiety and multiple time-zone travel, and examines a number of 'self-help' techniques for minimizing their ill-effects.

It is not the aim of this chapter to provide a comprehensive review of passenger problems and their possible counter-measures; rather it seeks to explore in relation to a limited number of examples the relatively novel idea that passengers can be taught a variety of skills directly aimed at preserving their well-being both during and after exposure to vehicle motion. The emphasis throughout will be on those things that the passenger can do for himself without the help of other agencies. In other words, we shall be concentrating on those actions and mental states over which the passenger has some degree of voluntary control. Clearly, passengers can exercise little direct influence over the manner of their travelling once they have selected their destinations and modes of travel. The average passenger cannot, for example, dictate the altitude at which his aircraft will fly, nor the route his bus, train or ship will take. Nevertheless, although the role of passenger imposes severe constraints upon action, it does not necessarily follow that he should abdicate all further responsibility for his well-being once he has delivered himself into the hands of the carrier. It is this common tendency, in particular, that is being challenged by what follows.

COPING WITH MOTION SICKNESS

Before describing the skills for coping with motion sickness, it is necessary to outline the essential nature of the motion sickness stimulus, and also the processes presumed to mediate the acquisition of protective adaptation. A more extensive discussion of these issues together with an evaluation of alternative theories can be found elsewhere (Reason, 1974; Reason and Brand, 1975).

The nature of the motion sickness stimulus

The variety and abundance of vehicles available to those who live in industrialized societies tend to obscure the simple biological fact that man was not designed to be moved passively. It is not just the case that we lack the ability to fly, to live under water, or travel at great speeds over land. These physical barriers to our locomotion have largely been overcome by the great technological advances of the last half-century. But the physiological and psychological barriers—shaped as they are by countless generations of evolutionary adjustment—do not yield so easily. That we ride in some form of vehicle nearly every day of our lives does not alter the fact that the human nervous system and especially the body's position and motion senses remain those of a self-propelled animal programmed to move at foot-pace over an essentially two-dimensional environment under conditions of normal terrestrial gravity.

If man had been intended to move about in any way other than under his own power, he would have been equipped with an altogether different orienting system, principally the eyes, the vestibular receptors and the nonvestibular proprioceptors. It is only under natural conditions of self-propelled locomotion that these senses function in harmony to convey correlated spatial information. That is, under biologically normal conditions, they all tell the brain the same story. But when we allow ourselves to be transported in some kind of vehicle, or when we are exposed to an atypical force environment such as that encountered in space or in a rotating device, this delicate concordance is disrupted to produce a mismatch between the signals communicated by these normally synergistic receptors. It is this condition, termed *sensory rearrangement*, that is present in all the many diverse situations that provoke motion sickness.

The sensory rearrangement theory of motion sickness (Reason, 1970) has two basic premises. First, that all circumstances which provoke motion sickness are characterized by some form of sensory rearrangement in which the motion signals transmitted by the various spatial senses are at variance one with another, but also more importantly, with what is expected on the basis of previous transactions with the spatial environment. The second premise is that irrespective of what other spatial senses are party to these conflicts, the vestibular system—the semicircular canals and otolith organs—is always implicated. This takes account of the well-established finding that the *only* people who are truly immune to motion sickness are those who have suffered some damage to the vestibular receptors. In addition, it also tells us something about the nature of the effective motion stimulus, namely that it must involve a changing velocity component since the vestibular receptors only respond to angular and linear accelerations.

The many different forms of motion sickness (seasickness, car sickness, air-sickness, train sickness, simulator sickness, Cinerama sickness, swing sickness, even camel sickness, and most recently, space sickness) indicate that essentially the same condition can be elicited by a wide variety of motion stimuli. From this, it can be deduced that sensory rearrangement can also take a number of different forms. In fact, as Table 7.1 shows, we can identify at least six distinct types of rearrangement.

The basis of this classification is that we can distinguish two major forms of sensory rearrangement: the one an *inter-modality* conflict arising principally between the visual and inertial receptors (which includes both the vestibular and nonvestibular proprioceptors); the other an *intra-modality* conflict occurring within the vestibular system between the semicircular canals and otolith organs. The former is termed *visual–inertial rearrangement*, and the latter *canal–otolith rearrangement*. When we are moving under our own power, both pairs of receptor systems work to provide compatible spatial information. But in unusual force environments, this harmonious relationship breaks down to produce three logically distinguishable types of conflict: type 1, where A and B simultaneously signal contradictory or uncorrelated motion information; type 2, where A signals in the absence of an expected B signal; and type 3, when B signals in the absence of an expected A signal (where A and B represent portions of normally congruent receptor systems—see Table 7.1).

Table 7.1 **Some everyday and laboratory examples of six kinds of sensory rearrangement that can provoke motion sickness**

	Visual (A)–Inertial (B)	*Canal (A)–Otolith (B)*
Type 1 (A and B)	1 Watching the waves over the side of a ship	1 Head movements made about some axis other than that of bodily rotation—cross-coupled angular accelerations
	2 Looking out of the side or rear windows of a moving vehicle	2 Head movements executed in conditions where the g-vector is greater or less than unity
	3 Making head movements while wearing some optical device that distorts vision	3 Low frequency oscillations (between 0·1–0·3 Hz)
Type 2 (A not B)	1 Cinerama sickness	1 Head movements in weightless flight (space sickness)
	2 Operating a fixed-base vehicle simulator with a moving visual display	2 Caloric stimulation of the outer ear
	3 Observing angular or linear oscillations of the whole visual field while stationary	3 Positional alcoholic nystagmus (see Reason and Brand, 1975)
Type 3 (B not A)	1 Reading a map or book in a moving vehicle	1 Rotation about an Earth-horizontal axis
	2 Riding in a vehicle without external visual reference	2 Counter-rotation (see Reason and Brand, 1975)

There are three points to be made about the six-part classification shown in Table 7.1. First, symptoms of motion sickness have been experienced in each of the six kinds of rearrangement. Second, more often than not these rearrangements occur in combination rather than singly. A pure canal–otolith rearrangement can only occur when vision is occluded. In most transport situations, canal–otolith rearrangements are usually exacerbated by being part of a wider visual–inertial rearrangement. Third, not all the circumstances that provoke motion sickness fall neatly into this scheme. Like many similar classifications, it is far tidier than the reality. For example, there is now a substantial body of evidence to show that motion sickness incidence increases sharply as the frequency of vertical oscillation falls from around 0·5 Hz to the region of 0·1 Hz. Above 0·5 Hz, little motion sickness is provoked, and above 1 Hz virtually no sickness can be elicited (Benson, 1973; O'Hanlon and McCauley, 1974). That some form of sensory rearrangement is involved in these low frequency oscillations is in little doubt, but since we do not fully understand the dynamics of the transduction of linear accelerations by the otolith organs and other gravireceptors it is not yet possible to specify the exact nature of this rearrangement with any confidence. However, in Table 7.1 it is speculatively entered as a type 1 canal–otolith conflict.

The mechanism of protective adaptation

A strong clue as to the functional processes underlying the acquisition of protective adaptation is given by the sequence of adaptive effects and after-effects. The appearance of symptoms on initial exposure to the provocative stimulus, their gradual reduction and eventual disappearance on continued exposure, and their reappearance (mal de débarquement) on returning to the previously typical environment are sufficiently uniform over a wide range of eliciting conditions to suggest that they are mediated by common central mechanisms. One type of explanation has been termed the 'neural mismatch' hypothesis (Reason, 1970, 1974; Reason and Brand, 1975) and postulates two neural components: (1) a *neural store* that retains the informational characteristics of previous inputs from the spatial senses; and, (2) a *comparator unit* that compares the most recently consolidated contents of the neural store with the prevailing sensory influx from the spatial senses.

It is suggested that during the initial period of exposure to the rearranged spatial influx, the contents of the neural store are markedly different from the signals currently arriving from the spatial senses. This discrepancy is detected by the comparator which, as a result, generates a signal reflecting both the sign and the extent of the mismatch. This mismatch signal is then directed along reflex pathways to the neuronal and neurohumoral mechanisms responsible for the production of symptoms. It is assumed that the severity of symptoms are in direct relation to the strength of the mismatch signal.

With continued exposure, the contents of the neural store are gradually updated by incorporating elements of information about the rearranged sensory inputs; so that, eventually, they are compatible with the characteristics of the provocative environment. When this occurs, the mismatch signal is no longer generated, and symptoms disappear. At this point, the individual is said to be adapted to the rearranged environment.

On returning to the previously typical environment, the recent contents of the store, having adjusted to the atypical conditions, are again at variance with the incoming sensory information. This causes the reinstatement of the mismatch signal and, with it, the reappearance of symptoms. On remaining in the typical environment, the contents of the store are rapidly readjusted to be compatible with the existing sensory influx. This part of the adaptation cycle is likely to occur much more rapidly than the initial adaptation to the rearranged stimulus since the informational characteristics of the typical environment will be overlearned. That is, the appropriate stimulus traces are well consolidated and readily retrievable from the store for matching within the comparator. Similarly, when the individual again encounters the same conditions of rearrangement, adaptation is likely to proceed more rapidly than on the first occasion (Reason and Diaz, 1970) owing to the presence of stored traces from the previous exposure. If the person continues to move in and out of this enviroment, the time should come when both transitions will be free from symptoms, as in the case of the experienced sailor who is evidently able to retrieve the appropriate stimulus traces from the store before a mismatch signal of sufficient strength to trigger motion sickness can be generated.

To summarize: it is believed that motion sickness is a maladaptation phenomenon which occurs at the onset and cessation of conditions of sensory rearrangement when the pattern of inputs from the vestibular system, proprioception and vision is at variance with the stored patterns derived from recent transactions with the spatial environment. Needless to say, this does not explain why motion sickness should occur at all, nor why it should take the particular form that it does. It is simply one of the penalties we pay for adopting a biologically alien mode of locomotion. Although it may be of little comfort to the troubled passenger, it is worth reminding him of the obvious but often neglected fact that motion sickness is a self-inflicted condition. The only sure way to remove it from the human scene is to revert to being a self-propelled species.

The distinction between active and passive locomotion

Before discussing possible counter-measures, it is worth commenting briefly on the marked difference in susceptibility displayed by passengers and vehicle controllers. The latter are rarely troubled by motion sickness while actually controlling the vehicle, even though they may be—and usually are—highly susceptible passengers. This suggests that the distinction between active and passive locomotion is not as clear-cut as it might first appear.

It seems more likely that wholly active locomotion and totally passive transportation represent the extremes of a continuum with a number of intermediate stages in between. The controller of a vehicle, the driver or pilot, is being transported passively, yet being an integral part of a closed-loop control system, where the consequences of his volitional control actions are fed back to him via his senses or instruments, he shares many of the important characteristics of an actively self-propelled individual. The passenger, by contrast, is completely 'out of the loop'.

It is probable that the intermediate status of the vehicle controller confers a powerful degree of protection against motion sickness. If this analysis is correct, then future theorizing about motion sickness must take greater account of the factor of volition. To be more specific, we need to incorporate within the theory something akin to von Holst's (1954) concepts of a 'command signal' and an 'efference copy' which compares the sensory consequences of actions ('reafference') with what is expected from a stored record of the command signal. But for our immediate purposes, it is clear that the closer the passenger is able to imitate the actions of the vehicle controller, the more likely he is to remain free from symptoms.

Counter-measures appropriate for short journeys

In specifying the passenger skills for increasing resistance to motion sickness, it is necessary to distinguish between short journeys of not more than a few hours duration and much longer journeys lasting days or even weeks. In the former, the issue of adaptation is of minor importance; but for longer journeys it is crucial and demands a different strategy from the passenger. Accordingly, counter-measures appropriate for the two kinds of journey will be considered separately.

As soon as we come to examine what the passenger can do for himself to combat motion sickness, it becomes apparent why his actions must be directed by a clear understanding of the provocative stimulus. Different modes of transport require different counter-measures, but the basic principles underlying them remain the same—being rooted in the sensory rearrangement theory described earlier. For short journeys, these principles fall under four headings: postural factors, visual reference, mental activity and dietary factors.

(a) *Postural factors*. There is now considerable evidence (see Money, 1970) to show that, where the situation permits, adopting the supine position markedly reduces the risk of motion sickness. Manning and Stewart (1949) compared the incidence of swing sickness in 14 different conditions and found that the lowest incidence occurred in the supine position with the eyes open and with a full view of the earth-stable surroundings. The incidence of sickness in the supine position was found to be one-fifth of that in the sitting position with the head upright, and similar results have been observed on ships and trains. Experimental studies indicate that when the imposed linear accelerations act perpendicularly to a line drawn from the outer canthus of the eye to the auditory meatus, the resultant incidence of sickness is significantly higher than when these forces act parallel to this line (McIntyre, 1943; Manning and Stewart, 1949).

The beneficial effects of the supine position have been attributed to the fact that the otolith organs are less responsive to vertically-acting linear accelerations than when the head is upright. This follows the general theory of Quix (1925) for which there is some recent support (Graybiel and Patterson, 1955; Graybiel and Clark, 1962). However, it is also likely that these prophylactic effects are due in large measure to the restraint imposed by the supine position upon independent movements of the head on the neck. It has been shown that the extent of these head wobbles are positively and significantly correlated with motion sickness susceptibility (Johnson et al., 1951). Certainly, the provision of some kind of mechanical head restraint is helpful in reducing the likelihood of sickness, particularly on aircraft during moderate turbulence (Johnson and Mayne, 1953). In a rotating environment or in weightless space flight, the nauseogenic stimulus is only applied when the head is moved, so that in these circumstances fixing the head will guarantee immunity against motion sickness. In a car with head rests, passengers can gain a considerable amount of protection from simply holding their heads against the supports. But even voluntary head restraint will be effective. Where head movements are essential, they should be carried out slowly and preferably when the vehicles is not engaged in a turning or braking manoeuvre.

How does limiting head motion afford protection against sickness? It seems likely that head movements executed in atypical force environments where the linear acceleration vector is less or greater than 1 g produce intra-labyrinthine conflicts in which the canals correctly transduce the changing angular velocity of the head while the otoliths simultaneously signal the presence of the unusual force vector. Whatever the underlying reason, however, it seems likely that restricting head motion eliminates or reduces sensory rearrangement, and as such constitutes a potent and easily applied counter-measure in all modes of transport.

(b) *Visual reference.* The sensory rearrangement theory indicates that a cardinal rule for combating motion sickness is that the passenger should seek to minimize as far as possible the discordance between inputs to his position and motion senses. However, once he has adopted a suitable posture, the only important sensory factor over which he usually has any direct influence is vision. And here the major factor is the view he has of the stationary world outside the vehicle.

In a land vehicle with windows, the ideal position is one in which the passenger has an unobstructed view of the way ahead. Not only is this the most 'natural' aspect, allowing the greatest opportunity for matching visual and vestibular inputs, but it also permits the passenger to anticipate potentially sick-making manoeuvres like braking and turning. Rear- or side-facing seats should be avoided by the highly susceptible passenger. Although the visual flow pattern observed from these positions is correlated with the inertial inputs, the matching is not one that conforms with stored expectations and so is likely to hasten the onset of symptoms.

Many passengers unwittingly increase their susceptibility by attempting to read a map or a book while travelling in a moving vehicle. This creates a type 3 visual-inertial conflict (see Table 7.1) in which the eyes are presented with a stationary visual field relative to the observer, while the inertial receptors are detecting the accelerations of the vehicle. In other words, the inputs from the inertial receptors are not corroborated by the expected visual input.

This same type of sensory rearrangement is present in all modes of transport where the passenger does not have a clear view of the environment outside the vehicle; that is, where he is denied 'external visual reference'. It contributes to the appearance of sickness in the sea traveller or aircraft passenger seated in an enclosed cabin with his view restricted to the stationary scene (with respect to him) within, while his inertial receptors are signalling changing patterns of linear and angular accelerations. Where such a conflict is inevitable, there is some evidence to suggest that the passenger can reduce his susceptibility by shutting the eyes and thus removing the discordant visual information in a fairly natural way (Money, 1970).

Certainly, the absence of external visual reference in a moving vehicle can markedly increase the passenger's likelihood of becoming sick. For example, Tyler (1946) found that when troops being transported from ship to shore in small landing barges were made to crouch below the sides thus restricting vision to the interior of the craft, the incidence of sickness was 30% as opposed to 11% when they were allowed to stand and look over the sides. This difference could not be attributed to head position since it was the same for both conditions. And this difference also occurred despite the fact that Tyler estimated that the ability to restrain independent head movements was better in the crouching position. Similarly, in aircrew the highest incidence of sickness is found among those crew members such as navigators and air electronics officers who are frequently denied external visual reference.

As the Tyler study showed, the presence of visual information that is in agreement with the inertial inputs can suppress the onset of symptoms. On a ship or an aircraft almost the only way that this concordance can be achieved is by fixating the horizon or some visible landfall. This provides a stationary datum against which the perceived motions of the whole body can be accurately and synchronously registered. Birren (1949) also suggested that the presence of some form of artificial horizon may also be effective in reducing symptoms when external visual reference is denied. This possibility seems worth pursuing particularly in view of a recent finding by Dichgans and Brandt (1973) that the prophylactic effects of visual information can be further enhanced by having the visual scene move counter to the perceived motion of the body and so appear to cancel it. There is considerable evidence to show that in any conflict between visual and inertial inputs, the visual information is dominant (Reason and Diaz, 1970; Lee and Lishman, 1975).

(c) *Mental activity*. The early motion sickness literature contained a number of suggestions as to how the susceptible passenger could best occupy his mind. Some writers urged him to 'strengthen the will to resist' (Stocker, 1881), while some advocated prayer, and yet others favoured the humming of cheerful tunes—partly to control respiration and partly to keep the spirits up (à la Winnie the Pooh). A French writer offered the wise counsel 'Fermez les yeuz et prenez patience'.

In addition, there were a number of anecdotal reports that concentration upon some difficult or engaging mental task, or a sudden demand on the total resources of an individual as in an emergency, tend to delay the onset of symptoms or to alleviate them once they are established. Many sailors relate how their seasickness vanished on a call to battle stations. Similarly, Hill (1936) describes how on one voyage seasickness '. . . was lost in an ecstasy of hymn singing.' On the reverse side of this coin, there is the phenomenon frequently observed by the present writer and others involved in the experimental manipulation of motion sickness in which an overconcern with the presence of minor symptoms leads to a more rapid onset of sickness. This is something of a vicious circle: the more the person worries about feeling sick, or, in an experiment, is directed to observe and report his sensations, the sicker he feels and the more wretched he becomes.

In recent years, some incidental experimental observations have provided strong support for these anecdotal reports. Guedry (1965) exposed two groups of subjects to the same level of cross-coupled angular stimulation in a large, enclosed rotating room. One group were required to solve problems (mechanical comprehension and spatial relations) while executing controlled head movements. The other group made the same head movements, but with their eyes closed in a semi-darkened part of the rotating room. Although the experiment was primarily concerned with the effects of vision on vestibular habituation, some striking differences were noted in the relative incidence of sickness in the two groups. In the mentally-occupied group, only 3 of the 10 subjects reported mild nausea, and this passed off quickly. But in the dark-unoccupied group, 6 of the subjects were severely disturbed by acute nausea and vomiting; in fact, 2 of them failed to complete the experiment. Four members of this group vomited several times. It would appear from this that the heightened mental activity of the problem-solving group exerted a powerful suppressive effect on the nausea syndrome. This conclusion is even more compelling when it is realized that at least three studies involving similar levels of cross-coupled stimulation have shown that, in the absence of differences in mental activity, the eyes-closed condition produces a significantly lower incidence of sickness than does a full view of the illuminated interior of the rotating device (Kennedy *et al.*, 1965; Reason and Graybiel, 1969; Reason and Diaz, 1970).

A second experiment (Correia and Guedry, 1967) involved exposure to constant rates of rotation about an Earth-horizontal axis; that is, subjects were strapped to a litter and turned like chickens on a barbecue spit. As before, a clear relationship was found between mental activity and susceptibility to motion sickness. Twenty subjects were rotated, but only 8 completed the experiment. The 12 subjects prevented by sickness from completing had all been asked to concentrate on their postural sensations with the purpose of giving accurate descriptions of the experienced motion. Of the 8 who survived, 4 had performed a task in which they signalled their orientation by pressing a key twice per revolution, and 4 had been required to carry out continuous mental arithmetic to enhance nystagmus.

Why demanding activity should increase resistance to motion sickness is not understood. It is possible that it involves pre-empting the cortical pathways implicated in the production of symptoms. But whatever the reason, the moral for the passenger is clear: keep the mind on other things than the state of the stomach and engage in some taxing form of mental activity—where this does not, like reading or writing, make matters worse.

(d) *Dietary factors*. Nineteenth century writers, in particular, were fond of giving bizarre advice as to what the intending passenger should eat or drink before travelling. These ranged from a pre-embarkation diet of pickled onions (to eliminate the near vacuum in the abdominal cavity that was presumed to cause sickness) to such splendid prescriptions as 'soup made of horse-radish and rice, seasoned with red herrings and sardines' to be washed down with liberal quantities of champagne or a 'light sparkling wine'. Red herrings indeed!

In actual fact, whatever is eaten before travelling, so long as it would not disturb the digestion anyway, makes very little difference to susceptibility. There is, however, one sound piece of dietary advice which is that the intending passenger should eat, if not a hearty meal, at least an adequate one before travelling. The writer's own experience of a fairly large number of experimental subjects exposed to sick-making motion is that those who do so on an empty stomach tend to succumb more rapidly. Once again, it is not clear why motion sickness should thrive on an empty stomach, but it certainly appears to be the case.

Accelerating the acquisition of protective adaptation

The counter-measures described above are primarily designed to combat motion sickness in journeys of relatively short duration. The skills required of a passenger on a lengthy sea voyage are somewhat more complicated. Not only does he need to use these short-term counter-measures to overcome the immediate risk of developing symptoms, he also has to employ a somewhat different strategy to accelerate the rate at which adaptation is acquired so that he may enjoy the larger part of his voyage in relative freedom from sickness. The problem can best be illustrated by considering the case of the astronaut in weightless flight. For all its exotic nature, the nauseogenic properties of zero-gravity flight are easier both to comprehend and to control than the motion of a ship. At the same time, lengthy space missions like those aboard Skylab share the same requirement for the speedy acquisition of adaptation.

As indicated in Table 7.1, astronauts are subject to a type 2 canal–otolith conflict whenever they make turning motions of the head in weightless flight. Being a gravity-independent system, the semicircular canals function normally in zero-gravity; but these inputs are not corroborated by the normally associated otolith signals. So long as the astronaut keeps his head perfectly still, he is in no danger of developing space sickness. But then neither will he acquire the necessary protective adaptation to enable him to carry out his operational tasks. For this, he must interact actively with the provocative stimulus—in other words, he must move his head, gradually at first and then more extensively.

This brings us to the crux of the long-haul passenger's dilemma: to obtain the benefits of protective adaptation he must expose himself to the risk of motion sickness. And there is a further problem. The evidence from a number of studies (see Reason and Brand, 1975) clearly shows that the presence of well-established symptoms seriously interferes with the acquisition of adaptation.

So how can this dilemma be resolved? One possibility is suggested by the characteristic way in which motion sickness reactions develop. When some index of the number and severity of symptoms is plotted against the duration of a steadily increasing provocative stimulus, there is a general tendency for individuals of moderate susceptibility to show a very gradual initial increase in the severity of the reactions until mild nausea, pallor and cold sweating are established. After that, well-being declines very rapidly, and severe nausea and vomiting quickly follow for most people (Reason and Graybiel, 1970). This final phase has been graphically termed the avalanche phenomenon. The relevant point here, however, is that prior to the onset of the 'avalanche', there is only a small loss of well-being during which adaptation can proceed without interference. Another important factor is that during these early stages of the syndrome, recovery occurs very rapidly once the stimulus is removed or reduced. This is not generally the case once the symptom build-up has progressed to the stage of severe nausea and vomiting. Recovery from this level of malaise can take several hours. Not only that, the will to take remedial action—or any action at all—is lost.

Thus, the skilled passenger on a long voyage has to tread something of a tightrope. He needs to take active steps to interact with a moderate level of motion stimulus, while at the same time closely monitoring his own state of well-being. As soon as an increase in symptoms is detected, he needs to take up a minimum risk posture until they have subsided. In the case of the astronaut, this is easy: he simply keeps his head still. But for the sea traveller, the problem is more difficult since he lacks the same degree of voluntary control over the nauseogenic stimulus. Perhaps the best he can do is to choose between maintaining the supine position with eyes closed, or else watching the horizon with his head movements restrained—though neither posture guarantees immunity. And in both situations, he should engage in some demanding mental activity.

Clearly, these are not easy prescriptions to follow. But if they are successfully carried out, they would surely justify the use of the term 'passenger skills'. If, however, these actions fail to produce the desired result of warding off sickness while hastening adaptation, the passenger should console himself with the thought that unless he is among the unfortunate few who like Lord Nelson seem to lack the ability to adjust to ship motion, he will eventually acquire some degree of adaptation even if he spends the first few days of his voyage prostrate on his bunk. The only difference is that it will take a good deal longer to achieve. There is also the further consolation that, once acquired, adaptation to a particular form of sensory rearrangement appears to be retained for long periods of time (Reason and Diaz, 1975). This is likely to be one reason why susceptibility to all forms of motion sickness declines markedly with age (see Money, 1970).

The use of anti-motion-sickness drugs

Although it was not the intention here to consider these in any detail, it is worth emphasizing that the correct use of drugs in combination with these behavioural counter-measures is likely to produce more effective protection than when either technique is used singly. It should be stressed, however, that these drugs are only effective as preventives and not as cures. In other words, they must be taken at the stated time *before* exposure to the sick-making motion, and not once symptoms are established. Their preventive action is not fully understood, but even the best drugs are far from perfect. They only serve to increase resistance to motion sickness, they do not confer immunity.

One question that falls within the scope of passenger skills is that relating to the choice of drug. What are the most effective motions sickness preventives, and in what circumstances should they be used? To some extent, the answer depends upon which side of the Atlantic you are. British investigators strongly favour l-hyoscine hydrobromide (an atropine-like drug which antagonizes the action of acetyl-choline), while Americans tend to favour antihistamines such as cyclizine. However, there is evidence (Brand and Perry, 1966; Wood, 1968) to indicate that both classes of drug are effective, but in somewhat different circumstances. When the passenger seeks protection against a short but potentially severe exposure such as a Channel crossing by ship or hovercraft, then hyoscine taken orally in doses of 0·3–0·6 mg one hour before departure is recommended. But for longer journeys in which the provocative stimulus is likely to be milder, the antihistamines are more appropriate since they are longer-acting and produce less marked side-effects. Cyclizine 50 mg, Dramamine 100 mg, Benadryl 50 mg and meclozine 50 mg will provide useful protection against motion of long duration where repeated medication is needed. Cyclizine, Dramamine and Benadryl act in about 2 h, and should be repeated after 4–6 h. Meclozine takes about 3–4 h to act and exerts an effect for between 12 to 24 h (Brand and Perry, 1967).

FURTHER SCOPE FOR PASSENGER SKILLS

Let us in this concluding section consider a more speculative question. If passengers can be taught to minimize the risk of motion sickness through their own voluntary actions, could they not acquire similar skills to combat other adverse effects of vehicle travel? The literature suggests that there are at least two further problems against which these self-help measures could be effective. Firstly, in reducing the physiological and psychological disturbances created by multiple time-zone travel; and, secondly, in the self-management of sub-clinical levels of anxiety provoked by vehicle travel. Each of these possibilities is explored briefly below.

Coping with multiple time-zone travel

The period necessary to resynchronize the passenger's 24-hour biological rhythms after a long-distance jet flight from east to west or conversely is of the order of one day for every time-zone crossed (Strughold, 1971). On average, therefore, it takes 3 to 4 days to resynchronize the 'body clock' after crossing four time-zones, as for example in flying across the United States from coast to coast. After a transatlantic crossing, covering five or six time-zones, it takes about 5 or 6 days for complete adjustment to occur. And after crossing 12 time-zones, involving a complete reversal of the day–night cycle, readjustment to local time may take up to 12 days. During this time, most people suffer discomfort and a general loss of alertness. As Strughold put it: 'They become hungry, sleepy or wide awake at the wrong time in relation to the new local time. Their head clocks, their stomach clocks, and their elimination systems are confused.' (Strughold, 1971, p. 57).

Strughold suggested a number of largely behavioural techniques for overcoming the worst of these effects. First, there is the method of pre-flight adaptation. If the passenger plans to attend an important meeting immediately upon arrival at some distant location, then he can avoid the adverse effects of desynchrony by presetting the physiological clock some days before the journey. For an eastbound trip, this can be accomplished by going to bed an hour earlier each night and waking an hour earlier the next day until the circadian rhythms are in phase with the local time at the destination. If the journey is to be westbound, the procedure should be reversed: go to bed an hour later and arise an hour later each day. Second, there is the method of post-flight adaptation. The passenger can fly to his destination several days in advance of an important engagement, thus giving the body time to adjust after arrival. This method has been used by heads of state flying to summit meetings on another continent. Third, the passenger can take some mild medication or use such expedients as physical exercise or warm baths to induce sleep and so help him adjust to the new local day–night cycle. Finally, those passengers who are unable to use these procedures should appreciate that the morning hours during the first few days after a lengthy eastbound flight, and the late afternoons immediately following a westbound trip, are not the times for entering into important negotiations or for taking major decisions, and should arrange their time-tables accordingly.

The self-management of vehicle-related anxiety

It must be made clear at the outset that we are not dealing here with *phobic reactions* to vehicle travel. Marks (1969) defined a phobia as a special kind of fear reaction that has four characteristics: it is out of all proportion to the situation, it cannot be explained or reasoned away, it is beyond voluntary control, and it leads to an avoidance of the feared situation or object. The treatment of true vehicle phobias is thus beyond the scope of passenger skills, and normally requires professional help. Fully-fledged phobic reactions to particular modes of transport are comparatively rare. Sometimes they occur as part of the extensive symptomatology associated with agoraphobia, while in other individuals they are specific to travelling in lifts, trains, tubes, aircraft and so on. However, there are few of us who have not experienced moments of anxiety, even panic, during take-off or landing, or during flight through turbulent air, or when high waves break over the bow of a ship, or even while being driven by certain individuals in a car. Some people remain chronically apprehensive while travelling in particular vehicles, usually aircraft. These feelings may not reach the crippling proportions of a true phobia, but they can be extremely distressing and may even provoke symptoms akin to motion sickness—though these reactions are better termed 'emotion sickness'.

Recent developments in behaviour therapy suggest that certain techniques used in the clinical treatment of phobias can profitably be taught as self-control skills for coping with anxiety (Goldfried, 1971; Jacks, 1972; Goldfried and Trier, 1974). Common to most of these procedures is the progressive relaxation training originally devised by Jacobson (1929) but which was not widely used for alleviating tension and anxiety until it was modified by Wolpe (1958) and incorporated into the therapeutic technique of *systematic desensitization*. This is based on the assumption that inappropriate and maladaptive emotional reactions are learned, and can accordingly be reconditioned by contemplating (desensitization in imagination) and by subsequently approaching (*in vivo* desensitization) the provocative stimulus while in a relaxed state.

Although the mechanisms by which muscular relaxation reduce anxiety are not clear, there is little doubt that it works while the training session is actually in progress. Not only do patients report an improvement in their subjective state, but there is evidence that relaxation has definite physiological consequences, including a decrease in blood pressure, pulse rate and skin conductance (Paul, 1966). However, as Goldfried and Trier (1974) have pointed out, its long-term benefits are more equivocal. They suggested that one reason for the inconsistent finding on relaxation training may be that people instructed in methods of relaxation are taught *how* but not *when* to use this skill. They investigated two ways of presenting relaxation training. In one condition, the subjects were told that relaxation exercises would more or less automatically reduce their anxiety level. In the second condition, relaxation was presented in a self-control context in which subjects were told that they were learning an active coping skill. It was found that, on a variety of measures, the latter condition produced the greatest degree of improvement. But perhaps more significant was the finding that subjects in this condition continued to improve after the actual study was finished. This was interpreted as being consistent with the view that anxiety-reduction achieved through relaxation training is a learned skill and in common with other skills requires repeated practice to maintain and improve its effectiveness. This, of course, holds true for all the passenger skills discussed here.

Space does not permit a full description of progressive relaxation training. This has been given at length elsewhere (Wolpe and Lazarus, 1966; Watson and Tharp, 1972). Briefly, however, it involves focusing the attention on each of the major muscle groups in turn. This usually begins with the arms, then progresses to the face, neck, shoulders, upper back, then chest, stomach and lower back, then hips, thighs and calves, and finally the whole body. At each stage, the muscle system being attended to is first tensed then relaxed, so that the muscles will relax more deeply than before they were tensed. For example, in Paul's (1966) manual for desensitization, the initial relaxation instructions are as follows:

'Make a fist with your dominant hand (usually right). Make a fist and tense the muscles of your (right) hand and forearm; tense it until it trembles. Feel the muscles pull across your fingers and the lower part of your forearm. . . . Hold this position for 5 to 7 s, then . . . relax. . . . Just let your hand go. Pay attention to the muscles of your hand and forearm as they relax. Note how those muscles feel as relaxation flows through them (20 to 30 s).'

The whole procedure may initially take something like 20 to 30 min. But with practice, the length of time required gets shorter. Similarly, the skilled relaxer may not need to tense his muscles first in order to attain deep relaxation. These skills are clearly within the behavioural repertoire of the passenger on most forms of public transport, and can be practiced without attracting too much unwelcome attention.

References

Benson, A. J. (1973). *Physical characteristics of stimuli which induce motion sickness: a review.* IAM Report No. 532, Farnborough, Hants. RAF Institute of Aviation Medicine

Birren, J. E. (1949). Motion Sickness: Its psychophysiological aspects. In *Human Factors in Undersea Warfare.* National Research Council, Washington DC

Brand, J. J. and Perry, W. L. (1966). Drugs used in motion sickness. *Pharm. Rev.,* **18,** 895

Brand, J. J. and Perry, W. L. (1967). *The use of drugs in the prevention of motion sickness in the services.* Medical Research Council. Royal Naval Personnel Research Committee. Report No. 08/1101. SS 178

Correia, M. J. and Guedry, F. E. (1967). Modification of vestibular response as a function of rate of rotation about an earth-horizontal axis. *Acta Oto-Laryngol.,* **62,** 297

Dichgans, J. and Brandt, Th. (1973). Optokinetic motion sickness and pseudo-Coriolis effects induced by moving visual stimuli. *Acta Oto-Laryngol.,* **76,** 339

Goldfried, M. R. (1971). Systematic desensitization as training in self-control. *J. Consult. Clin. Psychol.,* **37,** 228

Goldfried, M. R. and Trier, C. S. (1974). Effectiveness of relaxation as an active coping skill. *J. Abnorm. Psychol.,* **83,** 348

Graybiel, A. and Patterson, D. (1955). Thresholds of stimulation of the otolith organs as indicated by the oculogravic illusion. *J. Appl. Physiol.,* **7,** 666

Graybiel, A. and Clark, B. (1962). *The validity of the oculogravic illusion as a specific indicator of otolith function.* Naval School of Aviation Medicine Report No. 67, Pensacola, Fla

Guedry, F. E. (1965). Psychophysiological studies of vestibular function. In *Contributions to Sensory Physiology.* W. D. Neff (ed.) (New York: Academic Press)

Hill, J. (1936). The care of the sea-sick. *Br. Med. J.,* Oct–Dec, 802

Jacks, R. N. (1972). *Systematic desensitization versus a self-control technique for the reduction of aerophobia.* Unpublished doctoral dissertation. Stanford University

Jacobson, E. (1938). *Progressive Relaxation* (Chicago: University of Chicago Press)

Johnson, W. H., Stubbs, R. A., Kelk, G. F. and Franks, W. R. (1951). Stimulus required to produce motion sickness. I. Preliminary report dealing with importance of head movements. *J. Aviat. Med.,* **22,** 365

Johnson, W. H. and Mayne, J. W. (1953). Stimulus required to produce motion sickness. Restriction of head movements as a preventative of airsickness. Field studies on airborne troops. *J. Aviat. Med.,* **24,** 400

Kennedy, R. S., Tolhurst, G. C. and Graybiel, A. (1965). *The effects of visual deprivation on adaptation to a rotating environment.* Naval School of Aviation Medicine Report No. NSAM-918, Pensacola, Fla

Lee, D. and Lishman, R. (1975). Vision in movement and balance. *New Scientist,* 9 January

Manning, G. W. and Stewart, W. G. (1949). Effect of body position on incidence of motion sickness. *J. Appl. Physiol.,* **1,** 619

Marks, I. M. (1969). *Fears and Phobias* (London: Heinemann)

McIntyre, A. K. (1943). *The effect of head position on susceptibility to motion sickness.* RAAF, FPRC Report No. 86

Money, K. E. (1970). Motion sickness. *Physiol. Rev.,* **50,** 1

O'Hanlon, J. F. and McCauley, M. E. (1974). Motion sickness incidence as a function of the frequency and acceleration of vertical sinusoidal motion. *Aerospace Med.,* **45,** 366

Paul, G. L. (1966). 'Insight versus Desensitization in Psychotherapy' (Stanford, Calif.: Stanford University Press)

Quix, F. H. (1925). The function of the vestibular organ and the clinical examination of the otolithic apparatus. *J. Laryng.,* **40,** 425

Reason, J. T. (1970). Motion sickness: a special case of sensory rearrangement. *Adv. Sci.,* **26,** 386

Reason, J. T. (1974). *Man in Motion: The Psychology of Travel* (London: Weidenfeld and Nicolson)

Reason, J. T. and Brand, J. J. (1975). *Motion Sickness* (London: Academic Press)

Reason, J. T. and Diaz, E. (1970). *The effects of visual reference on adaptation to Coriolis acclerations.* Flying Personnel Research Committee Report No. 1303, Ministry of Defence, London

Reason, J. T. and Diaz, E. (1975). *Retention of adaptation to motion sickness induced by cross-coupled angular stimulation.* Flying Personnel Research Committee Report No. 1335, Ministry of Defence, London

Reason, J. T. and Graybiel, A. (1969). *Magnitude estimations of Coriolis sensations.* Naval Aerospace Medical Institute Report NAMI-1082, Pensacola, Fla

Reason, J. T. and Graybiel, A. (1970). Changes in subjective estimates of well-being during the onset and remission of motion sickness symptomatology in the Slow Rotation Room. *Aerospace Med.*, **41**, 166

Stocker, W. R. (1881). On seasickness. *Lancet* (ii), 1035

Strughold, H. (1971). *Your Body Clock* (London: Angus and Robertson)

Tyler, D. B. (1946). The influence of a placebo, body position and medication on motion sickness. *Amer. J. Physiol.*, **146**, 458

von Holst, E. (1954). Relations between the central nervous system and the peripheral organs. *Br. J. Anim. Behav.*, **2**, 89

Wolpe, J. (1958). *Psychotherapy by Reciprocal Inhibition* (Stanford, Calif: Stanford University Press)

Wolpe, J. and Lazarus, A. A. (1966). *Behaviour Therapy Techniques* (New York: Pergamon)

Wood, C. D. (1968). Use of drugs in the prevention of motion sickness. In *From the Symposium on the Role of the Vestibular Organs in Space Exploration.* NASA SP.187, Pensacola, Fla

8

The Train Driver

P. BRANTON

BACKGROUND AND HISTORY

The present writer cannot recall a time in his childhood when he wanted to be an engine driver (fire brigade having been his line at the time). Perhaps this earlier indifference becomes an advantage when turning from enthusiastic concern with technological perfection towards a psychological interest in the role of the driver as the key man in the system. Although many ergonomists and applied psychologists are known to be railway fans, remarkably little has been published on which to draw for a skill analysis. Recently, some work towards such an aim has become available (Rohmert, 1973, Mashour, 1974), certain detailed aspects have been dealt with by Davis (1966) and by Buck (1963a). Apart from these, there seems to exist a large body of directly relevant information emanating from the Japanese Railway Labour Science Institute. The present writer believes that his Japanese railway ergonomist colleagues may have covered some of the ground to be explored in this paper. Unfortunately, only brief summaries are available to readers not conversant with the Japanese language.

Train driving is not as uncommon an activity as it may seem. At any moment of the day tens of thousands of men all over the world drive trains and in Britain alone there are 30 000 footplate staff, about one-tenth of the total workers employed on the railways. They drive 4000 locomotives and 10 000 other traction units, moving 23 000 trains per day, transporting 4 million passengers a day and 200 million tons of freight each year. This represents about 19% of all goods moved and 8% of all passenger mileage. The railways' share of the total cost of transport and the social benefit the country derives from it is hard to estimate, but the train driver's contribution is clearly an integral part of it. This part is so much taken for granted that one only realizes how essential the service is when the men are absent on strike or in some other emergency.

To run a railway is to operate a system in the true sense of the word, in that all parts are effectively interactive and interdependent. From its earliest days, the system has a built-in, deeply engrained concern for safety and its human element forms perhaps the largest disciplined collection of men outside the military. Their jobs are circumscribed by a large set of rules, approximately 250 in number, with virtually statutory force, derived from practical experience and covering even remotely possible eventualities. With a high degree of awareness of responsibilities to the public, and the increasingly intensive use of track and equipment, operators are well aware of the 'ripple effect' of any incident snowballing delays down the line. The containment of the consequences of delay is an accepted part of the art of operating the service.

Figure 8.1   The driver's work station in a typical steam locomotive. A small forward window, not visible from this angle, gave limited vision along the body of the boiler. Drivers and firemen mostly leant out of the side opening to look ahead (By courtesy of British Railways Board)

ACQUISITION OF TRAIN HANDLING SKILLS

The training of drivers, or traction training as it is called in British Rail, is a fairly long and closely defined process in recognition of the fact that a highly complex skill is to be practised. The normal way to become a driver is through becoming a traction trainee. After an initial training course of about 6 weeks, the trainee passes to become Secondman for a number of years, the period being governed by agreements between management and trade unions relating to promotion and other aspects of manpower policy. During this time, the Secondman is subject to an extensive familiarization process, in which knowledge of and compliance with the Rule book and a large body of instructions and manuals is absorbed. It is an interesting sidelight on the strict division of responsibilities that the onus of judging competence, say, in regard to route knowledge, is on the driver. Whenever he deems to have learnt a route he is required to sign a card for this route irrespective of whether or not he has been examined on it specifically.

Considerable changes have, of course, taken place in the training arrangements of footplate staff, not only because of the change in traction mode from steam to diesels and later to electrics, but also with advances in training techniques. From the viewpoint of skill psychology one might characterize the old (steam days) type of preparation for the driver's job by likening it to osmosis. The aspiring man in those days had to go through all stages from cleaning the engine and polishing the brass to prolonged exposure to 'the road', literally soaking up on the way the lore and practice of the craft, as well as the social atmosphere of discipline and camaraderie. In such circumstances the notion of 'incidental learning' becomes blurred since almost all experience can contribute to the build-up in skill.

> I started my railway life at the age of 16 in the engine sheds at New Cross in 1897 . . . became a regular firemen in 1908 and my booked job was on a fast night goods from Horsham consisting of 50 loaded goods wagons. The engine had a big reversing lever—it was as much as the driver could manage to move it backward and forward. The engine was fitted with six wooden brake blocks fitted to the tender; the engine wheels had no brake at all and in wet weather the brake was almost useless. The small guard's van had wooden brake blocks. Sometimes when running down a bank with the signals against you, the driver had to reverse the engine and put on steam to make sure of stopping. When the old engine was taken off we had a modern one fitted with a Westinghouse brake—it was like living in another world, a pleasure to go to work . . . .

This recent reminiscence of a 93 year old ex-engineman breathes the spirit of steam. The situation of driver and fireman in those days was of a team working in close harmony like a small orchestra. Their score was a working timetable based on train diagrams and their time constraint was, and still is, considerably more exacting than that of any other transport mode. As the quotation indicates, it was physically very hard work to control such a large and complicated mechanical system, always dependent on the fireman's capability to provide power and tease out of an enormous engine just the right energy output to achieve their goal. The difference between then and now in control systems terms is in the functional distinction between the generation of power and its control. Then, primary motive power had to be skilfully modulated in the process of creating it; now the skill in the job is concentrated in husbanding the energy held, as it were, in reserve and available without great effort by the controller.

The steam driver's task, as far as can be said in retrospect, consisted both of scanning the outside world, the visual one in particular, and of directing the timing and volume of power generation. There had to be two men on the footplate at all times, and so the fireman shared in both parts of the task and could often be relied upon to apply his own route knowledge and initiative. This combined effort, needless to say, entailed a subtle social relationship and spread the skill. An element of joint achievement and awareness of interdependence mutually reinforced work satisfaction. By contrast, the diesel driver, even if a Secondman is present, is more unquestioningly in sole charge.

As far as acquisition of skill is concerned, it was in the nature of the combined effort that the occasions for practically taking over control of the locomotive were more easily grasped than is now possible. However, then as now, this is the way to 'get the feel' and to involve the 'self' of the man and thus pick up kinaesthetic and other information. 'Since the information needed to control motor skills is only generated by limb movements and postural changes there can be no learning without overt participation' (Singleton, 1967). Such involvement, be it noted, is much more than passively 'sitting by Nelly' in the training of factory operatives.

The more obvious, but in the present context less profound, differences between old and new traction are, of course, the immediate working environmental conditions. No one begrudges the modern driver the protection from the inclemencies of the weather, and that he should be seated all the time at the console in a clean cab, but the effects of changes on skill should not go unnoticed. For instance, thermal conditions are now stable and controllable, and might perhaps become monotonous, whereas on the open footplate they were positively arousing. Equally, the acoustic input on the open footplate enabled some drivers to use acoustic cues to identify their location at certain points along the route, a feat elegantly tested and described by Buck (1963b). On the other hand, the vast improvements in the size and quality of the visual field which the change to new traction allowed are wholly welcome for the exercise of skills. It is a moot point whether recent and proposed increases in *speed* of trains are so drastic as to affect visual perceptual functions. It is true that signal sighting times may have been shortened, but, on the

Figure 8.2   A modern traction unit in the high speed diesel train. This is a first attempt at 'design from the man out'. The driver is in a centre position with fully adequate forward view and controls are grouped around within easy reach (By courtesy of British Railways Board)

other hand, the efficiency of braking equipment has been improved apace. Nevertheless, Mashour (1974) has drawn attention to the possibility of visual information overload at high velocity of locomotion:

> As the deterioration of detection capacity is markedly greater at the periphery of the field of view than at its centre, a mobile observer is even more dependent on central vision for the detection of objects and events, than a stationary observer. For this reason an operator pays, in general, still less attention to (is attracted less by) things lying on the periphery of the visual field when he is moving at a higher speed than a lower one.

TASK ANALYSIS

While equipment and immediate environment of train drivers have changed beyond recognition, certain basic aspects or essentials of the task have remained the same. At least four factors remain common to the task in both modes of traction:
1. The allocation of system functions, e.g. between driver and signalman
2. The movement through signal block sections
3. The means of communications to and from the driver
4. The role of route knowledge.

In order to procede further towards a skill analysis, it is necessary to set out a list of variables in the face of which the skill is to be exercised.

For the present purpose, a variable affecting skilled performance is an external condition which may modify the driver's response by bringing into play internal functions such as memory and selective attention. The presence of these variables signifies a degree of inherent uncertainty and characterizes the openness of the system. As drivers are required to work over more than

Table 8.1　Task variables (in ascending order of predictability)

I *Climatic (variable during and between missions)*	*Liable to change*	*Driver's functions affected*	
1 Rain, fog, snowfall, clouds	momentarily	general visibility wheel–rail adhesion*	perception (mainly visual)
2 Position of sun (relative to duration of travel)	time of day	signal visibility	
3 Temperature (heat, cold, frost)	seasonal	wheel–rail adhesion*	

II *Train specific (variable between missions)*

4 Loads behind (e.g. Dining cars, unbraked freight waggons)	Timing and suddenness of power or brake application (rate of change of acceleration or deceleration**)	Experience, sensory–motor control
5 Traction power and brake performance a) type of engine or brake b) within-type variation ('individuality') c) state of maintenance		

III *Geographical locations (within-mission variables, invariant between missions)**

6 Gradients—up/down, steep/level	a) to be approached with various degrees of caution, and b) sequential cues for next location	*Memory* route knowledge, rules and regulations orientation
7 Curves—radius		
8 Junctions		
9 Points		
10 Cross-overs		
11 Neutral sections		
12 Level crossings		

* Variation in wheel–rail adhesion may cause traction wheelslip. Most traction units have an indicator of this event on the driver's console. On a recent, exceptional occasion, over a gradient of 1:75 on a main line, train speed had to be reduced to 20 m.p.h. 32 Km.p.h.); applying greater power, though available, would have created wheelslip.

** Occasionally, drivers claim to be 'dining-car-conscious', showing awareness of need for well-graded speed changes to avoid soup being spilt over passengers in the dining cars behind them.

*** In addition, incidental variables and fortuitous cues to action are utilized by drivers. These include landmarks, e.g. houses, church steeples, etc., as well as cuttings and bridges, or make-up of track, e.g. short or long-welded stretches, wooden or concrete sleepers and the resultant noise patterns.

Table 8.2 Line-side information specifically provided

I *Signals, multiple aspect colour lights or semaphore*

1 *Intended functions*	2 *Subsidiary function*
SYSTEMS INFORMATION CARRIERS a) acting as COMMAND SIGNALS (if aspect is 'red' or 'danger') b) the same signal provides STATUS INFORMATION, indicating state of the line 2 or 3 signal blocks ahead: i) 'green', 'clear' or 'off' or ii) 'yellow' or 'double yellow'	Aid to POSITION IDENTIFICATION along the path—signals may be unique in their environmental context

---

II *Boards, fixed or temporary*

Marking beginning and end of permanent or temporary speed restrictions

---

III *Mileposts, and other distance indicators*

Aids to identification of position as in I 2 above

---

one route in the course of a day or week, the characteristics of a given route become variables of the task. It will therefore be useful to regard each journey the driver makes as a 'mission'. Not only does this conform with the frame of reference used by researchers in other fields of transportation; it also underlines the essentially goal-oriented nature of the task. The list of these variables, grouped accordingly in ascending order of the degree of predictability of conditions is set out in Tables 8.1 and 8.2.

For the sake of completeness of description of the variable conditions in which train drivers operate, it should also be noted that the job necessarily involves shift work. Skilled performance is therefore possibly affected by consequent diurnal variability of bodily and mental states.

Against this background of task variables, it is interesting to quote from the official job description:

'Driving the traction unit whilst in service, and thereby control the movement of trains in a manner which:

(i) complies with the Rules and Regulations and Instructions of the B.R.B.,

(ii) ensures the safety and comfort of the public within the limits of his control at all times,

(iii) ensures optimum performance of the traction unit/train.'

In driving terms this means:

1. Optimize velocity of train
2. Maintain readiness to bring train to a halt, normally within at least one breaking distance from receipt of information about occupation of line ahead.

This analysis stresses the uni-dimensional and uni-directional nature of the task, clearly differentiating it from those of air, sea and road vehicle controllers. They have up to six degrees of freedom to move and their time constraints are not as severe as the train driver's. The extent of his discretionary control action is limited to starting, varying speed and stopping. In flying and car driving tasks, detailed mathematical applications of man–machine control systems theory have found great scope (cf. Bernotat, 1970). By contrast, train handling does not yet seem amenable to such exact treatment because, although it involves relatively limited control actions, the longer term consequences of these for safety and comfort of people in the rest of the system do not seem to allow this.

Control aspects of the task

Functionally, tasks are usually grouped into 'tracking' and 'monitoring' external events, depending on whether information intake and control output is continuous or intermittent. In train driving this division is not very useful because active control is intermittent but information intake virtually continuous. The driver has basically only two levers before him, one controlling motive power, the other the brake. Once activated, both have— in most types of modern traction—an element of automatically governed gradation, or stepping and notching function, built-in such that infinitely variable direct control of acceleration (positive or negative) is not possible.

Inside the cab the driver has relatively few instruments—a speedometer indicating actual speed, ampere meters and brake pressure gauges. (In the next generation of traction units, he is likely to have additionally, some indication of the maximum line-speed permitted on the section of the track.) These then are, so far, the only sources *in the cab* to give him information about deviations from his own planned or intended performance. In the light of these data—and of course by reference to the outside world—he exerts control action.

The train moves along a 'reserved' path, divided into block sections by visible signals, which the driver must monitor. These appear in his visual field at irregular intervals of anything between a few hundred yards and, say, 10 miles or more, the time intervals may be from less than one to about 20 min. He must watch these signals closely because they may command him to stop, although normally the previous signal would warn him of this contingency at least one braking distance beforehand. His destination or 'mission' goal is thus subdivided into a series of partial targets and the train may be regarded as moving in 'jumps' from one target to the next. It is as if a missile were propelled along a predetermined path from one target to another—with only one degree of freedom, namely velocity. The analogy with the skill of throwing a dart comes to mind and, indeed, railway engineers and operators speak of 'braking trajectories'.

However, the analogy breaks down with regard to knowledge of results and error correction. The controller of this missile, unlike the dart thrower, often does not have the target in his visual field. When no signal is in sight, information before him is so limited that there is considerable uncertainty in how punctually he will attain his target. Hence, any of his control actions in mid-trajectory must be based on judgements drawn from experiential memory. There is the added complication of 'lag in the system'. The time lag between initiation of control action and its effect on the behaviour of the train is such that, if he were to act only when a target (e.g. a signal) came into view the driver would proceed in fits and starts, rushing up to a signal post and, if commanded to halt, slam on the brakes and speed up again when the line is clear. Such a driving style would involve frequent changes of speed and could be both uncomfortable for passengers and uneconomical. In reality, the accomplished driver achieves optimal performance by smoothing out peaks and troughs of velocity; he arrives at part-targets at just the right speed to avoid sharp changes in rate of acceleration.

SKILL ANALYSIS

Many of the phenomena observed in train driving and similar slow-action, long-lag skills are difficult to explain satisfactorily by current theories. Normally, one would measure speed and accuracy of performance and economy of effort as the accepted parameters of perceptual-motor skills. Alternatively, attempts have been made recently to obtain measures of the information processed (Bainbridge, 1975). In our case unfortunately, the necessary controlled experimentation, measurement and consequent self-consciousness of the operator would seriously interfere with the exercise of the skill and might actually be dangerous. (A 'macroscopic Heisenberg principle' has lately been invoked for situations like this.) We shall therefore approach definitions, descriptions and explanations by other means, such as the interpretation of protocols, direct unobtrusive observation, critical incident interviews and the like, in order to narrow down the search for new measurables.

In this section we propose to set up a working definition of skilled acts and re-interpret observed facts in the light of it. We shall assume the existence of internal representations of the external world and suggest some characteristics of the operations required to fit the facts. To produce the skilled act, we shall conclude, the following would need to be represented internally:
1. The goal to be attained
2. The present position in time and space of the producer himself
3. The variables of the task
4. The potentiality of success.
First we shall consider what internal operations seem necessary to explain the observed success.

Working definition

The task analysis in the previous section contains some implicit assumptions about the nature of the skill elements in train driving. In the attempt to make them explicit, this writer has systematically questioned over 200 drivers and inspectors on the following lines: 'When you ride with a driver, can you tell whether he is a good or indifferent driver?' The answer is unfailingly in the affirmative, but to the next question, 'How do you tell the difference?', the answer is most hesitant and almost wholly uninformative. They just knew. On the face of it, our informants appear to be saying that,

1. Drivers carry out their task with a *quasi-automaticity* that is largely inaccessible to introspection and verbal expression
2. The *degree of skill* can only be judged intuitively and then only by someone who is himself skilled.

Both interpretations are a challenge to probe further. What they are in fact saying is: 'We have done this thing and therefore know that it can be done.' In other words, only he who has actually attempted and *succeeded*, knows how the potential becomes the actual. Success thus is the first criterion, and we recall that Bartlett (1951) described skill as having the specific 'character of *accomplishment* of an internally varied act' (italics added). Bartlett's formulation is particularly apt for the present purpose. For, if we propose a working definition of a skilled act as one in which *controlled internal processes and capabilities are successfully integrated with external goals*, we may perhaps explain certain points and test the validity of explanation by applying it to train driving.

A typical protocol

Consider for instance the protocol of a running commentary:

> 'As I cross this little bridge here, when I'm doing 80, with 8 coaches behind me, and I have to stop at Didcot, and I have plenty of time, and the weather is good and the lights are with me, then I shut off the power here and I'll coast nicely to the station. Just before the station entrance I give her a 5 lb rub on the brake before taking it off altogether and she'll stop about 4–5 yards from the signal post. I've done that many times.'

Our interpretation of this relatively simple statement is that, over and above his watching for danger signals, the driver makes running computations of the effect of gradients, curves, signal aspects, etc., upon his subjective, intuitive solution of the total time/distance equation which forms the current mission. On perceiving changes in any of the variables, he re-calculates his subjective trajectory by a process closely akin to partial differentiation and approximation, and he thus minimizes the difference (or error) between his forecast and the actual performance. However tentative and incomplete such an explanation of events may be, it directs us to an area in which we might seek quantifiable evidence.

Prediction and anticipation

Our working definition assumes the existence of internal representations of events external to the person (Craik, 1943). As to their function, Singleton (1967) suggested that they are 'models of the real world which can be manipulated to predict the consequences of certain actions and thus determine the optimum actions'. Our protocols tend to confirm that past experience is used to predict and anticipate. It should, however, not be inferred that anticipation means automatic, cue-triggered (stimulus–response) behaviour. In fact, in the railway case, anticipation must never become so automatic and uncontrolled that the driver would misread a line-side signal aspect commanding him to stop for one allowing him to proceed. Davis (1966) has classified the reasons given for incidents when signals were passed at danger, into 'failure to see', 'misjudgement' and 'misreading'. In each case a different form of anticipation is involved, depending on whether visual scanning, motor action or cognitive function is correctly anticipated or not. If correct anticipatory behaviour, once acquired, were rigidly automatic, such incidents could not occur.

Skill as constructive self-activation

We infer further that a number of models may be available to the man, one corresponding more closely than others to the real world around him. The skill rests then on choosing the most realistic model. That inference is quite respectable since Kelley (1968) used it in developing his Theory of Manual Control and applied it successfully in helping to put men on the moon. He treats 'human control decisions as a result of and choice among future possibilities'. The internal is integrated with the external by controlled choice among alternatives, and not merely by reeling-off a collection of routines, e.g. motor command sequences. This is autonomous, constructive self-activation. On passing the little bridge in our example, the driver brought together a set of variables before choosing to shut off power. He is 'in control' both nominally and in fact. Skilled integration is thus not automatic in the sense in which responses are inflexibly evoked by stimuli, as reflexologists would have it.

'Doing the sums'

We are on more difficult ground when we interpret the driver's actions as implicitly 'doing sums' in differential calculus. Indeed, he would be greatly surprised to hear it suggested. However, we are led to this conclusion by the exactitude with which he achieves his goals. His models must be so specific that he can accurately predict future states of the system.

It is neither intended to argue here, nor necessary, that these 'mental calculations' are carried out in the numerical, 'digital' mode of ordinary mathematics. Rather, they are to be regarded as quasi-mathematical or 'analogue' and their outcome need be no less exact for that. To attempt describing them, we start from the insight by Bruner (1964) that humans construct models of their world by way of three information processing systems: through action, through imagery or through language, resulting in three different types of representations, enactive, iconic or symbolic. We assume that our driver's representations are in the enactive mode, because he is manifestly able to perform on them but not so able to express his actions in language, let alone in numerical symbols. The ability to perform such internal operations in a non-symbolic yet exact manner is probably much more general than we realize.

Evidence can be drawn from behavioural physiology for the existence of neural equipment to deliver in very appropriate form continuous information about momentary states and relationships of all parts of the body. For instance, as part of the posture control function, the muscle spindle system signals two kinds of information to higher centres; one is the momentary *state* of tension in the muscles, represented by continuous discharge of very specific frequency, the other is *change* in tension, by magnifying (increasing) frequencies in accord with speed of change.

> Just like so many other receptors, the muscle spindle is simultaneously a measuring instrument for 'proportional quotients' and 'differential quotients' . . . every position corresponds to a specific pattern in the continuous afferent stream of impulses to the CNS. . . . No higher central area needs to be concerned with disruptive resistances and variations in loading which occur in the limbs, for example, in standing or running. *The muscle spindle system ensures that these effects are eliminated and that the momentary requisite posture or movement is 'successful'.* (Holst, 1973. Original italics)

If a summary of internal states is delivered in this quasi-mathematical form to the CNS, it is possible that the manipulations on the intrinsic model of the real-world are carried out in the same mode (c.f. Pribrom, 1976).

Handling the task variables

To use computer programming analogies, we might consider specific operations carried out in hierarchically ordered sub-routines from perceptual through central mediational to motor command functions. Initially, with practice on the job, each sequence would become more and more 'automatic' such that 'known' values are substituted for sub-routine calculations of unknowns. '. . . learning a skill involves the formation of a neural system of increasing redundancy' (Shallice, 1972). Determination of the degree of skill may then be related to the size of the repertoire of sub-routines available to the man and his capability to call them into play at the moment judged right by him. The real virtuoso gains the vital time saving advantages by cutting down on guessing by 'knowing'. Known values in terms of speed/ duration of 'jumps' (part-targets), to be substituted for calculations in sub-routines, would need to be contingent on preceding results and in a form usable in the next sub-routine. Such values are, in our sense, sequentially ordered conditional probability estimates. Cognitive psychologists claim that certain decision-making procedures follow the rules of Bayesian inference about subjective probabilities; an argument for similar operations on a non-verbal, non-symbolic level can be made to explain the observed high accuracy of success. The variables encountered along the driver's path would then be represented by estimated tolerance margins with

1. Upper limits compatible with the safety and comfort of the passengers, and
2. Lower limits below which successful achievement is in doubt.

Errors, successes and 'true' goals

The implicit operations upon these representations result, we assume, in statements of probable errors in *trajectory anticipation*, 'If I carry on like this, I shall be at least a minute late at X'. What is not immediately obvious, however, is that such statements necessarily imply an exact space–time representation of X, the goal.

It is unlikely that the goal representations merely take the form of visual imagery of the scene, say, 3 yards from the buffers in Euston Station. This would hardly be appropriate to allow calculations to be performed.

The whole idea of determination of errors and successes is inevitably bound up with, and necessarily depends on, having well defined goals. Errors are only deviations from goals, and success is nothing more than that small deviation from the 'true' target for which no control correction was required.

When we considered task variables and trajectory anticipation, we dealt with means to an end; when discussing goal achievement and goal anticipation we deal with the ends themselves and our argument shifts to a different level of discourse, namely to the process of goal setting. This change of gear is often overlooked when we move from the skill laboratory to the real life of skill practice. In the laboratory, the experimenter sets the targets and instructs the subjects to achieve them. Outside, whatever the task demands are, the operator makes them his own goals; he is also the arbiter of the limits to which he will go.

Beyond cybernetics

As any control engineer will confirm, there can be no success—and hence no error measurement to be fed back—without a specified value for 'true' target.

This thought applies all the more to the idea of *adaptive* feedback as a conceptual model for skill in man–machine interaction. Applied to technology the model has undisputed uses. In thinking about microbiology and genetics, adaption and feedback have also been fruitful as working models. In the explanation of human skill, when the goals are considered to which the system is supposed to adapt, the explanatory power of the usual cybernetic concepts is limited and we enter the area of 'meta-cybernetics'. The really skilled operator functions open-loop and is non-linear, as has been pointed out by Kelley (*op. cit.*) among others.

We have said that neither the mission goal nor even part-targets are for most of the time visible to the driver and yet he succeeds. The goal must be therefore represented inside him and, although exact in spatio-temporal terms, it and the real goal are only approached by approximation. The 'true' mission goal must remain an *idealized construct*.

Internal goals and time

One of the problems from which the apparent generality of feedback conceptual models distracts attention, is the relation of goals to the linearity of real time. The uni-directional nature of the train driving task brings this neatly to the fore, but it seems to be at the root of all goal direction of behaviour and inherent in the purposivity so characteristic of skill. As he expressed it so succinctly, we will call it Hull's Paradox of Time in Teleology:

> In its extreme form, teleology is the belief that the *terminal* stage of certain environmental–organismic interaction cycles somehow is at the same time one of the *antecedent* determining conditions which bring the behaviour cycle about (Hull 1943).

Hull's view is quoted by Boden (1972) in a discussion of purposive explanation in psychology. She adds:

> Such an interpretation would represent a purpose as a queer sort of event, a cause working backwards in time, which is all the more strange in that an action may be done for a purpose and yet that purpose may never be achieved.

Our train drivers seem to succeed rather well in letting the future determine the present. That paradox may be more apparent than real if internal representations exist and if manipulation of time is possible. Of course, real time is as uni-directional as a train and an action once done cannot be undone. But the lapse of time is predictable and the effects of an action on the future of the system can be subject to imaginative manipulation. This is our old friend, anticipation. We construct the consequences of an act *before* the act is carried out.

After all, one of the most obvious and the most important characteristics of man as a controller is his relative freedom from present time, his ability to remember the past and anticipate the future and to employ this capacity in control (Kelley, *op. cit.*).

If our assumption about internal computations holds, the most logical form in which the critical path computations would be carried out is by count-down or back-to-front, as it were like D-day, H-hour and M-minute.

Another interesting question is, whether it makes a significant difference to the form of representation that in our case the calculator/controller is *inside* the missile and not, as in the usual ballistic situation, outside as an onlooker who has full data on both origin and target. There could be a parallel here to the controversy over fly-from and fly-to presentation in aircraft display design. However, we said above that the train driver's internal representation was probably not in the form of imagery (iconic) and what he displays to himself, if anything, is not immediately to be taken for granted.

Representation of self-position

Just as we found it necessary to postulate the existence of a representation of the end point or goal, so also origin of the trajectory would need to be specifically represented. (As it is in the 'present', the teleogical problem does not arise.) This requirement can be found in control engineering terms as it can be shown that even in the simplest manual control system equation a 'position' component needs to be included for stability. (Birmingham and Taylor, 1954). The train driver too, must at all times first 'find his orientation'. The process of identifying his own location on the track means the driver must be able to refer to a capacious long-term memory store, namely route knowledge. It is here that he uses not only the line-side equipment specifically provided, but also any other landmark. Such reference points become especially important in diminished visibility, say, in fog or at night.

Without a coherent—and realistic—internal representation of present position of the 'self', goal-directed acts could hardly succeed, except by chance. The compilation and up-dating of such a representation may be a quite separate function, apart from any representation of the external world. It is used to provide the operator with a quasi-absolute internal reference scheme he carries around with him in what may be, to him at any given moment, a world full of uncertainties.

It seems a fact of life that, if the environment does not yield outside points of reference suitable for extending the self in the exertion of skill, one creates one's own reference system. At the most primitive level we skilfully exploit the juxtaposition of the thumb to the fingers to obtain a secure hand grip. At the other extreme, in the most complex tasks, when all outside cues are denied, we fall back on internal representation of ourselves in time and space to maintain our autonomy and independence from the environment in order to accomplish the task.

A motivational representation

Any description of skilled acts remains incomplete and lifeless without consideration of a motivating component. The exercise of skill is marked by the determination with which the operator explores the limits of his capability. Like the runner who knows the mile has been run in 4 min, the skilled operator strives for some kind of perfection: 'It *can* be done', is what the driver in our protocol meant by saying 'I've done this many times'. Having argued that success is a criterion of skill, it is essential for achievement that its potential is also somehow represented. Operationally, in the process of integrating the internally predicted with the externally observed facts, a closure must be effected and a decision taken when the approximation of the real is 'close enough' to the ideal. To stop 3 yards from the buffers at Euston is good enough, 10 yards is not. The indecision of obsessive accuracy could defeat success and be dangerous.

An interesting thought on the motivating effects of knowledge of results in connection with cybernetic models is the operational ambiguity or ambivalence of feedback. If knowledge of incipient failure engenders negative feedback and error-correction, success appears to generate positive feedback —re-inforcing correct behaviour—which might be thought of as growth of capability. There seems to be a moral here for Skinnerian explanations of the function of reward in skill training. Be that as it may, it is common knowledge that train driving, like other craft skills, carries intrinsic rewards with its exercise.

To sum up this section, we hypothesized that the driver's internal representations have an anticipatory function; they seem to be self-constructed, conditional probability estimates of deviations from idealized goals, arrived at by non-symbolic trajectory 'calculations'; these estimates would require prediction of position at an elapsed time in the future, and would need to be based on preceding knowledge of trajectory target and present self-position; the whole operation depending upon the motivating effects of a representation of the potentiality of the total system. It remains a matter for empirical research to show whether such an explanatory schema is true.

INFORMATIONAL NEEDS

From the foregoing outline of what we presume to be the ingredients of skill in the performance of the train driver's task, we may now extract some ideas of what sort of information might be deliberately provided to be helpful to him. Four demands suggest themselves:

1. To augment his capacity for self-orientation
2. To provide aids to his anticipatory efforts
3. To aid maintenance of motivational effort
4. To avoid impoverishment of the immediate environment.

Augmenting the driver's capacity to orientate himself

Orientation, or more exactly, the determination of one's present position by perception of external events (e.g. the passing of a signal or landmark) becomes meaningful only when the event is integrated with stored information, i.e. route knowledge. Presumably, the perceived object is compared with a 'cognitive map' (Tolman) of specific points in a sequence. To be able to do so in the brief moment of 'recognition', without having to run through the whole sequence, it is necessary to postulate the existence of a capability to interfere with the strict chronological order in which the sequence is stored. One must, in the words of Bartlett (1932) be able to 'conquer the sequential tyranny of past reactions'. The chain of perceptual events will match the cognitive map exactly and the anticipated position of his self will be highly correlated with the actual position, provided there was no distraction and the mission proceeded to plan.

In practice, with only intermittent monitoring, however, there will always be some distraction and hence an element of uncertainty about the next-following event. In the practical context of route knowledge, a procedure or device to enhance orienting capacity should aim at reducing any uncertainty by *increasing the confirmatory effect of uniquely identifiable passing points*. This means that in route-learning, emphasis should be given to committing to memory landmarks of visual and other uniqueness. It means, furthermore, that it would be advantageous if the learning process were so designed as to further the anchoring of each event in the context of the sequence, by explicit reference to what went before and what is to follow next. If devices for this purpose are to be provided, they should have as little visual uniformity as possible. Uniformly numbered 'mileposts' in themselves would seem to have little to recommend themselves, as the possibility of erroneous reading and even if correctly read, subsequently forgetting the number would be predictable. The provision of route maps to augment orientation is prone to the same possible errors of anchoring their symbols in the outside visual world. 'Moving maps', would have to overcome the additional handicap of being very costly to make fail-safe and reliable. The slightest unreliability of such a device is likely to create loss of confidence and greater confusion than constant reference to the outside visual world. Clearly, a great deal of work in this area would need to be done.

Aids to anticipation

The other area of support in the task of the driver lies in the goal-directedness of the skill. If 'the future determines the present', as we have indicated above, the driver is particularly interested in knowing
1. Whether and what changes in the state of systems variables occur
2. The effects of his own present control action on future performance.

The former will be dealt with below together with environmental considerations.

The topic of predictive displays has been treated extensively by researchers in other fields of transport, e.g. in relation to submarines and to aircraft (cf. DeGreene, 1970, Kelley, 1968) and precise theoretical and applied studies of the human factor in such control systems are available. In view of the fact that, as has been emphasized above, this capacity to anticipate constitutes the central characteristic of the train driver's skill, and because the exercise of this skill must never become so automatic that a change in the state of a variable information input (e.g. a light signal aspect) passes unnoticed because it is 'taken for granted', it would be unwise to design the predictive function out of the job, and automate it. Even if it were feasible it is unlikely that operation of train running will be made safer by such means. In the endeavour to increase safety, efforts should rather concentrate on providing the man with means for shedding some of the load which 'trajectory anticipation' would impose on him. For instance, if a device were to be designed which would fit in with the man's 'internal, quasi-mathematical processes', (the existence of which was postulated above), he could be provided with knowledge about the probable effects of any present control action to considerable advantage. We have in mind a combination of display-quickening and rate-of-change feedback information, in a form to be established empirically through co-operation between human factors engineers and highly skilled operators. The problem will be to decide on the extent to which the information should be coded or symbolized on presentation. Too much coding may be counterproductive and the driver may come to ignore the display, relying on his own functions rather than court confusion. Bernotat (1970) has reported that some pilots using certain types of display experienced vertigo when carrying out manoeuvres because of the conflict between visual and vestibular input.

Motivational involvement might be furthermore enhanced, if the present relative social isolation of the driver in the moving cab from the rest of the system could be relieved. It is known that continuous communications devices between train cabs, signal boxes and control rooms are costly and complex. However, being in frequent touch with someone who has an overall view of the system function could greatly enhance safety and reduce the stress, provided again that the communication function is arranged with the limitations of mental load of the driver in view.

Quality of the driver's immediate environment

While this is not the occasion to deal at large with the detailed design of the train driver's work station in the cab, it is obvious that inappropriate work-place design is certain to affect exercise of skill adversely. Grant (1971) and Branton (1970) have set out many of the requirements in railway terms, and it only remains to emphasize again that a designed environment may easily become an impoverished one, impeding the exercise of skill through lack of relevant information in terms of visual, acoustic and kinaesthetic cues. One driver made the point, comparing steam train handling and modern traction: 'You don't feel at one with the train these days'.

CONCLUSION

To ergonomists, the analysis of the train driver's task and skill has a strong appeal. He is so obviously a special case, because he acts in an isolated, mobile environment, dependent on long-delayed feedback with a uni-dimensional output, unlike that of air, sea and road vehicle controllers. He thus exhibits a paradigm case of skill and the measure of it seems to rest largely in the realism of his internal representations of the external world and the accuracy of his mental processes. He must rely on those representa-tions to make continuously updated long-range forecasts to achieve partial and final destinations. Furthermore, his situation as controller rather than provider of energy throws into relief the human factors/cybernetic problems arising when an extraordinarily large mass is moved and controlled by small physical effort.

There is no real railway equivalent of 'blind flying' an aircraft. The practical situation demands the fullest attention of the man and interference could be dangerous. It is therefore not easy to confirm or refute experimentally the hypothetical assumptions made about internal models and processes. Only some parts of the task can be taken into the laboratory for investigation. Even so, in the light of the consistency of the evidence found so far and presented above, this author is confident that the old basic skills, having changed relatively little since the steam days, can be merged with any new skills arising from new technology. Every experienced driver is conscious of his limitations and fallibility. Yet, if his skill is deliberately built into the system, given equipment well fitted to his own limitations, and if he is allowed to operate in an environment moderately and appropriately enriched so that he can again 'feel at one with the train', he will do the rest.

ACKNOWLEDGEMENTS

The author is indebted to his railway colleagues, the hundreds of drivers, inspectors and traction officers, and in particular the late Mr W. F. Thorley and Mr A. J. Powell, for their most valuable help and advice. Ms P. Shipley and Professor W. T. Singleton, the Editor, must also receive grateful acknowledgement for their encouragement and challenging discussions.

References

Bainbridge, E. A. (1975). The representation of working storage and its uses in the organization of behaviour. *In* W. T. Singleton and P. Spurgeon (eds.), *Measurement of human resources* (London: Taylor & Francis)

Bartlett, F. C. (1932). *Remembering* (London: Cambridge University Press)

Bartlett, F. C. (1951). The bearing of experimental psychology upon human skilled performance. *Br. J. Indust. Med.*, **8**, 209

Bernotat, R. (1970). Anthropotechnik in der Fahrzeugführung. *Ergonomics*, **13**, 353 (In German)

Birmingham, H. P. and Taylor, F. V. (1954). A Design Philosophy for Man–Machine Control Systems. Reprinted in H. W. Sinaiko (ed.), (1961). *Selected Papers on Human Factors in the Design and Use of Control Systems* (New York: Dover Publications)

Boden, M. (1972). *Purposive Explanation in Psychology* (Cambridge, Mass: Harvard U.P.)

Branton, P. (1970). *Train Drivers' Attentional States and the Design of Driving Cabs.* Invited Paper to 13th Congress, Union Internationale des Services Medicaux des Chemins de Fer (UIMC). Brussels

Bruner, J. S. (1964). The Course of Cognitive Growth. *Amer. Psychol.*, **19**, 1

Buck, L. (1963a). Errors in the Perception of Railway Signals. *Ergonomics*, **6**, 181

Buck, L. (1963b). Auditory Perception of Position and Speed. *J. App. Psychol.*, **47**, 177

Craik, K. J. W. (1943). *The Nature of Explanation* (London: Cambridge University Press)

Davis, D. Russel (1966). Railway Signals passed at Danger: The Drivers, Circumstances and Psychological Processes. *Ergonomics*, **9**, 211

De Greene, K. B. (ed.) (1970). *Systems Psychology* (New York: McGraw-Hill)

Grant, J. S. (1971). Concepts of Fatigue and Vigilance in Relation to Railway Operation. *In* K. Hashimoto, K. Kogi and E. Grandjean (eds.), *Methodology in Human Fatigue Assessment* (London: Taylor & Francis)

Holst, E. von (1973). *The Behavioural Physiology of Animals and Man* (London: Methuen & Co.)

Hull, C. L. (1943). *Principles of Behaviour: An Introduction to Behaviour Theory* (N.Y.: Appleton–Century–Croft)

Kelley, C. R. (1968). *Manual and Automatic Control* (New York: J. Wiley)

Mashour, M. (1974). *Human Factors in Signalling* (Stockholm: Almkvist & Wiksell)

Pribrom, K. H. (1976). Self-consciousness and Intentionality. In G. E. Schwartz and D. Shapiro, (eds.), *Consciousness and Self-regulation* (London: Wiley)

Rohmert, W. and Jenik, P. (1973). The Harmonogram as a method for investigating the Man–Vehicle–Work relationship. *Arbeitsmedizin*, **8**, 249 (In German)

Shallice, T. (1972). Dual Functions of Consciousness. *Psychol. Rev.*, **79**, 383

Singleton, W. T. (1967). Acquisition of Skill—The Theory behind Training Design. *In* J. Robinson and N. Barnes (eds.), *New Media and Methods in Industrial Training* (London: B.B.C.)

9

The Pilot

R. G. THORNE and
WING COMMANDER G. W. F. CHARLES

INTRODUCTION

In other places in this book attempts have been made to define skill, to describe how it is acquired and to discuss ways in which it can be measured. Perhaps the best definition of skill is that it is something acquired by training, since even people with an innate ability can usually improve it by practice. However, this implies that if we measure skill, assuming that this is possible, we measure an even more complicated factor made up of the innate ability of the subject, his ability to learn and the skill of his instructors.

The skill of the pilot is the mixture of dexterity, resourcefulness, proficiency and systems management which pilots often sum up as professionalism. This professionalism comes after expensive training both in the air and on the ground. The prime objects of this training are to promote flight safety and to increase their operational efficiency.

In this chapter we shall first describe the pilot's task and then discuss the ways in which he is selected and trained to perform safely and efficiently. We follow with some remarks on the ways in which the proficiency of the pilot is, or could be, assessed. We conclude with some comments on research aimed at improving our understanding of the skill of the pilot.

THE PILOT'S TASK

During recent years the relative importance of various tasks have changed and these changes will become more marked with the increasing use of automatic devices and on-board computing facilities. Exciting developments in control systems and in instrument presentations are leading to radically different approaches to the better integration of man into the overall aircraft system. We see changes in the role of the pilot from that of a highly skilled dextrous individual to that of a highly qualified technician operating as a computer controller, crew manager, monitor and planner. However, we continually face the paradox that the more clever we become in developing 'black boxes' to usurp man the more vital it becomes to define adequately, the role, the response, the performance and the limitations of man.

How far we should go down the technological path depends largely on the role of the particular aircraft and it is not possible in this chapter to consider the whole gamut of possibilities, so we shall merely attempt to define the more important aspects of the pilot's tasks. Smode *et al.* (1966) in an assessment of research relevant to pilot training have reviewed the literature relating to studies defining the pilot's task. Carol (1965) in considering the use of pictorial displays for flight has also discussed the analysis and description of the pilot's task.

The flying task

The use of automatic flight control systems has reduced the attention directed to manual dexterity and co-ordination which is seen at its best in the competitive aerobatic pilot or the low-flying military pilot. Basically the task reduces in its simplest form to the ability to perform a particular manoeuvre, in three dimensions, using the controls provided. A child can learn fairly quickly the use of a single two-dimensional control. However, ability of a completely different order is required to control any aircraft smoothly yet positively on the approach to a runway, to change its flying attitude over the runway threshold so that it lands smoothly at the correct speed, in the right place on the runway. Such an approach and landing requires constant assessment of the aircraft's actual position and attitude in relation to the desired approach path to the runway. This involves use of the flying controls to adjust the aircraft in possibly all three dimensions, coupled in all probability, with throttle movements to correct any deviation from the desired speed; the latter may have changed as a result of the previous adjustments to the aircraft's flight path.

A much simplified example may illustrate this point. Let us assume that an aircraft is approaching a runway at the correct speed but the aircraft is lower than it should be, the pilot moves the controls to cause a change in the attitude of the aircraft. He will in fact raise the nose of the aircraft in relation to the runway. This correction to the aircraft's attitude will cause it to lose speed so the skilled pilot would anticipate this by adjusting the throttles to obtain more power from the engines. If he applies too much power the aircraft will exceed the desired speed for the approach to land and this would then involve further corrective action to the aircraft's attitude and power settings.

Inept and unskilled corrections could result, at best, in the aircraft touching
down too far along the runway or at the wrong speed. Most people can
develop the ability to control in three dimensions but fewer can perform with
sufficient repeatability to achieve a reasonable level of safety. Perhaps this
stems from man's history as an animal mainly constrained to move in two
dimensions.

Figure 9.1 Typical view from Trident flight deck during approach to land (Photograph by
courtesy of British Airways)

As already seen above there are times when the pilot needs to maintain a
given speed. On other occasions he may be required to perform manoeuvres
whilst the aircraft is violently accelerating or decelerating. These factors are
particularly significant to the aerobatic and the military pilot, where the
effects of acceleration, coupled with instruments which may be difficult to
read because airframe buffet is causing them to vibrate, can produce disorientation. Davies (1971) in explaining the significant differences between
the flying qualities of jet and piston engined aircraft gives a detailed and
comprehensive review of the handling problems of modern transport aircraft.

Management tasks

Management tasks vary widely with the role of the aircraft. The private pilot
flying a light aircraft will check the weather for the route he wishes to fly, he
will then make some relatively simple navigation calculations to allow for the

wind and for the local magnetic variation so that he will know what magnetic course to fly. If he intends to fly through Controlled Airspace in or near major airports or airways his flight planning will be a little more complicated and will culminate in him completing a Flight Plan and having it formally cleared and accepted by Air Traffic Control. He will then execute some simple checks to ensure the aircraft and its equipment is fit for flight.

The military pilot and his crew may well spend several hours briefing for an operational sortie. At the end of this time they will have prepared a detailed navigational plan in which the timing is usually expressed in seconds. The timings and routing which are of particular interest to Air Traffic Control are incorporated in a Flight Plan which, as for the light aircraft pilot, has to be formally cleared and accepted. Between engine start up and reaching the take-off point, the military crew would have made an extensive check of all the aircraft's operating systems. These would have been done using prescribed check-lists and would culminate in the pre-take-off checks. Once airborne all the systems in the aircraft would be regularly monitored. On a low-level, high speed sortie the pilot would be largely pre-occupied with actually flying the aircraft so that he maintained the correct height above the ground and obstacles near his track; with maintaining the correct speed and in calculating and applying the corrections necessary to achieve the exact planned time over target. Throughout the sortie he must communicate as necessary with other aircraft or ground radio controllers; in a multi-crewed aircraft he must co-ordinate and direct his crew's activities and he must remain aware of the overall situation concerning the serviceability of the aircraft and its systems and any hazards that might affect the completion of the flight. Perhaps he shows the greatest skill in assessing and adjusting the conflicting requirements which inevitably arise during any operational sortie. In doing so he would be assisted and guided by the rules and procedures taught during his ground and flight training. System management is now a major part of the military pilot's task and will become increasingly important as the combat aircraft's navigation and weapons systems become more sophisticated to meet the demand for greater operational flexibility from the same aircraft.

For many years the civil commercial pilot has been greatly pre-occupied with the Air Traffic Control rules and procedures for leaving the controlled airspace around large airports to join the airways. There is the conflicting requirement that the airline captain wants to be allowed to climb his aircraft as quickly as possible to the economic cruising height for his type of aircraft and destination but he also wants to be kept a safe distance away from all other aircraft. This is achieved by air traffic controllers arranging for aircraft on the same airway to be separated vertically, or horizontally at the same height. The airline pilot then has to report when he reaches his height and subsequently at set reporting points. The combination of complying with these procedures, making the radio calls involved, and navigating and flying the aircraft at the same time as monitoring its systems has now produced the effect on short haul flights that sometimes it is difficult to complete all the prescribed check-lists. A major difficulty with check-lists is that it is easy to extend them and make them more comprehensive but it is very difficult to prune them. The management skill of the airline pilot is often shown in his ability to anticipate periods of high work-load when dealing with air traffic procedures and arrange to carry out the various aircraft checks either before or after such busy periods.

The communication task

Pilots talk to other crew members on their intercommunication radio and to the ground for reporting and receiving instructions. They also listen to other pilots communicating with the ground as this helps them to build up a mental picture of the activities of nearby aircraft. The times involved (in making and receiving such calls) can be a highly significant part of the total sortie time, particularly in civil aircraft operations. Military radio calls on combat, as opposed to transport type aircraft, are usually shorter than those required for civil operations but military pilots often have to contend with high noise levels in the cockpit especially when flying at high speed. Under these conditions they develop techniques for overcoming the difficulties. It would seem that routine messages in general are passed satisfactorily though there is the occasional lapse, but the main difficulties arise when unexpected messages are passed.

The monitoring task

Monitoring can take many forms. In multi-crew aircraft safety is often enhanced by deliberate cross-monitoring between the crew members. This procedure reflects the general understanding that man is a somewhat unreliable and imprecise device, prone to mental aberrations and forgetfulness. In modern civil and military aircraft, technology, though attempting to replace man, has not yet been able to demonstrate an acceptable level of component reliability. Paradoxically, man has been given the task of monitoring the function of complex systems and in modern aircraft, system warnings are presented to him visually and aurally. His task has now become a mixture of vigilance and fault diagnosis with system rectification the main objective, and it calls for alertness, clear thinking and quick reaction coupled with a complete understanding of the systems' operation.

SELECTION

The following paragraphs describe the way a candidate is selected for aircrew duties with the British Services. They portray one method of selection but it is reasonably typical and the procedures for civil aircrew selection in the

United Kingdom are similar, though there are certain significant differences.

Armstrong (1961) contains a description of the early analytical work undertaken in the United States to define job requirements for civilian and military aircrew. Cassie *et al.* (1964) in a selection of papers from the 1959 and 1961 meetings of the Western European Association for Aviation Psychology discuss Selection Methods and their Assessment. Trankell (1969) describes the selection system used by one major civil airline.

Before an individual can apply to become aircrew he has to meet certain academic standards. The attainment of these standards enables him to take the aptitude tests which form part of the overall selection process. The other aspects which are included are a medical examination and a series of interviews and exercises, to establish that he has the qualities to become an officer. However, as we are concerned mainly with flying skill we shall be concentrating on the flying aptitude tests which assess, amongst other things, natural physical co-ordination, perception and speed of thought—all vital for coping successfully with a modern, high-performance aircraft. The most effective means of predicting a person's ability to complete a flying course successfully is by a practical assessment of his performance in an aircraft. Because of the large number of applicants and the cost that would be involved, however, this method of selecting aircrew for training is impracticable. An alternative method, therefore, has been developed whereby a prediction of success in flying training can be made from a candidate's performance in a series of written and mechanical tests. To ensure that all candidates have identical conditions of testing, a standardized system of briefings is rigidly enforced and a triple check is carried out on the compilation of test results to ensure accuracy in marking.

The tests start with written papers which examine such aspects as logic and clear thinking, mechanical comprehension, and ability to interpret simple instruments. Such testing was first employed in the 1940s and has been refined by continuous experience gained since. However, for the pilot, the emphasis is, of course, on natural co-ordination and this is assessed on two machines. The first tests co-ordination between hand and eye and the second between hand, eye and foot.

When jet aircraft were first introduced it was found that aircrew were completing conversion on to such aircraft with similar success rates as with the previously slower aircraft, but that they were then having difficulty with the applied part of their training—for example, their instrument flying. As a result a further test was added to the aptitude tests previously described. The object of this additional test is to assess how well an individual can process rapidly changing information. This is effected by a special film during which a candidate is given a variety of pictorial information only some of which is of value to him in his assigned task. Work loads in a cockpit can be high and this test is of great value in highlighting those individuals potentially best suited to cope.

These aptitude tests have been meticulously validated and such validations are re-checked from time to time. They have given reasonably accurate predictions of those who are least likely to succeed in pilot training. The scores achieved during each of the aptitude tests are totalled, although one test may be given greater weighting than another. The tests do not attempt to establish a pass standard, but they do provide a sifting process which enables the Services, or training organization, to decide where to set the acceptable level for entry to pilot training.

TRAINING

It is convenient to discuss the training programme for military pilots since it generally covers a wider field of activities than those for civil pilots. Civil pilot training in the UK is described in a document published by The Air Transport and Travel Industry Training Board in their series of Training Studies (1973).

Basic training

Prior to starting the basic training stage of his flying course the student pilot is often given air experience in an elementary piston-powered trainer aircraft. For those who enter the Service direct from civil life this is likely to involve flying instruction to enable the student to become competent enough to go solo. On the other hand, the entrants from University will have gained their experience in the University Air Squadron and have gone solo and carried out various stages of further flying instruction on a similar elementary piston-powered aircraft. Both types of student pilot then start their basic flying training on a single-jet-engined aircraft. The course is divided into a ground phase which lasts about 1 month followed by a mixture of ground and flying training. The total time is 8 months.

The Ground School syllabus covers aerodynamics, mainly the basic and low performance aspects, but includes details of such things as range and endurance flying; airmanship including flying regulations; Air Traffic Control; a thorough grounding in the technical aspects of the aircraft he is to fly; meteorology; navigation and aviation medicine. Before completing Ground School the student has to pass examinations in the subjects he has been taught.

With this basic background and generally limited experience the student then starts his flying instruction. This comprises a total of about 100 hours dual and solo flying time and is divided into basic and applied stages. The basic stage involves approximately half the course's total flying. Initially the student is shown the effects of the controls, given general handling exercises, has circuits and landings demonstrated to him and is then guided through such exercises. During this initial stage, when he can carry out exercises to his instructor's satisfaction, he is given a pre-solo check. If he passes this he then makes his first solo flight. Complementary to these flying exercises the student is given exercises in a static procedural trainer, so that he is expected to be completely familiar with the aircraft cockpit and the various standard and emergency checks and actions.

Subsequently, his flying is made up mainly of dual sorties, but these are interspersed with solo flights where he is carefully briefed on the exercises he is to carry out. These often repeat those he has just completed with his instructor. As the course develops the student is introduced to more complicated handling exercises, including instrument flying, aerobatics, spinning, low flying, practice diversions to other airfields, practice emergencies both pre-briefed and surprise, and the use of navigation and radio aids. His instrument flying experience is increased by the use of an instrument flying simulator, in which he is put through representative exercises such as the correct instrument departure from, and let down to, his airfield. The simulator exercises are arranged to phase in with the instrument exercises in the air so that together they complement and enhance each other. The basic flying stage culminates in a Basic Handling Test, the satisfactory completion of which is necessary before starting the latter part of the course.

Throughout his flying training the student is assessed by his instructor and each dual sortie is 'written up'. If difficulties are experienced the student may be re-allocated to another instructor as this might overcome a lack of compatibility, or a personality clash between instructor and student. Such a switch also provides an opportunity for a second opinion on the student's ability. Should the student continue to experience difficulties the Flight Commander, who would have keen kept informed throughout, both by written reports and by discussion with his instructor, would probably check the student's ability. Depending on the student's performance on such a 'check flight' he may be suspended. Alternatively, subsequent instructional flights may concentrate on getting him to master one or two specific difficulties, which it is considered are hindering his overall progress.

Assuming the student completes the basic stage of his course he then starts the applied stage. This consists of more instrument flying so that he becomes sufficiently proficient to take his instrument rating test. More solo flying is included and this is extended to cover low level navigation techniques and procedures. A limited amount of night flying instruction and solo night flying takes place at about this stage. The student's experience is further widened by showing him any differences in handling at high altitudes and this would probably be combined with the use of the aircraft's radio and navigation aids and the services provided by Air Traffic Control Radar Units. At some stage he is tested, usually by an instructor other than his own, on his ability to navigate.

As with the basic stage of the course, exercises in the instrument flying simulator are planned to fit in with comparable flying exercises in the air.

Again, if a student is experiencing difficulties with instrument flying in the air, extra practice in the simulator is arranged. Throughout his flying the student's general flying ability is expected to improve. At the end of most dual sorties an instructor will probably ask the student to repeat manoeuvres or practice emergencies previously taught. The student is expected to consolidate on many aspects of his general handling during the solo flying periods. The applied stage of the course culminates with a final handling test which is often given by the Chief Flying Instructor or a Senior Instructor deputizing for him.

Advanced training

Once the basic flying training course has been satisfactorily completed the student is then ready to start his advanced flying training course. For the purposes of this paper it is assumed that he is selected for the single-engined advanced jet trainer course. Not surprisingly the course again starts with Ground School. Subjects covered in Ground School are the same as those for the basic course but with the addition of two subjects: Weapons and their Systems, and Signals.

The Ground School instruction revises on some of the subjects covered during the basic training course but uses it mostly as a foundation for expanding the subject. For example, during the aerodynamic lectures the theory of high-speed flight, shock waves and the aerodynamic implications of transonic flight are covered, as are stability, control, and inertia coupling. The lectures on airmanship are oriented to those aspects concerned with high-speed flight and the particular aircraft and its systems and the navigational instruction builds on the earlier lectures but then concentrates more on mental navigation and 'Dead Reckoning' methods. The additional lectures on Weapons cover warheads, fuzing and guidance systems, whilst the Signals phase deals in detail with those navigation aids in the aircraft which will be new to the student. The use of these aids and particularly their limitations are covered.

As during the basic training course, a cockpit trainer is employed in the Ground School phase to familiarize students with the cockpit layout and the standard and emergency drills. Ground School is concluded with examinations in all subjects which must be passed before the flying stage is started. The final part of the course comprises some 130 hours dual and solo flying. The exercises pre-solo are similar to those during the basic training course, but there is greater emphasis on the possible emergencies which could occur. Complementary exercises are programmed to be satisfactorily completed in a procedural instrument flying trainer at this and various stages of the course. Following first solo on type there is a period of 'consolidation' flying, both dual and solo, consisting of general handling, climb-out and let-down procedures and some instrument flying, including the use of the aircraft's navigational aids.

At this stage a progress check is carried out on each student by the Flight Commander. Assuming this check is passed satisfactorily the student is then made to concentrate on instrument flying until he is competent to pass his instrument rating test. The scope of the flying is then enlarged to include high-level navigation in transit to low-flying areas where low-level navigation is taught and practised. Night flying follows and then formation flying. As the end of the course approaches earlier exercises are revised by the student's instructor in preparation for the final handling test. The latter is usually carried out by the Chief Flying Instructor and as with all dual sorties the student's performance is assessed and recorded.

Operational conversion and role training

Once the pilot has completed his basic and advanced training he is ready to be sent to an Operational Conversion Unit (OCU) to gain experience on his operational aircraft and to receive instructions in the techniques and tactics to be used in combat. In this instance it is being assumed that the pilot is to join a Fighter Squadron and the examples given will be concerned with the Air Defence role.

The first month of the OCU Course is spent in Ground School. With the added complexity of the modern combat aircraft, most of this would be spent learning about the aircraft and its systems. It is here, if it is a two-crew aircraft, that the pilot will team up with his navigator. Together they will be put through exercises in the simulator, firstly to enable them to become thoroughly familiar with the layout of their cockpits and then with the use of the various systems, including all the standard and emergency drills. As in the earlier training courses, ground school examinations and simulator checks must be passed before the pilot and his navigator start the flying part of the course.

The flying is divided into various phases. The initial phase is concerned with converting the pilot to the aircraft. This involves dual instruction until he is fit to go solo. The remainder of this phase then quickly enlarges his experience on the aircraft by giving him general handling exercises, instrument flying, formation and a little night flying. A large proportion of this flying is under instruction but when the pilot flies solo exercises he will have his navigator with him. In this way every opportunity is taken to develop the necessary crew co-operation. This first phase takes up about a seventh of the total flying on the course. The bulk of the course is then devoted to developing the close crew co-operation so necessary in a high performance combat aircraft and to instructing both aircrew in all aspects of air defence and air combat. The flying includes a mixture of pilot instruction, which is more concerned with aircraft handling in given situations, and instruction by experienced staff navigators acting as the pilot's navigator in, for example, practice attacks on 'target' aircraft.

The pilot and his navigator are assessed by the Conversion Unit's Instructors on all exercises both in the air and in the simulator. They are then given a grading for each phase of the course and, subject to final checks, they are given an assessment of their overall proficiency for that aircraft and role. By now the pilot and his navigator will have reached the stage where they are considered fit to join an Operational Squadron. This is not meant to suggest that their periods of training and instruction are complete. They will still be closely supervised by their Flight and Squadron Commander, with the object of enabling them to become more and more proficient operationally. Their flying tasks will be monitored and efforts will be made to ensure that the flying tasks they are given are not too complicated nor possibly the weather conditions too demanding for their current skill and experience. The supervision will also include routine dual checks in the air and regular exercises in the simulator. Thus the training and assessing of the pilot, and also in this example his navigator, is a continuous process.

ASSESSMENT OF PROFICIENCY

It can be seen from the foregoing that a Service Pilot's proficiency can be assessed in three ways, first by his performance in Ground School, secondly in the simulator and thirdly in the air.

The knowledge he should have acquired in the classroom at Ground School reflects to some extent his previous standard of education. To this must be added the theoretical knowledge gained during the Ground School phases, and also his ability to soak up a great deal of information about aircraft and their mechanical, electrical, electronic, hydraulic or pneumatic systems. It is not too difficult to make an accurate assessment of an individual's work in the classroom. As a result of experience gained over the years with each new type of aircraft introduced, it is relatively easy to establish what should be the minimum pass mark in each examination and what overall level of knowledge the average student pilot should be able to attain.

The second part of pilot assessment involves simulators. These have been used for a long time in the training of pilots. They have varied from simple cockpit mock-ups which move slightly in pitch and $360°$ in azimuth and which were used for teaching basic instrument flying and instrument/radio navigation procedures, through those to train a pilot on a specific set of flight instruments, to a complicated and often large simulator which can simulate a long and realistic mission for a complete crew. It is this latter type of simulator which enables pilots to be tested on a whole series of emergencies and the appropriate emergency drills, which it would be considered imprudent to practice in the air on the real aircraft. All simulators, however simple or complex, enable the simulator instructor to compare the performance of different pilots, or crews, under almost identical circumstances. The performance of each pilot is 'written up' and this can be compared with the pilot's

behaviour in the air. The more advanced simulators enable crew performance as a whole to be assessed and are so realistic that a good indication of
the aircraft Captain's ability and manner as a Captain can be obtained.
Emergencies can be simulated and work-load increased so that the Captain's
or crew's ability under stress can be tested. This can be very informative to
the simulator instructors and can be beneficial to the individuals experiencing
such situations.

All simulators can be affected by the feeling in the back of the pilot's or
crew's minds that it is not real. Nevertheless, a simulator enables the experienced instructor to assess reasonably accurately a pilot's strong and weak
points. This knowledge can then be used either to arrange for extra practice
as necessary in the simulator or to forewarn the pilot's flying instructor of any
weaknesses. Training of pilots, or crews, in simulators provides many benefits in terms of the ability to familiarize aircrew with the cockpit layout, to
practice emergencies in reasonably realistic conditions, to teach instrument
and in some cases operational procedures and to do all these more cheaply
and safely than actually in the air. However, whilst the simulator can be used
to 'engineer' a situation of emergency or stress under virtually similar circumstances for each pilot it still poses the problem of how do you assess a pilot's
skill. There is no absolute value above which he is satisfactory or below
which he is inadequate. In fact, apart from being able to establish that a
pilot knows his standard and emergency drills either perfectly, adequately or
inadequately and applies them correctly and intelligently or otherwise, his
ability overall can best be assessed by comparing him with his predecessors
or the other pilots on the same course. Typical modern civil aircraft simulators are shown in Figures 9.2 and 3.

The third part of pilot assessment is carried out in the air. As already
outlined a Service student pilot is put through a series of stages of flying,
namely basic, advanced and operational, before reaching an operational
squadron. Within each of these stages there are distinct phases. For example,
in broad outline, each of them have conversion to the type of aircraft and
then a progressive expansion of the student's flying experience in terms of
general aircraft handling, instrument flying and other applied forms of
flying including training for combat.

Each of these phases introduces a new aspect of flying which, for the
student, may appear as another goal to be attained. The ease or difficulty
with which he attains this goal can be considered a measure of his skill, and
certainly a given instructor can compare his student's ability with others he
has instructed at a similar stage. However, assessment difficulties can arise.
For example, student 'A' may find one particular 'goal' easy to achieve
whilst another may find it difficult, yet for other 'goals', student 'A' may have
more difficulty than his colleagues. Moreover, an individual student's
motivation may well affect his performance. He may find the 'pure' flying
phase of his course necessary but somewhat boring whilst the applied phase,

Figure 9.2 Flight deck of a Trident flight simulator (By courtesy of Redifon Flight Simulation Ltd.)

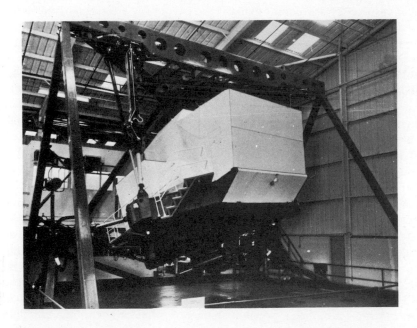

Figure 9.3 Tristar Flight Simulator (By courtesy of Redifon Flight Simulation Ltd.)

say practice bombing or low level navigation, enthralling, and hence his interest and enthusiasm may affect his apparent skill. This raises the difficulty of how an instructor can produce an overall assessment of his student for that phase of the course.

A further complication arises if, as can happen, the abilities of different flying instructors to teach certain phases of the course vary. This, too, can then be reflected in the ease or difficulty with which different students attain the 'goals'. It is at this point that the Flight Commander carrying out a progress check, or the independent instructor who is specially qualified to take students on, for example, instrument rating tests or on navigational tests is very useful. Not only will he be able to compare one student with another at the same stage but he can probably offer each useful guidance on how to improve his performance either generally or in specific areas.

ASSESSMENT CONSIDERATIONS

It must be apparent from the observation made in the preceding paragraphs that a student, or for that matter a qualified pilot converting to a new aircraft, can be tested, and be assessed objectively, on the knowledge he should have acquired during the Ground School part of his course.

A pilot can be further assessed in a simulator on his knowledge of the cockpit layout, the standard and emergency crew drills and actions and certain aspects of procedural flying. This part of his assessment can be near objective—that is, he either knows his drills and procedures to the required standard or he does not. In the modern simulator complete missions can be 'flown' and it can be arranged that the workload can be increased at similar parts of the mission. Consequently each pilot can be assessed on how well he handled the aircraft and the situation, and one pilot's performance can be compared reasonably fairly and accurately with another's. However, even under such controlled conditions it is still not possible to assess a pilot's skill in absolute terms.

The same situation applies, only more so, to assessing a pilot's skill in the air. In the first instance the training organization must decide and define what level of competence is required of a pilot at each stage of his flying training. This is not easy. How is the level of competence to be decided? Once this has been done, defining it in unambiguous terms can be a problem in itself. Once this level is decided an individual instructor must decide whether a student has achieved it satisfactorily. For example, one student may use his controls coarsely but keep the aircraft within the flying limits laid down, whilst another may fly smoothly but just exceed these limits. Which is the better pilot and who says so?

As previously outlined, when a student is some way through his flying course he will be expected to cope satisfactorily with practice emergencies. This is, in effect, not only a method of practising the emergency drills but of increasing the student's work-load; but at what stage of any flight should this increased work-load be applied and how can an instructor know that for comparative purposes, he is applying the same work-load to another student during a similar stage of flight? Another aspect affecting the assessment of a pilot is how well he 'commands' the situation or emergency in flight versus his actual skill at flying the aircraft. It is no use having a skilful pilot if he panics under pressure, nor conversely, an imperturbable pilot who cannot control the aircraft accurately, but what 'trade-off' between the two can be accepted?

So there are real problems in trying to assess a pilot's skill in absolute terms. It is possible to argue that when a Service pilot has reached the Operational Conversion Unit, his ability can be assessed objectively by his results when bombing, rocketing or in air combat, but this covers only one phase, albeit an important one, of his course. His instrument flying ability can be assessed during his instrument rating test and his 'pure' flying during a final handling test. But how good is his airmanship, discipline in the air and Captaincy when he is flying without an instructor or just with his own navigator or crew?

It seems, therefore, that a flying training organization can train a pilot by putting him through a series of flying, navigation and weapon exercises which lead on progressively and logically to more and more demanding flying tasks and eventually to his being either suspended or regarded as a reliable and safe pilot. This conclusion will represent an overall assessment of the skills he has demonstrated throughout the various phases of the course both on the ground and in the air. It must inevitably include an assessment of his character as his reliability and judgement will have been reflected in many of the decisions he had made in the air. Despite the various checks which the pilot will have been given by instructors other than his own, it will still not be possible to rate a pilot's skill in objective terms. However, the training system is so organized that the skill of every student pilot can be assessed with reasonable accuracy against that of his colleagues on the same course and against that of the pilots who have preceded him. His skill will therefore be graded as average, above the average or below the average, which implies that he is being compared with his colleagues of equal flying experience.

OPERATIONAL EFFECTIVENESS AS A MEASURE OF SKILL

As already stated the prime objects of aircrew training are to promote flight safety and to increase operational efficiency. The effectiveness of military pilots can be measured in exercises by recording miss distances of practice bombs or similar parameters, but the wide variability in the operational circumstances, e.g. visibility, wind, etc, do not usually enable such scores to be used for grading the ability of particular pilots. However, they are used in inter-squadron competitions and are assumed to reflect the skill shown by the contestants. They could be developed to give more objective marking of the pilots skill but would prove to be prohibitively expensive to apply in a useful fashion.

The main objective behind cost effectiveness studies of military operations is to meet economically the operational requirements which, since they must be forward looking to be worthwhile, must inevitably be somewhat nebulous and subject to change in emphasis and priority. Up to now it has been the practice to rely on the human operator to provide a large part of the flexibility in the operational use of any aircraft or weapon system. This has led to increases in cockpit workload, often accompanied by adverse cockpit environments in the form of cramped working space, acceleration forces, vibration, noise, extreme temperature and poor visibility. But at present our yardsticks for assessing the skill of the pilot in overcoming the environment and coping with the operational tasks are crude, so that any attempt to define the cost effectiveness of a system in which the man–machine relationship is important is highly unlikely to provide a definitive answer.

We have now entered an era where much more attention will be directed towards an integrated approach to aircraft systems and their human operators and any measure of skill should reflect how well the man integrates with his system. It should also recognize that the role of the pilot is no longer primarily that of the highly dextrous and resourceful Battle of Britain fighter pilot and that much more emphasis in future will be placed on his technical ability and his ability to manage, programme and monitor a sophisticated avionics system.

OPERATIONAL SAFETY

Civil and military pilots attain a very high level of operational safety. At present the fatal accident rate in scheduled civil flying is about 4 in 1 million flights. The rate for all types of flying in the RAF is about twice this figure. About one half of the accidents are superficially attributed to pilot error which might be deemed to indicate some lack of skill. There is also some evidence that the percentage of accidents attributed to crew error decreases as experience on a particular aircraft increases with the passage of time. This would confirm that pilots develop their skills partly from experience on the job, and that particular skills are needed for particular aircraft. However, when one studies accidents in detail the description of 'pilot error' becomes somewhat elusive. Whatever verdict is arrived at after studying an aircraft accident in detail, the resulting action, if any, must be either: to alter the aircraft to remedy defects in the aircraft or its system; to change some part of the operating system outside the aircraft e.g. air traffic control; or to alter the aircrew, that is by changing selection, discipline and training.

When a deficiency in pilots' skill is recognized after an accident almost inevitably training procedures are re-examined and possibly amended.

Luckily accidents happen too rarely for them to be regarded as any effective measure of pilots' lack of skill, but by studying accidents in some detail it is nevertheless possible to divide crew errors roughly in a somewhat arbitrary fashion. Figure 9.4 indicates such a breakdown of Civil Aircraft accidents attributed to Crew Error compiled by H. C. Black of the Airworthiness Division of the Civil Aviation Authority.

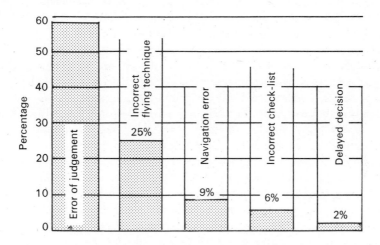

Figure 9.4   Causes of crew error accidents (Five types of aircraft)

Errors of judgement cover over 50% of the accidents listed. If a pilot takes a wrong decision it can only be because at a particular moment he was confronted with a task which was beyond his capacity, insufficient or wrong information was supplied to him or he was guessing. These factors we can study today in the flight simulators used for ground training purposes. The cost in time and money of introducing training programmes which would ensure that all pilots had been adequately trained to cope with all the possible situations which might arise in which judgement was required would undoubtedly be prohibitive. Civil airline and military training programmes today are a mixture of tradition and experience in which practical people try to ensure that the important lessons learnt from past accidents are incorporated in the training schedules, while keeping the total training costs down to a financially acceptable level. It would appear that for civil aircraft the perceptual and decision-making skills ought to rank high in the qualities required from a professional pilot. It is only under the heading of incorrect flying technique that motor skills appear and even here perceptual and decision making skills are probably equally important.

It is also clear that accidents occur too rarely for the lessons learned from them to be used in a systematic study of pilot skill. Some airlines are introducing reporting schemes which enable pilots to record anonymously, incidents that occur, but in general these are mainly used to record deficiencies of aircraft and air traffic control systems and do not give a useful commentary on pilot errors. The Advisory Group for Aerospace Research and Development of the North Atlantic Treaty Organization have organized a number of conferences to focus attention on the lessons to be learned from Accidents and Incidents. AGARD (1970) placed emphasis on Flight Mechanics but the importance of correct pilot training and drill was often emphasized whereas design implications were relatively less clear. AGARD (1971) discussed the incidents due to disorientation and AGARD (1973) looked at behavioural aspects of aircraft accidents. Beaty (1969) has reviewed the human factors which contribute to aircraft accidents and has indicated areas of research which are required to improve air safety.

It appears that for many years to come the skill of the pilot will be assessed by the 'check pilot', civil or military, who supervises his simulator and in-flight training. In making his assessment the check pilot will ensure that the subject understands the aircraft systems sufficiently well to enable him to rectify faults, he will check his flying, navigation and operational techniques, he will watch that he follows the agreed procedures and check lists and he will confront him with a number of arbitrarily chosen difficult situations to check the accuracy and speed of his response. The emphasis in training will be on decision making and management skills and the assessment will largely be based on the check pilot's own operational experience. Although it may be considered scientifically unsatisfactory, this approach to training and pilot skill obviously works fairly well, otherwise the accident rates now achieved in civil and military aviation would not be so low.

RESEARCH INTO PILOT SKILL

Since aviation research has given an enormous impetus to Applied Psychological, Human Factors and Ergonomic Studies, the conclusion in the previous paragraph that we still in practice rely on the judgement of his peers to assess a pilot's skill, may seem somewhat anachronistic and this is why we have given a lengthy account of their selection, training and assessment. A lot of work has been done to identify and describe the skills of the pilot based on detailed and objective studies of both military and civil aviation. These have shown that analysis of skills must pay due attention to the many different types of operation. For example, the single seat pilot's task is markedly different from those of the crews of multi-seat aircraft where work sharing and crew co-operation are so important. The ability of the pilot to display his skill in unusual environments and the particular stresses which are encountered in aviation are also important factors.

AGARD (1972) includes the papers presented at a Conference organized to cover the more important aspects of combined stresses in military operations which discussed heat, noise, vibration and acceleration. This was followed with a specialist meeting directed towards vibration effects, AGARD (1974). The Royal Aeronautical Society (1973) also arranged a symposium on the Flight Deck Environment and Pilot Workload. There have been a number of conferences organized by the Advisory Group for Aerospace Research and Development of the North Atlantic Treaty Organization directed towards the assessment of skill and the measurement of performance. AGARD (1966) reports a conference in Toronto in which R. E. F. Lewis compared the solo and dual navigation performance of helicopter pilots and E. Riis reported on the measurement of performance in a F-86K flight simulator. H. F. Huddleston described problems arising in measuring the pilot's contribution in the aircraft control loop. AGARD (1969) reports a conference to consider the flight deck workload and its relation to pilot performance which indicated that, despite the considerable effort expended on the recording of physiological variables in real and simulated flight, clarification of the interpretation of such data was still required. The proceedings include a paper by C. A. Brictson describing operational measures of pilot performance during aircraft carrier landings and a paper by C. L. Kraft and C. L. Elworth reporting a simulator assessment of night visual approach performance. A number of papers recording in-flight measurement of pilot performance are presented in AGARD (1974a) reporting a conference on Take-Off and Landing and this reference also contains some good descriptions of one of the more difficult parts of the pilot's task.

In general for fairly obvious reasons there have been more attempts to measure the performance of pilots in simulation than in flight. Typical are the papers by Perry and Burnham (1967) which looks at pilots' difficulties in turbulence and Tomlinson and Wilcock (1969 and 1970) which report on simulation studies of take-off and landing of the Concorde. A number of papers have attempted to correlate flight and simulator measurements with mathematical models to validate manual control theory, for example, Weir and McRuer (1972) and to extend the synthesis of displays, Weir and Klein (1970). Rolfe and Lindsay (1973) have examined some of the techniques that are being used to study the demands of the work situation upon the individual pilot and conclude that performance measures wherever possible should be supplemented by the addition of measures which can give an indication of the nature of the demands that the task imposes upon the individual and of the effort he expends to meet these demands—none of the reports and papers mentioned cover all these aspects.

We have now reached a stage where parts of the pilots task have been measured, sometimes with precision. Much of the human factor work undertaken has led to improved cockpit environments, better man–machine integration, better operating techniques and procedures. We are still a long way from a scientifically based rating which may be used to assess pilot's skill in absolute terms.

References

AGARD (1966). Assessment of Skill and Performance in Flying. *Advisory Group for Aerospace Research and Development Conference Proceedings No. 14 North Atlantic Treaty Organisation*

AGARD (1969). Measurement of Aircrew Performance. *AGARD/NATO Conference Proceedings No. 56*

AGARD (1970). Lessons with Emphasis on Flight Mechanics from Operating Experience, Incidents and Accidents. *AGARD/NATO Conference Proceedings No. 76*

AGARD (1971). The Disorientation Incident. *AGARD/NATO Conference Proceedings No. 95*

AGARD (1972). Performance and Biodynamic Stress—Influence of Interacting Stresses on Performance. *AGARD/NATO Conference Proceedings No. 101*

AGARD (1973). Behavioural Aspects of Aircraft Accidents. *AGARD/NATO Conference Proceedings No. 132*

AGARD (1974). Vibration and Combined Stresses in Advanced Systems. *AGARD/ NATO Conference Proceedings No. 145*

AGARD (1974a). Take-Off and Landing. *AGARD/NATO Conference Proceedings No. 160*

Armstrong, H. G. (1961). *Aerospace Medicine* (London: Bailliere, Tindal and Cox)

ATTIB (1973). Training Airline Co-pilots. Air Transport and Travel Industry Training Board

Beaty (1969). *The Human Factor in Accidents* (London: Secker and Warburg)

Carol, W. L. (1965). *Pictorial Displays for Flight.* Hughes Aircraft Company, Culver City, California

Cassie, A., Fokkema, S. D. and Parra, J. B. (1964). *Aviation Psychology* (The Hague; Paris: Mouton & Co.)

Davies, D. P. (1971). *Handling the Big Jets.* Air Registration Board, Redhill, Surrey

Perry, D. H. and Burnham, J. (1967). A Flight Simulation Study of Difficulties in Piloting Large Jet Transport Aircraft Through Severe Atmospheric Disturbances. *Aeronautical Research Council*, Current Papers No. 906, HMSO, London

Rolfe, J. M. and Lindsay, S. J. E. (1973). Flight Deck Environment and Pilot Workload: Biological Measures of Workload. *Applied Ergonomics*, **4.4**, 199

Royal Aeronautical Society (1973). Flight Deck Environment and Pilot Workload— *Proceedings, Royal Aeronautical Society*, 4 Hamilton Place, London

Smode, A. E., Hall, E. R. and Mayer, D. E. (1966). *An Assessment of Research Relevant to Pilot Training.* Aerospace Medical Research Labs. Wright Patterson AFB. AMRL 66–196

Tomlinson, B. N. and Wilcock, T. (1969). A Piloted Simulation of the Take-Off of a Supersonic Transport Aircraft, with and without a Take-Off Director. *Aeronautical Research Council*, Reports and Memoranda No. 3594, HMSO, London

Tomlinson, B. N. and Wilcock, T. (1971). Further Piloted Simulation Studies of the Handling Characteristics of a Slender-Wing Supersonic Transport Aircraft during Approach and Landing. *Aeronatucial Research Council.* Reports and Memoranda No. 3660, HMSO, London

Trankell, A. (1969). The SAS System for the Selection of Pilots. *Flight Safety V3*, Nos. 2, 3 and 4

Weir, D. H. and McRuer, D. T. (1972). Pilot Dynamics for Instrument Approach Tasks: Full Panel Multiloop and Flight Director Operations. *National Aeronautics and Space Administration*, Contractor Report CR 2019, Washington DC

Weir, D. H. and Klein, R. A. (1970). The Measurement of Pilot Scanning and Control Behaviour During Simulated Instrument Approaches. *National Aeronautics and Space Administration*, Contractor Report CR 1535, Washington DC

10

The Air-Traffic Controller

D. WHITFIELD and R. B. STAMMERS

INTRODUCTION

To the layman, air-traffic control is one of the more exotic jobs created by advanced technology, on a par with computers, high speed aircraft and complex chemical plant. For the applied psychologist, too, it presents a variety of interesting facets: it is a very new profession, concerned with rapidly developing procedures and equipment, and there is considerable evidence of high task demands on the human beings within the system. Air-traffic control (ATC) tasks are prime examples of the trend towards a reliance on perceptual and cognitive skills, and away from the more familiar motor skill demands of craft work.

Objectives

The objectives of an ATC service, as defined by the International Civil Aviation Organization, are to:
1. Prevent collisions between aircraft in the air,
2. Assist in preventing collisions between aircraft moving on the apron or on the manoeuvring area of an airport, and between aircraft and obstructions on the manoeuvring area,
3. Expedite and maintain an orderly flow of air traffic,
4. Provide information useful for the safe and efficient conduct of flights,
5. Notify appropriate organizations regarding aircraft in need of search and rescue aid, and assist such organizations as required.

Thus, safety, expediency, and orderliness are the essential desiderata of the ATC system. *Safety* is a self-evident objective in any transport system and no more so than in aviation, where the consequences of accidents can be very severe. This requirement most clearly conveys the criticality of the controller's task, and it underlies the sometimes rather conservative assessments which are applied to any proposals for amending ATC equipment and procedures. *Expediency* is rather less obvious, except perhaps to the airline passenger who regularly experiences a queue for take-off at a busy airport. However, the direct economics of expediency have been emphasized recently by the sudden rise in fuel costs, and airline companies are becoming much more aware of the quality of the ATC service they receive. More efficient ATC procedures, such as 'clean' descents into airports, without diversions or holding in 'stacks', can produce considerable savings in fuel. *Orderliness* implies adherence to established rules and procedures; this is important in that both pilots and air-traffic control officers (ATCOs) should be able to predict, or at least be prepared for, the actions of each other. It is important also that ATC systems, which operate in an international context, should deal impartially with the aircraft of different countries.

This discussion of the objectives of ATC should conclude with two qualifications. First, as Hopkin (1971) has pointed out, given that safety is the prime concern, there are inevitable conflicts between the various facets of the other two objectives. Human factors investigators must also take into account relevant measures of the effect of the system on the ATCO himself. Hopkin's paper is a detailed discussion of the various measures for evaluating ATC systems, and, while many of the problems are common to other complex man–machine systems, it is clear that ATC research is a very difficult area.

Second, we must remember that 'on-line' or 'real-time' ATC, as we are considering it here, is only the tactical front line of 'a hierarchy of control loops, each serving to convert a traffic demand into a potential traffic flow'. (Ratcliffe and Gent, 1974). Their model of the interlocking series of control loops is shown in Figure 10.1. Each control loop has a characteristic prediction time, over which it assesses potential problems and takes action to cope with them. Some unresolved problems, within the handling capacity of the lower loop(s), are left for resolution further down the chain. Thus, the ATCO is operating always within a framework of constraints set by the superior control loops, and any research must take account of this and perhaps contemplate changes higher up in the family of control loops.

Evolution of the ATC system

During the late 1930s the first formal ATC systems were introduced, to assist aircraft flying on defined 'airways' between airports. This pioneering system was very crudely equipped. Radio communication with pilots was rather limited, and often was indirect, the ATCO relying on a separate radio

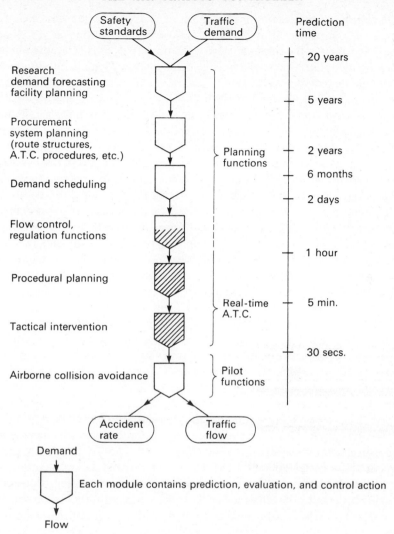

Figure 10.1 Hierarchy of ATC control loops (after Ratcliffe and Gent, 1974)

operator. The ATCO kept track of aircraft positions by listing the aircraft under his control and noting significant amendments as reported by pilots. Since then, the demands of air traffic have increased enormously: there are many more aircraft, and they travel much faster. These demands have been met partly by technological advances. Beginning in World War II, communications facilities and radar equipment became available to provide ATC with the tools it needed. Subsequently, the whole ATC system has been formalized on an international basis, and the major developments are listed below.

Standardization of rules and procedures: International agreement is obviously essential, and the International Civil Aviation Organization has developed precise definitions of the rules underlying the objectives of ATC quoted in our opening paragraphs. A good example is the concept of 'separation standards' —minimum spacing between a pair of aircraft, and below which the aircraft are considered to be 'in conflict' with each other. Typical separation standards for aircraft under radar control are 5 nautical miles horizontally and 1000 ft vertically, though these are subject to modification under defined circumstances. From the ATCO's point of view, the net result of developing this set of complex definitions is that there is a weighty rule-book to assimilate.

Communications: Radio-telephone (R/T) communication between pilots and ATCOs is now direct and efficient in operation. Typically, the controller broadcasts on a frequency which is received by all pilots under his control, and so they can all note his instructions to nearby aircraft. Communications on the ground have improved, too. Telephone or intercom links with other controllers and support staff are available, and computer-based communications systems are being introduced, one example being the automatic printing and distribution of 'flight progress strips' giving the intentions of aircraft, and another the instantaneous presentation of alphanumeric information on cathode-ray-tube displays. From the pilot's point of view, there have been major advances in the provision of electronic navigational facilities, and so he is able to follow ATC instructions much more accurately.

'Radar control' superseding 'procedural control': In the early days, information on aircraft position came solely from communication with the pilot. He notified his arrival at 'reporting points' along the route, and the ATCO recorded these reports in relation to the flight plan on the flight progress strip. The safe separation of aircraft depended on procedures which made use of these discrete indications of aircraft position, and so the technique is known as 'procedural control'. The advent of reliable radar facilities has made possible 'radar control' with a continuous indication of aircraft position. The major benefits to the efficiency of the ATC system are that radar separation standards can safely be smaller than procedural separation standards, and that the ATCO has an integrated visual presentation of the aircraft under his control. Procedural methods are employed as a back-up to radar systems, and they are still the principal method in some areas. However, the trend towards radar control is a very significant development in ATC, particularly in relation to the increasing traffic demand.

Developments in radar: Over the years, the actual geographical coverage of radar systems has improved, and the displays for the ATCO have become more effective. Displays may be bright enough for use in normal lighting conditions, 'visual noise' has been reduced, and maps are superimposed on the radar picture to help the controller. In some areas, primary radar is accompanied by a newer system, Secondary Surveillance Radar (SSR), which depends on aircraft being equipped with transponders, which are activated by the signal from the ground-based radar and which return a unique identification. In fact, suitably equipped aircraft will respond automatically with a code identifying the aircraft and giving a read-out of its altitude. With appropriate computer input to the radar display, this means that the 'blip' representing the aircraft can be labelled with the call-sign of the aircraft and its altitude, two items of information which are not directly available with the basic 'primary' radar system.

Computer assistance: Developments in ATC are beginning to involve on-line computers; indeed, on-line data processing is implicit in the SSR aircraft labelling scheme discussed above. There are several possible advantages in transmitting and displaying data such as flight plans by means of computer systems. However, those applications are fairly conventional examples of using a computer to process, store and display basic data. There are now investigations of computer techniques for helping the controller in his decision making. For example, the Computer Assisted Approach Sequencing (CAAS) program devised by the Royal Signals and Radar Establishment computes the optimum routes for a set of aircraft landing at London Heathrow airport. The aim is to maximize runway usage by having aircraft land at the minimum spacing, and the computer works out the length and pattern of flight for each aircraft from the holding stack to the runway. If the controller accepts these suggestions, the computer will then monitor progress and indicate when course changes are necessary (a more detailed description of CAAS is given by Peters, 1973). Further computer applications, such as predicting aircraft trajectories and arranging optimum queues of take-offs, will be discussed later. For the present, it is sufficient to emphasize that computer-assistance, and the difficult questions of specifying the optimum type and level of such assistance, are the latest features in the development of ATC systems.

ATC as a profession: Along with the development of procedures and equipment, ATC has emerged as a distinct profession. There are careful selection procedures, lengthy training schemes and a well-defined career structure. Commitment to the preservation of standards and interest in the job is represented by the existence of national and international professional bodies. The size of the profession is also a significant indicator; in the UK there are approximately 3000 fully trained ATCOs, in the USA 50 000, and the international total must be at least 200 000. (There are only rough estimates, and they comprise civil and military personnel. If the totals seem large, it must be remembered that most ATC services are operated 24 hrs a day, 7 days a week.)

Current and future demands on ATC

We shall be referring to these again in our later discussions, but it is useful to make some brief comments now. Increased fuel costs and general economic conditions have slowed down the increase in traffic, but a steadily rising demand is predicted. The airways network is divided into sectors, each of which is controlled by one ATCO or a small group of ATCOs, and a superficial solution to higher traffic densities could be to have more, but smaller, sectors. However, this would simply increase the amount of inter-sector communication necessary when handing-over aircraft, or otherwise co-ordinating activities, and the returns from this solution rapidly diminish.

Economic considerations dictate that fuel costs should be trimmed by the efficient handling of aircraft: this extends from the ATCO descending or climbing one particular aircraft, to the arrangement of efficient 'flow control' over an international area such as Europe (which in turn imposes constraints on individual ATCOs). Another facet of economics might be the most efficient use of the available manpower, and this is one possible benefit of computer applications.

This last point leads on to the effect of procedures and equipment on the ATCO himself. There is some evidence already that ATC tasks can involve high levels of strain in controllers (we shall discuss this further, later). Future systems must take account of this, and one particular aspect which concerns us at the moment is the effects of computer assistance. At the one extreme, some computer applications have actually resulted in *more* work for controllers in inputting data to the system, while the other extreme is for performance and motivation to suffer because tasks become dull and uninteresting. It is very important that the optimum balance is struck between controller and computer, and our discussion of ATCO skills will be influenced by this consideration.

Human factors in ATC

Historically, one of the first comprehensive human factors assessments of a man–machine system is that of Fitts (1951) on ATC. A more recent general examination of ATC in the United States, together with rather sketchy outline plans for further research and development, is given by Older and Cameron (1972). The standard reference is the large scale review by Hopkin (1970a), who categorizes human factors problems in ATC and relates to them the published research in ATC and in other man–machine systems.

Sources of more detailed individual papers are an issue of *Ergonomics* (vol. 14, no. 5, September 1971) and two AGARD Conference Proceedings (1975, 1976). Finally, a very readable and comprehensive description of the ATC system as a whole is given by Gilbert (1973), while an Open University text (Peters, 1973) covers limited aspects.

ATC TASKS

In the previous section we set out the objectives of an ATC system. These objectives—the primary emphasis on safety, but with increasing concern for efficiency of aircraft handling—extend to the various divisions of ATC, but the practical implications may vary. Thus, we must examine briefly the organization of ATC, and the major differences in the ATCOs' tasks. We have limited space here, but further detail is given in the general references discussed above (Gilbert, 1973; Hopkin, 1970a; Peters, 1973).

We shall discuss only *controlled air space*, where aircraft are required to fly under ATC guidance (although in the final, legal, analysis the pilot has ultimate responsibility for the safety of his aircraft), with reliance on flight instruments rather than on purely visual contact with the outside world. In controlled air space, aircraft fly along geographically defined corridors or airways. As mentioned already, the airways network is divided into sectors each controlled by individual ATCOs or groups of ATCOs: this type of control is known as *en-route* or *sector control*. Around major airports, Terminal Areas (TMAs) are defined, to deal with traffic merging from several airways and to direct aircraft on to the runway approaches: thus *TMA control* is another major division. The airport itself has separate control functions, dealing with landing and departing aircraft and with aircraft and other vehicle movements on the ground: this is defined as *aerodrome control*. Finally, *oceanic control* is another division, dealing in a fully procedural mode with aircraft flying across oceans, where full radar coverage is impossible. We shall discuss further only sector control and aerodrome control, they are the areas in which we are working at present.

In general terms, ATC tasks are management tasks, with special emphasis on planning the operation of a system involving a number of individuals (pilots) and on monitoring the success of these plans and re-planning if necessary. The planning aspect involves the allocation of resources (air-space runways, etc.) between individuals, within a complex framework of rules and procedures. As Kelley (1968) emphasizes, control is directed towards the future, and the controller must be able to identify possible future states of the system, choose one as a goal, and initiate a train of events leading to the goal. His monitoring of progress towards the goal then depends on receiving information from various sources.

The ATCO's training follows fairly conventional lines. In the UK, the basic training course can be up to 3 years, and it comprises a large academic component supported by simulation exercises and practical experience. The trainee gains extensive knowledge of aircraft operation, and he has often the opportunity of learning to fly. The essential ATC Licence is conferred by the Civil Aviation Authority on the successful completion of written, oral and practical examinations, together with a stringent medical test. The licence denotes what types of ATC service the holder is qualified to give: aerodrome control, various types of sector control, and so on. Thus, the ATCO has to be qualified for the particular type of control, but the rigours of assessment do not end here: the final requirement is to be 'validated' for a particular ATC installation, where he has to demonstrate, through oral and practical examinations, that he is thoroughly familiar with local equipment and procedures. He must repeat the validation process at each new unit in which he works, thoughout his career, and the annual renewal of his licence depends on continuing medical examinations.

Sector control

The sector controller receives advance warning of aircraft due to enter his sector, by means of the flight progress strips which are distributed to him. He then identifies, and takes over responsibility for, the aircraft when it enters his sector and has been handed-over by the controller of the preceding sector. This hand-over involves the aircraft pilot changing over his R/T channel while, at the ATC centre, the two controllers may consult each other by telephone or use a previously agreed 'silent' procedure if the aircraft is manoeuvring normally. For a given aircraft, the sector controller must preserve the legal separation from other aircraft while within his sector, provide if possible the required flight path (or, if not, he may 'clear' the pilot to a different level, or otherwise modify the requested path), give any other assistance which the pilot may require, and finally hand-over the aircraft to the next sector. For a given sector there may well be specific requirements, such as descending or climbing aircraft to certain flight levels before leaving the sector; if this is not achieved, the controller may be creating additional problems for his neighbour. Other complications may be junctions between two or more airways, and requests from aircraft to join an airway, or to cross it, from regions outside controlled air space.

   N. Vernon (1975) has listed the information required by the sector controller, and the sources of the information, as shown in Table 10.1.

   A typical radar display for a sector controller is shown in Figure 10.2. Note the SSR labels on some of the blips, and the superimposed geographical detail of the airway structure.

Aerodrome control

The aerodrome controller is concerned essentially with aircraft landing and taking off from an airport, and taxying or being manoeuvred on the airport surface. Other vehicles also come under control when they are moving on 'active' areas of the airport. An important element of control here is the 'visual' one, in that the aircraft and vehicles under control are usually within human visual range. Radar is used, but as an addition to the 'view from the window', rather than as an alternative, except under difficult weather conditions. The two main radars used are small daylight types, showing aircraft on their final approach to the runway (DFTI) and—an even shorter range— showing movement on the airport surface (UK: ASMI, USA: ASDE).

Table 10.1 Information required by sector controller, and sources of such information (from N. Vernon, 1975)

Information	*Source(s)*
Aircraft present position	Radar display or via R/T
Aircraft present height	Radar display (SSR) or via R/T
Aircraft intention	Flight Plan display or via R/T
Separation standards	Memory or documentation
Route structure	Memory or map display
SSR code allocation	Display list
ATC operating instructions	Memory or documentation
Meteorological information	Display
Aeronautical information, permanent or temporary (e.g. range, frequency and call sign of navigational aids; hazards to aircraft)	Display boards
Aircraft performance	Experience and documentation
Hand-over procedures	Standard or telephone
Flight Plan amendments	Telephone or R/T
Adjacent Sector or ATC Unit R/T frequencies	Memory or display lists
Emergency procedures	Display lists

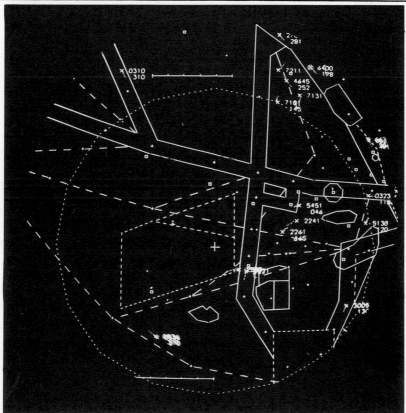

Figure 10.2 A typical radar display (with SSR labels) for the sector controller (Crown copyright)

Inasmuch as it is concerned with the processing of aircraft demands, the sources of information given in Table 10.1 for the sector controller are the same, with the addition of the 'real world display'. Figure 10.3 shows aerodrome controllers at work. Whilst it may be thought that aircraft manoeuvring at slow speed on the ground would be an inherently safer situation than in the air, it should be pointed out that 'conflicts' can occur in this area (Hopkin, 1973) and collisions have taken place.

Figure 10.3   The visual control room (VCR) at London Heathrow airport (Crown copyright)

The basic procedures involved again are similar to sector control in that, in response to aircraft demands via R/T and requested flight plan, the aircraft is 'cleared' through various areas of the airfield as it arrives or departs. In essence, each basic operation is a fairly simple procedure on its own; difficulties enter in when a number of aircraft are simultaneously manoeuvring. On a small airport one controller will cover all aspects of control, while at major airports the tasks will be divided between several controllers. At London Heathrow, there may be up to seven controllers and assistants in the visual control room (VCR) at busy periods.

ATC SKILLS

How does the controller undertake, and succeed with, the tasks which are assigned to him? To the best of our knowledge, the only attempt in the literature to list the ATCO's skills is that by Older and Cameron (1972). In Table 10.2, we have adapted their presentation (their Table 7, p. 45) to impose a further classification of input/processing/output skills.

Table 10.2 ATCO skills (adapted from Older and Cameron, 1972)

Input skills

Visual Monitoring (Display): to attend to a continuously changing visual information source and report system status on request.
(Examples: observation of CRT, meters, counters).
Visual Monitoring (Non-display): to attend to a continuously changing visual information source and report system status on request.
(Examples: observing aircraft patterns, signal lights, runways).
Auditory Monitoring: to attend to a continuously changing auditory information source and report system status on request.
(Examples: listening for radio, telephone, intercom. messages or warning signals).
Reading: the rapid and accurate extraction of relevant information from written or printed material, on the basis of limited exposure.
(Examples: reading flight progress strips, telex messages, weather sequences, frequency changes, tables, maps, charts).

Processing skills

Information Organization: the evaluation, synthesis, and integration of information from varied visual or auditory sources.
(Examples: simultaneous consideration of type of aircraft, relative speed, manoeuvrability and cockpit visibility; integrating weather information from a variety of sources).
Selecting Among Alternatives: predicting, on the basis of all available information, which of a number of alternatives optimizes system function.
(Examples: path selection, conflict detection, delay precaution).
Information Storage: the short-term retention of recently acquired material—information subject to immediate recall.
(Examples: remembering such information as radio frequencies, aircraft identification information, wind conditions and flight paths, sequences of aircraft).

Output skills

Recording: the preparation of written messages, information and reports.
(Examples: preparing flight progress strips and weather sequences; encoding flight data).
Reporting: transmitting oral messages, information, reports.
(Examples: oral flight path instructions, altitude instructions, weather reports, co-ordination with other sectors and centres).
Control operations: applying manual force to equipment or controls once a response has been selected and a decision to act has been made.
(Examples: manipulating tuning controls, cursors, tracker balls, touch wires; teletyping).

We find this 'system-oriented' classification useful, in that it forces us to consider the skills in relation to the dominant demands of the task. It clarifies also the major importance of those skills which we have listed under the 'Processing Skills' heading. The majority of the 'Input' and 'Output' skills listed are similar to other system control tasks, and indeed many of

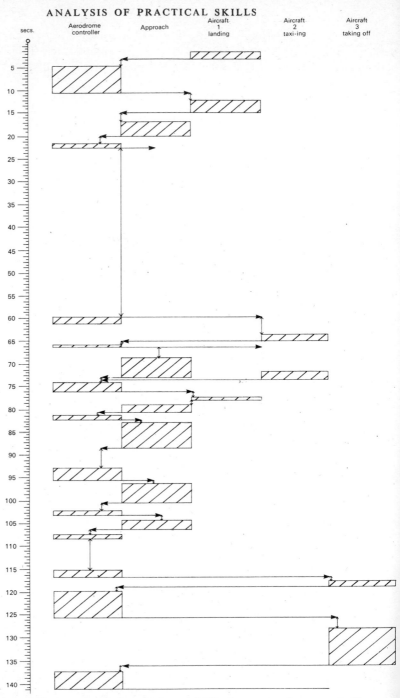

Figure 10.4 A typical sequence of time-sharing activities for an aerodrome controller (Shaded boxes represent messages, single arrows indicate direction of message, double-headed vertical arrows represent pauses)

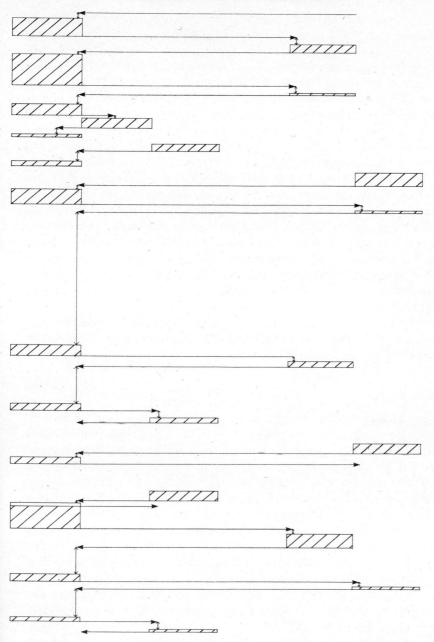

Figure 10.4

them, such as reading and operating controls, depend on very general experience. It is the central processing of information which characterizes the unique complexity of ATC tasks, and it is significant that here we find a greater diversity of strategies and tactics, both between different controllers and between the same controller's actions under varying conditions.

There is a pervasive feature underlying most of these separate skills, and we draw attention to it here because it seems to characterize the complexity and demands of the ATCO's job. It is very common for him to be handling a number of aircraft simultaneously. The en-route controller may have several aircraft at various stages through the sector; the TMA controller is responsible for a steady stream of aircraft approaching the major airport; the aerodrome controller takes over the stream, and has to insert outbound aircraft into the gaps. Although he has displays of the aircraft details, the controller will typically keep in short-term memory the major details of these constantly changing streams. He will respond to R/T calls from any of them, even if it interrupts some other control activity. This agile 'time-sharing' between transient aircraft is very striking. Figure 10.4 shows a short sequence of aerodrome controller activities which illustrates this, and Soede *et al.* (1971) have made similar observations.

We turn now to some of the detailed evidence which develops the brief descriptions given in Table 10.2, and we shall concentrate most of our discussions on the 'Processing Skills'.

Input skills

A major change relating to input skills has been the increasing reliance on radar control rather than on procedural control. Under procedural control alone, the controller's basic input came from the array of flight progress strips, and he arranged these by reporting points and flight levels, so as to create some representation of the overall traffic situation. Leplat and Bisseret (1966) made several studies of controllers' strategies of using such information and they distinguish two alternative approaches shown by different controllers. The more efficient means of predicting possible conflicts for a new aircraft entering the sector is to make comparisons first in terms of relative flight levels across the whole sector. A less efficient, but apparently more common, method is to put the initial emphasis on geographical position comparisons within each group of aircraft. Leplat and Bisseret demonstrate that the strategy beginning with flight level comparisons is both logically and operationally shorter in time.

It is obvious that the advent of radar control makes it easier for the controller to maintain an updated picture of the whole situation. The relative positions of the aircraft can be derived directly from the radar presentation, though with the 'unlabelled' displays which are still widely used, the identity and altitude of each radar blip must be confirmed from other sources. Identity can be established indirectly by reference to flight progress strips, and directly by asking the pilot to make a manoeuvre, such as a turn, which can then be observed on the screen. Altitude information is available similarly, from flight strips or by R/T report from the pilot. The latest radar displays present identity and altitude information directly, but even here we cannot assume that the controller's basic task of conflict (i.e. loss of separation standards) prediction is much simplified. For example, Sperandio and Bisseret (1973) report some later French research which suggests that conflict prediction from radar data is a rather more uncertain process for the controller. Procedural methods had involved a discrete sorting of aircraft pairs into conflict and non-conflict categories, based on the items of information contained in the flight strips. Radar control brings narrowed separation standards and an increasing reliance on visual 'time-extrapolation' of tracks on the screen: this is much more a case of decision making under risk. These features of 'tighter' control of aircraft, and the possibility of relying ultimately on visual extrapolation of tracks on radar screens, have encouraged research on such short-term prediction. Substantial studies have been undertaken by David (1969) and Hopkin (1963, 1965).

The sector controller has no possibility of direct visual contact with aircraft under his control, and so he must rely entirely on the 'artificial world' created by his displays. The aerodrome controller does have the opportunity of looking out of the window of the visual control room (USA—tower cab). Nevertheless, this important source of information may be interrupted by the design of the VCR itself, by airport buildings, or by weather conditions. In these cases also, some extrapolation of information may have to be undertaken.

A major feature of auditory input skills is the need to switch between a number of different auditory displays (R/T from aircraft, intercom. from other controllers, telephone, etc.). In general, each communication channel functions well and is easy to use—it is their profusion which creates difficulties, as pointed out in our previous comments on 'time-sharing'. Two other aspects of auditory skills should be mentioned. First, the controller has to interpret the standard ATC English communications as spoken by an international array of pilots. Although considerable redundancy results from the use of standard words and phrases, there is still wide variation in pronunciations. Such variation can help in rapid identification of the particular pilot, but interpretation is still a difficult task on occasions. Second, the controller may sometimes have to use R/T communication as a means of judging pilot strain under difficult conditions. It is fairly obvious that R/T messages do give this extra information on the pilot's psychological state, in addition to the formal content of the message. There is as yet only anecdotal evidence on this subtle aspect of verbal communications, except for a brief interview programme with controllers in San Francisco (Stuntz, 1969), who supported the phenomenon and suggested the important speech cues (rapid speech, increased pitch, self-interruptions, less clear enunciation, etc.).

Processing skills: information organization

Older and Cameron (1972) include in their report results of a questionnaire survey on two small samples of controllers. They were asked to make ratings of the skills involved, and this aspect of information integration and synthesis receives considerable emphasis, especially from the en-route controllers. There seems to be considerable similarity with the industrial process control operator, who has various sources of information about the plant, and who must merge the various items into a coherent understanding of the current situation.

The ATCO talks of 'getting the picture' or 'keeping the picture'. We have discussed already the major sources of information on aircraft movement— the radar and flight progress strip displays—but other important components of the 'picture' are the structure of the airways system and the typical patterns of movements within it, and the intentions of aircraft as expressed in flight-plans. Several anecdotal reports by ATCOs illustrate this psychological complexity. Even an experienced controller takes some time to understand the structure of a novel sector, and there can be similar problems in the handing over of a busy traffic situation between controllers on successive shifts. 'Unlearning' is a common problem, particularly under stress— as would be predicted from psychological theory: various details of the ATCO's background knowledge are liable to be modified and this can cause errors, annoying even if minor (a simple example is the ICAO phonetic alphabet, which has evolved through a number of versions).

In terms of computer assistance, there would seem to be several opportunities for improvement in this area. Computer-generated displays, with their inherent flexibility, could provide appropriate filtering, merging and organization of basic information. For example, in our investigations in an aerodrome visual control room, we have observed that much time is spent in organizing the flight strips for departures, and then in searching through the array when a particular aircraft calls the tower. Computer-based displays could offer various organizations of the data, on demand, and computer searching might be appropriate in some cases.

Processing skills: selecting among alternatives

Here again is a similarity with industrial process control, in that the ATCO is looking ahead, and trying to evaluate the consequences of alternative actions, before making a decision. Kidd (1961) has shown that increasing traffic load may cause controllers to plan less far ahead. Indeed, evidence from investigations in a variety of tasks confirm that human predictive skills are severely limited, and there have been several demonstrations of the benefits of predictive assistance, commonly in the form of a predictive display based on a fast-time simulation of the system being controlled (e.g. Kelley, 1968). The basic task of conflict prediction in sector control demonstrates three types of prediction based on increasing assistance for the controller:

1. Under procedural control, Leplat and Bisseret (1966) showed that controllers search for pairs of possibly conflicting aircraft by making successive judgements on different parameters of the situation. As mentioned above, they identified different strategies for organizing and comparing the aircraft information, providing a basis for revised training in the more efficient strategies.

2. With radar control, as discussed previously, the conflict prediction strategies include visual extrapolation of tracks on the radar screen. However, this is essentially short-term prediction, and more effective control should be possible using the third method.

3. This is an example of a predictive aid using a fast time computer simulation, as mentioned above. An experimental system is being developed (Ball *et al.*, 1975) which stores the typical trajectories for different aircraft, and uses these to predict dynamically the future paths of the group of aircraft through the whole sector. 'Zones of protection' are defined around each aircraft, and the computer program will detect any overlapping of these zones, which constitutes a predicted conflict. Thus, the controller has a device for planning any array of aircraft paths and testing for conflicts. If a conflict is predicted, he may change some aspect of the plan, and re-test it. This is a good example of radical extension of human capabilities by computer techniques, and it must be emphasized that the span of prediction is much greater than for visual extrapolation, in that it incorporates aircraft intention based on flight plans. A close analogy is the distinction between 'perceptual anticipation' and 'receptor anticipation' as expounded by Poulton (1957).

In some other decision situations, it may be appropriate to assess future alternative actions within a combinatorial framework. For example, the controller may be presented with a group of aircraft waiting to land or to take-off. Which is the optimum sequence for the queue? With even a few aircraft, the number of possible sequences is very large; moreover, certain sequences may be inadmissible under ATC rules. Providing an unambiguous criterion of optimality can be defined (a reasonable example would be minimum average delay over the whole group), the problem is ideal for computer assistance. The computer can exhaustively check all the permissible solutions within a short time, and present the controller with a recommendation of an optimum, or perhaps a 'short list' of good solutions. A short list is likely to be a better procedure where there are other, less well defined criteria to satisfy, and on which the controller can make the best judgement. This type of computer assistance may well have a useful application in ATC queueing problems, particularly at airports.

It will be noted that we are discussing computer assistance for the ATCO, rather than complete automation of control procedures. In future developments, it is essential that the correct balance is maintained between human and computer responsibilities. Equally important, computer assistance will have to be compatible with the changes of strategy which are characteristic of these processing skills. Sperandio (1971) examines the strategies followed by approach controllers under different traffic loads, and shows that the more flexible strategies selected under medium loads have to be replaced by more rigid procedures when the pressure builds up. Similar variations in the operations of TMA controllers have been observed by Coeterier (1971).

Processing skills: information storage

We emphasize here that the controller's 'picture' depends not only on the immediate information which he is receiving, but also on items carried over from other displays and communications. In psychological laboratory experiments Yntema and Mueser (1962) have demonstrated the severe limits on short-term memory for a number of items each of which can assume one of a fixed number of states. This certainly corresponds to some features of keeping track of a sequence of landing aircraft: as the head of the 'queue' disappears, another appears at the tail, and each of the others is moved up one step in the sequence. Leplat and Bisseret (1966) included some studies of 'operational memory', and demonstrated similar limitations. Their controllers seemed to have adapted to these limitations by remembering the most important parameters of the situation—they were able to begin the thought sequence of conflict detection without reference to flight strips. On the other hand, it is observed often that controllers make use of informal 'aides memoires', making temporary notes on flight strips and other sheets.

As well as this running memory, there is a great deal of static information, such as aircraft types and performances, which the controller may recall without any external aid. Table 10.1 has given other examples of memory as a source of such information: intricate variations in procedural standards have been mentioned as a particular problem. Computer storage of information which may be required in a long or short time may be useful, but the procedures for entering and retrieving data must not be time-consuming or interfering with other activities.

Output skills

The detailed procedures for operating radar and communications equipment constitute the specialized output skills in ATC, and they are similar to other jobs involving advanced electronic systems. Newer developments in interface devices include tracker balls and touch displays, and these require the development of some new skills; data entry for computer systems can create significant increases in workload.

Communication with pilots is a very heavy demand—the controller may spend up to 50% of his time using the R/T channel. There are also the communications with other controllers and assistants. Thus, verbal communication—though with a restricted language—is the major aspect of his output activities. Also, within the immediate work group, controllers may communicate non-verbally, with a variety of gestures and special signs.

In a recent paper, Hopkin (1974) has drawn attention to some useful aspects of voice communication which would be lost in any system which relied on automatic transmission of data between aircraft and ground. He notes that a pilot in an emergency situation may well derive confidence from the calm and highly professional manner of the controller on the R/T. Again, under both emergency and normal conditions, the controller will vary the pace and content of communication for foreign or unfamiliar pilots, and will often repeat a message which has even been repeated and acknowledged by the pilot, if he has the slightest suspicion that the understanding is not complete. These subtleties of verbal communication should not be overlooked in any assessment of the more systematic content of R/T messages.

HUMAN FACTORS RESEARCH IN ATC

This brief review concentrates on topics which have direct relevance to the ATCO's job. Obviously, there are general findings and concepts in human factors which may apply to ATC; indeed, in Hopkin's (1970a) report, the majority of references cited do not emanate from ATC itself and much of the discussion attempts to develop such a relationship. Hopkin is somewhat pessimistic about the generality of many human factors results, and, further, of the relevance of basic research in experimental psychology (see also his review of Peters (1973), *Ergonomics*, 1974). We agree with him that there is a disappointing gap between academic research and practical needs: this seems more defensible in the case of human factors studies involving a large number of independent variables, than in basic experimental psychology which aims to elucidate the underlying mental processes. There are two areas of current psychological research which are commonly supposed to have a bearing on ATC tasks: vigilance and selective attention. In fact, the first shows little resemblance to the ATC situation, where events are fairly predictable, incoming signals are well above thresholds, and controller activity levels are high; even in air defence systems, where uncertainty is greater, Kibler's (1965) well established objections cast severe doubts on the usefulness of vigilance research. Like vigilance, selective attention research developed originally from practical problems, in communication systems with competing messages. However, apart from demonstrating the difficulties resulting from simultaneous messages and the possible benefits of binaural listening (e.g. Rappaport, 1965), the subsequent avalanche of selective attention research has had no practical effect on ATC communications systems. For instance, we still know very little about the development of controllers' strategies for dealing with such problems over long periods of experience and practice.

In closing this argument, we ought to mention two other instances of the relevance of basic psychological research. In their analysis of conflict detection processes, Leplat and Bisseret (1966) are influenced by the work of Bruner *et al.* (1956) on categorization of problem situations in terms of combinations of variables. In a review of the extensive ATC simulation studies at Ohio State University, Kidd (1959) suggests that the susceptibility of short-term memory to interference is the main cause of failures in organizing, and extrapolating from, multiple input sources. These further references to basic psychological research indicate that the relevance is at a general conceptual level, and that specific guidance for real problems is much more difficult to derive.

Laboratory studies, simulation and field-work

An important aspect of human factors research is the conditions under which it is carried out. We have no need here to rehearse the relative advantages of laboratory experiments, such as their precise control of variables, and of field studies, such as their comprehensive realism. As a compromise, controlled simulation experiments have much to offer in complex systems like ATC, and there are several examples of this technique in action.

The advent of radar control prompted several laboratory experiments on the prediction of motion of targets on radar screens. The basic aim is to define the factors governing the controller's success in predicting conflicts. Various configurations of tracks of pairs of aircraft are presented to the controller and he is required to predict whether or not a conflict is imminent. David (1969) and Hopkin (1963, 1965) have used both static and dynamic simulations of the radar presentation in such studies. The validity of laboratory tasks should be checked: David cites one previous study where the effective speeds of the 'aircraft' were over 10 000 knots! Dunlay and Horonjeff (1974) have demonstrated how such information on controller performance might be incorporated in a mathematical model to predict the workload due to conflict detection.

The most successful attempts to date in elucidating the mental process of controllers are those by Bisseret and his colleagues, some results of which have already been discussed. Three basic methods are used to develop the flow charts ('organigrams') depicting sequences of information collection and processing by the controller. In general interviews, controllers are asked to describe their approach to typical control situations. Then, they are given a 'static simulation' of a traffic situation, with a problem such as the introduction of a new aircraft, and they are asked to describe their techniques for solving the problem. Finally, controllers are presented with a static simulation which they study before the flight strips are covered; questions about possible conflicts are posed and information about any specific flight strip is provided on request from the controller. From all of these techniques, the investigators synthesize a representation of the information handling processes. They justify the reliance on static simulation as highlighting the particular task component (in this case, conflict detection), controlling the test situation between subjects, and enabling relatively short and easy experiments. In some later studies, aimed at specifying the nature of the controller's 'operational memory', a dynamic simulation of the procedural control task was run under laboratory conditions, and the flight strip board was concealed unexpectedly. The controllers were then required to reconstruct the traffic situation as far as possible from memory.

Unfortunately, only four of these French papers are available in translation (Leplat and Bisseret, 1966; Bisseret, 1971; Sperandio, 1971; Sperandio and Bisseret, 1973). The first two describe the techniques of using flow diagrams to represent mental processes, the basic data being obtained from verbal protocols in simulated dynamic or static simulations. Sperandio's paper covers the work on strategy variation already discussed, and the final translated paper is a summary of several studies undertaken by the group. A further report (Bisseret and Girard, 1973), available only in French, presents a 'global description' of the mental processes in conflict prediction and solution, based on both procedural and radar information.

There are several examples of full-scale dynamic simulations of radar control systems. Parsons' *Man–Machine System Experiments* (1972) gives resumés of work in the US. In his introduction, he suggests that large scale man–machine research is fostered in the main by radar, advanced communications and displays, and computer-based systems—all facets of ATC development. The two major programmes were at the Ohio State University in the late 1950s, and under the Federal Aviation Administration from 1950; the latter continues at the National Aviation Facilities Experimental Center (NAFEC) in Atlantic City. In Europe, large scale simulations take place at the Civil Aviation Authority ATC Evaluation Unit at Hurn, England, and at the Eurocontrol Experimental Centre at Bretigny, France. The measurement of system performance, and of the contribution from the controllers, in such simulations is very difficult. There is systematic recording of many parameters, but the integration of these into a coherent picture is always controversial. In the UK studies, at any rate, questionnaires are used extensively to collect controllers' opinions on the systems. We have referred already to Hopkin's (1971) critique of evaluation measures.

Field studies of 'real-life' ATC systems are not very common, probably because the intrusion of a research team into this fairly sensitive system may cause operational problems. Informal observations often precede laboratory or simulation exercises, and there are examples of workload estimations made by experienced observers under various traffic conditions. Some activity analyses have been made of controllers under real conditions (e.g. Soede *et al.*,

1971). There is a great need to develop systematic studies of controller performance and strain under real conditions: nevertheless, the operational
constraints, and the difficulties of inferring mental processes, should not be
underestimated.

Controller performance and indicators of strain

It is readily appreciated that the ATCO's responsibilities are great, and any
casual observer would agree that there are periods of work when the activity
level is very high. Notwithstanding difficulties of definition, most people
would agree that the 'workload' can be severe, and that current research
(e.g. *Ergonomics*, vol. 14, no. 5, September 1971) into sources of stress in the
job and corresponding strain in the individuals is necessary. An organizational acknowledgement of this is that ATCOs, like airline pilots, have regular
medical examinations, their re-licensing depending on a positive result.
Obviously, as in any system, there are large fluctuations in the demands of
the task over any working period, but it is widely accepted that stress and
strain are problems. What objective support for this view has been provided
by human factors research, and what improvements have been developed?

The short answer is—not very much. The problems of measuring complex
system performance, operator performance, and operator strain are numerous
(e.g. Singleton *et al.*, 1971). In ATC, as discussed earlier, system performance
has several facets, and in any case the prime criterion of safety is rarely trans-
gressed. There is current research on a more sensitive and versatile measure
of system safety, known as the Index of Orderliness (Ratcliffe and Gent,
1974); this is based on predictions of potential conflicts which exist at a given
time, but which will probably be removed in due course. The complexities of
this measure are still being explored, but it has great promise in the context of
safety. Nevertheless, even with reliable measures of system performance,
their interactions and their tenuous relationships with operator performance
and strain are continuing difficulties in human factors investigations.

In simulated and field studies, measurements of overt activities are often
taken. A typical example is the percentage of his total time which the ATCO
spends on the R/T link with aircraft. As communication with pilots is one of the
main parts of his task, this seems reasonable as a first step towards measuring
his workload. However, it is a truism that overt activity is often independent
of the amount of 'mental work' involved; moreover, evidence is now appear-
ing (e.g. Sperandio, 1971; Coeterier, 1971) to support the suggestion that
controllers' strategies are modified by the demands of the task. This adaptive
nature of high level skills is reviewed in other tasks also, by Bainbridge
(1974). Such adaptability makes it almost impossible to define a stable
measurement of the effort expanded by the controller, though conceivably
the strategy variation itself could be used as an indication of his overall
effectiveness: an example is given by Kidd (1961), who reports that the

controller pays less attention to long-term problems and solutions as the number of controlled aircraft increases. Another subtle measure, suggested by Hopkin, is to observe how long it takes for a controller to hand over all the necessary background information and description of the traffic situation, when he is being relieved by a colleague on the next shift. Two other approaches have been the secondary or dual task method, and subjective ratings by skilled observers. In future it is likely that much more attention will be paid to parameters of job satisfaction, and there is something to be said for self-assessment of effort and workload by the highly skilled operator: this has been observed in studies of airline pilot strain during approach and landing (AGARD, 1969).

Physiological and biochemical indicators of strain have been investigated in several applied contexts. The results are nearly always complicated by large individual differences and by a rarity of suitable norms. Current research by the Federal Aviation Administration in the United States (Melton 1975) is showing some incidence of abnormally high responses in certain busy locations, but there are also reports of measurements typical of the general population. A related feature of ATC jobs, which we have not mentioned yet, is shift work. The relationships between shift work and human effectiveness and well-being are a complex of biological and social factors (Wilkinson, 1971). Hopkin (1970b) notes the lack of research specifically in ATC, but points out the importance of social factors in determining acceptable shift schedules. There is a very wide range of shift organization within ATC systems.

A significant part of the research on ATCO workload and effort is directed towards 'modelling' the controller so that quantitative predictions can be made of his capacity for handling increasing rates of traffic within future ATC systems. Sophisticated computer simulation is being applied to the planning and control of air traffic over the next decade or so, and there is a real need for taking account of ATCO capabilities and limitations therein. After the above inconclusive review of attempts to measure controller performance and strain, the reader will not be surprised to learn that estimates of the controller's capacity for handling simultaneously a number of aircraft range from five to twenty, for different aviation administrations! Ratcliffe (1970b) has reviewed some attempts at quantification.

Design of displays and controls

This traditional area of human factors has received much attention in ATC over the last 10 years or so. Hopkin's (1970a) review covers these topics in considerable detail, and he points out the ever-present danger in the application of automation and computer systems, that the man–machine interface may well be less flexible and convenient to use, thus increasing, rather than reducing, the controller's workload. For our purposes here, we shall comment briefly on the more significant developments in interface design.

We have already commented on the evolution of radar displays. The modern ATC radar picture is used in normal lighting conditions, and the information is processed to remove 'visual noise' and spurious echoes. The provision of tracking and labelling facilities for the aircraft 'blips', and the addition of important geographical information, enhances the interpretation of the display by the controller. Nevertheless, inadequacies remain: SSR labels for adjacent aircraft may overlap on the display, and controller adjustment is required; SSR responses from aircraft may be 'garbled' or the transponder in the aircraft out of order or incorrectly set up by the pilot.

Another important application of the cathode ray tube (CRT) which has emerged recently is for the presentation of computer-based alphanumeric information. Efficient transmission and dissemination of detailed information, such as flight plans, is obviously important for the controller, and some limited applications are becoming available. The standard problems of legibility and appropriate organization of the data require careful attention, but the instantaneous updating of the displays is their prime feature. The next advance in CRT displays will be the application of colour, and careful assessment will be necessary to ensure its most useful application.

The cathode ray tube is incorporated in the major advance in controller input, too. This is the so-called 'touch display' due to Johnson (1967). The CRT screen has wires running across parts of its surface, and the computer is able to sense the position of a finger on any of the wires. A computer-generated alphanumeric display produces labels on any of these points, and so we have a system which can display any configuration of possible responses, and sense which the controller selects. There are several advantages over conventional inputs, such as the standard typewriter keyboard. Sequences of different response ensembles can be displayed, to guide the controller through successive decision stages. At each stage, the computer will accept only one of the specified responses—'illegal' responses, the bane of system designers, are eliminated. Display/control compatibility is absolute, and the response of the system to the controller's command is virtually instantaneous. Current developments of the touch display will enable a computer-generated picture to be touched anywhere on the screen for control purposes, as determined by the program. Such a system allows for great flexibility of input, e.g. discrete touches for alphanumeric data and continuous path tracing to define required tracks for aircraft.

CONCLUSION

In this chapter, we have attempted to describe the major features of the controller's job and of the underlying skills. In doing so, we have emphasized the 'processing' or cognitive skills: there is still much to be done in developing our understanding of these complex processes, but some of the studies cited have begun this work. We have demonstrated also the influence of equipment development on the human skills required, and we have referred to current research and development in the application of on-line computers. This is the most recent impact of advancing technology on the ATCO's job, and there will be more sharing of tasks between men and computers in the future. One set of human factors problems will be in the design of the controller–computer interface, but more fundamental considerations are involved in the balance of responsibility between man and machine—or, as Ratcliffe (1970a) puts it—between controller and computer programmer. He suggests that the best form of computer assistance would be to produce a broad overall plan for traffic movements over the next 10 min or so, and then to have the controller responsible for the safe implementation of the plan and any necessary modifications. There is little real evidence for the optimum assignment of these decision making functions, and it is to be hoped that current developments in computer assistance, in ATC and in other fields, will provide some guide-lines in due course. Another facet of this problem is its effect on the attitudes and job-satisfaction of the controllers involved; Hopkin (1969) has drawn attention to such 'neglected psychological problems in man-machine systems', including attitudes towards automation, preferences for equipment and organizational psychology aspects. There is some evidence from various countries that, while ATCOs find their jobs inherently challenging and satisfying, they most often have complaints about the equipment provided and the management of the organization. The introduction of on-line computers is germane to these areas, and these wider human factors will have to be considered.

We hope that similarities between this and the other chapters of this book will lead to an increased understanding of human skills in complex systems, and of the problems outlined above. In the meantime, we are grateful to members of the ATC research group at the Royal Signals and Radar Establishment, Malvern, for comment and discussion.

References

AGARD (1969). Measurement of aircrew performance: the flight deck workload and its relation to pilot performance. *AGARD Conference Proceedings No. 56*

AGARD (1975). A survey of modern air traffic control AGARDograph 209 (NATO)

AGARD (1976). Plans and developments for air traffic systems. *20th Guidance and Control Panel Meeting/Symposium*, CP188 (NATO)

Bainbridge, L. (1974). Problems in the assessment of mental load. *Le Travail Humain*, **37**, 279

Ball, R. G., Lloyd, R. B. and Ord, G. (1975). Interactive conflict resolution in ATC. In *AGARD* (1976)

Bisseret, A. (1971). Analysis of mental processes involved in Air Traffic Control. *Ergonomics*, **14**, 565

Bisseret, A. and Girard, Y. (1973). Le traitement des informations par le controleur du trafic aerien: une description globale des raisonnements. *Institut de Recherche d'Informatique et d'Automatique, report 7303-R-37*

Bruner, J. S., Goodnow, J. J. and Austin, G. A. (1956). *A Study of Thinking* (New York: Wiley)

Coeterier, J. F. (1971). Individual strategies in ATC freedom and choice. *Ergonomics*, **14**, 579

David, H. (1969). Human factors in air traffic control: a study of the ability of the human operator to predict dangerously close approaches between aircraft on simulated radar displays. *Ph.D. Thesis, Loughborough Univ. of Technology*

Dunlay, W. J. and Horonjeff, R. (1974). Application of human factors data to estimating air traffic control conflicts. *Transp. Res.*, **8**, 205

Fitts, P. M. (1951). Human engineering for an effective air-navigation and traffic control system. *NRC Committee on Aviation Psychology, Washington DC*

Gilbert, G. A. (1973). *Air Traffic Control: The Uncrowded Sky* (Washington: Smithsonian Institution Press)

Hopkin, V. D. (1963). Laboratory studies in conflict detection. II. Track velocity, angle of approach and distance between tracks. *Flying Personnel Research Committee, FPRC/1208*

Hopkin, V. D. (1965). Laboratory studies in conflict detection. III. Turning tracks. *RAF Institute of Aviation Medicine, IAM Report No. 328*

Hopkin, V. D. (1969). Some neglected psychological problems in man–machine systems. *The Controller*, **8**, 5

Hopkin, V. D. (1970a). *Human factors in the ground control of aircraft*. (AGARDOGRAPH No. 142) (NATO)

Hopkin, V. D. (1970b). Work–rest cycles in air traffic control tasks. *AGARD Conference Proceedings No. 74* ('*Rest and Activity Cycles for the Maintenance of Efficiency of Personnel Concerned with Military Flight Operations*')

Hopkin, V. D. (1971). Conflicting criteria in evaluating Air Traffic Control systems. *Ergonomics*, **14**, 557

Hopkin, V. D. (1973). Human factors problems in conflict detection and resolution. *AGARD Conference Proceedings No. 105—'Air Traffic Control Systems*'

Hopkin, V. D. (1974). Changing pattern of stress. *Can. Air Traffic Control Ass. J.*, **6**(2), 20

Johnson, E. A. (1967). Touch displays: a programmed man–machine interface. *Ergonomics*, **10**, 271

Kelley, C. R. (1968). *Manual and Automatic Control* (New York: Wiley)

Kibler, A. W. (1965). The relevance of vigilance research to aerospace monitoring tasks. *Hum. Factors*, **7**, 93

Kidd, J. S. (1959). A summary of research methods, operator characteristics, and system design specifications based on the study of a simulated radar air traffic control system. *WADC Tech. Rep. 59-236 (Wright Air Development Center, Dayton, Ohio)*

Kidd, J. S. (1961). Some sources of load and constraints on operator performance in a simulated radar air traffic control task. *Aerospace Medical Laboratory, Wright-Patterson AFB Ohio, WADD Tech. Rep. 60-612*

Leplat, J. and Bisseret, A. (1966). Analysis of the processes involved in the treatment of information by the Air Traffic Controller. *The Controller*, **5**, 13

Melton, C. E. (1975). Comparison of U.S. air traffic control facilities by means of a stress index. *The Controller*, **14**, 28

Older, H. J. and Cameron, B. J. (1972). Human factors aspects of air traffic control. *NASA Report CR-1957*

Parsons, H. M. (1972). *Man–Machine System Experiments* (Baltimore: Johns Hopkins)

Peters, G. (1973). *Air Traffic Control—A Man–Machine System* (Bletchley, Bucks.: Open University)

Poulton, E. C. (1957). On prediction in skilled movements. *Psychol. Bull.*, **54**, 467

Rappaport, M. (1965). Increasing voice communications channels using man's binaural listening capability. *Hum. Factors*, **7**, 28

Ratcliffe, S. (1970a). Automation in Air Traffic Control. *The Controller*, **9**, 6

Ratcliffe, S. (1970b). Mathematical models for the prediction of air traffic controller workload. *The Controller*, **9**, 18

Ratcliffe, S. and Gent, H. (1974). The quantitative description of a traffic control process. *J. Navigation*, **27**, 317

Singleton, W. T., Fox, J. G. and Whitfield, D. (1970), (eds.), *Measurement of Man at Work* (London: Taylor & Francis)

Soede, M., Coeterier, J. F. and Stassen, H. G. (1971). Time analyses of the tasks of approach controllers in ATC. *Ergonomics*, **14,** 591

Sperandio, J. C. (1971). Variation of operator's strategies and regulating effects on workload. *Ergonomics*, **14,** 571

Sperandio, J. and Bisseret, A. (1973). Ergonomics of controller-computer interface in a CAUTRA environment. *Eurocontrol, Luxembourg: Seminar on the Controller–Computer Interface, May 1973*

Stuntz, S. E. (1969). Vocal indications of emotional stress in aircraft pilots (as perceived by air traffic controllers). *AGARD—Aeromedical Aspects of Radio Communication and Flight Safety* (N70-16962)

Vernon, N. (1975). (Personal communication)

Wilkinson, R. T. (1971). Hours of work and the twenty-four-hour cycle of rest and activity. *In* P. B. Warr (ed.), *Psychology at Work* (Harmondsworth: Penguin)

Yntema, D. B. and Mueser, G. E. (1962). Keeping track of variables that have few or many states. *J. exp. Psych.*, **63,** 391

11

The Process Controller

LISANNE BAINBRIDGE

INTRODUCTION

'Process' industries make such products as paper, electricity, steel and petro-chemicals. In these industries the men do not work directly on the product but control the process machines within which input materials are converted into products which meet required specifications.

As the process machines are complex and the required product specification may vary, the machines cannot be controlled by simple rote rules. In essence skill is adaptable to different contexts. Manual skills are of minor importance in process control, but the operator needs a wide variety of other interrelated skills. Keeping the process output within specification involves perceptual and control skills. The operator may also schedule the use of resources, for instance by allocating input materials to different machines after comparing alternative plans of action. He may carry out sequential drills as part of start-up or emergency procedures. If the process breaks down he may have to identify and correct the fault, or to control the process to maintain output despite the fault. When automatic process controllers are used the operator may be simply a machine minder, or he may be expected to set the set-points (the targets for the automatic controllers) or to take over control when the automatic controllers fail.

The actual tasks in controlling a particular machine will depend on the nature of the process, the allocation of decisions between different workers, and the use of remote control panels and automatic controllers. The level of technology available will interact with traditional attitudes to skill in a particular industry to affect whether, for example, scheduling or set-point control are done by operators or by management, and whether fault diagnosis or correction are done by operators or maintenance technicians.

Edwards and Lees (1972) describe the range of process operator tasks; they have also published a useful collection of process operator studies (Edwards and Lees, 1974). This paper is concerned with the general skill types which underly process operator activities. The next section of the paper will review operators' perceptual and control skills, and the relation of the operator's process knowledge to the way he checks the process variables and to his working memory. The following section will describe how an operator's behaviour is organized in some planning tasks. The final section will summarize what is known about the skill of a highly experienced process operator, and will discuss how this skill is affected by the introduction of automatic controls.

Figure 11.1   Pulp-mill control room (By courtesy of Neilson McCarthy Ltd. and Wiggins Teape)

DYNAMIC CONTROL

To control the process the operator must identify its present state, judge whether the state is acceptable and, if not, choose and make a change in the machine control settings. Perceptual skills are used to identify the state of the process output and machinery; the operator may make a direct judgement or he may read information from displays or laboratory tests. If he is working at a remote panel he must imagine how the process works, and its present state, solely from the display changes. The operator can compare the present process state with the requirements, or he can predict future process behaviour and events and take anticipatory action. The operator may have to set his own control targets if the specification given to him is in general terms.

The process needs changing if it is or will be off specification. The operator must judge what change is needed and choose new control settings to make this change. In making his choice he must allow for the size and timing of the effect of any change, and for the interaction of this effect with other parts of the process. Longer time lags and more complex interactions make the control decisions more difficult. Altering a control setting may involve movements varying from pressing a button to manually turning a valve. The operator checks whether his action has had the required effect, and if not he makes another change. The interaction between man and machine through information sources and controls is summarized in Figure 11.2.

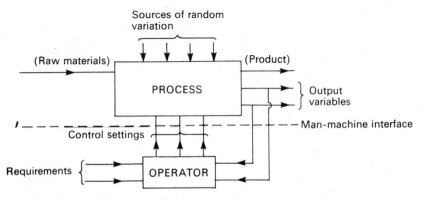

Figure 11.2   Man–machine interaction in manual process control (from Crossman *et al.*, 1964)

When the product is within specification the operator must still check the state of the process, as it can be disturbed by factors not under his control. With a complex multi-variable process the operator cannot check or control all the variables at the same time. Instead he must divide his attention between them and maintain a working memory for variables he is not currently looking at.

As an operator's job description, when it exists, may not give his detailed control methods these must be identified directly. An investigator interested in job and plant design may use simpler techniques to do this than someone interested in the detailed mechanisms of skill. Both however should start by talking about the process and task to several operators, foremen and managers. Any one person may not know the full context of plant operations and decision making, or may not know all the alternative control strategies. The limitations of verbal questioning as an investigation technique should be remembered. Often in skilled action several things are done together in a co-ordinated way which cannot be represented adequately by a sequential description. The operator may also not mention things which are noticed and done unconsciously when on the job. There is some evidence that operators' off-the-job reports of their process knowledge and the control settings used in given circumstances do not reliably represent their activity when controlling the plant (Cooke, 1965; King, 1976). The operator's report may also not reflect the priorities and strategy changes which occur under on-the-job pressures, and he may describe the official method rather than the one he actually uses. Despite these limitations however it is often true that simply gathering together process knowledge and control strategy tips and making this information explicitly available to all the operators can have a considerable effect on control performance.

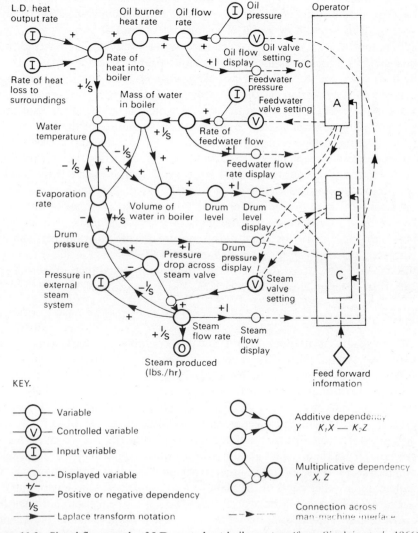

Figure 11.3 Signal-flow graph of LD waste heat boiler system (from Sinclair *et al.*, 1966)

Task description

The investigator has to arrange this information about the process–task system in a description which will help him both to check the completeness of his understanding and to identify the structure of the task as a basis for control panel design or training. The first step is to make two descriptions at a general level: a 'product oriented' account of the stages which material goes through in being processed, and a 'machine oriented' description of the flow of material between machines and the processes they carry out. These give a general understanding of the plant.

Next the characteristics of the process to be controlled must be described, i.e., the variables involved, and how they interact and affect the product quality. The signal-flow-graph is a convenient tool for this (see Beishon, 1967; Sinclair *et al.*, 1966). This representation is the inverse of the traditional box diagram; circles are used to represent variables and the causal relations between them are shown by arrows, see Figure 11.3. To develop such a graph it is simplest to start from the variables describing the process output and work backwards, representing the way in which variables affect each other, and including sufficient detail to account for the nature of the process. This form of diagram has several advantages. One can trace the process dependencies through from inputs to outputs and so identify the control loops available to the operator. Intermediate variables whose value is the result of an interaction can be identified; it is useful to display such values to the operator. Training procedures and the control–display panel layout should be arranged to reflect the relationships within the process. It is useful (if possible) to identify the quantitative nature of the relation between two variables, especially in the timing of effects, as this indicates the difficulty of the control task. It is also necessary to identify the range of permissable variation (tolerance) of output variables, and the costs of making an error.

Perceptual skills

The necessary technology is not always available for measuring process variables, so that their value must be judged by the operator. Any of the senses may be involved. For instance visual skill is used in assessing steel from the texture and colour of flames or metal surfaces, or in judging the rise and colour of cakes. A change in sound may indicate completion of a process stage (e.g., when a kettle starts boiling), or the texture of paper can be judged by feel. Information for these judgements may come from the machine, from the product at output or at intermediate stages, from displays or laboratory tests, or from other workers who may talk about what is happening in other parts of the plant or about events in the previous shift.

There has been very little explicit investigation of the discriminations which operators do make, and how these are used. Superficially, the obvious method would be to record examples of the possible values and to test the operator's discrimination or categorization ability by standard psychophysical techniques. Unfortunately the problem is not so simple. It may not be possible to capture important aspects of the stimulus texture on tape or film. Even when this can be done possible performance, test performance and task performance are not necessarily the same. For instance, operators may be able to see finer distinctions than they would make use of on the job, or inversely they may take more care on the job than in an artificial test. When perceptual skills have been studied in the development of training procedures this has usually been done by observing and questioning the operator at work.

The operator does not discriminate the process information as an isolated task but with the purpose of using it in his job. He may not mentally measure the process variables by numerical scale values but in relative terms, for instance it is more useful to know that 'power usage is well above target' than 'power usage is now at 65'. Probably relative judgement is encouraged by dial displays and accurate reading by digital displays (Bainbridge, 1971). It seems that the process variable values and their rates of change are categorized into overlapping bands with different implications for action: 'on target', 'going off target', 'action required', etc. The operator's thinking and remembering are probably done in terms of this scale of categories which includes relative judgements about the state of the process and actions required, rather than in terms of actual numerical scale values. This will be discussed further in later sections.

Control skills

If one wants to study the operator's control behaviour in more detail than he can give in reply to general questions then a considerable amount of work is involved. The standard shop-floor method of obtaining operator performance data is to log all the displayed variable values and all the operator's control actions and samples. These values are then plotted against time on an 'activity graph', as in Figure 11.4 (see examples in Crossman *et al.*, 1964; Beishon, 1967, 1969; Spencer, 1962; Attwood, 1970). From this graph it is possible to identify, on each occasion when the operator makes an action, what variable changes preceded the action and so what display–control connections he is making. If one wants to study the dynamics of his control skill, that is the mechanisms determining the size and timing of his actions, more detailed data are needed. It is difficult to obtain such data from shop-floor studies, though the reasons for this emphasize the operator's skill. It is difficult to monitor and log process variables which the operator identifies by perceptual skill or from talking to other workers, so the account may be incomplete. The need to work to commercial specifications means that the full range of control behaviours possible on the process is not observed, yet repeated tests of behaviour in exactly the same conditions are not possible. In addition, in many real tasks dynamic control decisions are interleaved with

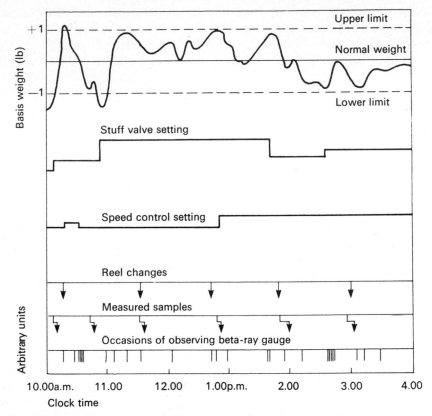

Figure 11.4   Activity graph for paper machineman (from Beishon, 1967)

other types of planning decision, so that the control-error to action-size decision link is not direct.

For these reasons all the systematic studies of dynamic control skill have been made in the laboratory. (For some reason most of the model processes involve hot water!) In the laboratory it is possible to test the full range of behaviour in controlled repeatable conditions using automatic data-logging equipment, and the controller can be asked to do special tests; the best potential for such studies is in control laboratories with fairly complex test plants controlled by full-time employees. In considering the results of laboratory studies it is important to remember their disadvantages. It is most difficult to reproduce the costs and values of a real task, but if the costs are unreal the controller may use different strategies, and may work with less or greater care. Usually the controller will co-operate and play the game of taking his laboratory task seriously, but this attitude can be disrupted easily; for example by using an arbitrary process which has no realistic meaning, by frequently interrupting his control for special tests during which the process is unattended, or by giving a work load which is too heavy. Laboratory processes are also usually simpler than the real equivalent, so there is not so much to keep in mind in deciding what to do and good performance is easier than in the real context. The skills of controlling very complex real plant may develop over many years.

The majority of laboratory studies have used fairly simple processes, and have looked at control behaviour in changing process output from one steady level to another (a step-change). These studies (e.g., Crossman and Cooke, 1962; Attwood, 1970; Clark, 1972; Kragt and Landeweerd, 1974; Brigham and Laios, 1975) show that when an inexperienced controller tries to bring process output to a new value the output oscillates wildly around the target value. Control falls into three stages, as shown in Figure 11.5: initial actions to bring the output towards the new value, stabilization on the target, and maintaining the value on target. With practice the second stage disappears and the controller changes the process output smoothly without oscillations. The amount of practice required to reach this stage seems to be a good measure of the difficulty of the control task, or of the usefulness of the process information provided for the controller.

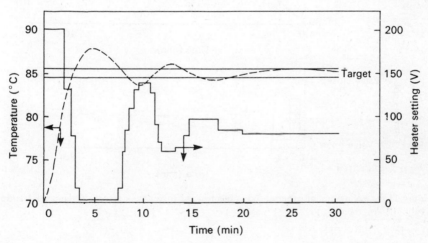

Figure 11.5 Performance on first trial by good subject in the water-bath task (from Crossman and Cooke, 1962)

We can ask how the controller chooses the size and timing of his control actions, and how he learns to do this. If the controller was acting by simple feedback the size of his control actions would be related to the size of the error in process output, and to the rate of change of the output value. The existence of these relations can be tested by correlation. In their classic study, of controlling water temperature via the power supply to an immersion heater, Crossman and Cooke (1962) found that the correlations, between size of controller's action and size of temperature error and its rate of change, decreased with practice. This indicates that while an inexperienced controller may act by simple feedback an experienced controller does not. To find how experienced controllers did do the task, Crossman and Cooke asked them to make a temperature change without seeing the thermometer, that is without any feedback. They were able to do this quite well. Crossman and Cooke suggest that the controllers know what will be the effect on process output of a given size of control setting used for a given time, from their past experience of process behaviour. They can use this knowledge in the normal task, first using settings which they know from experience will bring the output to the new target, and finally making small corrections by feedback, as in Figure 11.6.

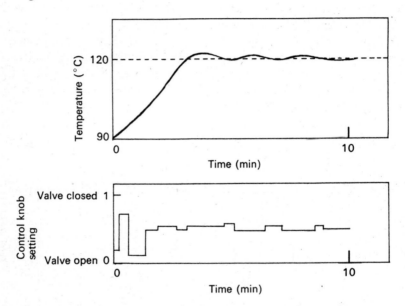

Figure 11.6 Behaviour of experienced subject in air mixer task (from Kragt and Landeweerd, 1974)

Figure 11.6 shows experienced control of air flow temperature, from Kragt and Landeweerd's (1974) study. To make the temperature change the controller used three control settings; one to bring output towards the target, one to stop the change on target, and a final setting to maintain output at the new value. The size and timing of such actions is critical; if they are wrong the output will oscillate around the target, so this controller must have learned the process dynamics very accurately. It is obvious that the control settings in Figure 11.6 are not related in any simple continuous feedback function to the temperature values at the time they were made, so correlation is inadequate to study this behaviour. It is necessary instead to identify typical patterns of controller action. When one looks at an activity graph one makes comments such as 'it looks as if he has noticed that change here', or 'he does that because . . .'. Instead of ignoring this ability of the investigator one should identify explicitly the cues for such comments, and so obtain operational definitions for such events. Clark (1972; summarized in West and Clark, 1974) has made an interesting attempt at this type of analysis, although he only identifies patterns of control settings and has not related these to display changes. He has begun to study changes in these activity patterns or 'strategies' with practice and task conditions. It would also be necessary to study the size and timing of experienced controllers' actions within each general strategy pattern, over a wide range of process changes and dynamic types.

Crossman and Cooke (1962) and Beishon (1969) suggest that the controller's knowledge of process dynamics is not continuous but divided into a limited number of categories, so that the controller reacts to a range of process behaviours in the same way. Bainbridge (1971) found that controllers grouped control errors into categories of 'alright', 'above', 'action required', etc. Categorized knowledge would require less memory storage space and would be simpler to refer to, also process states not previously experienced could be handled by grouping them with others. If controllers do categorize then these categories should appear in the size and timing of actions used; this needs testing.

The controller's knowledge of process dynamics is not necessarily explicit, he may control by subconscious 'feel'. If he can explicitly predict process behaviour however his knowledge is much more powerful as he can actively think out the effect of actions before making them. This prediction might also be done using categories. Cooke (1965) found evidence that controllers do predict the result of actions in choosing between them. Some work has been done on assisting the operator with computer-generated predictive displays, e.g., Ketteringham and O'Brien (1974). Very little is known about controllers' predictive ability. Specialized tests would be needed to study this, for example, covering the displays and asking the controller to continue control or to assess the process state after various time intervals. (Similar techniques could test the increasing accuracy of controllers' process knowledge with experience.)

In some cases an operator may appear to be using simple feedback, in which case one can look for a direct relation between process output values and control settings. Simple linear regression is usually inadequate to find this relation however, as the operator's response may be non-linear and non-stationary. His gain (relation between size of error and size of control action) may be asymmetrical if there is hysteresis in the process; his gain may also vary with the size of the output error or with the extent to which the output is under control.

These examples show that control behaviour is a function of the operator's knowledge of the process dynamics, which he uses in interpreting the present and recent past process behaviour and in predicting the future. The operator's knowledge of process dynamics is called his 'mental model' of the process. This includes his knowledge of the size and timing of effects in the process and of their interactions. Control by 'feel' could be acquired simply by associative learning, control by actively predicting the effects of alternative actions requires some generalized knowledge of patterns of process behaviour.

It might be better to limit the term 'mental model' to process knowledge which can be used in prediction, as prediction requires some sort of model while feedback control can be done by a simpler mechanism. A process controller may have responsibility for scheduling or fault diagnosis, tasks which require knowledge of optimum sequences or plant mechanisms beyond that needed for plant control. The term 'mental model' often refers to all the operator's knowledge of his process.

The operator learns the dynamics of a particular process, often by 'feel' rather than consciously, from his experience of the effects an action or process input has on the process output. The operator's ability to learn process dynamics may be invaluable, he can learn to control processes for which automatic controllers cannot be designed because the processes are not sufficiently well understood. This does not imply however that explicit training procedures are not useful. When the gains and lags of the process are known, instruction about these can increase the rate of learning a 'feel' for process characteristics. When it is easier to learn or identify process behaviour then the controller may develop more complex strategies such as prediction.

The ease with which process behaviour can be learned is particularly affected by the way process information is displayed. In essence, if the operator is to learn the effect of an action or input on process output he needs clear information about these effects, and verbal instructions are not sufficient. Technically it may be possible to calculate control error automatically by comparing output and target values, but it would be a mistake to display this error alone without the underlying output and target values. If the controller is shown only an error value he cannot work out whether changes in error are a result of his actions or of other process changes not under his control; consequently he cannot learn the process dynamics and cannot predict future process behaviour, he is thus constrained to simple forms of feedback control. It must also be easy for the operator to discriminate the size of action made and the size of the result; for example backlash or high sensitivity of controls make this difficult. If the process responds slowly it can be difficult to notice the changes, and chart recorders can help in this. Related displays and controls should be placed close together so that it is easy to see the relationship. Chart recorders can also help in recognizing process relationships when there are time lags between input and response. These records become more important the longer the time lag: for instance if an action does not have its full effect until several hours later in the next shift the operator will never learn this unless he can look at records of plant behaviour over longer periods than the one shift he observes directly. Learning process relations is also difficult if there is a delay in obtaining information, for instance if samples are sent for laboratory test; but if a log is made at the time the sample is taken the operator does not have to recall the related process conditions when the report returns.

In interacting systems the operator can identify interactions and predict later effects more easily if intermediate variables are displayed. Learning about interactions is also important in large plants with interdependent but separately controlled processes. Engelstadt (1970) found that output from the chemical pulp department of a paper-mill improved when the operators were trained to control all the processes and centralized information about the plant was provided. The operators also showed more interest in and responsibility towards their job. Presumably they had learned the process interdependencies, and how each one contributed to the final output. In many processes the operator is given the output values he must meet; for example weight of paper or thickness of steel sheet. In other cases he must choose the values himself; for example the ovenman studied by Beishon (1969) had to know the appropriate temperature conditions for each cake type baked. This type of knowledge could again be learned by experience, by comparing process conditions with success at meeting more general product specifications, e.g., the rise and colour of the cakes.

Sampling and working memory

The potential accuracy of an operator's control depends on his knowledge of the process dynamics. The actual accuracy achieved depends on how much attention he gives to his tasks, which in turn depends on his assessment of the costs of process error against the costs to him of doing something to check or correct it. Real processes are more complex than the ones used in the laboratory studies above; it is not possible to monitor all the variables at the same time so the operator must divide his attention between them, choosing when to check each part of the process and remembering relevant values of process variables not currently being checked. Consequently any factor which affects how he attends to part of the process may affect his control performance. Such factors include his knowledge of the process dynamics, the cost to him of checking or acting, and the efficiency of his working memory for the present state of other parts of the process.

It is not necessary to watch any process variable continuously; according to sampling theory a randomly varying signal can be reconstructed in full if it is checked or 'sampled' at twice the frequency of the fastest changing component in the signal. In process control the operator's process knowledge can allow him to predict future changes so he is less uncertain about process behaviour than he would be if it was random, and so he can sample even less frequently than indicated by sampling theory.

The controller's sampling behaviour can be studied by tests in which he has to make an overt action to obtain information, e.g., lifting a cover over a display or requesting a computer print-out. These methods put an unusual load on memory, but the costs of sampling can be manipulated directly. Less restrictively, sampling can be studied by eye-movement recording. Unfortunately studies of selective monitoring do not give a complete picture of sampling activity in a complex control room. Iosif (1969b) showed that when a process is within tolerance the operator frequently does general monitoring by a quick glance over the control panel. Dial displays can be checked easily against expectations about pointer position, an experienced operator can obtain a large amount of information very quickly using pattern recognition. (Operators talk about 'the expression on the face of the process'). This quick general monitoring could not be done with digital displays. It is difficult at present to see how this type of general monitoring can be studied rigorously on the shop-floor.

When the operator has made an action to alter process output he must check its effect. Crossman, Cooke and Beishon (1964) found that controllers sampled less frequently with increasing experience. This suggests that the controller learns the process dynamics; as he becomes less uncertain about the effect of an action he needs to check the process behaviour less often. The operator must learn the timing as well as the size of changes in his particular process. He must learn how long it takes for an action to begin to have an effect; this is the earliest time it is worth checking for the effect. He must also learn how long it takes for the action to have its full effect on process output. If he does not wait this long before sampling he will get a wrong impression about the size of the action/output relation, and the next action chosen will also be the wrong size. Crossman et al. mention a paper-mill operator who had learned to time his samples at this interval, although there was no clock on the plant and he could not name the interval. Attwood (1970) says that the control performance of the paper-mill operators he studied improved immediately when they were not allowed to make actions at intervals shorter than this. Finally the operator of some processes may learn the pattern of transient changes in process output as an action takes effect. He will then be able to sample and take actions at intermediate intervals, as in Figure 11.5.

When the process output is within specification the operator must check that this remains true; the output could be affected by factors not under his control, such as changes in ambient conditions or input material quality. In this situation he does not need to monitor at the maximum rate the process can change, as he does when checking the effect of an action, but only to sample at the maximum rate of possible process disturbances (ignoring disturbances which make output vary within the tolerance limits). Various studies (e.g., Crossman et al., 1964; Iosif, 1968) have shown that operators sample less frequently when output is within tolerance than after an action, although they sample more frequently when the output is near tolerance limits.

When the operator monitors a multi-variable process he must allocate his attention between the variables. In extensive studies of monitoring during manual control in electricity and petro-chemical industries Iosif (1968) showed that the rate of sampling of each variable varies with the rate of disturbances on that variable and with its importance. Functionally related groups of variables are sampled together. If the samples were timed randomly around some average interval, then more process disturbances should be detected late when the average inter-sample interval is long. Iosif (1969a) found no such correlation, he therefore suggests that the operator anticipates when samples should best be made. Anticipation could be based on knowledge of probabilities (itself based on experience), combined with monitoring the recent evolution of variable values and the state of related variables; it could be aided by visual extrapolation on chart recorders.

Three different suggestions have been made to account for the timing of an operator's samples. Crossman et al. (op. cit.) suggest that when the operator is not looking at a variable he uses his process knowledge to predict its behaviour, and he samples when his prediction about this behaviour reaches a certain level of uncertainty. Iosif suggests that an operator samples when he anticipates a critical event is about to occur; this implies that the operator is able to predict process behaviour fairly accurately. Beishon (1966) suggests that good sampling performance is not related to predictive ability. In his study the controllers had to prevent water overflowing from tanks; water was running into different tanks at different rates and the tanks were at different places in a largish building. An operator's ability to predict when a tank would overflow was not related to his efficiency at preventing overflow, rather it seemed to depend on the ability to think of an effective route round the building which was physically possible in the time available and within which each tank was visited sufficiently frequently. These three apparently incompatible suggestions have not been fully tested directly. The differences between them would be resolved if the different mechanisms apply in different circumstances. Further study might show for example that uncertainty influences sampling during learning and while the process is out of control, that anticipation determines sampling when the process output is within tolerance, and that sequencing strategy overrides prediction when the time and effort taken to sample limits the possible number of samples.

When the variables in a complex process interact, if there is a disturbance in process output the operator must work out which of the possible causes is responsible before correcting it. Inversely, there may be several alternative ways of making a particular change in process output. Whichever action he chooses the operator must allow for its effects on other parts of the process and be prepared to correct these secondary effects. Which of the strategies the operator uses may also be affected by the costs of sampling the information or making the actions involved (having to move, stopping the present activity, adding to the memory load). The greater the effort involved in carrying out a strategy the less likely it is to be used.

Changing from one task to another also involves costs, the costs of stopping one activity (which might vary from an important control task to sitting next-door reading the newspaper) and the costs of increased working memory. These costs are accentuated in the use of 'visual display units' on which the operator has to call up successively the information he requires. The call up procedure involves decisions which interrupt the main task decisions. Also the call up takes time and items are only available in sequence, these both increase the strain and load on working memory.

Non-optimal work loads emphasize the effects on sampling behaviour of costs and of probability of change. In task overload conditions when there is not time to sample all variables the operator will concentrate on the most important, and assume the values of the others instead of sampling them. His uncertainty about the unsampled variable values may become high enough to be an additional source of stress. Sub-tasks which require more effort on the operator's part (for instance extensive physical movement or complex mental work) will be the first to be left out in overload conditions, unless they are very important. The effect of different physical costs on choice between actions or samples can be reduced by using 'wrap-around' control consoles designed to human physical dimensions, so that movement distances and viewing distances and angles are minimized and equalized. Task 'overload' occurs when the tasks required cannot be done in the time available, or when more items should be remembered than can be. If the time taken to do each task is reduced then a larger number of tasks can be done in a given time period without overload. As well as physical movement times, all the factors which influence reaction time are important here. For instance, variable values which will never occur should not be displayed as they increase the time taken to read a display; display and control movements should be compatible and should fit with general expectancies. Display codes should have a direct meaning; dial displays are more compatible with human judgement processes than digital displays are, and can be read and remembered (roughly) very much more easily by pattern recognition.

When the operator checks the process and reads a display this usually gives information about the process state, but it might indicate machine or instrument malfunction. The operator's expectancies help him to evaluate whether the displayed value validly represents the process value (see Anyakora and Lees, 1972). Most simply he can do this by comparing the display with other displays of the same or related variables. He also has general expectancies about behaviour of variables, which may make him suspect constant or extreme values. He can assess whether displayed behaviour would be expected at this process stage from his knowledge of process dynamics. The operator's ability to identify the cause of process breakdowns also depends on his knowledge of relations in the process.

If the operator of a multi-variable process is going to compare variable values or use them together he must remember some values while looking at others. He apparently builds up a 'mental picture' of the state of the process in his working memory, and samples to keep this up to date. This term 'picture' does not imply a visual image of the process (though visual pattern recognition must be involved in rapid scanning of the control panel) but is used in the sense of 'being in the picture' or knowing what is going on. The operator's current knowledge of the process state, his mental picture, includes information about the present state and about predicted process behaviour and operator actions.

The operator apparently does not remember raw data about the process state, but remembers data which have already been processed so that they are in the most useful form for doing the task. For example, he considers process variable values in terms of what they imply for action, whether they are alright, off target, or action is urgently needed, etc. Displayed information may be remembered in groupings which are more convenient for rapid access in task decisions; for instance a furnaceman does not remember which state each furnace is in separately but remembers the list of furnaces in the same state. This working memory also retains items which are not displayed but are the result of previous thinking by the operator, such as predicted events and actions. The data about the future enable the operator to anticipate and so to be in better control of the process. The contents of the operator's working memory, or his 'mental picture', are not the same as his 'mental model' which covers his general long-term knowledge of all potential process behaviour and relationships. However, as the operator identifies important relations in the present process state and predicts future states by using his general process knowledge or mental model, obviously his current knowledge of the process state is highly dependent on his mental model.

An experienced operator's picture of the present process state is more integrated than the mental picture of a trainee, presumably because the experienced operator has wider general knowledge about process behaviour and relations. He can remember more items, presumably because the items are more interrelated, and so has a more extensive knowledge of the process state at any one time. This wider knowledge includes more predictions of future states and actions, so he is less uncertain about events and spends less time seeking explanations of them. These aspects of working memory have been more fully established for air-traffic controllers than for process controllers, but see Bainbridge (1974) and next section. If an experienced controller is more able both to predict future process behaviour and to remember process facts, he should need to sample the process less frequently than a less experienced operator to keep up to date with its state, and should be able to leave it for longer periods to do other tasks without feeling too much uncertainty. The more experienced operator should therefore be more able to cope with increased workload without increased strain.

The stored mental picture is used directly by the operator in decision making and in choosing his sequence of behaviour. One can suggest that the mental picture takes time to develop, as the component items must be sampled in sequence and the operator must assess and integrate the items. This is supported by the way that, in some industries, an operator will come on shift quarter of an hour before he is due to take over control, to get the feel for the process state. Also Iosif (1969a) showed that a higher proportion of process disturbance were detected late after the operator had been telephoning or making written reports. Iosif suggests that when the operator had not been monitoring his ability to anticipate events decreased.

PLANNING DECISIONS

In many tasks dynamic control of the process, although essential, is only a small part (10–20%) of the operator's skilled decision making or cognitive activity (e.g., Beishon, 1969). In dynamic control the operator chooses between quantitatively different settings of the same control variable. Another type of decision making is concerned with alternatives which are different in kind, for instance whether to cut off power to furnace A or to furnace B, or whether to put jam tarts or eclairs into an oven first. In process control these are typically planning decisions about how to use the available resources. A different type of cognitive activity generally called 'information processing' is involved; this requires different methods of investigation and description.

It is less easy here than in the case of dynamic control to analyse the relations between process and task and to give a general description of the operator's place in the system. One could describe what decisions should be made, but it is not possible to deduce *a priori* what decision making strategy the operator will actually use. Particular strategies can be encouraged in training for new processes, but in existing processes the strategy used must be identified empirically. Much more research is needed on typical information processing activities in process control.

As examples for discussion we will describe briefly the findings from two of the most detailed studies available. Bainbridge *et al.* (1968) and Bainbridge (1974) studied a simulated task of controlling power supply to five electric-arc melting furnaces. When a change in power usage was needed the controller had to decide in which furnace steel making would be least disrupted by a power cut, before making a quantitative decision about the size of the change. He alternated between checking the control error and other types of behaviour. When power usage was unacceptable he chose an action; when power usage was acceptable he monitored the present states of the furnaces, and predicted whether future events would affect power usage and if so what control action would be needed. Beishon (1967) made a shop-floor study of an operator controlling three cake-baking ovens. Different cake types in different quantities might arrive at unscheduled times during the day. The ovenman had to bake the cakes, getting the ovens to the correct conditions for given cakes, and sequencing the cake types through the ovens so that time was not wasted in making large changes in oven conditions. The optimum sequence could be affected by the unexpected arrival of another cake type. The ovenman therefore had to allocate his time between controlling the present state of the ovens and thinking out the best future baking sequence. To do this he maintained a 'future activities' list extending $\frac{1}{2}$–1 h ahead. In both furnace and oven control tasks therefore the operator sampled the present and predicted the future process state, as in dynamic control.

In both these studies the operator's behaviour was identified from verbal reports recorded while he was doing the task. Bainbridge *et al.* recorded verbal protocols from controllers who were asked to 'think aloud'; Beishon asked the ovenman questions about what he was doing. Verbal reports given on the job are a source of information which it is difficult to obtain by any other method, but they are incomplete in important ways. One can think faster than one can talk, so the reports tend to be a random selection of the possible material. Many thinking processes are not verbal. Visual or intuitive concepts may have no simple verbal labels so have to be translated before they can be described; this may constrain the controller to using more easily verbalized methods. Behaviour which was once conscious may be over-learned so that it is produced automatically without thinking out the reasons for it. It is of course not possible to collect verbal reports if the task involves verbal communication. Leplat and Bisseret (1965) used instead the explicit experimental technique of static simulation. They put the controller in a static example task situation, and asked him to say what further information he would like and what he would decide to do. This method allows controlled repeatable exploration of the possible task situations but has several disadvantages. The operator may be self-conscious about his behaviour. There are no real pressures or costs from the use of time, working memory or other simultaneous tasks. The technique also imposes a sequence on behaviour which might be done differently in the real situation, for example by glancing across part of the control panel.

As a basis for identifying the operator's information processing, given the verbal reports and other activity data, the sequence of behaviour can be divided into sections or blocks of activity with a single aim. Similar behaviour may occur in sections with a similar aim. By combining evidence from these similar sections the sequence of operations being carried out, the 'routine', can be identified; for example there are routines for choosing the furnace to change power supply to, for making a list of predicted events, etc. Algorithmic flow diagrams as used in describing computer programs are a convenient tool for describing the routines found. These routines make use of basic operations and facts; for example operations for doing numerical calculations, or for making dynamic control decisions as discussed above, or facts

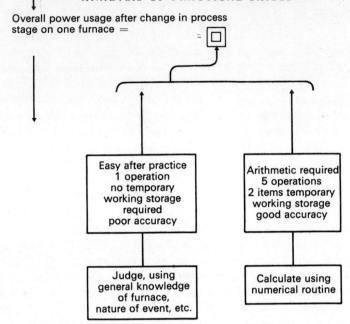

Figure 11.7 Example of alternative methods for finding a data item, with dimensions of choice between them

about the oven conditions required for a given type of cake. The routines differ in detail on different occasions. Some mechanisms additional to the usual flow diagram symbols can be useful to account for this (see Bainbridge, 1975). An item required is named separately from, but refers to, the routine(s) for finding it. An operator may use different routines for obtaining a given data item; for example using judgement or numerical calculation, doing this calculation by mental arithmetic or using a slide-rule, etc. This can be represented by giving a list of alternative routines at the point where the data item required refers to some routine for finding its value, as in Figure 11.7. Controllers' behaviour suggests that the routine used at a particular time is chosen according to the time and working storage available, the difficulty of the operations involved and the accuracy required. Different pay-offs and costs could lead to different choices of behaviour at this point; much research is still needed on this. If each item name has an associated location for storing the value found by the routine, see Figure 11.8, then the first time cognitive processing comes to an item with no associated value the routine will be used to obtain one, the next time this item is needed a value is available so will just be recapped. This gives behaviour which is not unnecessarily repetitive, although in practice the routine is repeated if this type of behaviour has not been done recently.

The routines may be used by the operator in a sequence which appears rather arbitrary at first glance. On-the-job verbal reports are usually just

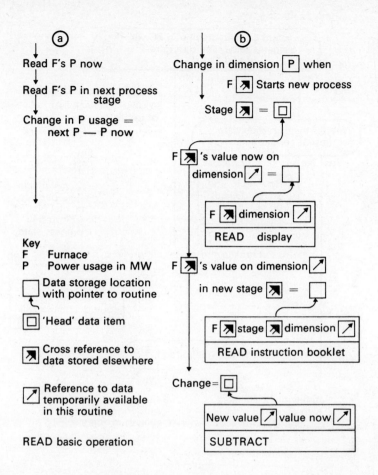

Figure 11.8 Example routine. (a) simple description of operations; (b) using 'box' notation to make working storage explicit

statements of fact with very few comments about the reasons for behaviour, so indirect methods must be used to find what determines the sequence of activity. In doing this one can treat the routines identified above as units of behaviour. One looks first for any repeated sequences of routines. At points where alternative behaviours occur one identifies all the dimensions of the task context, finds which of these differ consistently in value when the different behaviours occur, and assumes that these different values determine the operator's choice between behaviours. The tests for different values which lead to different behaviours can then be described by 'sequencing' flow diagrams including conditional statements, see Figure 11.9.

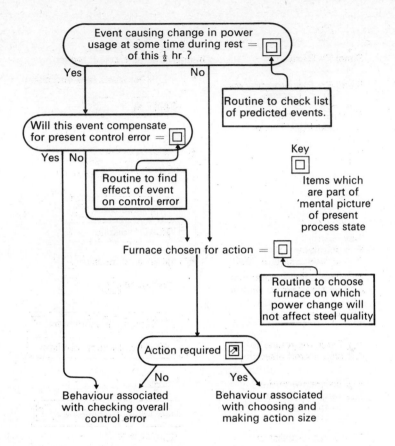

Figure 11.9 Simplified description of behaviour sequence determinants in power control task, when power usage is unacceptable

One of the operator's main problems, given his wide range of possible activities, is to choose behaviour which is both appropriate in the context of present and recent past activities by the process and by himself and which also takes into account new events which change the circumstances. One can suggest that the items which determine the sequence of behaviour (which are also the items found by the main routines) form the operator's 'mental picture' of the process state and provide the context in which task decisions are made, see Figure 11.9. These main items are stored for reference when needed, in comparison to items which may be stored temporarily for use during a routine but are not needed again. This mental picture is similar to but more complex than the process state knowledge which is needed in dynamic control. The operator looks at process variables during the routines so the sampling rate depends on which routines are used: however as the use and length of routines is mainly a function of the process state the pattern and rate of sampling are too, as in dynamic control. In addition, as indicated in Figure 11.9, the operator not only remembers present process values for use quickly in decision making but also remembers the results of his own thinking, such as lists of predicted events or best actions to take.

The operator may do different general types of behaviour in different overall contexts, for instance when process output is acceptable or when it is not. The factors determining the sequence of behaviour in these different overall contexts can be described in several 'sequencing' flow diagrams, one for each overall context. One might suppose that working storage, or the 'mental picture', would be local to each of these general contexts, but there is some evidence that operators can refer across from one to data found in another, and that values relevant in one context can be stored while another is being considered. The operator develops with experience his knowledge of available routines and items which should be remembered, and how both of these may be relevant in different parts of the task.

A further higher level of decision making is required for deciding which of the general types of behaviour is appropriate at a given time. In the power control task this decision was simple; there were only two main types of activity, which occurred when power usage was acceptable or unacceptable. Beishon (1969) suggests that the ovenman in the bakery study had an 'executive routine'. The ovenman had to control three ovens, and to adapt his behaviour if a different type of cake arrived for baking. He had to divide his time between checking and controlling the state of the three ovens and deciding on the best sequence of future activity. His 'future activities list' included when to check and control the present state of the ovens, in what sequence to bake the waiting cakes, and the checks and actions needed on the ovens to obtain correct conditions for the waiting cakes. This list of activities had to be revised if a different type of cake arrived which altered the baking sequence priorities. The future activities behaviour was recursive, keeping the future activities list up to date must be one of the activities on the future activities list. Beishon does not discuss whether the ovenman thought through possible alternative sequences of action. In some tasks the sequence may be clearly constrained by task priorities. A considerable amount of research is needed on the details of operator methods and priorities in thinking out future activities, particularly in control tasks in which plans for the future interact with the state of the process and its control requirements. The better an operator is at predicting future events and the future behaviour of the process the more adaptive will be his control.

These examples, and Figures 11.7 and 8, illustrate more fully some of the comments made about working memory in the previous section. Obviously in these examples the stored 'mental picture' items are not raw data about the process but are the result of mental operations by the controller. Items in the mental picture therefore depend on the controller's overall knowledge of routines and their use. With experience the controller becomes more aware that the same data can be cross referenced from different contexts, so his mental picture becomes more integrated. Figure 11.9 suggests a mechanism by which the controller's knowledge of the present system state is used in making task decisions and determining the controller's sequence of behaviour. This mechanism also implies that storage of items is intimately connected to the operations for both obtaining the items and using them.

MANUAL CONTROL SKILLS AND AUTOMATION

The skill of an experienced process controller is evidently complex. It includes general knowledge of process behaviour and mechanisms and of the operations the controller can carry out plus a structured overview of the present process state and its future behaviour. The controller's knowledge and abilities develop with more opportunities to recognize generalizations in the process and in his own behaviour. These process skills are needed just as much by a man who is expected to take over control of an automated plant when it develops a fault, but he has greatly reduced opportunities to develop and maintain his skill and process knowledge.

In summary, perceptual skills are used in discriminating aspects of the process or product which require different actions. A skilled controller knows the gains, lags and interactions of his process, so that he can make a smooth change in the state of the process or can keep it under control in unusual conditions. The controller also uses his knowledge of process dynamics and mechanisms to identify and correct plant faults, or to control the process despite them. The longer the lags in the process and the more complex the interactions, the more difficult it is both to learn the process dynamics and to make the control decisions. An experienced controller uses his process knowledge to predict process behaviour and take anticipatory action, rather than controlling by feedback. As he is able to predict process behaviour he needs to check it less frequently and so has a lower workload. He knows the optimum time interval for checking on the effects of an action, and also the probabilities of different process changes, which affect how he divides his attention between the parts of a multi-variable process. He maintains a mental picture of the present and future states of the process and his own activities; this working memory does not contain raw data about the process but items which have been assessed relative to his general knowledge and other aspects of the present state. The experienced controller can remember more items as his working memory is more structured, so he has a wider overview of the process state and needs to sample less often to check forgotten values. This picture of the present state can take many minutes to acquire.

In a process control task the operator may have to decide not only between alternative control settings but also between different ways in which the process can be used and his time can be allocated to his several responsibilities. Cognitive behaviour in these information processing tasks is organized in a complex way. The basic task operations consist of perceptual judgements and dynamic control plus information processing operations of calculation, judgement and prediction. The operations are organized together into routines; alternative methods and the pay-offs of using them must be identified. The operator must also learn which behaviour is appropriate in which context, and the ways in which the same routine or data may be relevant in different contexts. He must be able to identify these contexts and to predict the interacting effects of any behaviour he chooses to do. His choice of behaviour depends on a stored mental picture of the process state and on the costs and tolerances.

The tasks of an operator who is associated with an automated plant are different but not necessarily easier. If he has to monitor the automatic controllers' performance he needs to know the characteristics of good control and to identify the presence of faults, he therefore needs some dynamic control skill and process knowledge. If he has to set controller set-points he must decide what these should be. He must know not only the dynamics of the process but also the dynamics of the controllers; for example if the response of a three-term controller is 'sticky' he will use a different pattern of set-points. If he is expected to take over manual control he needs at least the same skills as a manual controller. The operator only takes over manual control if there is something wrong with the plant or the automatic controllers. If an operator with little skill takes over control he may send the plant into oscillation (see Figure 11.5) and so make the fault worse and his own task more difficult. It can be argued that an operator who takes over under fault conditions is faced with more complex control decisions and so needs more process knowledge and higher levels of control skill than are needed for normal manual control. The control exercised must vary according to the nature of the fault. The operator must be able to diagnose the fault and to allow for this in choosing his control actions. He needs flexible control skills so that he is able to control in different ways as necessary.

Manual take-over therefore requires highly developed mental control skills. Many automated plants are monitored by men who controlled the plants manually before automation. High level skills deteriorate rapidly if they are not exercised however, so it cannot be assumed that these men will retain their skills. Take, for example, a plant on which product quality has formerly been judged by the operators, using perceptual skills. When instrumentation to measure the product is added the operator is expected to control from the instrument readings. Product output may deteriorate, because the instrumentation does not measure all important aspects of the product and the operators lose the skills of patterning the direct visual information. New operators must learn to make control judgements and they can learn the process dynamics only by direct involvement in control. They can learn next to nothing about the feel of control from watching an automatic controller at work (Brigham and Laios, 1975), although skills can improve over many years of informal on-the-job experience.

We have seen that it is important for operators to maintain and develop their feel for process dynamics. As this can only be done by direct involvement in control this suggests that some control functions should be allocated to the human operator in an automated plant even when this is not technically necessary. One method which has been tried is for the automatic controller (computer) to suggest a control action, the operator assesses it and then presses an 'accept' button. However, when the computer very rarely makes a mistake the operator comes to 'accept' automatically without any check. This method may be good for giving an operator confidence in the computer's control, but it is no help in maintaining his control skill and useless as a way of monitoring automatic control performance. An alternative is for operators to control the process manually for a short period at the beginning of each shift. This is economically worthwhile if the costs of poorer productivity during this period are less than the costs of lost productivity during plant failure because the operator is not able adequately to take over control or assess failure. The only other alternative is to use special training sessions on high-fidelity simulators, as in aircraft pilot training.

Manual take-over involves some fault diagnosis, which also depends on a knowledge of process dynamics and mechanisms. There is some evidence that when an operator who formerly controlled manually has been monitoring automatic equipment for some years his knowledge of these relations deteriorates. (This deterioration of knowledge will be familiar to anyone who took an examination some years ago in a subject they have not used since.) The operator then no longer knows the symptom malfunction relations and alternative modes of control which are need to diagnose and deal with the breakdown. This is ironical as the operator is often retained in an automated plant mainly to deal with breakdowns. This suggests that operators on automated plant need frequent breakdown training exercises, perhaps by simple test 'games' rather than complex simulation, to remind them of process structure and relationships (see Duncan and Gray, 1975; Duncan and Shepherd, 1975).

A human operator uses not only a general 'mental model' of dynamic process behaviour but also a 'mental picture' of the present process state. The breadth and integration of this mental picture depend on the operator's general task knowledge, and the picture takes time to develop. When a human operator takes over from automatic controllers he may take several minutes to acquire and interrelate sufficient process information to make wise control decisions. He is working in high uncertainty. He knows nothing about the present process state, he also does not know what parts of the process are working normally, so more checks are needed than under normal conditions. This combination of time pressure, uncertainty and high sampling rate make a high workload, and very efficient behaviour is needed. A highly skilled operator should be able to identify, anticipate and control the normal aspects of the process behaviour more easily. He should also remember more items in a more integrated way and so should need to sample less to maintain the same amount of information. For both these reasons the inexperienced operator should have a lower workload to enable him to cope with fault conditions. However, these points suggest that the workload at plant break-down would be lowest, and the operator able to take over control most quickly and efficiently, if he always had an up-to-date mental picture of the present and possible future process states and events, ready for use as necessary. This ongoing mental picture cannot be maintained by making the operator fill out a formal log-sheet, as logging can be done almost auto-matically. Also the mental picture develops as part of doing the job; the pro-cess data remembered have been assessed and integrated, and are stored in close relation with the task decisions for rapid access. This therefore implies that to maintain a well-structured ongoing mental picture and so avoid delay between manual take-over and effective action the operator must again be actively involved in process control, and continuously rather than for short periods.

An operator who can take over manual control is needed on a process when it is not possible to shut down the process automatically and take over must be rapid so there is not time to call in someone else on the plant. As we have seen, only a highly skilled operator can take over adequately. He needs very flexible skills to control the plant in unusual conditions, he needs a highly organized mental picture so that he can anticipate process behaviour, and he needs considerable process knowledge to identify faults. Unfortu-nately, on the job experience in automated plants provides almost negligible opportunities to maintain or develop such skills.

The operator has little on-the-job opportunity to learn about the plant, both because his control experience is all gained under unusual fault condi-tions from which it is difficult to generalize, and because faults needing manual take-over are usually rare on automated plant. The low probability of events has other equally important effects. When a skilled manual con-troller has his process under control he is able to predict when the process will need attention again and can leave the task without much uncertainty. In automated plants the human operator is often retained as a machine minder to notice process faults which are unpredictable. He cannot leave the task, yet when there is a very low probability of change in an information source it is humanly impossible to attend continuously to it, ability to notice changes deteriorates badly within half an hour. 'Machine minding' tasks are therefore an inefficient use of a human operator not only because he has nothing to do for most of the time but also because the machine minding will not be done well.

When this type of task situation continues for longer periods of time it leads to the classic job-dissatisfaction symptoms of high accident rates, high sickness rates, high absenteeism and high labour turn-over. When the operators are both skilled and intelligent, the problems of job-dissatisfaction are increased, such people are less tolerant of boredom. Also a person's status in the plant, and his self-esteem, depend partly on his level of skill. When this skill is both usurped by the automatic controllers and also deteriorates because it cannot be exercised this leads to justifiable resentment. These points again suggest that operators should be actively involved in the control task; this will keep them more aware, more attentive and more interested.

This discussion suggests that it is imperative for the human operator to maintain and develop his general knowledge of process-dynamics and relations, for use in control, planning and diagnosis. The economy of his behaviour will depend on his mental picture of the present and future process states, which in turn depends on his general knowledge. While his knowledge of both long-term process behaviour and the short-term present and future states can be encouraged by good control panel design they must also be supported by training exercises and by ongoing involvement in the job.

ACKNOWLEDGEMENTS

Figure 11.3 is reproduced from a figure in Edwards and Lees (1972). Figures 11.2, 4, 5 and 6 are reproduced from figures in Edwards and Lees (1974). The writer would like to thank the authors and publishers involved for giving their permission.

References

Anyakora, S. N. and Lees, F. P. (1972). Detection of instrument malfunction by the Process Operator. *Chem. Engr., Lond.*, **264**, 304 (Reprinted in Edwards and Lees, op. cit.)

Attwood, D. (1970). The interaction between human and automatic control. In *Paper-Making Systems and their Control* (F. Bolam, ed.), p. 69. Br. Paper and Board Makers Ass., London (Reprinted in Edwards and Lees, 1974, op. cit.)

Bainbridge, L. (1971). The influence of display type on decision-making strategy. In *Displays, Conf. Publ. No. 80*, p. 209, Inst. Elec. Eng., London

Bainbridge, L. (1974). *Analysis of verbal protocols from a process control task.* (*In* Edwards and Lees, op. cit., p. 146)

Bainbridge, L. (1975). The representation of working storage, and its use in the organisation of behaviour. In *Measurement of Human Resources* (W. T. Singleton and P. Spurgeon, eds.), p. 165 (London: Taylor & Francis)

Bainbridge, L., Beishon, J., Hemming, J. H. and Splaine, M. (1968). A study of real-time human decision-making using a plant simulator. *Oper. Res. Q.*, **19**, *Special Conf. Issue*, p. 91 (Reprinted in Edwards and Lees, 1974, op. cit)

Beishon, R. J. (1966). *A study of some aspects of mental skill in the performance of laboratory and industrial tasks.* D.Phil. Thesis, Univ. of Oxford

Beishon, R. J. (1967). Problems of task description in process control. *Ergonomics*, **10**, 177

Beishon, R. J. (1969). An analysis and simulation of an operator's behaviour in controlling continuous baking ovens. In *The Simulation of Human Behaviour* (A. de Brisson, ed.), p. 329. Dunod, Paris (Reprinted in Edwards and Lees, 1974, op. cit.)

Brigham, F. R. and Laios, L. (1975). Operator performance in the control of a laboratory process plant. *Ergonomics*, **18**, 53

Clark, J. A. (1972). *Display for the chemical plant operator*. M.Sc. Thesis, Univ. Manchester Inst. Sci. Technol.

Cooke, J. E. (1965). *Human Decisions in the control of a slow response system*. D.Phil. Thesis, Univ. Oxford

Crossman, E. R. F. W. and Cooke, J. E. (1962). Manual Control of slow response systems. *Int. Congr. on Human Factors in Electronics, Long Beach, Calif* (Reprinted in Edwards and Lees, 1974, op. cit.)

Crossman, E. R. F. W., Cooke, J. E. and Beishon, R. J. (1964). Visual attention and the sampling of displayed information in process control. *Univ. of California, Berkeley, Calif., Hum. Factors in Technol. Res. Gp. Rep.* HFT 64-11-7 (Reprinted in Edwards and Lees, 1974, op. cit.)

Duncan, K. A. and Gray, M. J. (1975). An evaluation of a fault finding training course for refinery process operators. *J. Occup. Psychol.*, **48**, 199

Duncan, K. A. and Shepherd, A. (1975). A simulator and training technique for diagnosing plant failures from control panels. *Ergonomics*, **18**, 627

Edwards, E. and Lees, F. P. (1972). Man and Computer in Process Control. *Inst. Chem. Eng.*, London

Edwards, E. and Lees, F. P. (eds.) (1974). *The Human Operator in Process Control* (London: Taylor & Francis)

Engelstadt, P. H. (1970). In *Paper-Making Systems and their Control* (F. Bolam, ed.), p. 91. Br. Paper & Board Makers Ass., London (Reprinted in Edwards and Lees, 1974, op. cit.)

Iosif, G. (1968). La strategie dans le surveillance des tableaux de commande. I. Quelques facteurs déterminants de caractère objectif. *Rev. Roum. Sci. Sociales—Psychol.*, **12**, 147

Iosif, G. (1969a). II. Quelques facteurs déterminants de caractère subjectif. *Rev. Roum. Sci. Sociales—Psychol.*, **13**, 29

Iosif, G. (1969b). III. Influence de la correlation fontionnelle sur les paramètres technologiques. *Rev. Roum. Sci. Sociales—Psychol.*, **13**, 105

Ketteringham, P. H. A. and O'Brien, D. D. (1974). *Simulation study of computer-aided soaking pit scheduling* (*In* Edwards and Lees, op. cit., p. 260)

King, P. L. and Cincines, A. (1976). Manual control strategy determination using questionnaires. Warren Spring Laboratory, Stevenage. LR. 236 (CON)

Kragt, H. and Landeweerd, J. A. (1974). *Mental skills in process control* (*In* Edwards and Lees, op. cit., p. 135)

Leplat, J. and Bisseret, A. (1965). Analyse des processus de traitement de l'information chez le contrôleur de la navigation aérienne. *Bull. du C.E.R.P.*, **1–2**, 51

Sinclair, I. A. C., Sell, R. G., Beishon, R. J. and Bainbridge, L. (1966). Ergonomics study of an LD waste heat boiler control room. *J. Iron Steel Inst.*, **204**, 434

Spencer, J. (1962). An investigation of process control skill. *Occup. Psychol.*, **36**, 30 (Reprinted in Edwards and Lees, 1974, op. cit.)

West, B. and Clark, J. A. (1974). *Operator interaction with a computer-controlled distillation column* (*In* Edwards and Lees, op. cit., p. 206)

12

The Tea Blender

B. A. LACY

IMPORTANCE AND CONTEXT OF THE TASK

Tea is grown in a great number of locations across the world from Asia to South America at altitudes which range from sea level to many thousand feet. Tea plantations, normally called gardens, exceed 6000 in number and each garden has its own characteristics, rather like the variability between vineyards. There is an added complication, because unlike a vineyard, the crop is not all harvested at one time of the year. The tea picked at the beginning of the season, the first flush, is quite different from the autumnal teas picked at the end of the season. The seasons of course vary with the location and altitude. After tea is picked it is processed, at the garden, to change it from a green leaf to the dry black cut leaf that we use to make a pot of tea. There are at least three major ways of processing tea resulting in products with very different attributes. Some teas keep well and will last for up to 12 months, other teas have a very much shorter life. All teas deteriorate with age.

Tea is sold by private purchase or auction in the countries of origin and in London. It is normally sold in lots which can be quite small, perhaps only half a dozen 45 kg chests or the lots may be several hundred chests. It is also possible to buy complete crops from a garden in advance of harvesting. There are various conventions about when the purchaser pays for the tea and about the period for which the tea will be warehoused without charge after auction purchase. There is at least a 10 to 1 price ratio between cheap and expensive tea.

In the exposition which follows, the task of the tea blender is regarded as the whole function of enabling the growers to be interfaced with the consumers in the home. The task includes buying the tea because this is really the first step in blending the tea. In practice buying and blending may be done by two people but they work very closely, it is the workload and particular personality attributes which can make it convenient to split the task into two functions. Any particular group of tea blenders cannot be properly studied in isolation from other groups in other organizations. The task is essentially competitive, in the sense that they are competing for the same supply of tea and are trying to satisfy the requirements of the same consumers. This is of course a loose generalization, for example, not all organizations necessarily attempt to supply all consumer requirements. Fundamentally the task of the tea blender is to interpret the requirements of the consumer and to economically satisfy these requirements by the purchase and blending of tea.

In a large tea packing organization many millions of pounds will be spent annually on the purchase and storage of tea. The number of tea blenders could be not more than about half a dozen. So there are a few men who hold the key to whether the business is viable. A small drop in their effectiveness can wipe out the profit of the organization. Anything approaching a major error would certainly bring the business to a halt. Viewed in a wider context, if consumers are not supplied with their requirements at what they consider to be a reasonable cost they will drink other beverages and so effect the total tea trade with serious consequences for some countries which rely considerably on their tea exports.

THE TASK

Tasting

Each week, in a large organization, in excess of 1000 samples of teas will be received from brokers. These samples will be identified by their origin, type and date of manufacture. The broker will also add his tasting assessment of quality and likely sale price. Samples from brokers are accepted as being representative of the bulk from which they have been taken.

These samples of tea are sorted into homogeneous groups and put into a rough sequence of quality. The teas are then made up into tasting batches. This is done by weighing a precise quantity of each sample into separate pots which are then filled with a precise volume of freshly boiled water. The pots are like large mugs with lids. After brewing for a timed period the liquor is poured into a bowl until the mug is empty of liquor and the tea leaves are held on the lid of the mug. The lid is placed on the mug so that the leaves are exposed to view. A measured portion of milk is added to the liquor in the bowl. A batch usually consists of about 40 teas arranged on a long well lighted counter. Each tea is thus represented by a bowl of milked liquor, the spent tea leaves and a sample of the original tea leaves from which the liquor was brewed.

The first tasting task is usually done by a junior taster who will examine the appearance of the tea liquor and taste the liquor by taking a spoonful from the bowl, sucking it noisily from the spoon to the back of the mouth and then spitting into a large spittoon. The purpose of the examination is to put the teas in a better order for the tea buyer who will next examine the teas. The first order in which the teas will have been put on the counter will be according to the brokers assessment, which may not correspond with the way in which a particular organization uses teas and hence attaches value to specific features.

The teas will next be tasted by a buyer, who will do this at great speed, just taking sufficient time for the physical movements involved in spooning the tea from the bowl, sucking it from the spoon and spitting it into the spittoon. As he does this he will call out his assessment of the tea using an alpha-numeric code and occasionally adding remarks to amplify the code. A clerk follows the buyer listing his assessment on a sheet against the details of each sample tasted.

Buying

Separately from his tasting activity the buyer will have been involved in the creation of a buying strategy. This strategy is based on the expected availability and price of tea together with the forecasted demand for the various named blends of tea sold by the organization. The creation of this strategy is an iterative process, because the formulae for the blends can be changed to enable a viable strategy to be formed.

The next step is to decide which of the tasted and assessed teas should be purchased or bid for at auction. The aim of the purchase being to build the intended stock of particular types of tea at the time required to meet the strategy. If teas are purchased overseas, rather than in the London auction, account must be taken of the time required between purchase and availability in the United Kingdom. It is not usual to buy tea for immediate use because the price will probably be high, since the buyer cannot be so selective if he must purchase to meet immediate demand.

The decision process of whether or not to buy, although done against the quantified strategy, is in itself highly subjective. It is based on the buyers knowledge of the market in terms of the movement of prices and future availability of various teas. This knowledge is based on statistics of production and stock levels in various countries, published frequently by the tea trade, and intelligence supplied by brokers and on more informal exchange of information with many individuals.

Blending

There are two stages to blending, first there is the creation of the formula for a particular named blend and secondly the putting together of specific tea purchases to make up a mix of tea which can be packed and sold as the named blend.

Assuming the blend is an ongoing brand of tea, then the formula creation will be a modification of an existing formula, to take account of the price and availability of tea, or to meet or gain some competitive advantage over a rival blend which is competing for the same consumers. The structure and defining of the formula is discussed in a following section dealing with task analysis. Even a completely new blend is in reality a modification of the formula for one or more existing blends, since the blender will inevitably build on his past knowledge of blends. The formula is a statement of the number of parts of broad groupings of types of tea that are to be used in a blend.

The second stage of the blending task is to taste the teas that have been purchased so as to more carefully define each purchase. The mixes of teas to create the various blends are then compiled. This is done by selecting teas to meet the blend formula. The correct amount of each tea selected is then weighed out and mixed together to form a miniature blend. This blend is then brewed in the same way as the tasting samples and it is tasted against a brew made from a sample of a standard mix of that blend if it is an ongoing blend, or against a brew of any other blend which the blender may consider to be relevant. If the blender considers that the mix that he has compiled is satisfactory it is passed for making up as a large scale factory produced mix. A sample will later be taken from the factory mix and this will be tasted against the standard and possibly also against the miniature on which it was based.

CHANGES IN THE TASK

The basic task of the tea blender has not changed for many decades. Such changes as have occurred are in the way in which the information obtained by tasting is coded and used. There have been changes in the types and quantities of teas available to the blender and there has probably been a change in attitude causing a move away from the emphasis on the subjective art of blending towards a more cost effective justification of the task.

THE CONSEQUENCES OF UNDERSTANDING THESE SKILLS

When considering the analysis of a real skill it is essential to have a real objective. It is not sufficient to just hope that some good will come from the study. A real skill is so multi-faceted that it is not practical to pursue the study on all possible fronts. Very early on it is necessary to consider the justification for the study and this will cause it to be orientated in a particular way. There is of course the danger that as the study progresses, the analyst may miss an opportunity to change direction or emphasis that would be beneficial, because he has become too fixed on his original objective, but this is a risk which has to be taken and is not too great if borne constantly in mind.

The analysis described in this paper resulted from the classical conflict of interests between the quality controller and the producer. The producer thinks that the quality controller is turning down good production and the quality controller considers that the producer is not following standard procedures and therefore not meeting the quality standards. When the standard is a subjective thing like taste or general appearance the opportunity for misunderstanding is increased. The question posed by the management was: 'Are our quality tolerances too tight?' This led to a series of further questions. There was a need for a more objective measurement which could be communicated by a tea taster to a 'lay' person, so that the tasters could set a standard which was agreed to be necessary to satisfy the consumers requirements and was accepted as practical.

Consideration of measuring varying blend standards leads to the consideration of other uses for the measurement, than just quality control. Could the measurement be used in the formulation of the blend and then in the compilation of the individual mixes of the blend? If it were possible to create a common measure of the attributes of tea, regardless of whether the tea was an unblended original tea or blended tea, and if the way in which the attributes combined when tea was blended could also be measured, then the mathematical technique of linear programming might be used. This would enable vast numbers of possible combinations of teas to be explored mathematically and the total cost of tea purchases, financing and storage to be minimized whilst meeting the required quality standards and all the other restrictions imposed by the environment of the business.

In a business with a multi-million pounds turnover only a very small improvement in the cost optimization is needed to make very significant savings. Apart from the immediate tangible savings to be gained from objective measurement, the way would be opened to better consumer research because more precise hypotheses could be tested. Tea usage research in general would be improved because the researchers, usually chemists and not tea tasters, could be given a language with which they could communicate more precisely with the tea tasters. Simulation of various approaches to the buying and blending of tea would become possible on a much larger scale, than would be possible with the traditional information and handling methods.

The possibilities outlined above were achieved by analysis of the skills of tea blending and in addition there was a general benefit by enabling the tea tasters themselves and people of various other disciplines to understand each other and work together on common problems.

THE ANALYSIS

General approach

The task of analysing the function of tea blending at first seems daunting. The tea trade terminology is incomprehensible to the uninitiated, for example, pekoe, fannings, brokens, breaks, chests, spot, legge-cut, scribe, and thousands of names of tea gardens, are just part of the maze that must be penetrated at the start. Combine this with a mass of facts about where and how tea is sold, copious statistics of production, prices and stocks of original teas and the analyst starts to get overwhelmed. Additionally the tea trade is very traditional, almost a sort of closed society, where the outsider, although treated most courteously feels he does not belong.

A possible reaction to the situation is to regard it all as mystique, be completely cynical and declare no real skill exists until it is proved measurable and consistent between various blenders. This is a mistaken approach, if the analyst cannot measure the skill, it is he who has failed. The skill manifestly exists, since it creates order out of the 'chaos' of available teas which are the input to the system.

The most fruitful approach is to set up a rapport with the tea blenders. Seek the pieces which can be fitted together rather than concentrating on the anomalies. Find blenders of experience who can agree about what they are doing, gain from them an understanding of what the effective person does. This helps to avoid the confusion of inter-subject differences and later the results will be more readily accepted because the information used to arrive at conclusions has been obtained from people of some seniority. This approach may seem to be not sufficiently rigorous or not to take advantage of the curiosity which is often stimulated by the piece that does not fit in the experimental findings and then leads to the real discovery. It is a matter of degree. Too rigorous and the work will grind to a halt. Too lax and the results will not stand the test of practical use. The analyst must be continually aware of the risks that he is taking and make his own judgement.

Tasting analysis

At the time of the study, the terminology used by the tasters to describe the tea they had tasted, had an emphasis on general quality. The terms were not orientated towards attributes that the tea possessed relevant to its use in a blend of tea. Nor were the terms very concise in their meaning. During observation of tasting and discussions with the tasters, it became apparent that some form of psycho-physical scaling would be possible. From these discussions and much trial and error with tasting, six dimensions of tea quality were agreed to be the basis of the construction of a blend of tea. These attributes are shown in Table 12.1.

Table 12.1 **The six attributes of tea quality for construction of a blend**

Attribute*	Description
B. Brightness	A bright tea has a lively fresh appearance, a dull tea looks matt and dead
C. Colour	Teas range from a yellowish grey to a red brown
T. Thickness	The tactile sensation of the tea in the mouth ranges from watery to creamy
S. Soft/Coarseness	Tea can range from lacking in any astringency to being harsh and acidy
P. Briskness/Pungency	This is a tea tasting term referring to a desirable strength in the tea
F. Flavour	This is a special use of the word 'flavour' and refers to a very desirable tea taste sensation, somewhat akin to the roundness of a smooth good quality wine

* All these attributes refer to a milked infusion of tea.

Validation of analysis

It was then decided to build up a library of teas, which would be tasted using the scale marking standards, so that each tea in the library would be numerically defined in respect of each attribute.

Over a period of several weeks a sample of 40 teas was drawn from the library each day and was tasted by three tasters. The results were correlated with the original tastings and differences between tasters was tested. Correlation coefficients greater than the 0·9 were obtained and were significant at $P = 0.001$. Inter-subject differences were minimal between the three tasters involved, who had all been concerned with defining the attributes and creating the measuring scales. Later in the project when other tasters were introduced to this concept of tasting, a learning period was required before they accepted the concept and were able to produce consistent results.

Although these repeat tastings were successful the problem of drifting standards was recognized. For example, the brightness of teas used as tasting standards, apart from gradually becoming exhausted in quantity as they were used, were also deteriorating. It would therefore be very desirable to be able to replace these standard teas, using some completely objective physical measurement of the attributes, or to be able to measure something which was correlated with the attributes.

Brightness and Colour measurement. The attributes which were considered most likely to lend themselves to physical measurement were brightness and colour. Attempts in the past had been made to correlate the tasters assessment of brightness with the normal scientific measurement of brightness defined as the percentage of light reflected from a standard magnesium carbonate block. This was not successful and the attempt to make this correlation showed a lack of understanding of what the tea taster means when he refers to brightness. A tea can be bright yet dark in colour and so reflect less light than a dull tea which has little colour. It was apparent that brightness must be considered in the context of the colour of the tea. It was also apparent that any physical measurement of these two attributes would require a sophisticated instrument.

Within quite wide tolerances the taster will make allowances for a drop in the temperature of the tea he is examining. He knows that the brightness is lowered as the temperature drops and he is able to make some allowance for this, unless the temperature drop is considerable in which case he will not evaluate the tea. A leaf floating on the surface is ignored by the taster, whereas any meter will integrate the colour value of the leaf with the rest of the surface of the tea infusion.

Chemical analysis of attributes. In addition to the physical measurement of the visual attributes of the tea infusion, gas chromatography was used to measure the coloured polyphenals (theaflavins and thearubugins) and the colourless polyphenols (which include caffeine and gallic acid). The heights of the peaks of the chromatograms obtained, were correlated with the tasters evaluations of the six defined attributes. Indices of determination between the height of a particular peak and any single attribute were not better than 0·46. However, significant equations were found linking all peak heights with some of the attributes and these had indices of determination as large as 0·70.

Although these results were not of practical use, they did indicate that the taster is indeed measuring things which have references which are external to the subjective tasting system. Again, it is interesting to compare the perceptual ability of the taster who can evaluate 100 or more teas in an hour, with the considerable effort required by the chemist who needs about 4 h to evaluate a single tea.

Blending. The attributes and their measurements, to be of use, had to be valid in the context of blending tea. It was necessary to know what are the resultant attributes when individual teas of known attributes are mixed. Experiments were performed starting with mixing 2 teas and finally with mixes of 20 teas, which at the time was the maximum number of different teas normally used in a blend.

The crucial test of blending validity using the concept of attributes which had been defined, was to get the tasters to measure the attributes of the blends of tea which were being marketed, and then for the analyst to create matching blends from teas in the library of teas which the tasters had evaluated. These 'analysts blends' were then tasted against the marketed blends. Tests consisted of repetitions of six samples of the 'analysts blends' with six samples of the marketed blend, randomly sequenced and tasted 'blind' by the tasters. The tasters attempted to identify the 'analysts blends' but could not significantly distinguish between the two blends.

Reliability and validity. The objective of the blender's task is to economically satisfy the consumer demand. The analysis described so far, has been concerned with understanding the reliability of tasting tea and mixing teas to create specified blend characteristics. Although the term validity has often been used, in fact, it is the internal reliability of the system which has been examined without testing its validity relevant to an external reference. Such a reference is the differential threshold of the consumer. Is the taster measuring attributes which are meaningful to the consumer and are the blends he is creating properly matched to consumer preferences?

These questions can be tackled by a laboratory assessment of consumer behaviour or a field assessment in consumer's homes. The former approach is unreliable because it is likely to standardize many of the random factors which are a feature of real consumer behaviour such as, brewing time, amount of tea used, or amount of milk used. It would of course be possible to build all these factors into laboratory experiments, but having assessed their effects it would then be necessary to find out how they occurred in the consumer universe. Apart from this objection there is also the difficulty that tea is normally drunk in the context of meeting a need. This context is different in the laboratory to the home situation.

The field experiment because it does pick up all the random features of the home situation, is likely to lead to totally inconclusive results. This can only be overcome by a very large well planned experiment. What is required is to distribute a number of blends of tea to a large number of households. The blends put into each household need to be controlled so that certain attributes are held constant whilst others are varied. A questionnaire about preferences for the blends is completed by each household. Such an experiment was made possible by using the attribute concept and by using a computer with a linear program package, to produce a complete set of blend formulae which would meet the experimental design. With traditional blend quality definitions this would have been a most time-consuming and almost impossible task.

In designing an experiment of this type one quickly realizes that a totally rigorous approach is impractical. For example, a complete block design would require 29 400 different blends, from which 432 165 300 pairs can be selected for paired comparisons. Even an incomplete block design is not practical because many of the theoretically possible blend combinations of attributes are not possible in practice. The approach adopted was to do two separate experiments. In the first only one attribute in a paired comparison of two blends was changed. This experiment used 100 different blends, tasted in pairs, and with each pair replicated between 20 and 50 times depending on the importance of the pair, this gave a sample size of 2500 households. A second experiment was undertaken in which two attributes were varied in each comparison, so as to test the interaction between attributes. The choice of attributes which were varied depended on the sensitivity to the attribute discovered in the first experiment. Initially only interactions between major changes in the attributes was tested, and if significant results were obtained, then the interaction of smaller changes was tested. This second set of experiments involved a similar sample size to the first experiment.

The results of these experiments showed that the consumer was sensitive to the attributes which the blender was manipulating in a blend of tea and that they were most sensitive to those attributes which were most costly to increase in the blend. This latter finding was disappointing, in as much as it precluded any economically revolutionary change in marketed blends, but it substantiated that the chosen attributes were in keeping with previous practice. Some attributes were shown to be less important than had previously been supposed. It was now possible to be confident that it was a valid concept to measure the quality of original tea in terms of attributes and to have a blending objective which is to make these attributes reach certain magnitudes. The desirable magnitudes can be determined by market research.

PUTTING THE STUDY TO USE

The exercise of helping to make an objective analysis of what they are doing when they taste and blend tea, was in itself helpful to them. They could start to make more use of the information that they gain when tasting tea, because they were now annotating this information much more thoroughly and it was being quantified. The possibility of blending teas, with advantage, which it was not customary to put together, could be explored more easily.

To progress beyond the development of a tasting method which improved the information gained, it was necessary to consider how the information could be put into a form to enable it to be used in the total buying and blending system.

Information grouping

The tea blender traditionally thinks in terms of grouping teas according to their country of origin and then refines his groups according to location within the country, time of harvesting and type of manufacture. He will also have a concept of cheap, medium and expensive teas within the country of origin. Although he makes these groupings he regards each purchase of tea as being unique. When he specifies a mix of tea, he will state how much tea from each of a number of purchases is to be used. He does not just specify how much tea from a number of generic groups is to be used.

Statistical cluster techniques might have been used to determine the minimum number of groups which would include all the combinations of attributes which occur and the extent to which this number could be reduced if infrequently occurring combinations were included in adjacent groups. It was found to be easier to use the experience of the blenders on a trial and error basis. Starting by making a rough analysis and gradually refining the groups to eliminate those which were ambiguous. In this way we ensured that the groups were conceptually relevant to the blenders. They could think of a group as containing certain types of tea and then superimposing on it, the value of its attributes. This enabled them to hold in memory several hundred groups.

Linear programming

Very early in the study of the skill of tea blending it was decided to orientate the work towards examining the possibility and advantages of using linear programming to blend tea. At this stage we had a method of placing all purchases of tea into defined groups and we knew the linear functions governing the way in which these groups combined to form blends of tea. The next task was to specify all the restrictions involved in buying and blending tea and to state the objective function of the linear programme. There is probably no better way of finding out exactly how a task is performed than trying to computerize it. Any faults in the logic of the analysis of task will be ruthlessly exposed by the computer. Possible branches in the logic of the task which are not at all apparent, but are being handled intuitively by the human operator, cause the computer to abort or produce nonsense results.

The task must be stated to be the minimization or maximization of an objective, subject to a set of restrictions relating to a set of parameters. The objective was defined as minimizing the total cost of buying tea and holding it in stock. This objective has to be put into the context of a finite period of time. The time period requirements are both short-term and long-term. Short-term because tea needs to be bought every week and long-term because optimization of the immediate future can set up a difficult situation for the next period. So the task must be seen as a series of time periods each feeding into the next period and finally ending with a far away advantageous situation, which in practice is never achieved because the plan is updated before the first horizon is reached. In other words it it no good blending cheaply in the immediate future if at the end of this period a properly balanced stock is not available to enter the next period. It is not the intention of this paper to attempt to provide a detailed specification of the inputs and outputs of the tea buying and blending linear programme. The purpose of mentioning the topic is to show that mathematical models have a role in task analysis and to give an indication of the amount of information that the tea blender is handling.

During the course of specifying the programme the blenders introduced a number of restrictions which were overlaid on the basic attributes of brightness, colour and the rest, these restrictions were safeguards to ensure that a number of traditional indicators of blend quality and style were not contravened too drastically. The linear programme matrix which resulted from all the requirements and restrictions was very large indeed. First attempts to run the programme on an IBM360/50, in a 250 K byte partition of the core using the then current IBM mathematical programming system resulted in running times in excess of 20 h. It was only when a faster machine was used with a more efficient LP package that a running time of less than 2 h was achieved. This is an indication of the immense amount of information that the blender is handling, it is true that no one person solves the whole blending problem in detail as is being done by the computer, but the senior blender certainly has a grasp of the total situation.

Effect on blender's confidence

When an investigation is made into a system which has gradually evolved and which has become the accepted way of doing a job, there is a danger that the staff will lose their traditional references and anchors. During a period of questioning a senior tea taster, he asked whether the analyst had heard the tale of the centipede who was asked in what sequence he used his legs, and had laid helpless in the ditch ever since. This cautionary tale needs to be heeded. Several times during the study the blenders felt that there was a danger that they would 'lose their place'. What they meant was that various streams of information were brought together by them and fused to produce a result, a Gestalt effect. Any disturbance of this situation could cause chaos. The change to the attribute grading and blending concept was made very slowly and all the staff were involved in the decisions taken as the change was implemented.

THE SKILLS OF THE BLENDER

At the end of long study and implementation of a new way of doing the task that was studied, it is still hard to say what the blender can do that other people cannot do. There are two aspects to the task, tasting tea and knowledge of the tea trade.

Tea tasting

There is no evidence that tea tasters are a specially selected group who have any physiologically superior sensory ability in respect of taste, smell or vision. Nor do they themselves take any action that might be expected to keep these senses in an enhanced condition. They are commonly heavy smokers and the tea trade is by no means abstemious. The tasting skill is very much a trained skill. The tasters have been alerted to the presence of various features of the taste, smell and appearance of tea so that their absolute and differential thresholds for these features are different to those of non-tasters. This is more so in respect of taste than of vision. This was a finding of the consumer research previously described.

These lowered thresholds enable a taster to work at great speed. An unusual feature of their performance is that their sensory abilities do not seem to become fatigued. Whereas a non-taster having tasted say 10 teas, would require major changes in the teas to differentiate between them, a taster will taste 40 or more teas in a batch quickly one after the other. Indeed the secret may well be in the speed of tasting so that one tea does not saturate the senses before moving on to the next. Also the lingering sensation from the previous tea is probably used so as to make a differential judgement when the next is tasted. This is supported by the fact that tasters prefer to taste a batch of similar teas. When tasting teas offered for sale they have the teas tasted previously by a junior taster who puts the teas into fairly homogenous and graduated groups.

Knowledge

The blender has an immense knowledge of what type of tea comes from each area and even each tea garden throughout the world. He also knows how the tea varies at different times of the year. This knowledge enables him to:
1. Know what to expect when he tastes a tea, so that he is alerted to particular attributes and readily detects differences from expectation
2. Judge the value of tea very precisely from its likely price, origin and date of manufacture. He knows whether certain teas will be good or bad buys and whether they will fit into his strategy
3. To work quickly when producing blends because he knows which teas are likely to have the attributes he requires, even without studying the tasting results. His knowledge also enables him to counteract errors in the system information because he is quick to see that facts do not fit and need to be investigated.

Mental abilities

The blender is very used to considering alternatives and evaluating likely or actual results. His mental arithmetic is extremely fast and the speed at which lots of tea are auctioned is impressive. This whole area of information handling is characterized by the immense familiarity that the blenders have with their subject, enabling them to communicate and manipulate data with a minimum of redundancy.

CONCLUSION

The analysis of this task was essentially achieved by the tea blenders themselves. They were guided towards an analysis which would be useful and they were prevented from going up too many blind alleys. From the outset it was recognized that the most important, almost the only, source of information for the study were the tea blenders. The achievement of the study was that it demonstrated to the tea blenders that they were wasting much of the information that they obtained when tasting teas. This valuable information was recorded in terms which could be fundamental to the whole process of buying and blending tea.

It was shown that these terms used to record tasting information could be the language which would enable researchers to communicate accurately with the tea blenders. Once it was possible to quantify the previously only qualitative tasting information, mathematical programming could then be used to examine the vast array of alternative solutions which confront the tea blender. The study emphasized that man has perceptual abilities which when properly harnessed, together with his ability to store and handle data, make him a most economical sensor and processor of information.

13

The Information System Designer

R. B. MILLER

INTRODUCTION

The primary purpose of this chapter is to make some useful distinctions between job skills and job competences. Inevitably the criteria for making these distinctions will be relative and loose rather than rigorous. The operational significance of the differences is all that counts, however, and should be found in useful extensions to concepts and practices in job analysis and specification, training and assessment, possibly in selection, and certainly in career planning.

Let skills be provisionally defined as the effective application of the more or less sequential procedures of the job or profession. These procedures may be quite complex and performed, like keyboard exercises, with great virtuosity. On the other hand, competences are shown by the incumbent's coping with a larger context of information than is normally required for procedural adequacy: it may be the effective adaptation to the unusual and unexpected in problem situation or resource. More largely, competences can be viewed as coping conceptually with strategic variables for arriving at innovative compromises that, taken together, tend to optimize the solution itself and the operations taken for arriving at a solution. In layman's words, the competent man thinks constructively both before and while he is exercising his task skills. The distinction between skill and competence may range from wrapping packages to directing an enterprise.

A job is a collection of tasks. A person may be more skilled in some tasks than in others. Similarly a person may have some competences but not others.

But to simplify exposition in the following text, let us call the person 'proficient' if he is limited to the usual skills of the job and 'competent' if he can go beyond these limitations. A more colourful pair of terms would be 'artisan' and 'virtuoso'. We will have to recognize attitudinal and motivational components as well as performance capabilities as we explore examples of the distinction.

The meaning of 'information system' is as wide and diffuse as are the practices for designing one. An arbitrarily chosen, but legitimate, subset is the design of an application specification for data based, computer terminal oriented operations for the logistics and control level of activities in a large business. This is application system design as contrasted with designing the implementation in computer hardware and software. No attempt will be made here at a complete task identification and analysis of application design. Highlights in the design process will be examined in order to distinguish in principle between a skilled handling of work segment and an approach and execution that represents an individualized competence. The phases of design can be outlined as:
1. Conceptual approach to the problem and solution
2. Bounding the problem to be solved
3. Analysing the transactional structure of the defined problem
4. Developing a design concept
5. Creating the design specification
6. Testing the specification.

The reader is asked to accept an important caveat. The analysis which follows avoids the entire problem of budget restrictions, cost and cost analysis. As any realistic planner knows, this sidesteps a crucial constraint on every stage of design from problem concept to implementation. The inclusion of the cost dimension, however, would have imposed an impossible burden on the brevity and exposition of the chapter. But expertise in the costing dimensions of information system design would be almost a complete parallel for the expertise and creative imagination which designs for application 'benefits'.

CONCEPTUAL APPROACH TO THE PROBLEM

A strategy fundamental to human affairs in general is particularly important to every level and stage of design: proceed in a way that uncovers and allows the maximum number of feasible alternatives available for any next design or decision step or phase. Counter to this strategy is the practical limit of time and schedules. The merely skilled will tend to perceive and define a problem according to his job speciality and expertise. The highly competent person will tend to have several conceptual models, at least some of which will be more embracing than his speciality skills. Thus, the artisan's perception of an information system may be dominated by the objective of automating one or more segments of activity heretofore performed manually. He will tend to perceive the transmission, processing and storage of data as an end in itself. The virtuoso may perceive information in terms of its meaning for action and action decisions and its support for human and physical processes. He will approach the information system problem as an opportunity to create a new service or a new way of doing things. Or he will suspect that new interfaces can be created between the mechanism to be designed and the properties of the users of the mechanism. For example, the possibility of using the interactive computer to teach while the user is doing his daily work with the device may occur to him as a broadened base for the design of the application. To over-simplify: the mere artisan sees the design job as that of creating a mechanistic entity; the virtuoso sees the design job as that of creating an organic entity.

More subtly, the artisan sees an assignment as an opportunity to exercise his existing expertise, whereas the virtuoso sees an assignment as an opportunity to explore and expand the range of his expertise.

BOUNDING THE PROBLEM TO SOLVE

The potential extensibility of information systems is virtually infinite. It may encompass not only all the non-material processes in an enterprise, but its interactions with other enterprises, the government and the public at large. With some vision, even the design of so apparently well-bounded a problem as a company payroll processing may have hundreds of potential implications for the enterprise.

But the proficient artisan will seek to identify the functions which his sponsor wants automated. He will tend to accept the problem and its limits as given by the statements of his sponsor, and if it occurs to him to explore a deeper or broader context, to feel insecure and even anxious. To impose upon himself a larger responsibility than is explicitly assigned may be an unwelcome challenge.

The person of competence, by definition, will be bolder. He treats with respect the problem as stated, but at least initially as a point for departure and exploration. Thus, he may be asked to develop an 'information system' for the purchasing department. He may quickly sketch out actual and potential operational, hence informational, dependencies between purchasing, inventory control, accounting and the financial office, as well as between the purchasing and the requesting functions. This is extensibility of the 'problem' in breadth.

The person of competence may also distinguish at the outset between transaction structures that are essentially programmable or formatted from those which may be largely unformatted in the sense that Simon (1969) writes of non-programmed decisions. A non-programmable decision is one in which the objectives may be conflicting, or not enough information about situation or resource is available for a rational choice, or the problem parameters are not well known. The making of the decision requires human art and intuition or judgement. The opportunity to stockpile an expensive but possibly critical part from a key vendor threatened by a lengthy strike could be the opportunity for such a decision. This would not be a routine purchasing decision.

The competent designer may also search beyond the requirements of day-to-day purchasing operations and perceive the possibility of a historical data base about experiences with vendors. If such relevant data could be rapidly retrieved and presented to the purchasing agent, he could in effect bring a higher level of sophistication even to run-of-the-mill choices of vendors in filling purchase requisitions. The distinction between programmed and non-programmed purchase decisions, and the concept of a system that learns from experience are examples of extensibility of the 'problem' in depth.

It would seem likely that the competent person must have developed a variety of conceptual structures (models?) for organizing a large body of otherwise inchoate ideas. This kind of thinking contrasts with the single conceptual format for assimilating information that applies to the performance of a skill. The virtuoso's conceptual versatility may be manifest by rapidity in applying a modular structure even in sketching out a pattern of design elements. The block diagram is at least a primitive expression of modularity in function or in mechanism.

When, after exercising various feasibility criteria, the virtuoso decides on the boundaries of the problem he will actually tackle, these boundaries will have open interfaces to extensions of what he will accomplish. His preliminary proposal to management of the actual design problem he will solve may outline, more or less in operational terminology, reasonable extensions to the problem subset he is tackling and perhaps the means whereby such extensions could readily be attached to his present problem solution.

If the artisan, however, feels impelled to suggest a broader problem base than the one he has accepted, it will be expressed vaguely as a laundry list of 'potential add-on functions'. The names in the list may be more like well-used slogans high in the abstraction ladder, than pointing to operational significance.

PROBLEM ANALYSIS

The expression 'problem analysis' assumes a variety of meanings. The definition used in the present paper is indeed arbitrary: problem analysis is finding out what the application system has to do and the major parameters of the information that enables the work to get done. In personnel subsystems the expression 'task analysis' would be used for this activity. Data gathered in the process of bounding the problem would be carried over into this phase of effort.

The artisan will tend to examine the 'as is' operations with a view towards developing more efficient 'tools' for existing operations. He may therefore tend to turn at once to particulars in operations in order to move quickly towards design specifications. He will be uncomfortable until he gets to the level of concrete details, partly because he finds it difficult to abstract the problem from implementation technique.

The virtuoso will be more likely to try out a variety of conceptual structures for representing complex processes. He will want to learn the 'as is' behaviour as a starting point for determining 'what ought to be'. In order to do so, he may represent the 'as is' picture at a number of levels of abstraction. He will be not only concerned about cost reductions but also about new or extended benefits which technology may provide.

Gross functional flow. A flowchart which identifies and links organizational and specialized roles and 'functions' serves as a mnemonic structure with which to organize progressively more detail. Commentary about function modes may include actual data about frequencies and kinds of errors, bottlenecks, transmission failures, crises and other perturbations. He studies what happens when the existing application system is overloaded, or for one reason or another breaks down. He identifies those errors which, when they occur, are trapped locally, and those which are propagating. (An example of propagating error is a misplaced decimal point in a multiplier number, but this is not a representative example of the problems examined by the analyst.)

Detailed analysis tends to emerge progressively from the gross analysis. This is the level of specifying the transaction and decision structure of individual modes: presumably of operators performing assigned tasks at terminals. A widely useful structure for the analytic description of a transaction consists of: (a) the essential data categories of the message output from the transaction; (b) the essential data categories contained in the input message plus (c) the data categories of reference content that supports the input data for (d) the transformation or decision rules that convert input and reference data into the output message. (Some readers may want to substitute the expression 'parameter' or 'variable' for the term 'data category'.) The sum of these categories or data names for entities (e.g., 'part name') and their transactionally relevant attributes (e.g., 'part price') becomes the semantic structure of the data base.

The output message content of the one transaction becomes at least partial message input to a transaction later in the process flow. Thus, another characteristic of transactional structure is the queue or in-basket of input messages which are really demands for action. Temporal relationships of entry, queue lengths, and transactional processing to respective outputs enable analysis of the dynamics of the individual transaction structure of chains of transactions. In many real life cases, the control of large variability in processing delay (from any cause) may be more important than reductions in average throughput time.

Parenthetically, it is my observation that the ability to think in practical terms about variability and its control is uncongenial to businessmen, factory managers, engineers and technical people in general. Having had a course in 'statistics' seems to make little difference. This blind spot in the *practical* education of many of us leads to risky oversimplifications in design and procedure.

The general reader should bear in mind that the rules whereby data put into a computer are to be correctly retrieved must be complete, explicit and precise. The art of developing data names combines the criteria of meaningfulness to the human user, task relevance and sufficiency. Parsimony in data is significant in two ways: cost in storage space and cost in retrieval time and facility. For routinized tasks, such as computing payroll, withholding tax and so forth, the necessary and sufficient data categories for input are relatively easy to identify. The data variables sufficient and relevant to the decision to market a new product are less well fixed. Difficulty in identifying the variables for maintaining day-by-day and week-by-week management control of a complex manufacturing plant will lie between that in the payroll and that in the marketing decision if the criteria of relevance and sufficiency are applied. These criteria are not absolute; they have only statistical validities. Approximations of Zipf's law seem to hold: about 20% of the information is used about 80% of the time. Almost by definition, the unprogrammable type of decision demands large amounts of rarely (if ever) used information accumulated in storage.

If the information system designer has complete freedom of scope, it might seem wiser to proceed from the well-known to the less well-known. That is, he would first establish the information requirements at the *operations* level of the enterprise where the transactions and their necessary and sufficient data categories are likely to be well defined. He would then proceed to the management *control* levels which maintain a balance between needs and resources at the operations level. Control is maintained by taking standard samples of standardized data categories from the operations level. Actual results in operations are compared with expected or 'normal' results, and deviations from norms initiate control decisions such as reallocation of resource or adjustment to schedules. The competent analyst understands the dynamics of control systems not only in the abstract, but in terms of organizational realities.

With a platform of operations and of operations control to stand on, the information system analyst may dare the much riskier job of studying the data 'requirements' of higher management's long-range planning and design of change. Obviously, some classes of data should filter upward in summarized form. But what will be clutter and what may be useful? The novice designer may try to 'store everything' because the relevance and sufficiency criteria seem like applying a yardstick to the clouds. The problems of naming subsettable data for retrieval become astronomical. Data bases for problem-solving purposes have, for obvious reasons, been among the least successful kinds of endeavour in the computer world.

Like any other designer, the information system specialist must decide whether to respond to what the system user *wants* to have, or what the designer believes he *should* have. The designer's temperament and background may largely influence the choice. Realities may dictate compromises. Perceiving these compromises calls for social and psychological insights. If the designer hopes for adoption of his design, it is imperative that he interact effectively with the eventual users in the varied roles of colleague, student, teacher and servant. The techniques of the interview are his equipment. To the artisan all data are equal grist so his mill grinds slowly. The virtuoso professional is sensitive in determining the one or two workers in the work group who have insight into their operations rather than mere loquaciousness. He may learn from them in an hour what the artisan will not learn in a week about the essentials in a class of organizational activities.

The results of the analysis phase should be a map of what the segment of the enterprise being studied actually does, and perhaps of what it is trying to do, or should be trying to do. This latter issue carries over into the next stage: the development of the design concept.

THE DESIGN CONCEPT

The artisan is likely to skip this phase of constructive thought. He will select from one or two exemplar models which are his stock in trade for implementing a class of problem, or seek immediately to adapt the application requirements that result from the study and analysis. In consequence many of the liabilities and limitations inherent in the old operations will be performed at higher speeds and, from some standpoints, more efficiently. He will take for granted that innovation is an interative process and thus rationalize the shortcomings of the first design cycle. Successive 'improvements' may require either complete recyclings from ground zero (after periods of costly disillusionment by his sponsor) or result in a patchwork of local fixes.

The virtuoso is likely to examine and reflect at each of the several levels of description of the application. He will search for structural alternatives in simplifying and improving the information system as such. He will also seek new relationships of work processes in the enterprise as a function of an improved information technology. As a single example, manual reordering of rejected parts may require batched reordering with costly delays that could be dramatically reduced by an automatic ordering process tied in with the parts-testing operation. Other feed-forward information could enable better tuning of the scheduling operations. He will understand that the primary objectives of control design are not only to identify and correct for perturbations, but to keep fluctuations (outside the limits of acceptable range of system slop) from occurring, or if they occur, to remain localized.

He can think in terms of dynamics and time cycles. For classic examples in formalizing this kind of thinking see Forrester (1961) and Beer (1966).

The virtuoso will also be guided but not tyrannized by working principles for modularizing information flow and storage. One such principle is that in a good modularization much data may flow within a module, but relatively little data flows from one module to another. (That 'little' may be highly essential, of course, and in any event is only relative.) But this principle has tradeoff criteria. For example, if something goes wrong anywhere in the system, degradation can be minimized if operational information has been distributed. Efficiency for normal operations is usually the enemy of flexibility and coping with the abnormal. The virtuoso, unlike the artisan, plans and designs for contingencies as well as for the normally expected events. But since no backup capabilities can be either complete or guaranteed effective in all cases, he must exercise imagination and comprehension of the essential values in the enterprise. In summary, any principles for the organization of information in an enterprise will be tested by the organization's response to stress and local impairments as well as by its normal operations. Capacity to cope with local failures implies the ability to redistribute information effectively.

In formalizing the design concept (principles for the organization and distribution of information) the knowledge, insights and ethics of the virtuoso may require him to challenge the sponsor's picture of what the information system should do and be. Skill and courage are required for these interpersonal confrontations. The designer may be mistaken in his assumptions, incomplete in his facts or misled in his projection of the organization's value structure. In his study, he may become more enlightened than his sponsor. But if recriminations can be avoided, the interpersonal communication process has benefits for all parties.

Fundamental to an information system design concept is an explicit picture of the role to be played by the human users of the information system. For example, will they be essentially passive and 'computer-program-driven', or essentially active and initiating? Will the role be primarily that of monitoring programmed activities and decisions with takeover for unprogrammed situations, or that of continuous interaction? These are not arbitrary decisions. They should take into account the climate and personality of the organization and its people, the prevailing style of interaction between manager and employee, and the characteristic image the employee has of his role and his job.

The general system design concept should extend to the tactics for introducing the system into the operations of the enterprise. Thus it may be introduced all at once, or gradually over a period of time. It may be started in the mainstream of operational and control activities, or peripherally in service and ancillary activities. Changes put into the mainstream are inevitably more risky to the enterprise than changes to peripheral activities, although the payoff can be much greater. The risks may be hedged by maintaining one or more layers of standby capability (usually meaning manual operations) but these are sustained at a cost.

It is axiomatic that any information system will change, and very possibly grow in range and penetration of enterprise activities. The design concept, and its major modularities, should make changes and extensions relatively painless and accomplished with little or no disruption of then-existing operations. Design for extensibility will add costs to the current project, but ingenuity may reduce the size of this increase.

But throughout this broadly based conception, the designer will (or should) periodically bring forward in his thinking the key nodes of the set of operations for which he is developing an information support. For example, in the Purchasing Department subsystem, the key operations consist of:

1. The requestor making a 'correct' request
2. The purchase agent making 'optimum' selection of vendor
3. The purchasing department effectively controlling pending purchase orders according to priority and other criteria
4. The purchasing department assimilating and digesting its experience with vendors for future access
5. The purchasing department (or other) confirming delivery and product acceptance, and handling payment.

This list is hypothetical and not exhaustive, but it is brief and deals with essentials. Specific experience might show that an additional key factor is feedback from purchase agent to requestor that confirms an order or requires respecification of a request. This list describes a 'critical path' of operations, hence of information flow. It is the thematic reference for design conceptualizing.

A test of completeness in describing an information system has two parts. One is the identification of input source data for all parameters of information needed to come into the system as the system is defined. The other part of this test is corollary to the first: Is a purge specification of some kind made for all data parameters in the system? Purge may consist of actual erasure of data, or it may consist of shipping it outside the system perimeter, or it may consist of statistical assimilation for archival purposes. This consideration blends into the next phase of system design which is that of creating the detailed specification for construction. The design concept phase may conclude with an informal documentation of the major strategies that should guide the construction of the detailed specification to be implemented. If explicit and brief, they can be negotiated with the sponsor who will then share the risks.

CREATING THE DESIGN SPECIFICATION

In this stage the design philosophies, operating strategies, application system sketches and commentary will be translated into relatively unequivocal specifications for implementation by programmers and machine system people. Traditionally the specification and implementation phases have been telescoped because the application analysis has generally been performed by programmers or persons with a strong programming orientation. But the increasing range of tasks that are being adapted to the capabilities of terminals connected to computers in conversational modes is requiring a range of knowledge and expertise about tasks and transaction structures generally outside the domain of the professional programmer. The foregoing statement will certainly be challenged in some quarters. The development of a detailed specification of the application does, however, demand the periodic interaction between the application specialist, who formulates a description of what is more or less ideally desirable in function, and the computer specialist who has a working knowledge of what is feasible to implement and where the major costs to implement will lie. If we wish, we may assume that one person has two sets of knowledge and skills, one of which is application analysis and specification and the other in the computer arts of programming and engineering.

The application specification may proceed into detailed transactional scenarios for each class of task for which the computer provides a direct or indirect service to an individual or organizational task role. This task role may be centred around the concept of what is to go on at a given one or more specialized 'work stations'. From these transactional scenarios the following information will be derived:

1. Identification of the control functions required for the user
2. Procedural protocols associated with user and work station
4. Data categories and data sets for given tasks, and what data will only be referenced and what data be subject to updating
5. The network of data context flow, action nodes and work queues
6. Provisions for data security and control of access
7. Fallback capabilities for various kinds of system failure, human failure or system overload.

It is insufficient to state these factors in general terms. To be useful, they must be associated with specific transactional contexts and behaviours.

The next level of specification is the development of quantitative estimates of load imposed by the application when it is implemented in order to determine capacity requirements. Quantitative modelling is essential where the computer is expected to respond to demands with very rapid as well as fixed limits (statistically speaking) in response time but with a highly fluctuating rate of overall demands that are imposed by many active terminals.

The virtuoso who has profited from experience learns to make realistic estimates of resource requirements. The novice or artisan may be quite as industrious in gathering and processing quantitative data, but tends to gross underestimates, perhaps by hundreds of per cent, of what turns out to be really needed. This optimism may come from failure to anticipate such factors as outages, maintenance, additional resource required for unanticipated changes, and a variety of overhead operational demands. The virtuoso has developed and will apply strategies for using limited resources (system costs) in creating an implementation for maximum services. The artisan who copes with one factor at a time cannot optimize resources among several factors.

The competent designer can finish a specification quickly because he knows or can guess what needs to be spelled out very completely to the expected implementer, and what needs only to be sketched. In cases where he is unable completely to detail the specification of an element, he may describe one or more tests by which the implementer can check the adequacy of that element in a tentative implementation. He recognizes that a specification is not an end in itself but a communication to implementing specialists who may be experts but who are also human with skills, competences and frailties.

The virtuoso has learned to make design decisions rapidly even when he is uncertain. The artisan may stew for hours or days while uncertainty becomes anxiety. The virtuoso becomes aware when trying to get more information for a rational decision is impossible or impractical, and that he will be as badly off tomorrow as today if he procrastinates. He may trust his intuition or flip a coin but he makes the decision that enables action to progress. If he can hedge, he will. This is rationality not impulsiveness. Unless design decisions are made more or less at a given rate, the design job never gets done. Coping with uncertainty in defining problems and in making decisions of commitment is a general dimension in a competence as contrasted with the see-sawing and hesitancies of the merely proficient.

TESTING THE SPECIFICATION

A practical sign of one kind of sophistication in design is the simplicity by which it can be checked out. This is another desideratum of planned modularity in the organization of the design effort as well as in the organization of the entity to be designed. A design should be integrated, but integration means that the parts fit and work together as a whole, not that the whole is not made up of divisible parts.

Tests of specifications apply to many design dimensions. One may be the consistency with which the rules and stipulations for the design entity have been followed in specifying what is to be implemented. An impulse in a wire cannot travel faster than the speed of light, nor can two solid objects occupy the same space at the same time. This class of test can be administered by a computer programmed with the design rules if the design data are submitted to it.

Another form of test applies to the operational validity of the specification to implement. If the designer took the trouble to create specific transactional scenarios preliminary to the design concept and specification stages, a useful tool is at hand. It is possible, perhaps laboriously, to perform a paper test with the scenarios serving as sample problems. Each transactional step required by the scenario has its operational implications traced through the specification. Gaps and inadequacies may be spotted in this way, although undesirable redundancies of facilities are not likely to be found, especially if the designer himself is making the test. It will be obvious to the competent person that more than one set of sample inputs is essential for any useful test conclusions. One of the major difficulties in information systems is the problem of contention of more than one demand for the same function or data at the same time, or overlapping in time. This difficulty is especially acute if one of the demands is for the update of data in a transactional data base. An example is that of two order clerks in different locations who want to requisition the same parts from an inventory listing at the same time. Scenarios and paper testing may reveal missing or inadequate functions, but are incomplete for dynamic testing of the system stressed by different loads and load mixes. Computerized simulation models are necessary for this task.

The programming or adapting of simulation models can be a costly and time-consuming chore. But here, too, a thoughtful design of modularity can simplify the development of the simulation model as well as reduce the extensive computer costs of running the simulation. The modularity is a basis for segmenting the application into parts that can be tested more or less independently of the other parts so that a wider range of sample inputs can be put into each segment with the same overall test time, or the same range of samples run overall in less time. The diagnosis and correction and checkout of design inadequacies can be made more efficiently with well-defined and well-chosen modularities. Recall that creating a system modularity was a major strategic goal during the design concept stage for the competent designer.

Perhaps the virtuoso is more concerned than the artisan with checking out and debugging his specifications because he has a greater identification with his client-user. The artisan may be content, even eager, to complete the last page in a set of specifications and let others take the responsibility for translating his design into a useful entity. These motivational factors take the competent beyond the mere exercising of skills within the specific limits of a job definition. His sense of responsibility extends beyond the edges of his speciality and even of his expertise. In this he may take personal risks to which the artisan will not expose himself. One should expect that in a defensive organizational climate the virtuoso, if he survives at all, lives a comparatively hazardous life. By definition, a defensive climate is one where, when things go wrong, it is important to assign blame to individuals and blame is regarded as equivalent to failure. The virtuoso sticks his neck out for it.

So it turns out that the care with which the virtuoso oversees the checkout of his design specifications is not completely altruistic. It is also a realistic protection of his professional reputation which he may regard as at least as important as his job.

SUMMARY AND CONCLUSIONS

The following is a list of highlights that characterize the competent professional in the design of an information system application.

Conceptual approach: Multiple reference models in mind enabling search for
model answers to novel needs, environments and constraints.

Problem definition: Seeks purposes of the resulting system it is essential to
know; seeks relationships between design task to be accomplished and the
contexts in which the results will be useful.

Problem analysis: Search for strategic variables to be optimized in the problem
environment and reflected in the application tackled. Sensitivity to the
dynamics of tradeoff variables. Search for modularizing the problem and its
solution in order to find partitions valid for design work, implementation and
operation and maintenance respectively.

Design concept: Multiple levels of conceptualizing problem and tentative
solutions; realism in anticipating and designing for system contingencies
and for change and growth.

Creating design specifications: Strategies for using limited resources (system
costs) in creating and sustaining an implementation for maximum services:
optimizing benefits and costs. Coping with decisions in uncertainty.

Testing the specifications: responsibility for operational validity.

By contrast, the artisan tends to identify an assignment with one of relatively few, fixed reference models, does the job he is handed to do, works
more or less procedurally with the limited context of a step or two at a time,
plans primarily or solely to 'normal' expected flows of situations, may be
concerned with local rather than systemic optimization, and tests out his work
mainly to assure he has not made procedural mistakes. His responsibilities
are identified more with his job and his supervisor than to his client and eventual users of the system. Within this purview, his skills may be substantial.

An abstract from the summary of competence reads much like a list of
platitudes associated with successful executives. They get the big picture, have
long-term as well as short-term views, have a strategic sense, can organize
and plan disparate activities, make decisions in uncertainty and are capable
of combined theoretic and practical thinking. They also have a strong sense of
responsibility to achievement and to their organization. Abstractions at this
level tend to be meaningless, at least for training purposes.

Every job and task I have ever examined, from digging post holes to
system designer, from floor sweeper to airplane pilot, has had opportunities
for what I will summarily call 'strategic' thinking and doing. Rarely if ever
have I seen behaviour at this level reflected in a set of training requirements
or in formal training content. No doubt it is this level which is addressed by
some high-priced 'coaches' especially in professional athletics and the fine
arts. This statement is not intended to imply that the rationales are understood even there except in the practical sense.

I think a good case could be made for the hypothesis that a major basis for transfer of training, either vertically or laterally, rests more on what I have characterized as competences than from learned procedures and skills. They could be the conceptual centre of career planning based on psychological grounds. Despite individual student differences in response, I would also make the substantive content of task and job *competences* the central axis of training.

Unfortunately it seems to require unusual technical competences in the psychologist or training analyst to educe task competences. They are slippery to identify as training content and to measure as proficiencies. They have no clear place in a mechanistic psychology of training that is anchored to 'clear-cut training objectives' and reliability in the measurement of acquired abilities. The paradigm of the current philosophy is the small step unit in training a student. Whereas it would be unfortunate to forfeit the tremendous gains made in training technique by this paradigm (and the subject matter that lends itself to it) it seems equally unfortunate thus to limit the universe of what can be learned by formal instruction.

This idea of competences is not new. Several decades ago the proposal was made that all training in electronic maintenance be developed from and point to the conceptual axis of troubleshooting strategy. That troubleshooting separates the men from the boys in maintenance is axiomatic. I do not know of any follow-up. 'Theory of system operation' is taught in lieu of 'theory of diagnosis' and psychologically the two have only incidental overlap.

In conclusion it should be clear that as of this time the understanding of human performance and the technologies of task analysis and of training present major opportunities for innovation.

References

Beer, S. (1966). *Decision and control* (New York: Wiley)
Blumenthal, S. G. (1969). *Management information systems* (Englewood Cliffs, N.J.: Prentice Hall)
DeGreene, K. B. (ed.) (1970). *Systems psychology* (New York: McGraw-Hill)
Forrester, J. (1961). *Industrial dynamics* (Boston: MIT Press)
Kirk, F. G. (1973). *Total system development for information systems* (New York: Wiley)
Martin, J. (1973). *Design of man–computer dialogues* (Englewood Cliffs, N.J.: Prentice Hall)
Simon, H. A. (1969). *Sciences of the artificial* (Boston: MIT Press)

14

The Architect as a Designer

B. R. LAWSON

INTRODUCTION

Architectural design has become a complex and high level kind of skill. Todays architect requires a most unusual and demanding combination of technical, social, artistic, analytical and managerial skills. The kernel of the architect's task is the production of a three-dimensional structure of space and form to accommodate an abstract structure of related human activities. While this paper will deal only with that central task, it must be recognized that it has become a small kernel in a rather large nut. The architect today must co-operate with a formidable array of technical, financial and legislative experts as well as being able to coax the brief from his client and the edifice from his builder. Although most schools of architecture now try to teach many of the necessary supporting skills, the development of spatial thinking still remains the dominant and central part of most courses.

Until quite recently architects believed almost exclusively in intuitive design methods. It was widely felt that design ability is innate and unteachable. This Beaux Arts attitude towards design resulted in an educational procedure based on demonstration and practice. Design methods as such were learnt and not taught. The inevitable reaction to such a philosophy generated a movement which became inspired by the role of scientific method and drew on the techniques of operations research. The movement culminated in a conference held at the Hochschule für Gestaltung at Ulm in 1967 which discussed methods of teaching architectural design skills. Attention was focused on building models of the design process which would enable teachers to concentrate on related sub-processes in turn. Most models identified at least five major tasks to be completed by an architect between receiving his brief and the start of construction; preparation, analysis, synthesis, evaluation and communication.

The names of these basic tasks have been in our vocabulary for so long that they are now seldom questioned as representing real activities. What is still very much under debate is the precise sequence and amount of overlap that occurs in practice. Since most architects do not work in a self-analytical mode it is difficult to answer these questions from practice or controlled observations and experimentation becomes necessary. Observation has led some designers to produce simple models of the design process, while others have considered the process at a more philosophical level. Asimow (1962) declared that 'Engineering design is a purposeful activity directed towards the goal of fulfilling human needs'. He laid down the principles of design as he saw it and carefully defined all his terms. Archer (1965) and his team have developed, and worked to a decision framework for the design process held together by a critical path network.

Other writers such as Rosenstein, Rathbone and Schneerer (1964) have proposed various 'anatomies' of the design process. Wehrli (1968) reported a series of experiments to demonstrate the existence of several common behavioural patterns shared by architects when designing, but the work does little to show how these patterns are inter-related. Lawson (1969) pointed out that design models must take account of the apparent reversal of procedure as the designer moves from solving primary problems, (what function is required?) to secondary problems (how is it to function?). That is, in the case of most architectural schemes, moving from questions of human activities, and their system or organization to questions of building technology. Considering only primary problems, Lawson suggested that the design process can be seen as one of breaking the problem down into the smallest analysable (by the designer) units, 'isolates', grouping these into meaningful 'sets' and establishing the 'relations' between these sets. Secondary problems seem to cause the designer to work back towards the micro end of the scheme again as he 'details' his building, according to the performance specifications laid down by the systems design decisions. This model is closely analogous to that put forward by Miller, Galanter and Pribram (1960) who were considering cognitive performance in a more general context.

Markus (1969) has listed four basic sources of information available to a designer faced with a complex problem: his own experience, others experience, existing research work and new research work. Quite different design strategies result from the use of these sources. It is, perhaps, the inevitable mixing of these four strategies that contributes towards the appearance of random behaviour that the designer often portrays. At the one extreme his own experience may be so thorough that his performance seems intuitive, while at the other his organization of the search for data is much more self conscious. Thus he may appear to almost skip over some of the activities or stages hypothesized by design models. The Beaux Arts School considered the most important set of factors contributing to the nature of the design situation to be those associated with the final solution. Students were trained on a series of schemes graded for complexity of solution, and indeed the scheme was described more as a task of producing a solution than one of solving a problem. A student would be asked to design a porch or a church, not to solve the environmental problems of entering or worshipping. This thinking still has an influence on current architectural practice where designers can be seen to 'specialize' in solution types such as schools or libraries.

However, classifying the design situation by its end product would seem to be rather putting the cart before the horse, for the solution is something which is formed by the design process and has not existed in advance of it. Design is defined by Wehrli (1968) as 'the man–machine problem-solving process which results in a scheme or schemes'. Clearly then, the nature of the solutions is a function of the nature of the problems and their solvers, and the design situation can be altered by varying any of these three. For example, the real world problem caused by fires in multi-storey hospital buildings might well be solved differently by an architect and by a psychologist. The architect might suggest a scheme of fire doors and escape stairs, while the psychologist might suggest better fire drill training for the staff. Thus although the solution to some extent describes the design situation, it is really only an incomplete picture and a fuller description may be obtained from studying both the problem and its solver.

THE STRUCTURE OF ARCHITECTURAL PROBLEMS

Traditionally architectural problems have been defined by the goal rather than the obstacle. The goal, or solution, must be a building, that is why one goes to an architect. It is perhaps because of the obvious differences between the solutions of the various environmental designers that they have been classified this way. A planner produces towns, an architect buildings, an interior designer interiors, and so on. However, it is not just that their goals, or solutions, are different, but also the obstacles that they meet are different. They do in fact perform quite different jobs, as is quite apparent from even a superficial knowledge of them.

Any architectural problem involves countless sub-problems which tend to be organized hierarchically from planning to component design. The architect's main concern is, however, not with grand plans or furniture details, but with the organization of forms and spaces and the activities contained by them. Spaces vary in plan, section, shape and size, and in their geographical relation to other spaces. They may be connected in many different ways in a building—by human movement, by service cables, pipes, ducts and roads, acoustically, visually, and any combination of these types of connection is possible. The central problem of all architectural design is the translation of functions (human activities) into three dimensional forms (buildings).

> Form follows function is the catchphrase that spells modern architecture to most laymen. (Blake, 1963).
> Every problem has a structure of its own. Good design depends upon the designer's ability to act according to this structure and not to run arbitrarily counter to it. (Chermayeff and Alexander, 1963).

Having abandoned systems of visual rules for generating his forms, the architect now seeks visual pattern or structure in the complex interaction of functions that are to be housed in his building. Chermayeff and Alexander (1963) succintly identify the main difficulty here.

> Too many designers miss the fact that the new issues which legitimately demand new forms are there, if the pattern of the problem could only be seen as it is and not as the bromide image conveniently at hand in the catalogue or magazine around the corner.

First then, the architect must be able to perceive the structure or pattern of his problem directly rather than reflected in the form of an already designed building of similar function. This latter procedure leads to the transmission of errors, irrelevant pre-conceptions and innacurate extrapolations, with a possible tendency to establish new traditions of form. This structure is composed of two main sets of relations between the variables of the problem. Both of these sets of relations place constraints on the designer's freedom of action, and thus provide the 'obstacle' to reaching the 'goal'. I shall call these constraints the internal constraint and the external constraint.

The internal constraint is composed of the various interactions between the variables of the architectural system being designed. An interaction exists between two variables if they are not completely independent. Thus, if the architect alters the state of one variable and consequently finds he must change another variable, then these two variables are not independent. There is an interaction between them, and this interaction constrains the architect's freedom. For example, he may find that a space he is designing could be a variety of lengths, widths and heights. The volume, however, may be rather more carefully specified, and this relatively fixed volume relates the other variables and restricts the total number of design possibilities. As often as not the variables may interact in more than one way. In the same example there may be critical combinations of height and area which produce acceptable acoustics, yet these same two variables may interact so that certain other combinations produce the best visual solution. To simultaneously satisfy these acoustic and visual criteria there may only be a small overlap to meet this condition. If there is not overlap, and both acoustic and visual standards cannot be met in one solution, the architect must compromise and make a value judgement on the relative importance of the two criteria. In either case he obviously needs accurate and easily understood information about the relationships of the variables, the performance criteria and they way they influence one another.

In addition to internal constraint there is a second constraint on design— external constraint. This constraint is supplied not by the architectural system alone, but by its interaction with the environment at large. This constraint differs from internal constraint in that the interaction is between the internal variables and fixed external factors. The architect has control over the internal variables, but he cannot, of course, exercise any control over the external variables. To return to the earlier example again, the shape of the site may prohibit certain combinations of width and length for our space. The sources of external constraint are legion, they may range from the direction of the prevailing wind and aspect of the site, through considerations of surrounding buildings, roads and pedestrian access, to planning and building legislation. As with the internal constraint, the architect needs to be able to perceive the range of acceptable options that is defined by these external constraints.

Both internal and external constraints may be generated more or less explicitly. A desired relationship between some elements of the building may be quite clearly stated. The client may brief his architect that two functions are closely related and that the spaces housing those functions should be adjacent, thus explicitly generating an internal constraint. However architects also generate rather less explicit constraints during the design process. An overall visual form for the building implicitly imposes constraints upon the relationships between the spaces inside. An architect may feel it inappropriate to provide a large scale effect on an elevation of a building which is to be adjacent to an existing small scale edifice. This may imply an external constraint relating the larger spaces of the building to the site in a particular way. It may only be at a later stage in the design process that the architect becomes fully aware of this constraint and perhaps realizes that it is in conflict with achieving certain explicitly stated internal relationships. In such a case the architect must assess the relative value of the explicit and implicit constraints which are in conflict. Several courses of action are open at this stage, which illustrate the essential structure of architectural problems.

Firstly the architect may decide that his original concern not to produce a large scale elevation is relatively unimportant. Thus the constraint is set aside once the full restrictions of its interactions are understood. Secondly, a less than optimal internal relationship may be accepted, and the implicitly generated constraint allowed to dominate the decisions. Thirdly, the architect may decide to fully satisfy the internal constraints, leaving the problem of large elevational scale to be solved at a later stage by the detailed design of walls and window openings. The generation and handling of these implicit constraints is what separates architecture from building. Architects are not just expected to satisfy the explicit wishes of their clients and meet the legislative requirements, but are also expected to provide a structure of space and form which offers an aesthetic experience for those who use it. As the amount of structure, or constraint, in a problem is increased then the range of freedom of the designer decreases and the nature of the solution becomes more prescribed. Eventually there is little or no room for manoeuvre and the form of the final product is inevitable. At this point the designer himself is totally redundant and his job, such as it is, would be better done by a computer.

There is no risk of this happening in architecture. There is a long tradition of respect for implicit constraints, and the sheer size of architectural problems and the nature of the variables is such that a designer has many potential ways out of any difficulty. This is not so in all environmental design. Compared with the architect, the civil engineer has few variables and few possible solutions to any problem. The result is much more a foregone conclusion. His choice is so limited that he can often count the basic alternatives on one hand. For example, the main variable of bridge design is the structural system employed; it must be an arch, beam, cantilever or catenary, and the external constraints may rule several of those out. This sort of restriction is inconceivable in architecture. At the other extreme, theatre design is relatively unconstrained. Apart from the external constraints of the stage and the script there is little to restrict the designer and he has an almost unlimited set of alternatives.

Architecture clearly lies near the middle of this spectrum with both explicit and implicit constraints being considered important, and given roughly equal balance. At different times, the architect may have to deal with either heavily constrained or lightly constrained problems. Wehrli (1968) introduced the notion of 'open endedness' of architectural problems, but he implicitly assumes that open and closed ended problems are discrete categories. Lawson (1970) has suggested that architectural problems can be seen as varying in the degree of open endedness which they exhibit:

> The more open ended problem is typically rather unconstrained with respect to the number and variety of its solutions. It is also frequently not easy to see just what the obstacle to its solution is.

Basically the architect always starts with a very open ended problem; no-one would dare predict what the outcome will be. However, as he works and some decisions are made a structure grows and the architect encounters more closed ended problems. Lawson (1970) has also pointed out, as did Wehrli (1968), that the typically open ended problem presents the architect with a substantially different sort of task to that presented by the typically closed ended problem. The former needing a creative, imaginative kind of thought to generate alternatives and the latter calling for a clear examination of the problem structure so as to develop a sufficient understanding to pinpoint the optimal solution.

THE COGNITIVE SKILLS OF THE ARCHITECT

Introduction

Ryle (1949) notes that the term 'thinking' is a polymorphous concept, like the term 'farming'. Thinking, he suggests, consists of many different kinds of activity which may have little in common with each other, indeed two persons engaged in two kinds of thinking may not share any common activities. In the past psychologists have attempted to study thinking by dividing it up into sub-divisions which could be examined separately. Perhaps the most well used categories are those of 'reasoning' and 'imagining' (Vinacke, 1952). In 'reasoning' the individual is said to carry out mental operations within some coherent symbolic system. Reasoning is considered purposive and directed towards a particular conclusion. This category is usually held to include logic, problem-solving and concept formation. When imagining the individual is said to draw from his own experience, combining material in a relatively unstructured way. Artistic, creative and autistic thought are normally considered 'imaginative'.

This kind of simplistic taxonomy is perhaps as misleading as it seems helpful. If 'reasoning' and 'imagining' really were independent categories of thought one should not be able to sensibly speak of 'creative problem-solving', or a 'logical artistic development', which are both meaningful concepts. Some kinds of problems, even in such apparently logical disciplines as engineering, can be solved creatively. Certainly art can be logical and have well developed structure (Mueller, 1967). The fact is that rarely can one find an instance in the world outside the experimental psychologist's laboratory when one kind of thought is employed in isolation. The mode of thinking adopted in any particular situation is dependent on many factors. However, most writers seem to concentrate on two main related factors, the thinker's relation to the external world, and the nature of the directional control he exercises over his thought processes.

When problem-solving the normal person is attending more to the demands of the external world than to his inner needs; in imaginative thinking the individual is satisfying inner needs through cognitive activity that may be quite unrelated to the real world. This is precisely the distinction between design and art as cognitive tasks. Design is directed towards solving a real world problem while art is self motivated and centres on the expression of inner thoughts. This does not mean that imaginative thought should be excluded from the design process, but that its products must always be evaluated by rational thought, in order that the designer's work should be relevant to his real world problem.

Guilford (1956) in a review of factorial research into intelligence concluded that intellectual factors could be sub-divided into two major groups— thinking and memory factors. The thinking factors are composed of cognition (discovery) factors, production factors and evaluation factors. Further to this Guilford found two types of production—convergent and divergent production: 'The cognition factors have to do with becoming aware of mental items or constructs of one kind or another.'

These factors reflect the individual's ability to recognize classes of objects or ideas. Guilford maintains that recognition of a class may depend upon 'figural', 'structural' or conceptual content of its elements. One might recognize a class by perceiving its members, and relating their figural properties. One might recognize a rule or class by some structural relations between its members (as in the 'complete the series of symbols' type of IQ test question). Finally one might recognize a class conceptually, such as the class of all men with degrees in psychology. The cognition (discovery) of conceptual factors Guilford says is 'an ability to define or structure problems'. Guilford notes that this category includes the ability to recognize the existence of a problem. Guilford continues:

Whether we shall ever find parallel factors for seeing problems of deficiencies of figural and structural types (as opposed to conceptual) remains to be seen. Problems of a figural type are faced in such aesthetic pursuits as painting and architecture.

Guilford specifically refers to architecture again when discussing what he refers to as perceptual foresight ability (as measured by maze tests). 'This ability may be important for the architect, the engineer and the industrial layout planner.' Guilford's second group of thinking factors is concerned with the production of some end result. 'Having understood a problem we must take further steps to solve it.' As with cognition (discovery) factors Guilford lists three types of content, figural, structural and conceptual. That which is produced has value primarily at the perceptual level, or because of the relations between elements, or because it has meaning. Guilford expected that subjects would show both an ability to perceive order and an ability to generate it.

In the investigation of planning abilities it was hypothesized that there would be an ability to see or to appreciate order or lack of it, as a feature of preparation for planning. It was also hypothesized that there would be an ability to produce order among objects, ideas or events, in the production of a plan. A single ordering factor was found.

Thus Guilford found not two abilities to handle structure, or order, but one which seemed to belong amongst the production factors rather than the cognition factors. Guilford separates his production factors into two subgroups he calls divergent and convergent production. A study of the nature of architectural problems reveals that the central task of the architect is to discover the inherent structure of his problem and produce a three dimensional expression of that structure. It would seem that what Guilford calls 'production factors' will play a large part in his thinking processes. The ability to recognize and produce order or structure as identified in Guilford's work will be all important in the design of buildings.

Productive thinking

Wertheimer (1945) first introduced the notion of 'productive thinking'. He was concerned with the directional quality of thought; 'what happens when, now and then, thinking forges ahead?' He showed with a whole series of small experiments how, when in a problem situation, thinking can be productive if it follows an appropriate direction. There are at least two fundamental questions the experimental psychologist can ask here. Is the thinker trying to control the direction of his thinking and if so is the direction productive or not?

It is clear that mental processes are bipolar in their directional quality just as in their relation to the external world. The thinker can wilfully control the direction of his thought, or he can allow it to wander aimlessly. The normal person does not engage solely in either one kind of thought, but varies the degree of directional control he exercises. Here is another distinction between design and art. The designer must consciously direct his thought processes towards a particular end, although he may deliberately use undirected thought at times. The artist, however, is quite able to follow the natural direction of his mind, or to control and change the direction of his thinking. Bartlett's (1958) classification could be used to support this argument distinguishing as it does between the artist's thinking and that of the designer.

> There is thinking which uncovers laws of finished structure or of relations among facts of observation and experiment. There is thinking which follows conventions of society or of the single person, and there is other thinking still which seeks and expresses standards.

Clearly the search for, and expression of standards is pure artistic thought. The designer must primarily indulge in Bartlett's first kind of thinking in order that he can appreciate the relationships of the elements of his problem. The amount of purely expressionistic thinking he can do is a function of the structure of the particular problem in his problem (see p. 297). Guilford (1950, 1956) has identified two modes of productive thinking which he calls convergent and divergent production.

> In convergent thinking, there is usually one conclusion or answer that is regarded as unique, and thinking is channelled or controlled in the direction of that answer. .... In divergent thinking, on the other hand, there is much searching or going off in various directions.

He goes on to state that divergent thinking is most clearly seen when there is no unique conclusion, and treats convergent and divergent thinking as separate and independent dimensions of ability which, he says, can occur in any proportions in an individual. He maintains that, even though few real world tasks require exclusively convergent or divergent thought, the distinction is still valid and useful.

The distribution is not so clear in some problem-solving tests, in which there must be, and usually is, some divergent thinking or search as well as ultimate convergence towards the solution. But the processes are logically and operationally separable, even in such activities.

This realistic attitude towards problem-solving makes Guilford's work ideally suited for studying architectural design. Bartlett (1958) suggests that there are two main modes of thinking both of which can be 'productive' in Wertheimer's sense of the world. These two modes of thinking he calls 'thinking in closed systems' and 'adventurous thinking'. Bartlett defines a closed system as possessing a limited number of units which may be arranged in a variety of orders or relations. Formal logic is such a closed system as are arithmetic, algebra and geometry. Bartlett identifies two processes in closed system thinking, interpolation and extrapolation. Here again we see the concept of the directionality of the thinking processes being used to distinguish between them.

Genuine thinking is always a process possessing direction. In interpolation the terminal point and at least some evidence about the way there are given, and all that has to be found is the rest of the way. In extrapolation what is provided is some evidence about the way; the rest of the way and the terminal point have to be discovered or constructed. So it is in extrapolation that directional characters or properties are likely to become most prominent.

These two processes of interpolation and extrapolation are most attractive concepts, and it is easy to think of many examples of them. Indeed Bartlett was able to go further and examine the characteristics of people thinking in these ways with simple laboratory tasks. However, when we consider real world design conditions, the situation loses some of its clarity. Rarely in design does one know or not know the terminal point, but rather one has some information about it. Indeed it is a matter of degree rather than absolute extremes. In some kinds of design one knows almost exactly where one will end up, in other kinds one has very little idea. Architectural design seems to be near the middle of this spectrum being neither entirely open or closed ended.

Bartlett's other mode of productive thought, adventurous thinking is less clearly defined than thinking in closed systems. The repertoire of elements which can be considered is not prescribed in this mode of thought. Indeed it often depends for its success upon elements normally thought of as in different ensembles being considered together, hence its adventurous nature. Adventurous thinking is usually at its most productive when this kind of juxtaposition leads to a genuinely new direction. The difference between adventurous thinking, and thinking in closed systems seems to be basically that of directional control. In most of Bartlett's discussion he seems to assume that the thinker is consciously and deliberately dealing with the needs of the external world. He does not consider for example, the kind of autistic thought that goes on when we daydream, and in this his writings seem to relate easily to the design activity. However, Lawson (1970) pointed out that when considering design, the distinction between Bartlett's 'adventurous thinking', and 'thinking in closed systems' becomes as blurred as the distinction between interpolation and extrapolation.

One can easily find closed systems, as defined by Bartlett, in architectural problems if one looks for them. The problem of arranging tables and chairs in a restaurant certainly requires 'thinking in closed systems'. Such examples, however, do not bear too close an examination. Most sensible architects would try to design a restaurant from the inside out. The architect is not given a 'kit' of parts. If a particular arrangement will not fit, the architect may try different sizes or shapes of tables or he may alter the shape of the restaurant. The ensemble of elements that the architect works with is neither closed nor entirely open. He often needs to combine adventurous thinking with thinking in closed systems to deal adequately with his problems.

Structural thinking

To think sensibly about a large system, one must consider both its constituent parts and their relationships. It is the recognition that relations are at least as important as parts that characterizes the modern systems approach to architectural design, and it is with the cognition of relations that this section is concerned. Just how do we perceive order and structure in a system external to ourselves which we are studying?

When an architect reaches the central problem-solving stage of design he has identified the constituent parts of the system he is working with. Next he must develop an understanding of the way in which these parts are interrelated and also relate to the macro-system (internal and external constraints). Traditionally this task has been embedded in the complementary one of building up a three-dimensional structure incorporating the parts in suitable relations. The architect seems to be learning about the structure of his system while he is attempting to design it. This phenomena is perhaps not very surprising in the light of Guilford's finding that there seems to be only one ability covering the recognition and production of order. Few psychologists seem to have considered both the recognition and production of order at the same time, and if one is to learn from other work in this field one must first turn to studies of man's recognition of structure.

In their now classical 'study of thinking' Bruner, Goodnow and Austin (1956) attempted to discover how we recognize structure in multi-dimensional stimuli. The experiments reported in their study have been developed many times by other workers seeking to understand how both children and adults develop concepts. The format of these 'concept attainment' experiments is a useful tool in exploring all kinds of multi-dimensional thinking, and was first used to probe the design process by Lewis (1963) who examined communication within design teams. More recently Lawson (1969) developed the idea further to examine the way in which individual subjects looked for and processed information about multi-dimensional structures such as those to be found in design problems.

SOME EMPIRICAL STUDIES OF ARCHITECTS' DESIGN SKILLS

Like any other professional group, architects appear to have a distinct and recognizable cognitive style. This seems to be a function both of personality and education. Contrary to popular belief, students typically arrive at a school of architecture with no great calling to be an architect, and with a widespread but unremarkable set of abilities, save for a generally high spatial sense. It seems likely that many students now select architecture because they do not have an obvious first subject at school which could be read at university.

The vast majority of students attend schools of architecture between the ages of 18 and 23. It seems reasonable to suppose that many lasting attitudes, habits and interests will form in these years and that the intellectual environment of a school of architecture will have some influence on them. Architectural education depends largely upon a succession of exercises of increasing difficulty and complexity, and by his final year the architectural student has been solving similar problems in a fairly intensive manner for nearly 5 years. It seems reasonable to hypothesize that he will have developed some strategies and tactics which he employs more or less consciously when problem-solving. The whole language of communication used by architects is visual. Problems are expressed visually as much as possible, and solutions always are. This spatial language may well reinforce some cognitive strategies and discourage others. This seems especially likely in the case of the typical student who comes to the school with an apparent preference for tasks calling for high spatial ability.

Architects seem to have fascinated those psychologists who search for the personality correlates of creative talent. MacKinnon (1962) tells us that:

It is in architects, of all our samples, that we can expect to find what is generally most characteristic of creative persons . . . in what other profession can one expect better to observe the multifarious expressions of creativity?

MacKinnon studied architects who had been judged by their peers to be highly creative, along with other groups of architects, whom he had no reason to believe had exceptional creative talent. He found that highly creative persons tend to exhibit certain common personality traits. Oversimply stated, his architects generally showed these traits and in a more pronounced manner in the 'highly creative' group. More than this, MacKinnon claims that the typical creative architect can be distinguished in some ways from creative individuals in other occupations such as science, mathematics or art. He summarizes the creative architect as agressive, dominant, self-confident, not especially sociable, self-centred, persuasive, relatively uninhibited, and independent. MacKinnon also found that creative architects were not interested in 'striving for achievement in settings where conforming behaviour is expected or required'. With reference to their college work it was found that:

> In work and courses which caught their interest they could turn in an A performance, but in courses that failed to strike their imagination they were quite willing to do no work at all.

This rings very true to those familiar with architectural education. It is nearly always the less distinguished students who have the broad and comprehensive grasp of their subject. The more creative students reinforce their natural spatial abilities, and often turn in quite inadequate performances in the other more technical aspects of the subject. Perhaps one of MacKinnons most disturbing findings is that it was the less creative architects who described themselves as showing a 'sympathetic concern for others'. In contrast the more creative architects felt that they showed high individuality and determination. It would perhaps be more appropriate to show sympathetic concern than individuality in the design of environments for other people.

Lawson (1970, 1971, 1972) reports a series of experiments in which the thinking strategies of first and final year architectural students were compared with those of the sixth form pupils and post-graduate science students. The experimental situations required subjects to design patterns using coloured blocks of wood or card shapes. The arrangements had to satisfy certain unstated structural relations and achieve other stated criteria, but no technical expertise was required. Lawson found that although first year architectural students behaved very similarly to sixth form pupils, the fifth year science and architectural students used quite different methods. Both the groups of older students achieved a higher standard of performance at the tasks but by employing quite different, highly developed strategies. Fifth year architectural students appeared to show considerably more interest in the production of solutions than in the recognition of problem structure. More importantly, they integrated these two activities more than their scientific peers. The fifth year science students worked more logically through phases of problem structure investigation and then solution structure generation. In design, solutions take on a visual form, while problems have structure only in the abstract. Since designers are on the whole selected and trained for visual awareness, it is not surprising that they are more interested in visual solutions than abstract problems.

Eastman (1970) reported an experiment in which subjects designed bathrooms under controlled conditions, and concluded that the most important finding from his study is the significance of representational languages to problem-solving ability. Eastman found that his subjects explored possible solutions by representing them, usually graphically, in a variety of ways. The problems discovered and hence solved depended largely on the nature of the means of representation. Those subjects who did not choose to draw a section through their bathroom failed to discover that there was a problem of young children not being able to reach the taps on the sink. Eastman observes the inherently flexible nature of the designers skill:

> One of the strengths of the human problem-solver is his ability to use several representations—words, numbers, floor diagrams, plans, sections, perspectives—to represent, compare and manipulate information. . . . It can be argued that most methodologies are in fact new representations that allow explicit comparison of information not previously relatable.

In a series of experiments into 'open-ended problem solving in design' Wehrli (1968) studied architectural students designing in model form using modular blocks. The results parallel those of Eastman showing how the means of representation, in this case models, influence the type of problems considered. Subjects were shown to concern themselves with the spatial ordering of the blocks in a way which is meaningful to the observer of the model but not necessarily to someone moving around the real building. Wehrli found that subjects tended to begin by stacking the blocks by size and shape. The largest blocks were frequently positioned first and then smaller ones related to them. The use of such models, it seems, emphasizes the importance of the overall spatial massing of the building. Wehrli not only found subjects producing symmetrical forms, but consistently choosing the north/ south or east/west axis of the model baseboard as the basis of this symmetry. This in spite of the lack of any apparent symmetry in the functional relationships of the building being designed. Thus the solution may present a well ordered overall form, with inadequate internal relationships.

In his introduction Wehrli discussed intuitive, rational, metaphorical and empirical modes of thought in the design process. These ideas have been developed in an original way by Campbell (1971), who related architectural and political activities. This work argues that both architecture and politics are similar kinds of *practical* activity, and that the same ideological dimensions can be found in each. Several experiments are reported which show the use of rationalism and pragmatism as major modes of thinking about architectural problems.

Considering architecture as an activity like politics immediately emphasizes the importance of those aspects of values and decisions which psychologists have not traditionally been interested in, that is the interrelationships between values, attitudes, opinions and ideologies and the meaning of these in behavioural terms.

Thus this work takes as its central premise that architecture is not a value-free activity, and concentrates on the effects of the architect's value system on his problem solving behaviour. These notions share much in common with those of an increasing number of psychologists who seek to use personal construct theory to reveal the importance of the way in which individuals structure their worlds. Much current work in this field concentrates on the importance of the construct system of the architect and its relation with the construct system of his clients. Thus architectural problems can no longer be assumed to be given by clients, but rather 'perceived' by designers.

SOME METHODOLOGICAL IMPLICATIONS

All the experiments referred to in the previous section demonstrate some inadequacies in the performance of architects as designers. Those traditionally considered creative were described by MacKinnon as typically self-centred and dominant and by Campbell as operating with rationalist ideologies. Such people hardly sound suitable to analyse the many interactions of environmental problems at least without some objective help. Lawson showed that architects tend to analyse problems by focusing their attention on the successes and failures of alternative solutions, and Eastman and Wehrli demonstrated the strong influence that the means of representation of these solutions had on the understanding of the problem. This aggravates the design methodologists who quite reasonably feel that better buildings could be designed more quickly and cheaply if only the design process was more accurate. Almost invariably this implies the use of computerized techniques.

An early example is the program of Whitehead and Eldars (1964) which can design single storey buildings from projected inter space flow figures. However, such programs can only optimize quantities and not qualities. Lawson (1971) has pointed out that for the architect much of the structure of a design problem consists of value relations between factors which cannot be reduced to a common metric. Whitehead and Eldars program relies upon costing the movement time of building users. Often, however, the kind of movement is as important as the distance moved. Many human circulation problems are very subtle and delicate. A manager's room must often only be accessed by visitors through his secretary's room, but he must be able to leave without being seen by those waiting for him, and to reach the board room without encountering any other members of the committee. This sort of factor cannot be meaningfully costed, and the architect must consider it separately from many other similar factors.

The human problem solver in the form of the architect remains the better decision maker in the face of all this complexity of information. However, he cannot make sensible decisions until he has fully grasped the structure of the problem. In his now classical work Alexander (1964) proposed a problem structuring aid to design. This was perhaps the first genuine attempt at computer-aided architectural design. Here the computer does not generate solutions but rather presents the designer with the problem structured in a particularly visual way. Alexander's technique suffered many restrictions and potential inaccuracies. The designer was only allowed to input binary codes which indicated whether he considered that two elements interacted or not. The program then factor-analysed the data and output the results in the form of a cluster diagram. All interactions were treated as if they were identical in strength and kind, and the architect could never tell what distortions had been caused by this gross oversimplification. Even with these weaknesses, however, Alexander's technique showed how man and computer could work together in the design situation.

A number of workers are now busy developing the extensive software necessary for computer aided architectural design systems. Unlike Alexander's earlier work most efforts are now concentrated on generating interactive systems in which the architect and computer exchange information throughout the process. Negroponte (1970) has reviewed many of the more spectacular ideas which often utilize computer graphics and seem more directed towards assisting the architect to understand his solutions than his problems. Davis and Kennedy (1970) report their efforts to develop 'EPS', a program for the evaluation of problem structure. However, apart from some work by Cross, little effort is being expended to determine how beneficial computer aids actually are to the designer. Such research is vital, and the consequences of using various problem structuring aids should be fully investigated.

Just what roles should be allocated to man and computer in architectural design? Clearly we must not just allocate a role to the computer based on what it can already do in rather more deterministic design areas. Controlled experimental usage of interactive computer design systems is necessary before we can be sure of their effectiveness. However, research already carried out into the problem solving strategies of architects begins to suggest the form that these experimental systems might take.

Human circulation patterns might be studied by the architect developing a link diagram aided by computer generated tables, matrices and cluster diagrams. The link diagram might be assembled interactively on a graphics terminal with the computer suggesting which link should be included next. The architect could continuously manipulate the diagram to achieve a better pattern, which could be stored if required. At any time the architect could refer back to the interaction chart and change his weightings on different user groups, getting immediate feedback by observing the resultant distortions to his link diagrams. This sort of system would allow the architect to develop an understanding of this section of the problem enabling him to integrate it with other aspects in a meaningful way. This raises another questions, how much of this integration is done by the computer? We can easily imagine a system in which the computer interrupts the designer every time an external constraint is violated. For example, as the architect reorganizes a staircase to achieve a better relationship between two spaces, the computer interrupts by informing him that fire regulations have been contravened. Will the architect respond gratefully to all such interruptions, should he be able to turn them off? As yet this sort of question remains largely unanswered.

SOME EDUCATIONAL DEVELOPMENTS

The period of 'high methodology' seems to have passed by into the history of architectural education. In the late sixties design method became an important part of the formally taught course in many schools of architecture. Method was indeed taught rather than discussed, and the inevitable reaction against such dogmatism gave rise to the present unfortunate position where methodology rarely receives more than passing references. Research, some of which has been described here, has enabled us to develop a clearer definition of the architect's skill as a designer than was possible a decade ago. However we still seem to understand remarkably little about the acquisition of that skill. Both the experience and research of academics show that beginners at design do not naturally use the methods of the more experienced and sophisticated practitioners who teach them.

Experiments have been quoted (Lawson 1972) which show a strong tendency for students who benefit from an architectural education to develop methodologies more suited to the production of solutions than the understanding of problems. In 1964 the Royal Institute of British Architects Board of Education advised that 'the schools of architecture must produce, the RIBA must welcome those whose excellence is towards "problem understanding" as well as those whose excellence is towards the design of solutions'. It is not easy to detect the evidence of any such development in the intervening decade. Most courses in architecture are still organized around the principle that students learn *by designing* rather than learn *to design*. It is during these formative developmental years that students learn design processes whilst their performance is assessed in terms of the end products of those processes.

Architectural educationalists are now turning to techniques which do not so much teach design skills but rather mirror those skills already acquired back to the student for his critical self evaluation. Such techniques usually involve some form of gaming or simulation exercises often performed by groups rather than individuals. In this situation the emphasis is placed on the study of the manner in which decisions are made and how that influences the final outcome, rather than any critical assessment of the absolute success of the solution. Students may also learn to identify the role of communication and of personality, political and social factors in design decision making.

Increasingly research workers are seeking to develop parallel techniques for use in the real world, in which building users take part alongside the designers. Thus the architect's role as a designer is beginning to change its nature. Perhaps the architect of the future will not take so great a personal responsibility as he does today, nor will be be so isolated a figure, but rather he will become more of an advocate and consultant to those groups of ordinary people who wish to participate in the design of their built environment.

References

Alexander, C. (1964). Notes on the synthesis of form (New York: McGraw Hill)

Archer, L. B. (1965). Systematic method for designers. A *Design* reprint

Asimow, M. (1962). *Introduction to design* (Englewood Cliffs: Prentice-Hall)

Bartlett, F. C. (1958). *Thinking* (London: George, Allen and Unwin)

Blake, P. (1963). Encyclopaedia of modern architecture (London: Thames and Hudson)

Bruner, J. S., Goodnow, J. J. and Austin, G. A. (1956). *A Study of thinking* (New York: Wiley)

Campbell, S. *Ideological dimensions in design decision making*. M.Sc. Thesis, University of Strathclyde

Chermayeff, S. and Alexander, C. (1963). *Community and Privacy* (Harmondsworth: Penguin)

Davis, C. F. and Kennedy, M. D. (1970). EPS: A computer program for the evaluation of problem structure. *In* G. T. Moore (ed.), *Emerging methods in environmental design and planning* (M.I.T. Press)

Eastman, C. M. (1970). On the analysis of intuitive design processes. *In* G. T. Moore (ed.), *Emerging methods in environmental design and planning* (M.I.T. Press)

Guilford, J. P. (1950). Creativity, *Amer. Psychol.*, **5**, 444

Guilford, J. P. (1956). The structure of intellect, *Psychol. Bull.*, **53**, 267

Lawson, B. R. (1969). *A study of set formation in design problem solving*. M.Sc. dissertation, University of Aston, Birmingham

Lawson, B. R. (1970). Open and closed ended problem solving in architectural design. *In* Honikman (ed.), 1971. A.P. 1970 Conference (London RIBA)

Lawson, B. R. (1971). Problems structure displays in computer aided architectural design. *Paper given at Ergonomics Research Society Conference 1971*

Lawson, B. R. (1972). *Problem solving in architectural design*. Ph.D. Thesis University of Aston, Birmingham

Lewis, B. N. (1963). Communication in problem solving groups. *In* J. C. Jones and A. Thornley (eds.), *1963 Conference on design method* (Oxford: Pergamon)

MacKinnon, D. W. (1962). The personality correlates of creativity: a study of American architects. *In* G. A. Nielson (ed.), *Proceedings of the 14th Congress on Applied Psychology, vol. 12, Munksgaard*, 11–39

Markus, T. A. (1969). *Design and research*. Conrad, July 1969, vol. 1, no. 2, 35–38

Miller, G. A., Galanter, E. and Pribram, K. H. (1960). *Plans and structure of behaviour* (New York: Holt, Rinehart and Winston)

Mueller, R. E. (1967). *The science of art: the cybernetics of creative communication* (London: Rapp and Whiting)

Negroponte, N. (1970). *The architecture machine, toward a more human environment* (Cambridge, Mass: M.I.T. Press)

Rosenstein, A. B., Rathbone, R. R. and Schneerer, W. F. (1964). *Engineering communications* (Englewood Cliffs: Prentice Hall)
Ryle, G. (1949). *The concept of mind* (London: Hutchinson)
Vinacke, W. E. (1952). *The psychology of thinking* (New York: McGraw Hill)
Wehrli, R. (1968). *Open-ended problem solving in design*. Ph.D. Thesis, University of Utah
Wertheimer, M. (1959). *Productive thinking* (New York: Harper)
Whitehead, B. and Eldars, M. Z. (1964). An approach to the optimal layout of single storey buildings. *Archit. J.*, 17th June, 1964, 1373

15

Final Discussion

W. T. SINGLETON

THE INDIVIDUAL COPING WITH THE PHYSICAL WORLD

Before embarking on a reappraisal of skill in the context of these papers it is necessary to remind ourselves of the limited range of human activities under discussion. It was a deliberate decision that this book should be restricted to the individual coping with the physical world. There are reasonable grounds for assuming that this is the simplest way of entering the enormously complex field of human skill. Such individuals currently rely heavily on hardware technology and this at least is something we understand thoroughly. The skills are shaped, and sometimes almost created, by the technology and thus we have one anchor from which to extrapolate to the human activity. Some authors such as Taylor (machine tools) and Whitfield and Stammers (Air Traffic Control) have carefully explained the current state of the technology as it influences the tasks, while others such as Miller (Information Systems) and Thorne and Charles (Aircraft) while acknowledging its importance, have assumed that the reader knows enough to appreciate how the hardware affects the tasks. For some jobs technology has initiated enormous changes which are still in progress, notably the forest worker (Pettersson) and the farm worker (Matthews), for others technology has had little impact for a long time, e.g. the sewing machinst (Singleton) and the tea-blender (Lacy). Branton suggests that the skills of the train driver have not changed as much as one would expect given the dramatic changes in railway engines, perhaps because the remainder of the system; the track, the stations, the signalling and so on, has not changed very much.

Eccles points out that dentistry involves a complex interaction of skills, tools and materials and that the latter in particular change rapidly. Bainbridge notes that the process control skills are affected not only by the processes themselves and the control technology (direct, remote or automatic) but also by the history of the industry such as whether particular kinds of decision are traditionally made by on-line operators or by managers. The conditions for the passenger (Reason) changed with the introduction of better road transport suspensions, ship stabilizers and jet aircraft around 20 years ago. The Reason paper differs from the rest in that the passenger does not dominate the system that he is a part of, nonetheless his skills can be active rather than passive in the objective of resisting motion sickness. The difference is that his goal is a negative one while all the other papers are concerned with individuals pursuing positive goals. With different degrees of immediacy and directness the operators are serving the needs of other people.

From this broad point of view they are all functioning within western society with its characteristic technological, social and economic standards and beliefs but, having noted this underlying pervading influence, it need not detain us. We are discussing experienced, rational, relatively unemotional human operators pursuing objectives about which there is no disagreement. Another common factor sometimes mentioned explicitly and always present implicitly, is the pursuit of orderliness. This might even be used as a broad definition of the purpose of skill. As the natural scientists have pointed out, the physical world has a pervading tendency to drift towards disorder and the more complex the system the greater the potential to move in this direction. The skilled man is the opponent of chaos, the corrector of degeneration and the creator of structure.

There is some ambivalence in this role which emerges most clearly in controlling transport vehicles. Thorne and Charles consider that 'we have entered an era where more attention will be directed towards an integrated approach to aircraft systems and their human operators and any measure of skill should reflect how well the man integrates with the system' (p. 204) and Branton concludes that the train driver should be provided with 'an environment moderately and appropriately enriched so that he can again "feel at one with the train" ' (p. 187). The obverse of this unity is that the man must retain his identity and his separateness in that he is the dominant element opposing some natural trends and providing the objectives. There is an analogy with leadership in that the leader must be close enough to other members of the group to facilitate communication but remote enough to retain his authority. The automatic resistance to digression and irrelevance is another characteristic of the skilled operator.

The impact of technology is most evident in the increased availability of power. This is changing the skills of the forest and farm workers dramatically from manual activities involving muscle power to those involving manipulative and monitoring activity. Important aspects of the skills of the machine tool operator, the sewing machinist, the train driver and the pilot are concerned with the controlled release of power which is amply available. Branton makes the point that this was much less true of the steam engine driver who actually controlled his system by the generation of power rather than by its direct release from storage. Singleton describes the power release system of the sewing machine as clumsy and difficult to control, justified on economic grounds of simplicity and rapidity of response but of necessity creating considerably demands for skill. The proximity of so much potential energy has important consequences for some skills in relation to safety. This is obviously true for the air traffic controller, the pilot and the train driver. It does not arise for the passenger because, in all transport systems it is accepted that the responsibility for safety is not with him. Safety is still in principle a problem in dentistry, but danger has been almost eliminated by training and design of procedures. It is a well recognized problem for the machine tool operator and for the forest-worker (at least in Sweden) but it is still increasing in severity for the farm worker. Taylor (machine tools) mentions the different potential strategies of the safe operator and the safe work place. The design problem of safe work places has an inevitable limitation in that the versatility of the operator is restricted, thereby lessening the extent to which his skill can be employed. The safe operator concept is very much in line with skill although the parallel techniques of training and procedure design could do with more detailed study and exploration.

There is, at present, little concern with power husbandry although it has recently become a more important objective to the pilot and also to the air traffic controller. Taylor suggests that an analogous change of emphasis may be about to occur in machine tool operation and, more remotely, it affects the architect who has to take building heat conservation more seriously than he used to.

Precision is the objective of graded power application. The second main contribution of technology is instrumentation used for sensing of position, velocity, acceleration, voltage, temperature, etc. The dentist seems to have little support from instrumentation and perhaps this is one reason why he requires such a long training. The same is true of foresters, farm workers, sewing machinists and even passengers. Instrumentation is crucial to the machine tool operator, the train driver, the pilot, the air traffic controller and the process controller. They can perform without it, but only in a crude way and if circumstances are favourable. Given relevant instruments the skill might be said to decrease, although it takes time and effort to learn to use them. Their advantage is in the increased range of potential performance, particularly in respect of accuracy.

Instrumentation brings with it the requirement for new perceptual skills, particularly those involving symbolism. Instruments may use either an analogue or a digital convention or a mixture, as in a pointer/dial display. These have the advantage that the operator can either extract digital information or analogue information as described by Bainbridge (process controller) where the operator often uses the angular position of a pointer rather than a reading. He may also perceptually divide the dial or scale into regions related to actions such as 'no problem/needs monitoring/take action'. Bainbridge also points out that chart recorders have a critical function in presenting data about the immediate past thus helping the operator to take a broader view than the present. The potential stress of presented information is noted also by Thorne and Charles who mention that one selection criteria for the pilot is the ability to scan instruments and rapidly assimulate the overall message contained in them. This kind of 'quickness' may have little connection with a fast reaction time in the laboratory sense. All this emphasizes the sensitivity to operator skills required of the good systems designer. There is a complex iterative relationship as technology develops in that instrumentation design is modified to take account of the perceptual skills of the operator but it in turn changes these skills.

Technology began with substitution for muscle power, moved on into supplementation of sensory and perceptual abilities by instrumentation and is now entering the field of support for cognitive processes. Whitfield and Stammers suggest that this most recent area is very much the current design problem for air traffic control systems. It is beginning to effect also the process controller and the architect and it is of course the central concern in the design of information systems. As Miller points out, the transmission, processing and storage of data are not ends in themselves but parts of the process of decision making. They have meaning in relation to action and as support for human and physical processes (p. 285).

We do not yet have very well developed principles of allocation of function between human operators and computers in relation to decision making. As with all other kinds of machine design, if we know exactly what is required and how to do it then the machine is usually better than the man, but we do not know how cognitive decision making is done. The best strategy at present seems to be that mentioned by Whitfield and Stammers, namely to allow the hardware to prepare a short list based on the defined parameters of the problem and then ask the human operator to select within this short list using as criteria other less definable but equally relevant parameters.

All the jobs have in common the reconciliation of two conflicting requirements, the quality of the product and the cost of producing it. This unique human facility for trading off values on totally different scales is mentioned specifically by Lawson as an ability needed by the architect (p. 297), but in fact it applies to all our skilled operators.

CONCEPTS OF SKILL

There is a bewildering variety of taxonomies of skill mentioned by the different authors. Some authors have attempted to relate skills closely to the task required in the particular industry, some have tried to use the academic terminology of experimental psychologists and almost every author eventually reaches a rather uneasy compromise between these two extremes. Each tries to get away from the specific jobs of his particular skilled operator but finds generalization based on current psychological thinking inappropriate or at best inadequate for his purposes. We have a long way to go to reconcile this mismatch.

Pettersson notes the stresses and dangers for the forester arising from temperature extremes, mobility in difficult terrain and the hard physical work which is still necessary. Nevertheless, the differences in skill are concerned with assessment and judgement, e.g. direction of fall, position of butting cuts, ease of removal, in other words in planning rather than in execution. Matthews describes a similar position for the farm worker. There are still climatic problems and heavy manual work and with these there are associated skills in the minimization of energy expenditure and the positional and directional application of forces for optimum effort. However, the transition to manipulative as opposed to manual activity is well under way. Much of this manipulation is not in carrying out processes but rather in setting them up, versatility remains the central feature of this job. There are higher level skills of diagnosis: the health of animals and the readiness of ground states and crop states for further processes. All we know about these is that they involve the weighting and integration of many different factors and vary according to the specific content. They are timing problems but on a very long, essentially seasonal, time scale.

Taylor describes four kinds of machine-tool operators: semi-skilled, versatile, numerical control operation and metal forming. Semi-skilled jobs such as lathe operation and metal forming (e.g. forging or machine feeding) require manipulative or timing skills where the operator's activity is phased together with the machine activity. The man–machine system is a very close partnership, the machine providing the power and precision, while the operator controls the sequencing and timing. The versatile operator is much closer to the craftsman since he uses machines as tools which are extensions of his hands to execute the decisions arrived at by planning to suit the specific case.

The operator of a numerically controlled machine is a monitor of the programmer's effectiveness. He is needed because of the difficulties which the human operator has in functioning simultaneously in four dimensions; three space and one time. The sewing machinist has much in common with the semi-skilled machine tool operator, although she is closer to the material, indeed in physical contact with it and she has a more limited range of controls to manipulate. Versatility, manipulation and timing are the central features. The exactness of timing of this activity has been explored in unusual detail, including the precision of short bursts and needle stopping positions, the use of machine inertia to oscillate about a required average speed and the phasing of speed changes with curvature changes. This is common also in car driving and it is relevant to quote a car driving enthusiast with an unusual feel for these timing, phasing aspects of skill.

'It seemed important to find a rhythm, to flow along efficiently and in harmony with the road. To see the curves as wholes, and to link up successions of curves with one smooth, sinuous line. To match the efforts of the engine, the brakes, and the steering to the road so that there was never a sensation of violence. To pick up the first hint of changes in the road surface, the potholes, the patches of sand, the stones fallen from the rock faces, the sudden severe bumps and depressions and twists of camber, the abrupt crests and dips. I wanted to pick them up quickly enough, smoothly to adapt my rhythm to them, all the while going quickly but not quite so quickly that the tyres sounded harsh. (From an article by Pete Lyons in *The Motor*, November 2, 1974).

Eccles proposes that the skills of the dentist can be divided into three categories: cognitive, psychomotor and affective. The cognitive skills are associated with acquisition and selection of relevant information leading to diagnosis and treatment decisions, starting, incidentally, from a broad background knowledge of the patients history. The importance of the personal context seems to be common to all clinical decision making. Psychomotor skills include the use of mirror vision and it is interesting to note that given adequate practice there seems to be no problem in integrating data from mirror vision and direct vision. This lack of harmony within visual data doesn't seem to have any motion sickness effect as does conflict between visual and inertial channels or within inertial channels. The particular difficulties of planning and working in three spatial dimensions are noted. This aspect is mentioned also for the passenger, the pilot and the air traffic controller. As Reason puts it, the passenger is an organism accustomed to functioning in a self-propelled fashion within an essentially flat or two dimensional space and anything beyond this is inherently stressful. The provision of power and the addition of another dimension create a demand for different skills which are not easily acquired.

In contrast the train driver functions in only one space dimension but he has to operate in much closer relationship to clock time than do any of the others. Branton considers that he does it fundamentally by an elaborate body-image or enactive model which incorporates an ideal goal plus tolerance margins and analogue computation of trajectories. Thorne and Charles divide the pilots' skills along dimensions of dexterity, resourcefulness, proficiency and systems management. The whole is described as professionalism, a word used also by Eccles for the dentist. It refers to accepted, if undefined, standards of performance, including adherence to rules and procedures. Thorne and Charles mention another kind of anticipation in which the pilot plans his activity to take account of potential or actual changes in work-load within different phases of the flight, he also monitors his own performance in this dimension. Self-monitoring of learning, strategy success, progress towards a goal etc. are other facets of human skill worthy of much greater exploration.

The air traffic controller and the process controller are similar in that there is a negligible manual component and the manipulative component does not involve craft or timing since it is confined to actuating communication devices. There is a high information load arriving in many different streams, through different instruments and concerned with different events. To make decisions, or even to monitor effectively, the operator must have an integrated model of the total scene not only as it is but as it will be with or without particular decisions and actions. Bainbridge calls this a picture rather than a model in that it is recognized for both these jobs that the first task after coming on duty is to 'get the picture', the time required to do this may be up to 15 min. A picture is an on-line model, although Bainbridge prefers to regard it as not a model at all since for her, models have an element of timelessness. Although they are, of course, subject to up-dating, they are the consequences of learning rather than merely the consequences of operating. Whitfield and Stammers have particular difficulty in separating skills from tasks, possibly because the air traffic controller works almost entirely on artificially displayed information. They use the psychological 'input/processing/output' distinctions and within input aspects they conceive of the skill of monitoring the real world as different from that of monitoring displays visually which is different again from monitoring displays auditorally. They divide processing skills into information organization, selecting among alternatives and information storage. Bainbridge divides the process control tasks into dynamic control, planning decisions and manual control and subdivides control skills into perceptual, control and sampling and working memory.

Lacy points out that the tea blender needs trade knowledge and mental (computing) abilities as well as discrimination. Here again we see the importance of context, the tasting does not take place *in vacuo*. Given such a fine discrimination it is interesting that high speed seems to be not merely an actual but also an essential characteristic of the process. Lacy mentions also that the discrimination may be more precise than the available ways of describing it although he is careful to check that the precision of selection and blending does not exceed the fineness of discrimination of the customer, at least in the UK.

Miller makes a valuable distinction between the competent and the virtuoso which is reflected in the whole style of how they operate respectively. Their skills are qualitatively different. He describes the main dimensions as performance, motivation and attitudes. Lawson separates technical, serial, artistic, analytical and managerial skills. He points out that for the architect at least a solution is very much a function of the solver as well as the problem and its situation. This is an extreme manifestation of the range of individual differences which seems to increase with level of skill in both senses, that is, degree of learning within a problem area and hierarchical nervous system function. He reminds us of the useful distinctions made by others, internal and external constraint (Garner), closed system and adventurous thinking (Bartlett), cognitive–discovery and production–evaluation (Guilford) and intuitive, rational, metaphorical and empirical modes of thought (Wehrli).

An evaluation of the various models of skill proposed by the different authors would involve oversimplification, and it would be premature to attempt to produce a consensus. Nevertheless there are some underlying consistencies which are worth further delineation. The information theory model of inputs/processing/outputs can be useful but it can also be a rather dangerous oversimplification. It underemphasizes the continuity of skill in space and time, the basic nature of control and orderliness as the essence of skill and the inherent time and timing phenomena of learning, fatigue, and phasing, the importance of context and purpose, and the range of individual differences. The concepts of meaning and control through different kinds of models seems entirely apposite and perhaps this is the way to begin a taxonomy of skills. There are *enactive models* where the individual controls with his whole body through a body image. These vary from applications of optimum expenditure of energy and application of forces to projected timing mechanisms as in control of transport vehicles. There are *spatial models* where the control is based on topographical representations of a fixed world containing mobile units including the individual himself. These are used from manipulative and assembly tasks to design tasks. There are *symbolic models* varying from iconic to completely abstract models used for problems requiring predominantly cognitive processes.

Finally it should be stressed again that these comments are based on the activities of a small number of investigators studying a particular range of occupations. Studies of other jobs by other research workers may well require a considerable extension or even a complete revision of these ideas.

SKILL APPRAISAL

All the investigators rely extensively on discussions with skilled performers. This always starts informally but there are various attempts to provide structure, for example, by protocol analysis when the skilled practitioner is asked to talk continuously about what he is doing as he does it. There is surprisingly little mention of questionnaires and check lists. The limitations of verbal communication are discussed in detail by Bainbridge. In particular the tendency to describe the official rather than the actual method, the difficulty of expressing in words intuitive decisions and actions based on complex combinations of factors and the natural failure to report the many activities which have little conscious intervention. Nevertheless the method has to be used as the primary means of access to what is going on when all that is detectable visually is an immobile operator such as the process controller doing very little except occasionally glancing at instruments and performing apparently casual control manipulations.

Even when there is extensive overt activity as in forestry, farming, skilled machine tool operating and dentistry, it is clear from these studies that the interesting differences in skill are in the planning and decision making rather than in the action. Only in sewing machining and in semi-skilled machine tool work does the overt activity reasonably adequately reflect the skill and these limb and body actions defy analysis beyond the pictorial level. We seem to have made most progress in understanding how control of sequences and patterns of activity are maintained.

Another pervading theme is that it takes an expert practitioner to assess another expert practitioner in the same field. Making due allowances for professional exclusiveness there is obviously a strong case for this when the decision about level of expertise must be made with little or no measurement and on the basis of an inadequate sample of behaviour. The senior dentist, pilot, air traffic controller or train driver takes a gestalt view of a trainee and makes a decision which he could not defend logically in any detail. There is an awareness of the potential fallibility of this procedure and checks are provided, for example, by spreading the decision over a group, as in a dental examining board, or of ensuring that personality clashes are compensated for, as in the case of pilots.

A more analytical approach is exemplified by Miller's description of the information system designer. He separates out the sequence of problem solving activities into definition, analysis, design concept, design specification and solution testing. For each he is able to define in detail the difference between the approach of the merely competent and the virtuosos. This method of contrast between very different skill levels is used also by Petterson (forester), Singleton (sewing machinist), Thorne and Charles (pilot), and Eccles (dentist). It is one general way of getting some structure into what otherwise remains an amorphous problem.

Lacy tackles what to most investigators would seem the impossible problem of analysing the skills of the tea blender. He relies on an essentially psychophysical approach. He tries to get at the main dimensions of the taster's decision and to provide a scale of measurement for each of these dimensions. He concludes that there are six dimensions of tea quality: brightness, colour, thickness, coarseness, pungency and flavour, and that although some are reasonably correlated with factors which can be measured by instruments, others are not. He provides standards or bench marks for each dimension and carries out field surveys to check that the distinctions made have operational significance. Tea blenders are now in a position to improve the buying policy by computerizing the more structured aspects of their decision making.

Lawson has, in some respects, an even more difficult problem because the undefined quality of creativity is present in the decision-making of the architect. He distinguishes between design which has control and direction externally imposed (although it must be perceived), and art, which has a much more personal direction. He separates the internal and external constraints on the design process and finds that for creative thinking the terminal point or objective is neither known nor not known but rather it is something which emerges gradually. He uses experiments to try to gain a greater understanding of the process of problem solving or thinking used by his particular specialist.

OPERATIONAL UTILITY

In principle these studies can effect selection, education, training and work design. Eccles for dentistry and Thorne and Charles for the pilot are particularly concerned with selection, but they accept that the best that can be achieved by tests and interviews is rejection of the probably unsuitable rather than prediction of relative success. The same point is made by Singleton for the sewing machinist. Professional education is the main concern of Eccles for the dentist and Lawson for the architect and their studies have already effected their activities as teachers. Training has been influenced most obviously for the sewing machinist and the forest worker and is beginning to affect the farm worker and the tea blender. Miller on information systems, Bainbridge on process control, Whitfield and Stammers on air traffic control, Thorne and Charles on the pilot, Branton on the train driver, Taylor on machine tool operation and Matthews on the farm worker are attempting to understand and modify the impact of advancing technology on job designs. In each case it can reasonably be claimed that the policy makers and system designers do take some note of their activities and conclusions. Safety is a dominant objective for all those concerned with systems where there is a high power content.

RESEARCH NEEDS

All these investigators would welcome greater help from the experimental psychologists mainly in the area of cognitive process e.g. memory, as described by Bainbridge in her discussion of the process controller, involves storage of routines, trends, predicted events, data, switching of data between routines, reference back to specific earlier time phases, flexible executive routines and so on. It is obviously a fascinating dynamic complex of processes which we need to understand in much more detail. Miller mentions purging as a necessary process and design topic in relation to all information stores, how far does this apply to the human memory and how is it done?

Decision making involves shifting about in a subjective time domain with the future dominating the present, the resolution of conflicts, support from data, rules and procedures, the participation of computers, the integration of data and values represented in different metrics and so on. Contextual information often not directly relevant seems to be very important to all practical decision-makers, nothing is done in an *ad hoc* fashion.

Turning to the impact of technology, apart from computer aided decision making the pressing topic seems to be teams; the allocation of tasks between a group of individuals working towards a common purpose, their training and leadership. Although we know a great deal about training for semi-skilled jobs it seems that these techniques are less successful for more advanced skills and that these latter need more self-development. This not only makes the necessary allowance for versatility and individual differences but it also seems to provide the optimum motivation. It is accepted that all effective training demands a mixture of techniques and aids. Simulators, for example, are always mixed with exposure to the real situation and it is the optimum combination which we need to know more about rather than characteristics in isolation.

CONCLUSION

The knowledge of any expert can be divided into what has been established in terms of principles and data and what is accepted from experience as the procedures for adding to these principles and data. In other words, we have models and methods.

Principles of human skill

Man is conceptually a model-builder and categorizer and operationally a map-maker and navigator. His models vary from elaborations and extensions of a body image through mental pictures to symbolic abstractions. He uses them to make sense of (that is to interpret and predict from) what is happening in the real world and in particular to escape from the limitations of the here–now data coming in through the senses. Meaning comes from relating present data to past data within a particular context and the overall purpose is not so much to understand the present as to anticipate the future. As his skill at functioning in a particular category of situations increases, a sequence of almost immediate stimulus–response reactions gradually becomes parallel chains of receptor and effector processes. The effector processes become increasingly programmed and serial (that is dominated more and more by past and future rather than present) and consequently smoother. The receptor processes are less directly linked to the effector processes and have increasing mobility so that attention can shift longitudinally in time and laterally across streams of events. The overall control system is dominated by objectives of widely different degrees of immediacy and determinacy and operates through a hierarchy of self-monitoring systems. The individual is capable of checking his own activity and progress at many different levels, from immediate kinaesthetic feedback to a conscious management-type control. The more skilled the man is the more the control at all levels is by exception, events are more planned and if they proceed according to plan there is no intervention, there is also increasingly likelihood that they will go according to plan.

General procedure for skill appraisal

Lacking more specific direction one would approach the problem of appraising a skilled operator by the following procedure:

1. Discuss the skilled activity almost *ad nauseam* with the individuals who practise it and with those to whom and for whom they are responsible. It is not enough to pop in at intervals, the investigator must spend whole shifts and weeks with the practitioners to absorb the operational climate
2. Try to make this verbal communication more precise by using protocol techniques, critical incident techniques, good/poor contrast techniques and so on
3. Observe the development of the skill in trainees and by analysis of what goes on in the formal and informal training procedures and in professional assessment. Make due allowance for history, tradition, technological change and so on
4. Structure the activity. Identify the dimensions of the percepts, the decision making, the strategies of action and the overt activities, and try to provide scales of measurement along each dimension
5. Check as many conclusions as possible by direct observation, performance measurement and by experiment
6. Implement the conclusions and provide techniques for assessing the limitations and successes of the innovations.

Finally it should be emphasized once more that these generalizations are restricted to a particular category of skilled activity in a particular society at a particular time.

Author Index

Bold numerals refer to names cited in reference list at chapter ends

Subject Index